THE PRINCIPLES OF
COMPUTER HARDWARE

THE PRINCIPLES OF COMPUTER HARDWARE

Alan Clements

Department of Computer Science
Teesside Polytechnic

OXFORD UNIVERSITY PRESS
1985

Oxford University Press, Walton Street, Oxford OX2 6DP

Oxford New York Toronto
Delhi Bombay Calcutta Madras Karachi
Kuala Lumpur Singapore Hong Kong Tokyo
Nairobi Dar es Salaam Cape Town
Melbourne Auckland
and associated companies in
Beirut Berlin Ibadan Nicosia

Oxford is a trade mark of Oxford University Press.

Published in the United States
by Oxford University Press, New York

British Library Cataloguing in Publication Data
Clements, Alan
The principles of computer hardware.
1. Electronic digital computers
I. Title
621.3819'583   TK7888.3
ISBN 0–19–853704–2
ISBN 0–19-853703–4 Pbk

Library of Congress Cataloging in Publication Data
Clements, Alan, 1948–
The principles of computer hardware.
Bibliography: p.
Includes index.
1. Electronic digital computers
I. Title
TK7888.3.C62 1985   001.64   84–27205
ISBN 0–19-853704–2
ISBN 0–19-853703–4 (pbk.)

Filmset by Latimer Trend & Company Ltd, Plymouth
Printed in Great Britain by
Butler and Tanner Ltd, Frome, Somerset

For Norman Buddin
and David Crowe

PREFACE

This book is intended for students in universities and polytechnics taking a first-level (i.e. introductory) course in the principles of computer hardware.

The principles of computer hardware course has been constructed to achieve two goals. The first is to teach students the basic concepts on which the stored-program digital computer is founded. These include the representation and manipulation of information in binary form, the structure of a computer and the flow of information within such a machine, and the exchange of information between its various peripherals. That is, this book answers the question 'How does a computer work?' The second is to provide students with a firm foundation for further study in the second year of their course. In particular, the elementary treatment of gates and Boolean algebra provides a basis for a second-level course in Computer Design.

At the moment, computer science is not taught in all schools, and a prior knowledge of computer science is not an entry requirement to many courses in universities and polytechnics. Consequently, the level of this book is aimed at those with no previous knowledge of computer science. The only background information needed by the reader is a knowledge of elementary algebra which is required in Chapter 2 dealing with Boolean algebra. As all students following a course in computer science or computer technology will also be studying programming in a high-level language (typically Pascal), no attempt is made to deal with this topic, and it is assumed that the reader will be familiar with many of the basic concepts underlying a high-level language.

While there are some excellent books dealing with the individual topics of computer hardware (Boolean algebra, logic circuits, binary arithmetic, computer architecture, memory technology, assembly-language programming, input/output devices), there are very few really good books dealing with all these topics together at a satisfactory level. It is my intention to provide the reader with an insight into all the above topics.

In writing this book, I have tried to do three things. By adopting an informal style, I hope to increase the enthusiasm of the otherwise faint-hearted programmer who may be put off by the formal approach of other, more traditional books. I have also tried to give the student an insight into computer hardware by explaining why things are as they are, instead of presenting him with information as a piece of dogma to be learned and accepted without question. Moreover, I have included some topics which would seem out of place in an elementary first-level course. Such topics (e.g. advanced computer arithmetic, timing diagrams, reliability) have been included to show how the computer hardware of the real world often differs from that of the first-level course in which only the basics are taught. Finally, I have discovered that stating a formula or a theory is not enough—many students like to see an actual application of the formula. Consequently I have, wherever possible, given worked examples. In addition to the above, I have also broadened the range of topics normally found in first-level courses in computer hardware. I have provided sections giving an introduction to operating systems and to local area networks as these two topics are so intimately related to the hardware of the computer.

Like most introductory books dealing with the architecture of computers, I have chosen a specific microprocessor as a model. The advantage of the microprocessor as a vehicle for teaching the basic principles of computer architecture is its relative simplicity. Most mainframe- and many mini-computers have sophisticated architectures which confront the students with too much fine detail early in their course. The microprocessor has almost all the important features of the mainframe computer and few of its complexities. The microprocessor I have chosen to illustrate this course is the 6502 8-bit microprocessor, which has been selected simply because many of the low-cost teaching and personal microprocessor systems use this particular chip. I would emphasize that this book is not designed to provide a practical course in assembly-language programming on the 6502. It is intended to illustrate the operation of a central processing unit by means of assembly language. A concession has been made to modern trends in the design of micro-processors by including details of the 6809 CPU which represents today's most sophisticated 8-bit microprocessor.

Although intended for first-year degree students in a computer science course or to students of electrical engineering on a computer technology course, this book should appeal to those on Higher National BEC/TEC courses in computing studies, to those taking Part I of the BCS examination, and to the layman who just wants to find out how computers work.

Reading guide

It has already been stated that this book contains material appropriate to traditional introductory courses in computer hardware and architecture, plus other material broadening its scope and filling in some of the gaps left in such courses. As students following an introductory course might find it difficult to distinguish between foreground and background material, I am including a guide to their reading.

Chapter 2: The first part of Chapter 2 governing gates, Boolean algebra, and Karnaugh maps is essential reading. However, Section 2.5 on bistables and flip-flops requires a quantum jump in understanding over earlier sections on gates and similar logic elements. For the purpose of this book the basic idea of the flip-flop and its application as a memory element in registers is all that is needed. That is, by the end of this course students are expected to be able to design moderately complex circuits built from gates, but are expected only to appreciate the role of sequential circuits. A fuller treatment of sequential circuits belongs to second-level courses in digital design. Sections 2.7 and 2.8 both deal with some real-world problems in computer design, and may be omitted on a first reading.

Chapter 3: This chapter deals with the way in which numbers are represented inside a computer, and the way in which they are manipulated in simple arithmetic operations. Apart from Huffman codes in Section 3.3.9, almost all of this chapter is essential reading. Section 3.7 on floating-point arithmetic goes into more detail than some other texts, but this has been necessitated by difficulties that a few students have in understanding how floating-point numbers are represented and manipulated.

Chapter 4: This is the heart of the book and is concerned with the structure and operation of the computer itself. Section 4.2 deals with the operation of the computer's control unit and may be omitted on a first reading. The control unit is normally encountered in a second- or third-level course, and has been included here for the purpose of completeness, and to give the student an insight into how the computer actually turns a binary-coded instruction into a sequence of events which carry out the instruction. Section 4.5 on the 6809 provides background material and may therefore be omitted on a first reading.

Chapter 5: This chapter deals with input/output techniques and associated computer peripherals. It is essential reading and should not be omitted.

Chapter 6: This chapter deals with the way in which information is actually stored within the computer. The student should be aware of the principles governing the operation of both immediate access memory and backing stores. However, some of the detailed description (thin-film memory, codes for recording) embedded in this section may be omitted on a first reading.

Chapter 7: It may come as a surprise that this chapter, dealing with the way in which computers handle multiplication and division, may be entirely omitted—unless, of course, the topic falls within the student's particular syllabus. The fine details of multiplication and division are often relegated to second level courses in digital design techniques. I have included this chapter to illustrate how some operations such as multiplication may be carried out in a surprisingly large number of ways, and how they may be carried out either by means of special-purpose hardware or by means of software.

Chapter 8: The techniques whereby networks of computers communicate with each other, do not appear in many first level courses. Therefore, this chapter may be omitted. However, it is probable that computer communications will soon worm its way into such courses because of its great importance and impact on computing. For this reason I would expect students to read this chapter even if it does not fall within their syllabus.

Chapter 9: Operating systems and system software as such do not fall within the scope of this book. I have included a brief discussion of operating systems because it leads to the ideas of multiprogramming and memory management—Sections 9.2 and 9.3. These topics are intimately connected with interrupt-handling and data-storage techniques, and serve as practical examples of the use of the hardware in Sections 5.2 and 6.4.

The history of this book

Like people, books are born. This book was conceived in December 1980. At the end of every Christmas term the first-year students on the degree course in computer science at Teesside Polytechnic are given tests in each of their subjects in order to monitor their progress. The results of the test in the 'principles of computer hardware' were rather poor, so I decided to do something about it. I thought that detailed lecture notes, written in a style accessible to the students, would be the most effective solution.

Unfortunately, I had volunteered to give a short course on computer communications to the staff of the computer centre during the Christmas vacation, and did not have enough free time to produce the notes. By accident I found that the week immediately preceding Christmas was the cheapest time of the year for package tours. So I went to Tenerife for a week, plonked myself down by the pool with folders full of reference material and a bottle of Southern Comfort, and wrote the core of the book—number bases, gates and Boolean algebra, and binary arithmetic. Shortly afterwards I added the section on the structure of the CPU.

These notes appeared to produce the desired improvement in the end-of-year exam results and were well received by the students. In the next academic year the data preparation department of the computer centre began to offer an important new facility to lecturers. They would enter our notes into a Univac 1100. This enabled me to add new material and clean up the existing text. At this time I decided to convert the notes into a book. This process involved adding topics, not in our syllabus, to produce a more rounded text. One aspect of this approach to book writing is the 'ink-blot effect'. Once text is stored in a computer it tends to expand in all directions because it is very easy to add new material at any point. This would have been very difficult to do if a conventional typewritten manuscript had been produced because all changes involve retyping or 'cutting and pasting'.

Teesside
October 1983   A.C.

ACKNOWLEDGEMENTS

Few books are entirely one-man affairs, and this is no exception. I would like to thank those who wrote the many books about computers on which my own knowledge of, understanding of, and more importantly, attitude towards computers are founded. One of the most unpleasant tasks confronting an author is the translation of his handwritten manuscript into a typewritten document. This job was tackled by the data preparation department of the computer centre at Teesside Polytechnic. Without the help of Marlene Melber and those who work with her, this book may not have appeared. It certainly would not be in its present form.

The greatest help came from my wife, Sue, who proof-read the text, removed my spelling mistakes, modified my punctuation, and blunted my worst assaults on the English language.

As this book has grown out of my lecture notes, I have received many helpful suggestions from my students. Some have checked early drafts, while others have pointed out some of the more incomprehensible sections which have been modified accordingly. I gave a copy of the draft manuscript to a neighbour, Alan Tulo, who is a mathematician but is otherwise unconnected with computer science, and asked him for an overall comment. He not only read it but suggested several modifications to improve the clarity of the text. More importantly, he found some of the blunders I had not noticed.

ACKNOWLEDGEMENTS

CONTENTS

1 Introduction   1

  1.1 The digital computer   4
    1.1.1. The computer as a data processor   5
    1.1.2 The computer as a number cruncher   6
    1.1.3 The computer in automatic control   7
    1.1.4 The computer as a component   8
  1.2 Mainframe, mini and micro   9
  1.3 The stored program computer—an overview   11

2 Logic elements and Boolean algebra   14

  2.1 Basic gates   16
  2.2 Some applications of gates   22
  2.3 An introduction to Boolean algebra   29
    2.3.1 Karnaugh maps   39
    2.3.2 Special purpose combinatorial logic elements   52
  2.4 Tri-state logic   58
  2.5 Bistables and registers   62
    2.5.1 The RS flip-flop   63
    2.5.2 The D flip-flop   68
    2.5.3 Clocked flip-flops   69
    2.5.4 The JK flip-flop   73
  2.6 Sequential circuits   74
    2.6.1 Special purpose sequential logic elements   79
  2.7 Some practical considerations in logic design   86
  2.8 Reliability   93
    Problems   98

3 Computer arithmetic   104

  3.1 Characters, words, and bytes   104
  3.2 Number bases   106
  3.3 Number-base conversion   107
    3.3.1 Decimal to binary   108
    3.3.2 Decimal to octal   108
    3.3.3 Decimal to hexadecimal   108
    3.3.4 Binary to decimal   109
    3.3.5 Octal to decimal   109
    3.3.6 Hexadecimal to decimal   109
    3.3.7 Conversions between binary, octal, and hexadecimal   109
    3.3.8 The conversion of fractions   111
    3.3.9 BCD and other codes   112

3.4 Binary arithmetic 120
    3.4.1 The half adder 121
    3.4.2 The full adder 122
    3.4.3 The addition of words 124
3.5 Negative numbers 126
    3.5.1 Sign and magnitude representation 127
    3.5.2 Complementary arithmetic 128
    3.5.3 Two's complement representation 129
    3.5.4 One's complement representation 133
3.6 An introduction to computer arithmetic and assembly-language programming 134
3.7 Floating-point numbers 139
    3.7.1 The representation of floating-point numbers 141
    3.7.2 The normalization of floating-point numbers 142
    3.7.3 Some typical floating-point systems 144
    3.7.4 Floating-point arithmetic 147
    3.7.5 Some worked examples 150
    Problems 156

4 The central processing unit 162

4.1 The structure of the CPU 163
    4.1.1 A programming example 169
4.2 The control unit 174
    4.2.1 Microprogrammed control unit 175
    4.2.2 Random logic control unit 180
4.3 The 6502 microprocessor 188
    4.3.1 An introduction to the 6502's instruction set 192
4.4 Addressing modes 197
    4.4.1 Immediate addressing 198
    4.4.2 Indexed addressing 201
    4.4.3 Relative addressing 206
    4.4.4 Indirect addressing 208
    4.4.5 The stack 210
4.5 The 6809 microprocessor 220
    4.5.1 Addressing modes and the 6809 221
    Problems 230

5 Input/output 236

5.1 Programmed I/O 240
5.2 Interrupt-driven I/O 242
5.3 Direct memory access 246
5.4 Channel I/O 248
5.5 Input/output devices 249
    5.5.1 The VDU 249
    5.5.2 The printer 259
    5.5.3 User-orientated interfaces 266

6 Computer memory 271

  6.1 Semiconductor memory 274
  6.2 Ferrite-core memory 285
  6.3 Thin-film memory 292
  6.4 Memory hierarchy 296
    6.4.1 Magnetic recording 297
    6.4.2 The disk drive 305
    6.4.3 The tape transport 315
  6.5 Magnetic-bubble memory 322
  Problems 326

7 Advanced computer arithmetic 329

  7.1 Multiplication 329
    7.1.1 Unsigned multiplication 330
    7.1.2 Signed multiplication 332
    7.1.3 High-speed multiplication 336
  7.2 Division 339
    7.2.1 Restoring division 342
    7.2.2 Nonrestoring division 342
    7.2.3 Division by multiplication 343

8 Computer communications 347

  8.1 Serial data transmission 349
    8.1.1 Asynchronous serial transmission 349
    8.1.2 Synchronous serial transmission 351
  8.2 Protocols 359
  8.3 Local area networks 367

9 Operating systems 378

  9.1 System software 381
  9.2 Multiprogramming 386
  9.3 Memory management 390

Appendixes

  A1 Some worked examples 405
  A2 The 6502 instruction set 421

Bibliography 435

Index 437

1 INTRODUCTION

To begin with I feel I ought to define the terms hardware and software. Of course I could give a deeply philosophical definition, but perhaps an empirical definition is more helpful. If any part of a computer system clatters on the floor when dropped, it is hardware. If it doesn't it is software.

The hardware includes all the physical components which make up the computer system. These range from the central processing unit to the memory and input/output devices. The programs which control the operation of the computer are called the software. When a program is inside a computer its physical existence lies in the state of electronic switches within the computer, or the magnetization of tiny particles on magnetic tape or disks.

It is interesting to note that there is often a trade-off between hardware and software. Some operations may be carried out either by a special purpose hardware system or by means of a program stored in memory. In general, the fastest way to perform some task is to build a circuit dedicated exclusively to the task. This may be a very costly step. Writing a program to perform the task on an existing computer is much cheaper, but the task may take very much longer to carry out, as the hardware of the computer will not be optimized to suit the task. Hence the term 'trade-off' refers to the exchanging of speed for money. A similar trade-off exists within human activity. For example, a factory may wish to protect its goods from theft. One possible approach is to seek a hardware solution and position electronic sensors to detect and report any movement. An alternative technique is to program a human being to act as a nightwatchman. In this case the software is the 'program' which lies in the brain of the general purpose machine (the human). The brain is often referred to as 'wetware' by computer scientists.

Why do we teach the principles of computer hardware? After all, I can watch a television programme without understanding how a UHF receiver operates, or fly in a jumbo jet without ever knowing the meaning of thermodynamics. Why then should a computer scientist's or programmer's life be made miserable by forcing them to learn what goes on inside a computer?

There are several reasons for teaching the principles of computer hardware, the most important of which are:

1. Programming itself involves implicit hardware operations. Whenever a programmer inputs or outputs data he† is using a hardware device about which he must have some prior knowledge. Often this involves a knowledge

† For 'he' or 'she' please infer 'he or she'.

of the format of the data (columns per line and lines per page). For example, if data were to be presented on a television-style display (VDU), it would be sensible to break it up into segments or pages ending at some logical point, rather than by ending a screen in the middle of a sentence, so that when the next screen is displayed the poor reader has to remember the first half of the sentence.

2. Hardware defines the limitations of the computer. Any computer user must be aware of its restrictions. Clearly, there is no point in buying a computer to, say, allow 80 students simultaneous access to 80 terminals if the computer operating flat-out can service only 40 terminals. Similarly, an on-board navigation computer in an aircraft must have circuits operating at a sufficiently high speed to compute a course correction before the aircraft has strayed too far off track.

3. Programming cannot always be divorced from hardware. While a computer programmer writing packages in COBOL to calculate wages in a local government office is, largely, far-removed from the finer details of hardware, other programmers are often involved with interfacing a computer to a system. For example, a microprocessor may be used to control the temperature of a chemical reaction. Such a system involves converting a temperature into a voltage, transforming the voltage into a digital or numerical value, reading it into the computer, processing this number, outputting another number to a device which converts it into a voltage, and finally using this voltage to control the heater. This sequence of events requires the expertise of the electrical engineer and the programmer. If the job is to be done at all well, they must be able to communicate with each other. Sometimes, they may even be the same person; a programmer well versed in electrical engineering or vice versa.

4. It is aesthetically pleasing to understand hardware. The examples given at the start of this section are not entirely appropriate. The passenger is not interested in the workings of a jet engine but the pilot is. A detailed knowledge of the engines is not vital to his job, but understanding them gives him a measure of satisfaction. Similarly, the programmer who understands precisely what happens after his job has been submitted to the computer also has more personal satisfaction than his counterpart who regards the internal operation of a computer as a type of black-magic. *

It is very difficult to know just what should be included in a course in computer hardware, or excluded from it. Any topic can always be expanded to an arbitrary extent. If we start with gates and Boolean algebra, do we go on to actual semiconductor devices and then to semiconductor physics? In this course, I have attempted to include those topics relevant to points (1) to (4) above, at an introductory level. However, some of my material may surprise those familiar with more conventional introductory texts. I have included a somewhat wider range of material because the area of influence encompassed by the digital computer has expanded greatly in recent years. I have also gone out of my way to highlight the divergence between theory and practice. For example, while including the 'usual' introduction to gates and Boolean algebra, I have also made it clear that the designer is concerned with other (economic) considerations as well as logic design. The major subject areas dealt with in this course are as follows.

Computer arithmetic Our system of arithmetic based on the radix ten has evolved over thousands of years. The computer carries out its internal operations on numbers represented in the radix (or base) two. This anomaly is not due to some magic power inherent in binary arithmetic but simply because it would be uneconomic to design a computer to operate in denary (base ten) arithmetic.

Basic logic elements and Boolean algebra It is the type of technology we have today that determines what a computer can do. By starting with the basic logic elements, or gates, from which a computer is made up, we can see how the operation of these gates affects both the way in which the computer carries out arithmetic operations and the way in which the functional parts of a computer interact to execute a program. An introduction to flip-flops and their application to sequential circuits is also included. The flip-flop is a logic element which can store (remember) a single binary digit, and is the basic component of many memory units.

Computer architecture This topic is concerned with how a computer actually operates at the conceptual (i.e. block-diagram) level. That is, we show how the computer goes about reading an instruction from memory, decoding it, and then executing it. The structure of a computer in terms of its functional units is known as its architecture.

Assembly language The primitive instructions which directly control the operation of a computer are called machine-code instructions and are composed of a sequence of binary values stored in memory. As programming in machine code is exceedingly tedious, an aid to machine-code programming called assembly language has been devised. Assembly language is a form of shorthand permitting the programmer to write machine-code instructions in a simple mnemonic or abbreviated form of plain language. Sometimes high level languages (Pascal, COBOL, BASIC, FORTRAN, etc.) have their statements translated into a series of assembly language instructions by a compiler. A programmer writing in assembly language requires a detailed knowledge of the architecture of the machine he is using, unlike the corresponding programmer operating in a high level language.

Input/output It is no good having a computer unless it can take in new information (programs and data), and output the results of its calculations. In this section we will show how information is actually moved into and out of the computer. The operation of three basic input/output devices is described. These are the keyboard, the VDU, and the printer.

Memory devices   A computer needs memory to hold its programs, data and any other information it may require at some time in the future. In this section we look at the 'immediate access store' and the 'backing store'. Basically, an immediate access store provides a computer with the necessary data in a fraction of the time it takes the computer to execute one of its assembly language level operations, while the backing store is very much slower. Backing store is used because it is immensely cheaper than immediate access store. The most popular forms of backing store are the disk and tape units; these rely on magnetizing a moving magnetic material to store data.

Advanced computer arithmetic   A section is included on some of the ways in which multiplication and division is implemented in a digital computer. This is one of the more advanced sections and may be omitted by the student on a first reading.

Computer communications   Some people thought that the advent of the microprocessor would spell the end of large computer systems. In many ways the reverse has proved true and computer systems have grown even bigger as individual computers are now being linked together to form networks. This has many advantages, not least of which is the ability of a number of computers in a network to share expensive peripherals such as line-printers. Consequently, a section has been devoted to showing how computers communicate with each other. This chapter examines three aspects of computer communication. The first is the way in which digital information in a computer is encoded in a form suitable for transmission over a serial line, and how it is reconstituted at the receiver. The second section deals with the protocols or rules enabling the computers to conduct an orderly conversation with each other. The third section provides a brief overview of local area networks. These are networks of computers which are distributed over one site (e.g. an office, or a complex of buildings).

Operating systems   An operating system is a large chunk of software which coordinates all the functional parts of the computer. A major reason for mentioning operating systems in a book on hardware, is that two hardware features found on most computers (interrupt-handling mechanisms and the stack) facilitate multiprogramming, an important characteristic of many operating systems. Multiprogramming is the ability of a computer to run two or more programs apparently simultaneously. At the end of this section a short introduction to memory management is given. Memory management is a technique enabling a computer with a small, high-speed random-access memory, and a large, low-speed serial-access memory to appear as if it had a single large, high-speed random-access memory.

1.1 The digital computer

Before beginning the discussion of computer hardware proper, it is necessary to say what a computer is (and is not) and to define a few terms. If ever an award were to be given to those guilty of misinformation in the field of computer science, it would go to the creators of HAL in 2001 and of K9. These, and other similar machines, have generated the popular myth that a computer is a repository of all knowledge, so that somewhere in its memory banks it contains an infinite accumulation of data. The reality is a little more mundane: a computer is a machine which takes in information from the outside world, processes it according to some predetermined set of operations, and delivers the processed information. This is a remarkably poor definition as it tries to define the word 'computer' in terms of the equally complex words 'information', 'operation', and 'process'. Perhaps a better approach is to give four examples of what a computer can do.

1.1.1 The computer as a data processor

Figure 1.1 represents the more conventional idea of the computer. Here is a system designed to deal with the payroll of a large factory. I am going to call the whole thing a computer, in contrast with those who would say that the CPU (Central Processing Unit) is the computer and all the other devices are peripherals. Somewhere inside the CPU's immediate access memory is a program, a collection of primitive machine-code operations, whose purpose is to calculate an employee's pay based on the number of hours worked, the basic rate of pay, and the overtime rate. Of course, this program would include many sophistications so that tax, national insurance, and any other deductions could be dealt with. The purpose of the printer is largely self-explanatory. It is an electromechanical device which prints letters and numbers on a piece of paper and can directly produce the wageslips. Because the computer's immediate access memory is relatively expensive, only enough is provided to hold the program and the data it is currently processing. The mass of information on the employees is normally held in backing store as a 'disk-file'. Whenever the CPU requires information about

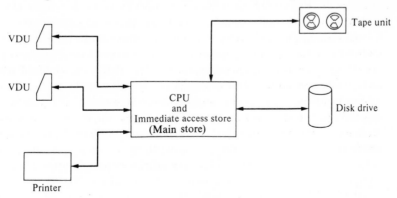

Fig. 1.1 The computer as a data processor

a particular employee, it is taken from the disk (or, more accurately, copied) and placed in the immediate access store. The time taken to perform this operation is a small fraction of a second but is many times slower than reading from the immediate access store. However, the cost of storing information on disk is very low indeed and this compensates for its relative slowness.

The tape transport provides a form of backing store which is much cheaper than the disk. In many installations the data on the disks is copied on to tape periodically (say every four hours) and the tapes stored in the basement for security reasons. Every so often (more often in some installations than others) the system is said to 'crash' and everything grinds to a halt. When this happens the last 'tape dump' can be reloaded and the system assumes the state it was in a short time before the crash. Incidentally, 'crash' had the original meaning of a failure resulting from a read-write head in a disk drive crashing into the rotating surface of a disk and physically damaging the magnetic coating on its surface. In practice, 'crash' has come to mean any system failure.

The visual display units (VDUs) allow operators to enter data directly into the system. This could be the number of hours an employee has worked in the current week. Conversely, the VDU can be used to ask specific questions, such as 'How much tax did Mr XYZ pay in November?' To be a little more precise, the VDU does not actually ask questions but it allows the programmer to execute a program containing the relevant question. The VDU may even be used to modify the program itself so that new facilities may be added as the system grows.

1.1.2 The computer as a number cruncher

In the example above the computer devotes much of its time to the manipulation of data in the form of symbols representing information about the employees of a firm. In such applications of the computer, the amount of time spent performing arithmetic (as understood by a mathematician) on numbers is quite small compared with data processing operations.

'Number crunching' refers to computer applications involving very large numbers of mathematical operations—often billions of operations per job. There are numerous applications of number crunching, many of which are described as 'scientific'. For example, consider the application of computers to the modelling of the processes governing the weather. The atmosphere is a continuous, three-dimensional medium made up of the molecules of a number of different gases. The scientist cannot easily deal with a continuous medium, but can make the problem more tractable by considering the atmosphere to be composed of a very large number of cubes. Each of these cubes is considered to have a uniform temperature, density, and pressure. That is, the gas making up the cube shows no variation whatsoever in its physical properties. A cube has six faces and the scientist can create a model of how the cube interacts with each of its six immediate neighbours.

The scientist may start by assuming that all cubes are identical (no initial interaction), and then consider what happens when a source of energy, the sun, is applied to the model. The effect of each cube on its neighbour is calculated, and the whole process is repeated cyclically (iteration). In order to get accurate results, the size of the cubes should be small, otherwise the assumption about the cube being uniform will not be valid. Moreover, the number of iterations needed to get the result to converge to a steady state value is often very large. Consequently, this type of problem often requires very long runs on immensely powerful computers, or supercomputers as they are sometimes called.

Another area in which number crunching pops up is in certain real-time applications of computers. Here, 'real-time' means that the results of the computations are required within a given time of the start of the computations. For example, consider the application of computers to air-traffic control. A rotating radar antenna measures the bearing and distance (range) of each aircraft (target). At time t, target i at position $P(i,t)$, returns an echo giving its range $r(i,t)$, and bearing $b(i,t)$. Unfortunately, because of the nature of radar signals, a random error is associated with the value of each echo from a target which must be taken into account.

The computer is given the data from the radar receiver for n targets, updated p times every minute. From this raw data, it must compute the position of each aircraft, its track, and warn the controller of any possible conflicts. All this requires considerable high-speed numerical computation.

1.1.3 The computer in automatic control

The vast majority of computers are employed in this role rather than the two above. The computer as a control element is normally embedded in some larger system and is 'invisible' to the observer. By invisible I mean that the operator (or the general public) may not be aware of the existence of the computer. For example, a computer is installed in a petrol pump to count and check the cash it receives and then deliver a measured amount of fuel. The user does not care whether the pump is controlled by the latest microprocessor or by a clockwork mechanism as long as it operates correctly.

A good example of a computer in automatic control is an aircraft's automatic landing system illustrated in Fig. 1.2. In this example, the aircraft's position (height, distance from touch down, and distance off the runway centre-line) and speed are determined by various radio techniques in conjunction with a ground-based instrument-landing system. This information is fed to the three computers which, individually, determine the error in the aircraft's course. This error is the difference between the aircraft's measured position, and the position it should be in. The resulting outputs from the computer are the signals required to move the aircraft's control

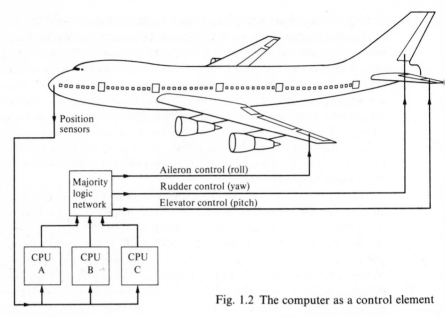

Fig. 1.2 The computer as a control element

surfaces (ailerons, elevator, rudder) and, if necessary, adjust the engine thrust. In this case the computer's program is held in immediate-access memory of a variety called 'read-only memory' (ROM) which can be read from but not written to. Once the program to land the plane has been developed it should not need modifying. Note that there are three computers each working on the same problem with the same inputs. The outputs of the computers are fed to a majority-logic circuit. If all three inputs to the majority-logic circuit are the same, its output is identical to its inputs. If one computer fails, the circuit selects its output to be the same as that produced by the two good computers. This makes the system highly reliable.

1.1.4 The computer as a component

This example is really an extension of the case of the computer in an automatic landing system. When the microprocessor first appeared, one of its social impacts was to generate friction between departments of electrical engineering and departments of computer science in universities and polytechnics. Both departments thought that the microprocessor belonged to them. A computer scientist sees the microprocessor as little more than a low-cost minicomputer with rather basic facilities. An electronic engineer, on the other hand, sees the microprocessor as just another component, albeit a sophisticated and complex one. In fact, the vast majority of microprocessor applications do indeed fall into the category of the microprocessor as a component.

Consider the application of a microprocessor to a hi-fi cassette deck. At first thought, a microprocessor may seem a little out of place in a system devoted to the processing of analogue signals. Microprocessors currently take no part in the processing of the speech and music signals themselves, but they do facilitate the control of the cassette deck in three ways. Since 1983 audio systems using digital storage and processing techniques have appeared, but these do not use general purpose microprocessors to do the signal processing.

1. The control of the mechanical parts of the system. In older (and cheaper) cassette recorders, the controls (record, play-back, pause and rewind) were large buttons which directly moved the various cogs and mechanical linkages inside the recorder. Today most good cassette decks employ electronically operated switches, called solenoids, to perform these functions. By using a microprocessor to read the position of the switches on the front panel, an advanced level of control is possible. For example, if the user presses fast rewind while the deck is in the fast forward mode, the microprocessor can slow, stop, and put the tape in a rewind mode, all in an orderly manner. If this operation were performed manually, without a pause to let the tape slow down, the tape would at best be stretched, and at worst would snap.

2. The control of a tape counter. In older cassette decks the tape position indicator is simply a mechanical revolution counter, displaying (typically) from 000 to 999 as the tape moves. By allowing a microprocessor to perform this function it is possible to gain a number of new facilities. For example, it is now feasible to ask the cassette deck to rewind from its current position to a given point on the tape and to replay the previous section. As there is a relationship between the tape counter value and the length of the tape, it is possible to indicate either the time elapsed since the beginning of the tape, or the time to go before the end of the tape.

3. The setting up of the bias and equalization systems. All audio recording systems have two parameters associated with them, bias and equalization. On nearly all cassette decks a switch selects one of three pairs of values of bias and equalization corresponding to the three basic types of tape (ferro, chrome, and metal). On some of the more advanced decks a microprocessor records a series of tones at the beginning of the tape and then adjusts the values of bias and equalization to the optimum for that particular tape.

1.2 Mainframe, mini, and micro

The four above examples should help to make clear the distinctions between the terms 'mainframe computer', 'minicomputer' and 'microprocessor'. In the beginning there was only the mainframe computer. This was a physically large and fabulously expensive beast complete with a priesthood of programmers, operators, and maintenance engineers. Such a colossus was found only in large installations and often tended to be employed as a general-purpose machine. In industry, the mainframe is used to design products and simulate their behaviour as well as to deal with such mundane operations as payroll calculations. Perhaps one of the most notable features of a mainframe is its wide range of peripherals—VDUs, printers, card readers and punches, disk and tape drives.

Not only the rich and powerful needed computer power. Scientists in small laboratories wanted to speed up their analysis of scientific data, and engineers, for example, wanted to control dams by measuring the flow of water upstream and hence predict the future level of the water. In both these cases the mainframe would have proved prohibitively expensive. The computer manufacturers provided a handly solution to such problems in the form of the minicomputer. There is no precise definition of a minicomputer, but the following attributes may be used to describe it.

Cost   The minicomputer is much cheaper than a mainframe. Typically, a mini falls in the £5000 to 50 000 price range.

Physical size   The mainframe takes up a largish chunk of real-estate, often a whole floor of a building. A mini, on the other hand, is frequently quite small, sometimes no larger than the average wardrobe.

Peripherals   A single mainframe almost certainly has a wide spectrum of users (especially in a university, polytechnic, or research establishment), each with their own particular demands. This leads to large numbers of peripherals: disks to store user programs and data, VDUs and printers, and now graphics equipment capable of producing complex diagrams. The mini is frequently dedicated to a single task (say controlling and evaluating an experiment) and often has few peripherals: perhaps a single disk drive, a couple of VDUs, and a printer. Having said this, it must be pointed out that some mainframe computers are gradually being replaced by minicomputers or groups of minicomputers in the form of a network.

Performance   The latest mini has only a fraction of the computational power of the latest mainframe. I say latest because the advance in computer technology is so rapid that today's low-cost mini is often far more powerful than yesterday's mainframe. One of the reasons for the mini's lower computational power is that it uses smaller word-lengths than mainframes. The word-length of a computer is the number of bits (ones and zeros) in its basic unit of information storage and manipulation. The effects of this will be dealt with later, but here it is sufficient to state that one result of a short word-length is to increase the number of arithmetic operations needed to perform a particular calculation to a given level of precision.

The microprocessor is nothing more than a CPU on a single chip of silicon. The importance of the microprocessor is a consequence of its staggeringly low cost and minute size. A microprocessor alone can do nothing. In conjunction with memory, a power supply, and the necessary peripherals it can be said to form a microcomputer. At the current level of technology most microcomputers have a performance below those of existing minicomputers. A microcomputer costs from £200 to 5000 (although educational 'toys' can be bought for under £100, and simple microprocessor-based controllers may also fall in this price range). It is worth noting that several minicomputer manufacturers have themselves, or in conjunction with others, brought out microprocessors which are functionally equivalent to the CPUs of their own minicomputers. In this way existing minicomputer software can be run on these microcomputers (which run more slowly than their bigger 'mini' brothers).

1.3 The stored-program computer—an overview

Before discussing the stored-program computer, consider first the human being. It is natural to compare today's wonder, the computer, with the human just as the Victorians did with their technology. They coined expressions like 'He has a screw loose' or 'He has run out of steam' in their endeavour to see their technology in human terms. There have been times when the computer has been compared with the human brain, and periods when the computer has been contrasted with it, and the poor computer called 'a high-speed moron'.

Figure 1.3 shows how a human may be viewed as a system with inputs, a processing device, and outputs. The inputs are sight (eyes), smell (nose), taste (tongue), touch (skin), sound (ear), and position (muscle tension). The information from these sensors is processed by the brain.

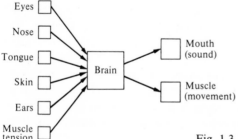

Fig. 1.3 The organization of a human being

The brain performs two functions. It stores new information, and processes the inputs from its sensors. The storage aspect of the brain is important because it modifies the operation of the brain in a process we call learning. Because the brain learns from all new stimuli, it does not always exhibit the same response to a given stimulus. Once a child has been burned by a flame it reacts differently the next time it encounters fire.

The output from the brain is used to generate speech, or to control the muscles needed to move the body.

Figure 1.4 shows how a computer can be compared with a human. It may

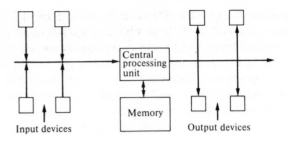

Fig. 1.4 The organization of a computer

have all the inputs a human has, and inputs for a few things we cannot detect. A computer can directly sense ultraviolet light, infrared, X-rays, or radio waves. The output from the computer is also more versatile than that of humans. It can produce mechanical movement (by means of motors), or can directly generate light (TV displays), sound (from loudspeakers), or even heat.

The computer counterpart of the brain is the central processing unit plus its storage unit (memory). Like the brain, it processes its various inputs and produces an output.

This is not a treatise on the differences between the brain and the computer. However, it is probable that the processing and memory functions of the brain are closely interrelated, while in the computer they are normally distinct. There are people who believe that the major breakthroughs in computing will come when computer architecture takes on more of the features of the brain.

Stored in a computer's memory is a program. The word 'program' has the same meaning as it does in the expressions 'program of studies', or 'program of music'. A computer program is a collection of actions to be carried out by the computer sequentially. The classic analogy of a computer program is a recipe in a cookery book. The recipe is a sequence of commands which must be obeyed one by one, and in the correct order. This analogy is particularly appropriate because the cookery instructions involve operations on ingredients, just as the computer carries out operations on data stored in memory.

The central processing unit reads the instructions making up the program one-by-one, and executes each instruction as it is brought from memory. The word 'execute' means carry out. For example, an instruction 'add A to B' causes the addition of a quantity called A to a quantity called B to be carried out. The actual nature of these instructions does not matter here. What is important is that the most complex actions carried out by a computer can be broken down into a number of more primitive operations. But then again, the most sublime thought of Einstein can be reduced to a large number of impulses transmitted across the synapses of the cells in his brain.

The computer performs its operations on information called 'data' held within its storage unit. This is also the memory in which the program is located. That is, the program and data used by the computer are located in the same memory but, of course, in different regions of it.

Note Throughout this book square brackets denote 'the contents of' so that in the example below, [4] is read as 'the contents of memory location number 4' and is equal to 2.

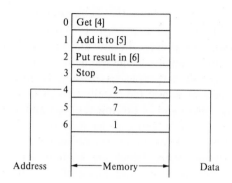

Fig. 1.5 The program and data in memory

Figure 1.5 illustrates how the program (instructions) and data coexist in the same memory. This memory has seven locations, numbered from 0 to 6. Memory is normally regarded as an array of storage locations (boxes or pigeon holes). Each of these 'boxes' has a unique location or address, and it is said to contain data. In Fig. 1.5 address 5 contains the number 7. One great difference between computers and people is that we number things from 1 to m, while the computer numbers things from 0 to $m-1$. This is because 0 is a valid identifier. Unfortunately people often confuse 0 (an identifier) with 0 (meaning 'nothing').

The program occupies successive memory locations from 0 to 3, and the data locations 4 to 6. The first instruction, 'get [4]', means get (fetch) the contents of memory location number 4 from the memory. The next instruction, 'add it to [5]', means add it to the contents of location 5. Thus, the computer adds 2 and 7 to get 9. The third instruction, 'put result in [6]', tells the computer to put the result (i.e. 9) in location 6. This it does, and the 1 that was in location 6 before this instruction was obeyed, is replaced by 9. The final instruction in location 3 tells the computer to stop.

2 LOGIC ELEMENTS AND BOOLEAN ALGEBRA

In this chapter we are going to examine the behaviour of the basic components from which a computer is constructed. Two distinct classes of component are found in a digital computer—the gate and the flip-flop. These are known as combinational and sequential logic-elements, respectively.

This chapter begins by describing the properties of some simple gates and then shows how such gates can be connected together to carry out useful functions in the same way that bricks can be put together to build a house or a school. Following the description of gates comes a section on Boolean algebra which provides a formal tool for the analysis of circuits containing gates. This leads on to Karnaugh maps which are nothing more than a graphical technique for the simplification and manipulation of Boolean equations.

The second part of this chapter is concerned with sequential circuits built from flip-flops. As their name suggests, these circuits involve the time factor and we are interested in their behaviour as a function of time.

The final part of this chapter takes a brief look at some of the aspects of computer circuits of interest to the designer. This is included to provide an overview and is not intended to be comprehensive. Topics included are the electrical characteristics of gates, their economics, and the reliability of systems in general.

One of the more remarkable facts about the digital computer is that all its circuits can be considered as nothing more than the interconnection of a few primitive elements called gates. There are three fundamental types of gate AND, OR, and NOT (INVERTER), plus two gates which are derived from the other three (i.e. NAND and NOR). Later we shall see that all other gates and therefore all digital circuits, may be designed from the appropriate interconnection of NAND (or NOR) gates alone. Thus, the most complex digital computer can be reduced to a mass of NAND gates. This fact does not devalue the computer, as the human brain itself is just a lot of neurons joined in a particularly complex way.

We don't use gates to build computers because we like them or because Boolean algebra (i.e. the arithmetic used to describe the properties of gates) is great fun. Information inside a computer is represented in digital form. In a digital system all variables and constants must take a value chosen from a set of values called an 'alphabet'. In decimal arithmetic we have an alphabet composed of the symbols 0, 1, 2, . . . , 9, in Morse code we have an alphabet composed of the four symbols dot, dash, short space, and long space. Other digital systems are Braille, semaphore, and the days of the week. An advantage of digital representation of information is that a symbol may be distorted, but as long as the level of distortion is not sufficient for one symbol to be taken for another, the original symbol may always be recognized and reconstituted.

The alphabet selected for digital computers has two symbols, 0 and 1 (sometimes called false and true, or low and high, or off and on). The advantage of such an alphabet is that the symbols can be made as unlike each other as possible so as to aid discrimination. Some computers store binary information on paper tape—a hole representing one binary value and no-hole representing the other. When reading paper tape the computer has only to distinguish between a hole and no-hole. Suppose we decided to do away with the binary computer and to replace it with a decimal computer. Imagine that paper tape were still being used. A number on the tape would consist of no-hole or a hole in one of nine sizes (ten symbols in all). How do we tell a size six hole from a size five or a size seven? Such a system would require extremely precise electronics.

A single binary digit is known as a bit (BInary digiT) and is the smallest unit of information possible. That is, a bit cannot be subdivided into smaller units. In current technology, the binary values of information inside a computer are represented by two ranges of voltage. Figure 2.1 illustrates these ranges for a typical logic element found in digital computers.

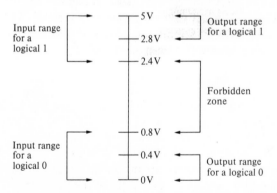

Fig. 2.1 The two states of a typical logic element

A manufacturer of digital components makes a number of promises or guarantees to the user. Firstly, he guarantees that the output of a gate in a logical zero state shall be in the range 0 V to 0.4 V, and that the output of a gate in a logical one state will be in the range 2.8 V to 5.0 V. Similarly, he guarantees that the input of a gate will recognize a voltage in the range 0 V to 0.8 V as a logical zero, and a voltage in the range 2.4 V to 5.0 V as a logical one. By making the input range (for a given logic value) greater than the output range, the designer allows for noise or unwanted signals. For example, a logical zero output of 0.4 V may have a noise spike of 0.2 V added to it to give a total of 0.6 V. This is still guaranteed to be recognized as a logical zero. The difference between the input and output ranges for a logic value is known as its guaranteed noise immunity. A further discussion of the electrical characteristics of logic elements is given in Section 2.7.

Notes on logic values

1. There are always two discrete states and every logic value must assume one of these states. There is no such thing as a valid intermediate state (a state which is neither 1 nor 0).

2. Each logic input or output can exist in only one state at any one time.

3. Each logic stage has an inverse or complement which is the opposite of its current state. The complement of a true (one) state is a false (zero) state, and vice versa.

4. A logic value can be a constant or a variable. If it is a constant it always remains in that state; if it is a variable it may be switched between the states 0 and 1.

5. A variable is often named by the action it causes to take place. The following logical variables are all self-evident: START, STOP, RESET, COUNT, ADD.

6. The logical value which causes a variable to carry out the function suggested by its name is arbitrary. If a logical one causes the action, the variable is called active-high. If a logical zero causes the action, the variable is called active-low. Thus, if an active-high variable is labelled START, a logical one (i.e. START = 1) will initiate the action. If it is active-low and labelled $\overline{START}$, a logical zero will trigger the action.

2.1 Basic gates

In this section we are going to define the properties of the five basic gates from which all digital systems are constructed The word 'gate' conveys the idea of a two-state device—open or shut. A gate may be thought of as a black box with one or more input terminals and an output terminal. The digital signals at the input terminals are processed by the gate to produce a digital signal at its output terminal. The nature of the gate determines the actual processing involved. If a gate has two input terminals A and B, and an output terminal C, then the output may be written C = F(A,B). This equation is expressed in conventional algebra, where A, B, C are two-valued, and F is some logical function.

To demonstrate that the idea of gates is not only simple but also commonplace, consider an example from the analogue world. An equation is defined as $y = F(x)$, where $y = 2x^2 + x + 1$. If x is thought of as the input to a black box, and y its output, the circuit of Fig. 2.2 shows how y is generated by a sequence of operations on x. Here the operations performed are those of

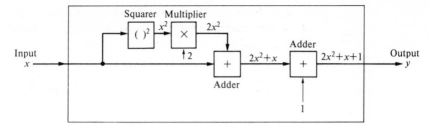

Fig. 2.2 The analogue processor

addition, multiplication, and squaring. The boxes carrying out these operations are entirely analogous to gates in the digital world.

Before dealing with the gates themselves and their interconnections to form digital (or switching) circuits, it is necessary to define a few elementary conventions. Because we write from left to right, many (but not all) logic circuits are also read from left to right. This means that information flows from left to right with the inputs of gates on the left, and the outputs on the right. As there are often many information paths, and the diagram is drawn on paper in a two-dimensional format, it is frequently necessary for information paths to cross one another. Figure 2.3 shows how this is done. In

The dot indicates
the intersection (connection)
of two lines

These lines are
not connected
together

Fig. 2.3 Circuit conventions

general, the standard procedure is to regard two lines which simply cross as not being connected. The actual connection of two lines is denoted by a dot at their intersection. The voltage at any point along a line (i.e. conductor) is constant, and therefore the logical level is also constant. That is, if one end of a conductor is in a logical state P, then every point along the line is in the same state.

The AND gate

The logic symbol for an AND gate is given in Fig. 2.4(a) The output of the AND gate is true if and only if each of its inputs is true. The classic way of looking at an AND gate is in terms of an electric circuit or a roadway as illustrated in Fig. 2.4(b).

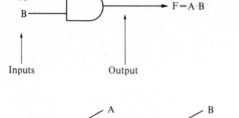

Fig. 2.4(a) The AND gate

Fig. 2.4(b) The representation of an AND gate by a switching circuit

Electric current (or traffic) can flow along the circuit (road) only if switches (bridges) A and B are closed. The logical symbol for AND is a dot so that A AND B is written as A·B. As in normal algebra the dot is often omitted and A·B is written AB.

A useful way of describing the relationship between the inputs of gates (and other circuits) and their output(s) is the truth table; see, e.g. Table 2.1. In a truth table the value of each output is tabulated for every possible combination of the inputs. As the inputs are two-valued, a circuit with n inputs has 2^n lines in its truth table. The order in which the 2^n possible inputs are taken is not important but by convention the order is 0 ... 00, 0 ... 01, ..., 1 ... 10, 1 ... 11.

Table 2.1 Truth table for the AND gate

| Inputs | | Output |
A	B	F = A·B
0	0	0
0	1	0
1	0	0
1	1	1

0 0 0 ⎫
0 1 0 ⎬ False as one or more inputs are false
1 0 0 ⎭
1 1 1   True as all inputs are true

In this example we have taken a two-input AND gate. There is no reason why we cannot have any number of inputs to a gate—some real gates have three or four inputs, and one gate, the 74133, is a 13 input NAND gate. Section 2.3.2 contains details of some of the types of gate widely available. Later, when we come to computer architecture and assembly language programming we will see that the AND operation can be applied to words. A word is a group of bits normally dealt with as a single entity. For example, consider the ANDing of the following two words:

```
1 1 0 1 1 1 0 0  A
0 1 1 0 0 1 0 1  B

0 1 0 0 0 1 0 0  A·B
```

Here we have applied the AND operation to each pair of bits so that the *i*th bit of A is ANDed with the *i*th bit of B. The AND operation, when applied to words, is called a 'logical' operation to distinguish it from an 'arithmetic' operation such as addition or subtraction. A logical AND is used to mask off certain bits in a word. For example, if we wish to clear the four left-most bits of an eight-bit word to zero, ANDing the word with 00001111 will do the trick.

The OR gate

The logic symbol for an OR gate is given in Fig. 2.5(a). The output of an OR gate is true if either (or both) of its inputs is true. This gate may be represented by the switching circuit of Fig. 2.5(b). The logical symbol for an OR operation is a plus sign, so that A OR B is written as A + B.

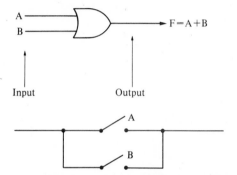

Fig. 2.5(a) The OR gate

Fig. 2.5(b) The representation of an OR gate by a switching circuit

The circuit of Fig. 2.5(b) is complete if A or B is closed. Note that the use of 'OR' here is different from the English usage. The Boolean OR means (A or B), or (A and B), whereas the English usage means A or B but not (A and B). We shall see that the English use of OR corresponds to the Boolean function known as EXCLUSIVE OR. The EXCLUSIVE OR is an important function and is sometimes written EOR or XOR.

Table 2.2 Truth table for the OR gate

Inputs		Output
A	B	F = A + B
0	0	0	False as both inputs are false
0	1	1
1	0	1	True as one or more inputs are true
1	1	1

A computer can also perform a logical OR on words as the following example illustrates.

```
1 0 0 1 1 1 0 0   A
0 0 1 0 0 1 0 1   B
```

```
1 0 1 1 1 1 0 1   A + B
```

The logical OR operation is used to set one or more bits in a word. Set means make a logical one, and clear means reset to a logical zero. For example, the least significant bit of a word may be set by ORing it with 00 . . . 01.

The NOT gate

The logic symbol for a NOT gate is given in Fig. 2.6(a). The NOT gate (inverter or complementor) inverts the state of the signal at its input. The operation of the NOT gate may be visualized in terms of the relay illustrated in Fig. 2.6(b).

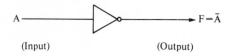

A ─────────────▷○─────────────► $F = \bar{A}$

(Input)   (Output)   Fig. 2.6(a) The NOT gate or inverter

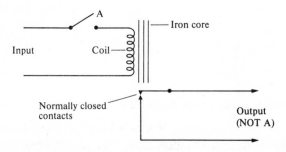

Fig. 2.6(b) The representation of a NOT gate by an electronic relay

If switch A is open no current flows through the coil and the iron is unmagnetized. The normally-closed contacts are closed so that they form a switch which is on when A is open. If A is now closed, a current flows through the coil, the iron is magnetized and part of the normally-closed switch is pulled towards the iron, breaking its circuit and assuming the opposite state to switch A. The relay is used by a computer to control external devices and will be discussed further in Section 5.5.3.

Table 2.3 Truth table for the inverter

Input A	Output $F = \bar{A}$
0	1
1	0

The NOT function can also be applied to words:

1 1 0 1 1 1 0 0 A
0 0 1 0 0 0 1 1 $\overline{A}$ or NOT A

The NAND and NOR gates

The logic symbols for the NAND and NOR gates are given in Fig. 2.7. These two gates are dealt with together because they correspond to an AND gate followed by an inverter (Not AND), and an OR gate followed by an inverter (Not OR), respectively.

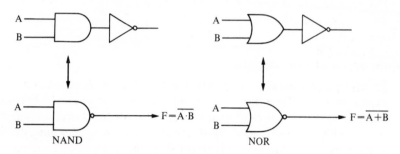

Fig. 2.7 The NAND gate and the NOR gate

It should be noted here that $\overline{A \cdot B}$ is not the same as $\overline{A} \cdot \overline{B}$ just as $\overline{A + B}$ is not the same as $\overline{A} + \overline{B}$.

Table 2.4 Truth table for the NAND gate

Inputs		Output
A	B	$F = \overline{A \cdot B}$
0	0	1
0	1	1
1	0	1
1	1	0

Table 2.5 Truth table for the NOR gate

Inputs		Output
A	B	$F = \overline{A + B}$
0	0	1
0	1	0
1	0	0
1	1	0

In order to give students a feeling for the different effects that the various gates have on two inputs, A and B, Table 2.6 compares the outputs of the four gates described above. The EXCLUSIVE OR and its complement, the EXCLUSIVE NOR, are also included in this table for reference. The EXCLUSIVE OR is derived from AND, OR and NOT gates, and will appear later in this chapter.

Table 2.6 Truth table for six basic gates

Inputs		Outputs					
		OR	AND	NOR	NAND	EOR	EXNOR
A	B	A + B	A·B	$\overline{A+B}$	$\overline{A·B}$	A⊕B	$\overline{A⊕B}$
0	0	0	0	1	1	0	1
0	1	1	0	0	1	1	0
1	0	1	0	0	1	1	0
1	1	1	1	0	0	0	1

2.2 Some applications of gates

In this section a number of applications of gates are presented in the form of examples. It is my intention to demonstrate that a few gates can be connected together in such a way as to realize a circuit whose function, and importance, may readily be appreciated by the reader. Following this introduction to gates a more formal section is devoted to the analysis of logic circuits by means of Boolean algebra.

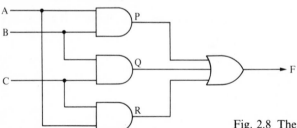

Fig. 2.8 The use of gates—Example 1

Example 1   From Fig. 2.8 we can create a truth table (Table 2.7) to obtain an output F as a function of the three inputs A, B, and C. There are three inputs, so there must be eight lines in the truth table. To simplify things the intermediate values P, Q, and R are included in the truth table.

Table 2.7 Truth table for Fig. 2.8

Inputs			Intermediate values			Output
A	B	C	P = AB	Q = BC	R = AC	F = P + Q + R
0	0	0	0	0	0	0
0	0	1	0	0	0	0
0	1	0	0	0	0	0
0	1	1	0	1	0	1
1	0	0	0	0	0	0
1	0	1	0	0	1	1
1	1	0	1	0	0	1
1	1	1	1	1	1	1

The output function, F, is given by: $F = P + Q + R$, where $P = AB$, $Q = BC$, and $R = AC$. Therefore, $F = AB + BC + AC$. If the truth table is inspected it can be seen that the output is true if two or more of the inputs A, B, and C are true. That is, the arrangement represents a majority logic circuit whose output has the same value as the majority of inputs. We have already seen how such a circuit may be used in an automatic landing system in an aircraft.

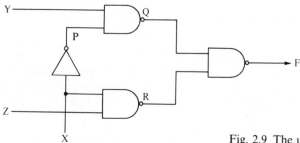

Fig. 2.9 The use of gates—Example 2

Example 2 As in the previous example, the circuit of Fig. 2.9 has three inputs, one output, and three intermediate values.

Table 2.8 Truth table for Fig. 2.9

Inputs			Intermediate values			Output
X	Y	Z	$P = \overline{X}$	$Q = \overline{YP}$	$R = \overline{XZ}$	$F = \overline{QR}$
0	0	0	1	1	1	0
0	0	1	1	1	1	0
0	1	0	1	0	1	1
0	1	1	1	0	1	1
1	0	0	0	1	1	0
1	0	1	0	1	0	1
1	1	0	0	1	1	0
1	1	1	0	1	0	1

By inspecting the truth table (Table 2.8) it can be seen that when the input X is 0, the output, F, is equal to Y. When X is 1, the output is equal to Z. That is, the above circuit is an electronic switch, connecting the output to one of two inputs, Y or Z, depending on the state of a control input X. This circuit is called a two-input multiplexer and may be represented by the arrangement of Fig. 2.10. Because the word multiplexer is used so often it is frequently abbreviated to MUX or MPLX.

From the circuit diagram of Fig. 2.9 an equation for F can readily be derived by considering the effect of the gates on the inputs.

$F = \overline{QR}$, $Q = \overline{PY}$, $P = \overline{X}$;

therefore $Q = \overline{\overline{X}Y}$, $R = \overline{XZ}$;

therefore $F = \overline{\overline{\overline{X}Y}.\overline{XZ}}$.

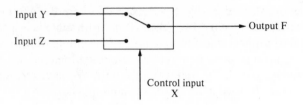

Fig. 2.10 The logical representation of Fig. 2.9

When we come to Boolean algebra we will see how this type of expression can be simplified. Another way of obtaining a Boolean expression is to use the truth table. Each time a one appears in the output column we can write down the set of inputs that cause the output to be true. Thus, the output is true when:

$$\text{(i) } X=0, Y=1, Z=0 \quad (\overline{X}Y\overline{Z}),$$

$$\text{(ii) } X=0, Y=1, Z=1 \quad (\overline{X}YZ),$$

$$\text{(iii) } X=1, Y=0, Z=1 \quad (X\overline{Y}Z),$$

$$\text{or} \quad \text{(iv) } X=1, Y=1, Z=1 \quad (XYZ).$$

There are four possible combinations of inputs which make the output true. Therefore, the output can be expressed as:

$$F = \overline{X}Y\overline{Z} + \overline{X}YZ + X\overline{Y}Z + XYZ.$$

That is, the function is true if any of the above four conditions is true. A function represented in this way is called a sum of products because it is the logical OR of a number of variables ANDed together.

Each of the terms, (i) to (iv) above, are called minterms. A minterm is an AND (product) term which includes each of the variables in either its true or complemented form. For example, in the case above $\overline{X}YZ$ is a minterm but $\overline{X}Y$ is not because the latter includes only two of the three variables. As the output of the circuit must be the same, whether it is derived from the truth table or from the logic diagram, the two above equations must be equal, with the result that:

$$\overline{\overline{X}Y.\overline{X}Z} = \overline{X}Y\overline{Z} + \overline{X}YZ + X\overline{Y}Z + XYZ.$$

the multiplexer may seem a long way from programming, but I have included it here to demonstrate the relationship between hardware and software. The power of a digital computer (or a human brain) lies in its ability to make decisions. In the world of computing, this 'decision taking' corresponds to the conditional branch or jump. For example, in high level languages we have the following constructs:

IF (X − 2.0*Z)10,20,30   FORTRAN
IF X = 5 THEN Z = 27   BASIC
IF t > = 0 THEN I := I + 2;   Pascal

The BASIC and PASCAL statements demonstrate two-way branches, and the FORTRAN a three-way branch. In practice, a three-way branch is implemented as two consecutive two-way branches. The conditional branch is implemented by testing for the specified condition (e.g. X = 0) and then executing the 'then' part of the construct if the condition is true, or continuing with the next instruction if it is false. The actual branching is done by loading one of two possible numbers into the program counter. The program counter is the part of the CPU which holds the address (i.e. location) of the next instruction to be carried out. By changing this address we can choose between two alternative courses of action. Consider now the arrangement of Fig. 2.11. This example may be skipped until the reader has read Chapter 4 if he is not familiar with the basic structure of the CPU.

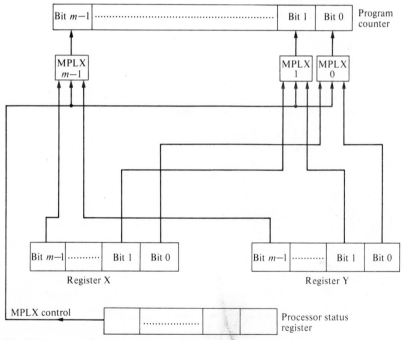

Fig. 2.11 An application of the multiplexer

Two registers X and Y contain *m*-bit addresses. The *m* bits of these registers are fed to *m* multiplexers whose *m* outputs supply the *m* bits of the program counter. The control inputs of the multiplexers are wired together and connected to one bit of the processor status register. The processor status register (PSR) has its contents determined by the results of certain calculations, and its various bits tell us whether the results of the last operation were zero, positive, negative, etc. In Fig. 2.11 we can see that a particular bit of the PSR can directly feed the contents of registers X or Y to the program counter, and therefore dictate which of two possible sequences of operations are to happen next. This example has been selected to show how a software operation may be implemented. In practice, the way in which conditional jumps are handled in real computers is somewhat different to the procedure I have outlined above.

Example 3   The truth table (Table 2.9) for this circuit (Fig. 2.12) has two inputs, two intermediate values, and one output. This circuit is one of the most important circuits in digital electronics. The output is true if one of the inputs is true but not if both inputs are true. We call this the EXCLUSIVE OR function and it corresponds to the normal English use of the word 'or'. Because this function is so popular, it has its own symbol:

$$F = A \oplus B$$
$$F = A \text{ EOR } B$$

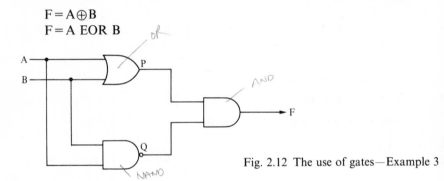

Fig. 2.12 The use of gates—Example 3

Table 2.9 Truth table for Fig. 2.12

Inputs		Intermediate values		Output
A	B	$P = A + B$	$Q = \overline{AB}$	$F = PQ$
0	0	0	1	0
0	1	1	1	1
1	0	1	1	1
1	1	1	0	0

Fig. 2.13 The EXCLUSIVE OR

Figure 2.13 gives the symbol for an EXCLUSIVE OR gate. From the truth table F is true when $A = 0$ and $B = 1$, or when $A = 1$ and $B = 0$, so that $F = \overline{A}B + A\overline{B}$. From Fig. 2.12 we have:

F = PQ,
P = A + B,
and Q = $\overline{AB}$.
Therefore F = (A + B)·$\overline{AB}$.

As these two equations (i.e. F = $\overline{A}B + A\overline{B}$ and F = (A + B)·$\overline{AB}$) must be equivalent, we can therefore build an EXCLUSIVE OR function in the manner depicted in Fig. 2.14. It is in fact perfectly possible to build an EXCLUSIVE OR with a single integrated circuit containing four NAND gates (Fig. 2.15). I leave it as an exercise for the reader to verify that the above arrangement is indeed an EXCLUSIVE OR.

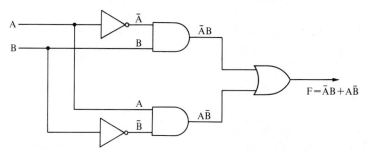

Fig. 2.14 An alternative representation of the EXCLUSIVE OR

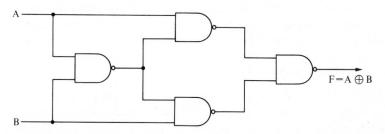

Fig. 2.15 An EXCLUSIVE OR circuit constructed with NAND gates only

The EXCLUSIVE OR is a remarkably versatile logic element which pops up in many places in digital electronics. The output of an EXCLUSIVE OR is true if its inputs are different, and false if they are the same. This feature allows us to build an equality tester which indicates whether or not two words are identical (Fig. 2.16). If the two words are equal, the outputs of all EXCLUSIVE ORs are zero, and the output of the *m*-input NOR gate is a logical one. This output may be connected to one of the bits of a processor status register so that it can determine which of two courses of action may be taken when a conditional branch is encountered. The processor status register, and its role in the operation of the central processing unit, is discussed in Chapter 4.

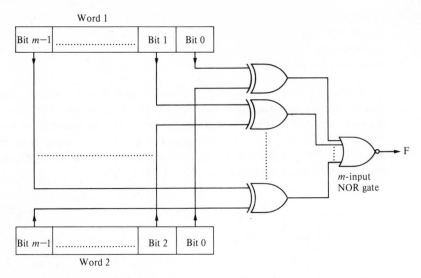

Fig. 2.16 The application of EXCLUSIVE OR gates in an equality tester

It should now be apparent that not only can a given function be represented by more than one Boolean expression, but that different combinations of gates may be used to implement the function. This is not the place to go into great depth on the detailed design of logic circuits but it is interesting to see how the designer goes about selecting one particular implementation in preference to another. Some of the basic criteria by which circuits are judged are given below. In general, the design of logic circuits is often affected by other factors than those described here. Section 2.7 discusses some of these factors.

Speed   The speed of a circuit (i.e. how long it takes the output to respond to a change at an input) is approximately governed by the maximum number of gates through which a change must propagate. In Fig. 2.12 there are only 2 gates in series, while in Fig. 2.14 there are 3 gates in series. This makes the first circuit 50 per cent faster. Note that not all real gates have the same propagation delay: some gates respond more rapidly to changes than others.

Number of interconnections   It costs money to wire gates together. Even if a printed circuit is used, somebody has to design it, and the more interconnections used the more expensive it will be. One parameter of circuit design is the total number of inputs to gates. In Fig. 2.12 there are 6 inputs, while in Fig. 2.14 there are 8 inputs.

Number of packages   Simple gates of the types being discussed here are normally available in 14-pin packages (two pins of which are needed for the power supply). As it costs virtually nothing to add extra gates to the silicon chip, the total number of gates is limited only by the available pins. Thus, an inverter requires two pins, so 6 inverters are provided on the chip. Similarly, a two-input AND/NAND/OR/NOR gate needs three pins, so four of these gates are put on the chip. As each of these circuits uses three different types of gate, both circuits require three 14-pin integrated circuits. Even so, the circuit of Fig. 2.12 is better than that of Fig. 2.14 because there are more unused gates left in the ICs, freeing them for use by other parts of the computer system.

2.3 An introduction to Boolean algebra

George Boole was an English mathematician who, in the 19th century, developed a mathematical analysis of logic. Boolean algebra would probably have remained a tool of the philosopher had it not been for the development of electronics in the 20th century.

In 1938 Claude Shannon applied Boolean algebra to switching circuits using relays. Such circuits originally appeared in connection with telephone exchanges and later digital computers. Today, Boolean algebra is used to design digital circuits, analyse their behaviour, and often, to simplify them.

When I was first introduced to algebra as a twelve-year-old schoolboy, I asked my teacher why we had to learn algebra, as I did not see any point in solving equations. 'Clements', he said, 'We teach algebra to make the life of schoolboys miserable.' A similar question about Boolean algebra often lies at the back of my students' minds. Digital design is concerned with the conversion of ideas into actual hardware, and Boolean algebra is a tool which facilitates this process. In particular, Boolean algebra permits an idea to be expressed in a mathematical form, and the resulting expression to be simplified and then translated into the real hardware of gates and other logic elements.

Boolean algebra deals with variables which have two possible values 0 or 1. Literals or constants also exist and likewise also have the values 0 or 1. Only three operations are permitted in Boolean algebra. The first two are the logical OR represented by a plus ' + ', and the logical AND represented by a dot '·'. The use of these symbols is rather confusing because they are the same as those used for addition and multiplication in everyday life. The reason that these particular symbols have been chosen is that they behave (subject to the postulates of Boolean algebra) rather like conventional addition and multiplication. Some texts use a $\bigcup$ (cup) or a V to denote $+$, and a $\bigcap$ (cap) or a $\wedge$ to denote a dot.

The third operation permitted is that of negation or complementation, and is denoted by a bar over a literal or a variable. The complement of 0 (i.e. $\bar{0}$) is 1, and vice versa. The equation '$X + Y\bar{Z} = A$' is read as 'X or Y and not Z equals A'. The priority of an AND operator is higher than that of an OR operator so that this expression means $A = X + (Y\bar{Z})$ and not $A = (X + Y)\bar{Z}$. Note that when this equation is read out its meaning is ambiguous. It should be appreciated that the arithmetic operations of subtraction and division do not exist in Boolean algebra.

The effect of the operations $+$, $\cdot$, NOT, is best illustrated by means of truth tables (Table 2.10). These rules may be extended to any number of variables.

Table 2.10 Boolean operations on constants

NOT	AND	OR
$\bar{0}=1$	$0\cdot 0=0$	$0+0=0$
$\bar{1}=0$	$0\cdot 1=0$	$0+1=1$
	$1\cdot 0=0$	$1+0=1$
	$1\cdot 1=1$	$1+1=1$

Boolean variables obey the same commutative, distributive, and associative laws as the variables of conventional algebra, listed as follows.

$A+B=B+A$
$A\cdot B=B\cdot A$

The AND and OR operators are commutative so that the order of the variables in a sum or product group does not matter.

$A\cdot(B+C)=A\cdot B+A\cdot C$
$A+BC=(A+B)(A+C)$

The AND operator behaves like multiplication, and the OR operator like addition. The distributive property states that in an expression containing both AND and OR operators the AND operator takes precedence over the OR.

$A\cdot(B\cdot C)=(A\cdot B)\cdot C$
$A+(B+C)=(A+B)+C$

The AND and OR operators are associative so that the order in which sub-totals are calculated does not matter.

The basic rules of Boolean algebra are given below.

$$0\cdot X=0, \qquad 1\cdot X=X, \qquad X\cdot X=X, \qquad X\cdot\bar{X}=0.$$

$$0+X=X, \qquad 1+X=1, \qquad X+X=X \qquad X+\bar{X}=1.$$

$$\bar{\bar{X}}=X.$$

These equations may be proved by substituting all the possible values for X (i.e. 0 or 1). For example, consider $0\cdot X=0$. If $X=1$ we have $0\cdot 1=0$ which is true. Similarly, if $X=0$ we have $0\cdot 0=0$ which is also true. Therefore, $0\cdot X=0$ is true for all possible values of X.

Using the above rules we can readily derive some theorems to help in the simplification of expressions.

Theorem 1 $X+XY=X$.
Proof: $X+XY=X(1+Y)=X(1)=X$.

Theorem 2 $X + \overline{X}Y = X + Y$.
Proof: $X + \overline{X}Y = (X + XY) + \overline{X}Y$ (by Theorem 1)
$= X + XY + \overline{X}Y$
$= X + Y(X + \overline{X})$
$= X + Y(1) = X + Y$.

Theorem 3 $XY + \overline{X}Z + YZ = XY + \overline{X}Z$.
Proof: $XY + \overline{X}Z + YZ = XY + \overline{X}Z + YZ(X + \overline{X})$ (remember
$(X + \overline{X}) = 1$)
$= XY + \overline{X}Z + XYZ + \overline{X}YZ$
$= XY(1 + Z) + \overline{X}Z(1 + Y)$
$= XY(1) + \overline{X}Z(1)$
$= XY + \overline{X}Z$.

Theorem 4 $X(X + Y) = X$.
Proof: $X(X + Y) = XX + XY$
$= X + XY$
$= X(1 + Y)$
$= X(1)$
$= X$.

Theorem 5 $X(\overline{X} + Y) = XY$.
Proof: $X(\overline{X} + Y) = X\overline{X} + XY = XY$.

Theorem 6 $(X + Y)(X + \overline{Y}) = X$.
Proof: $(X + Y)(X + \overline{Y}) = XX + X\overline{Y} + XY + Y\overline{Y}$
$= X + X\overline{Y} + XY$
$= X(1 + \overline{Y} + Y)$
$= X$.

Theorem 7 $(X + Y)(\overline{X} + Z) = XZ + \overline{X}Y$.
Proof: $(X + Y)(\overline{X} + Z) = X\overline{X} + XZ + \overline{X}Y + YZ$
$= XZ + \overline{X}Y + YZ$
$= XZ + \overline{X}Y$ (by Theorem 3).

Theorem 8 $(X + Y)(\overline{X} + Z)(Y + Z) = (X + Y)(\overline{X} + Z)$.
Proof: $(X + Y)(\overline{X} + Z)(Y + Z) = (XZ + \overline{X}Y)(Y + Z)$ (by Theorem 7)
$= XYZ + XZZ + \overline{X}YY + \overline{X}YZ$
$= XZ(Y + 1) + \overline{X}Y(1 + Z)$
$= XZ + \overline{X}Y$
$= (X + Y)(\overline{X} + Z)$.   (by Theorem 7).

An alternative proof for Theorem 8 is provided later.

Theorem 9 $\overline{X \cdot Y \cdot Z} = \overline{X} + \overline{Y} + \overline{Z}$.

Theorem 10 $\overline{X + Y + Z} = \overline{X} \cdot \overline{Y} \cdot \overline{Z}$.

Theorems 9 and 10 are collectively called de Morgan's theorem.

Observations

I am including the following observations because they represent the most frequently encountered misconceptions.

Observation 1: $XY + \overline{XY}$ is not equal to 1;
$XY + \overline{XY}$ cannot be simplified.

Observation 2: $\overline{X}Y + X\overline{Y}$ is not equal to 1;
$\overline{X}Y + X\overline{Y}$ cannot be simplified.

Observation 3: $\overline{XY}$ is not equal to $\overline{X}\overline{Y}$.

Observation 4: $\overline{X + Y}$ is not equal to $\overline{X} + \overline{Y}$.

Some examples of the use of Boolean algebra

Having presented the basic rules of Boolean algebra, the next step is to show how it is used to simplify Boolean expressions. Such equations are not 'pulled out of a hat', they are often derived from the description of a particular logic circuit. By simplifying these equations it may be possible to produce a cheaper version of the logic circuit.

(1) Simplify the following expressions.

(a) $X + \overline{Y} + \overline{X}Y + (X + \overline{Y})\overline{X}Y$

(b) $\overline{X}\overline{Y}\overline{Z} + \overline{X}YZ + X\overline{Y}Z + XYZ$

(c) $\overline{\overline{XY}.\overline{XZ}}$

(d) $(X + \overline{Y})(\overline{X} + Z)(Y + \overline{Z})$

(e) $(W + X + YZ)(\overline{W} + X)(\overline{X} + Y)$

(f) $WX\overline{Z} + \overline{X}YZ + WX\overline{Y} + XYZ + \overline{W}YZ$

(g) $\overline{W}XZ + WZ + XY\overline{Z} + \overline{W}XY$

(h) $(X + Y + Z)(\overline{X} + Y + Z)(\overline{X} + Y + \overline{Z})$

Solutions

Note: When I simplify Boolean expressions I try to keep the order of the variables alphabetical. This makes it easier to pick out logical groupings.

(a) $X + \overline{Y} + \overline{X}Y + (X + \overline{Y})\overline{X}Y = X + \overline{Y} + \overline{X}Y + X\overline{X}Y + \overline{X}\overline{Y}Y$

$$= X + \overline{Y} + \overline{X}Y \text{ (as } A\overline{A} = 0)$$

$$\;. \quad = X + \overline{Y} + \overline{X} \text{ (as } A + \overline{A}B = A + B)$$

$$= 1 \qquad \text{as } A + \overline{A} = 1.$$

Note: When a Boolean expression can be reduced to the constant (literal) 1 the expression is always true and is independent of the variables, i.e. X, Y.

(b) $\overline{X}\overline{Y}\overline{Z} + \overline{X}YZ + X\overline{Y}Z + XYZ = \overline{X}Y(\overline{Z} + Z) + XZ(\overline{Y} + Y)$

$$= \overline{X}Y(1) + XZ(1)$$

$$= \overline{X}Y + XZ.$$

(c) $\overline{\overline{XY}.\overline{XZ}} = \overline{\overline{\overline{XY}}} + \overline{\overline{XZ}}$ (by Theorem 9)

$\qquad = \overline{X}Y + XZ \qquad$ as $\overline{\overline{F}} = F$.

Note: Both expressions in examples (b) and (c) simplify to $\overline{X}Y + XZ$, demonstrating that these two expressions are equivalent. These equations are those of the multiplexer with (b) derived from the truth table and (c) from the circuit diagram of Fig. 2.9.

(d) $(X + \overline{Y})(\overline{X} + Z)(Y + \overline{Z}) = (X\overline{X} + XZ + \overline{X}\overline{Y} + \overline{Y}Z)(Y + \overline{Z})$

$\qquad = (XZ + \overline{X}\overline{Y} + \overline{Y}Z)(Y + \overline{Z}) = (XZ + \overline{X}\overline{Y})(Y + \overline{Z})$

$\qquad = XYZ + XZ\overline{Z} + \overline{X}\overline{Y}Y + \overline{X}\overline{Y}\overline{Z}$

$\qquad = XYZ + \overline{X}\overline{Y}\overline{Z}.$

(e) $(W + X + YZ)(\overline{W} + X)(\overline{X} + Y) = (W\overline{W} + \overline{W}X + \overline{W}YZ + WX + XX$
$\qquad\qquad\qquad\qquad\qquad\qquad + XYZ)(\overline{X} + Y)$

$\qquad = (\overline{W}X + \overline{W}YZ + WX + X$
$\qquad\qquad + XYZ)(\overline{X} + Y)$

$\qquad = (X + \overline{W}YZ)(\overline{X} + Y)$

$\qquad = X\overline{X} + XY + \overline{W}\overline{X}YZ + \overline{W}YYZ$

$\qquad = XY + \overline{W}\overline{X}YZ + \overline{W}YZ$

$\qquad = XY + \overline{W}YZ(\overline{X} + 1)$

$\qquad = XY + \overline{W}YZ.$

Note: The above procedure could have been shortened if we had noticed that $(\overline{W} + X)(\overline{X} + Y)$ was of the form $(A + B)(\overline{A} + C) = AC + \overline{A}B$. Continuing along these lines we get:

$(W + X + YZ)(\overline{W} + X)(\overline{X} + Y) = (W + X + YZ)(XY + \overline{W}\overline{X})$

$\qquad\qquad = WXY + W\overline{W}\overline{X} + XXY + \overline{W}\overline{X}X$
$\qquad\qquad\quad + XYYZ + \overline{W}\overline{X}YZ$

$\qquad\qquad = WXY + XY + XYZ + \overline{W}\overline{X}YZ$

$\qquad\qquad = XY(W + 1 + Z) + \overline{W}\overline{X}YZ$

$\qquad\qquad = XY + \overline{W}\overline{X}YZ$

$\qquad\qquad = XY + \overline{W}YZ.$

(f) $WX\overline{Z} + \overline{X}YZ + WX\overline{Y} + XYZ + \overline{W}YZ$

$\qquad\qquad = WX\overline{Z} + YZ(\overline{X} + X + \overline{W}) + WX\overline{Y}$

$\qquad\qquad = WX\overline{Z} + YZ + WX\overline{Y}$

$\qquad\qquad = WX(\overline{Y} + \overline{Z}) + YZ$

$$\text{(note that } YZ = \overline{\overline{Y} + \overline{Z}} \text{ so that we can}$$
$$\text{invoke } A + \overline{A}B = A + B)$$
$$= WX + YZ.$$

(g) $\overline{W}XZ + WZ + XY\overline{Z} + \overline{W}XY = Z(\overline{W}X + W) + XY\overline{Z} + \overline{W}XY$

$$= Z(X + W) + XY\overline{Z} + \overline{W}XY$$

$$= XZ + WZ + XY\overline{Z} + \overline{W}XY$$

$$= X(Z + Y\overline{Z}) + WZ + \overline{W}XY$$

$$= X(Z + Y) + WZ + \overline{W}XY$$

$$= XZ + XY + WZ + \overline{W}XY$$

$$= XZ + XY(1 + \overline{W}) + WZ$$

$$= XZ + XY + WZ.$$

(h) $(X + Y + Z)(\overline{X} + Y + Z)(\overline{X} + Y + \overline{Z})$

$$= (Y + Z)(\overline{X} + Y + \overline{Z})$$
$$\text{(as } (A + B)(A + \overline{B}) = A)$$

$$= Z(\overline{X} + Y) + \overline{Z}Y$$
$$\text{(as } (A + B)(\overline{A} + C) = AC + \overline{A}B)$$

$$= \overline{X}Z + YZ + \overline{Z}Y$$

$$= \overline{X}Z + Y(Z + \overline{Z})$$

$$= \overline{X}Z + Y.$$

The application of de Morgan's theorem

Theorems 9 and 10 provide the designer with an exceedingly powerful tool because they enable an AND function to be implemented by an OR gate and inverter, or they enable an OR gate to be implemented by an AND gate and inverter. This is of great importance when the implementation of logic functions in terms of NAND and NOR gates only is considered. When an entire function is complemented, de Morgan's theorem states that the ANDs are changed into ORs, and vice versa. Variables (and any literals) are complemented. It should be noted that here 'variables' means also groups of variables.

The reader may wonder why we should wish to implement circuits in NAND (or NOR) logic only. There are several reasons for this, but in general NAND gates work at a higher speed than AND gates and NAND gates may be built with fewer components. Later we shall examine in more detail how a circuit can be designed entirely with NAND gates only. The following examples illustrate the application of de Morgan's theorem.

(1) $F = \overline{\overline{XY} + \overline{XZ}}$ The ' $+$ ' becomes ' $\cdot$ ' and the two groups of variables are complemented.

$= \overline{\overline{XY}} \cdot \overline{\overline{XZ}}$ The process is continued by applying de Morgan

$= (\overline{X} + \overline{Y})(\overline{X} + \overline{Z})$.   to the two complemented groups.

(2) $F = \overline{\overline{AB} + \overline{CD} + \overline{AD}}$

$= \overline{\overline{AB}} \cdot \overline{\overline{CD}} \cdot \overline{\overline{AD}}$

$= (A + B)(C + D)(A + D)$.

(3) $F = \overline{AB(C + \overline{BD})}$

$= \overline{A} + \overline{B} + \overline{C + \overline{BD}}$

$= \overline{A} + \overline{B} + \overline{C} \cdot \overline{\overline{BD}}$

$= \overline{A} + \overline{B} + \overline{C}(B + D)$.

(4) A proof of Theorem 8 by de Morgan's theorem

$$(X + Y)(\overline{X} + Z)(Y + Z) = \overline{\overline{(X + Y)(\overline{X} + Z)(Y + Z)}}$$

$$= \overline{\overline{X + Y} + \overline{\overline{X} + Z} + \overline{Y + Z}}$$

$$= \overline{\overline{X}\overline{Y} + X\overline{Z} + \overline{Y}\overline{Z}}$$

$$= \overline{\overline{X}\overline{Y} + X\overline{Z}} \qquad \text{(by Theorem 3)}$$

$$= \overline{\overline{X}\overline{Y}} . \overline{X\overline{Z}} = (X + Y)(\overline{X} + Z).$$

The design of a two-bit multiplier

So far all the examples have been 'text-book questions' without any real application other than to provide a test-bed for the rules of Boolean algebra. The following example illustrates how Boolean algebra is applied to a practical problem. Suppose a designer wishes to produce a two-bit by two-bit multiplier. We have not yet come to binary arithmetic (Chapter 3), but nothing difficult is involved here. We start by considering the block diagram of the system (Fig. 2.17(a)) and constructing its truth (Table 2.10).

There are four inputs (indicating a 16-line truth table) and four outputs. Each 4-bit input represents the product of two two-bit numbers so that (for example) 1110 represents 11×10 or 3×2. The corresponding output is the 4-bit product which in this case is 6 or 0110 in binary form.

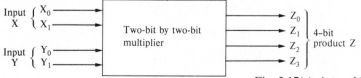

Fig. 2.17(a) A two-bit multiplier

Table 2.10 Truth table for a 2-bit by 2-bit multiplier

	Inputs				Outputs			
	X		Y		Z			
$X \times Y = Z$	X_1	X_0	Y_1	Y_0	Z_3	Z_2	Z_1	Z_0
$0 \times 0 = 0$	0	0	0	0	0	0	0	0
$0 \times 1 = 0$	0	0	0	1	0	0	0	0
$0 \times 2 = 0$	0	0	1	0	0	0	0	0
$0 \times 3 = 0$	0	0	1	1	0	0	0	0
$1 \times 0 = 0$	0	1	0	0	0	0	0	0
$1 \times 1 = 1$	0	1	0	1	0	0	0	1
$1 \times 2 = 2$	0	1	1	0	0	0	1	0
$1 \times 3 = 3$	0	1	1	1	0	0	1	1
$2 \times 0 = 0$	1	0	0	0	0	0	0	0
$2 \times 1 = 2$	1	0	0	1	0	0	1	0
$2 \times 2 = 4$	1	0	1	0	0	1	0	0
$2 \times 3 = 6$	1	0	1	1	0	1	1	0
$3 \times 0 = 0$	1	1	0	0	0	0	0	0
$3 \times 1 = 3$	1	1	0	1	0	0	1	1
$3 \times 2 = 6$	1	1	1	0	0	1	1	0
$3 \times 3 = 9$	1	1	1	1	1	0	0	1

From Table 2.10 we can derive expressions from Z_0 to Z_3. Note that where there are m output columns in a truth table, a set of m Boolean equations must be derived. One equation is associated with each of the m columns. To derive an expression for Z_0 the four minterms in the Z_0 column are ORed logically.

$$Z_0 = \overline{X}_1 X_0 \overline{Y}_1 Y_0 + \overline{X}_1 X_0 Y_1 Y_0 + X_1 X_0 \overline{Y}_1 Y_0 + X_1 X_0 Y_1 Y_0$$
$$= \overline{X}_1 X_0 Y_0 (\overline{Y}_1 + Y_1) + X_1 X_0 Y_0 (\overline{Y}_1 + Y_1)$$
$$= \overline{X}_1 X_0 Y_0 + X_1 X_0 Y_0$$
$$= X_0 Y_0 (\overline{X}_1 + X_1)$$
$$= X_0 Y_0.$$

$$Z_1 = \overline{X}_1 X_0 Y_1 \overline{Y}_0 + \overline{X}_1 X_0 Y_1 Y_0 + X_1 \overline{X}_0 \overline{Y}_1 Y_0 + X_1 \overline{X}_0 Y_1 Y_0$$
$$\quad + X_1 X_0 \overline{Y}_1 Y_0 + X_1 X_0 Y_1 \overline{Y}_0$$
$$= \overline{X}_1 X_0 Y_1 (\overline{Y}_0 + Y_0) + X_1 \overline{X}_0 Y_0 (\overline{Y}_1 + Y_1) + X_1 X_0 \overline{Y}_1 Y_0 + X_1 X_0 Y_1 \overline{Y}_0$$
$$= \overline{X}_1 X_0 Y_1 + X_1 \overline{X}_0 Y_0 + X_1 X_0 \overline{Y}_1 Y_0 + X_1 X_0 Y_1 \overline{Y}_0$$
$$= X_0 Y_1 (\overline{X}_1 + X_1 \overline{Y}_0) + X_1 Y_0 (\overline{X}_0 + X_0 \overline{Y}_1)$$
$$= X_0 Y_1 (\overline{X}_1 + \overline{Y}_0) + X_1 Y_0 (\overline{X}_0 + \overline{Y}_1)$$
$$= \overline{X}_1 X_0 Y_1 + X_0 Y_1 \overline{Y}_0 + X_1 \overline{X}_0 Y_0 + X_1 \overline{Y}_1 Y_0.$$

$$Z_2 = X_1 \overline{X}_0 Y_1 \overline{Y}_0 + X_1 \overline{X}_0 Y_1 Y_0 + X_1 X_0 Y_1 \overline{Y}_0$$
$$= X_1 \overline{X}_0 Y_1 (\overline{Y}_0 + Y_0) + X_1 X_0 Y_1 \overline{Y}_0$$
$$= X_1 \overline{X}_0 Y_1 + X_1 X_0 Y_1 \overline{Y}_0$$
$$= X_1 Y_1 (\overline{X}_0 + X_0 \overline{Y}_0)$$
$$= X_1 Y_1 (\overline{X}_0 + \overline{Y}_0)$$
$$= X_1 \overline{X}_0 Y_1 + X_1 Y_1 \overline{Y}_0.$$
$$Z_3 = X_1 X_0 Y_1 Y_0.$$

We now have the simplified expressions for Z_0, Z_1, Z_2, and Z_3,

i.e. $Z_0 = X_0 Y_0$,

$$Z_1 = \overline{X}_1 X_0 Y_1 + X_0 Y_1 \overline{Y}_0 + X_1 \overline{X}_0 Y_0 + X_1 \overline{Y}_1 Y_0,$$

$$Z_2 = X_1 \overline{X}_0 Y_1 + X_1 Y_1 \overline{Y}_0,$$

and $Z_3 = X_1 X_0 Y_1 Y_0$.

It is interesting to note that each of the above expressions is symmetric in X and Y. This is to be expected: if the problem itself is symmetric in X and Y (i.e. $3 \times 1 = 1 \times 3$) then the result should also demonstrate this symmetry. There are many ways of realizing the expressions for Z_0 to Z_3. Figure 2.17(b) illustrates one possible way.

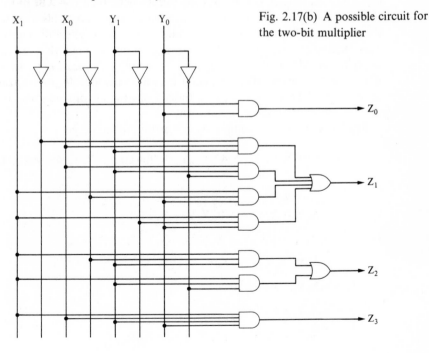

Fig. 2.17(b) A possible circuit for the two-bit multiplier

Implementing logic functions using NAND gates only

As has already been stated, some gates are intrinsically better than others. The NAND gate is both faster and cheaper than the corresponding AND gate. The same is true for the NOR gate and the OR gate. Consequently, it is sometimes necessary to realize a circuit using one type of gate only. This is often because that gate is cheap and plentiful. It should be noted that the range of gates open to the designer is not uniform; for example, there are many types of NAND gate, from the quad two-input NAND to the thirteen-input NAND, but there are few types of AND gates. To construct a circuit solely in terms of NAND gates, de Morgan's theorem must be invoked so that by negating a ' + ' it is converted to a '·'. For example, if we wish to generate $F = A + B + C$ using NAND gates only, we perform the following operations.

$$F = A + B + C$$

$$F = \bar{\bar{F}} = \overline{\overline{A + B + C}} \qquad \text{Double negation has no effect on the value of a function}$$

$$F = \overline{\bar{A}.\bar{B}.\bar{C}} \qquad \text{Apply de Morgan's theorem.}$$

We have now converted the OR function into a NAND function. The three NOT functions can be implemented in terms of NOT gates, or by means of two-input NAND gates with their inputs connected together. If the inputs of a NAND gate are A and B, and the output is C, then $C = \overline{AB}$. But if $A = B$ then $C = \overline{AA}$ or $C = \bar{A}$. The reader can better understand this if he refers to the truth table for the NAND gate, and imagines the effect of removing the lines $A,B = 0,1$ and $A,B = 1,0$. It is important to note that we are not applying de Morgan's theorem here to simplify Boolean expressions. We wish only to convert the expression into a form suitable for realization in terms of NAND (or NOR) gates. Indeed, the final expression may be much more complex than the original form.

Applying the above techniques to our multiplier we get

$$Z_0 = X_0 Y_0 = \overline{\overline{X_0 Y_0}} \text{ (i.e. NAND gate followed by NOT gate} = \text{AND gate).}$$

and

$$
\begin{aligned}
Z_1 &= \bar{X}_1 X_0 Y_1 + X_0 Y_1 \bar{Y}_0 + X_1 \bar{X}_0 Y_0 + X_1 \bar{Y}_1 Y_0 \\
&= \overline{\overline{\bar{X}_1 X_0 Y_1 + X_0 Y_1 \bar{Y}_0 + X_1 \bar{X}_0 Y_0 + X_1 \bar{Y}_1 Y_0}} \\
&= \overline{\overline{\bar{X}_1 X_0 Y_1} \cdot \overline{X_0 Y_1 \bar{Y}_0} \cdot \overline{X_1 \bar{X}_0 Y_0} \cdot \overline{X_1 \bar{Y}_1 Y_0}}, \\
Z_2 &= X_1 \bar{X}_0 Y_1 + X_1 Y_1 \bar{Y}_0 \\
&= \overline{\overline{X_1 \bar{X}_0 Y_1 + X_1 Y_1 \bar{Y}_0}} \\
&= \overline{\overline{X_1 \bar{X}_0 Y_1} \cdot \overline{X_1 Y_1 \bar{Y}_0}},
\end{aligned}
$$

and

$$Z_3 = X_1 X_0 Y_1 Y_0 = \overline{\overline{X_1 X_0 Y_1 Y_0}}.$$

Figure 2.18 shows the implementation of the multiplier in terms of NAND logic only. Note that it performs exactly the same function as the circuit of Fig. 2.17b.

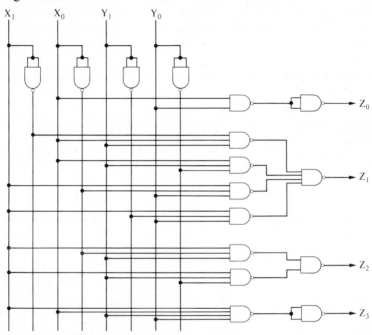

Fig. 2.18 Implementing the multiplier in NAND logic only

Implementing logic functions using NOR gates only

The procedures described above may equally be applied to the implementation of circuits using NOR gates only. By way of illustration, the value of Z_3 above will be converted to NOR logic form.

$$Z_3 = X_1 X_0 Y_1 Y_0$$
$$= \overline{\overline{X_1 X_0 Y_1 Y_0}}$$
$$= \overline{\overline{X_1} + \overline{X_0} + \overline{Y_1} + \overline{Y_0}}.$$

Note that $\overline{X}$ may be implemented by an inverter or by a NOR gate with its inputs connected together.

2.3.1 Karnaugh maps

The Karnaugh map, or more simply the K map, is a graphical technique for the presentation and simplification of a Boolean expression. Although the

Karnaugh map can simplify equations in five variables, it is best suited to equations in three or four variables. Other techniques, beyond the scope of this book, may be applied to the simplification of Boolean expressions in more than four variables. I find that students like Karnaugh maps because they show unambiguously when a Boolean expression has been reduced to its most simple form. When students use algebraic techniques to simplify an expression, they often reach a point at which they cannot proceed as they are unable to find further simplifications. However they are not certain whether the equation is indeed in its most simple form or they just cannot see the next step.

The Karnaugh map is a two-dimensional form of the (one-dimensional) truth table, drawn in such a way that the simplification of a Boolean expression can immediately be seen from the location of ones on the map. The key to the Karnaugh map is that adjacent squares (horizontally and vertically, not diagonally adjacent) differ by only one variable.

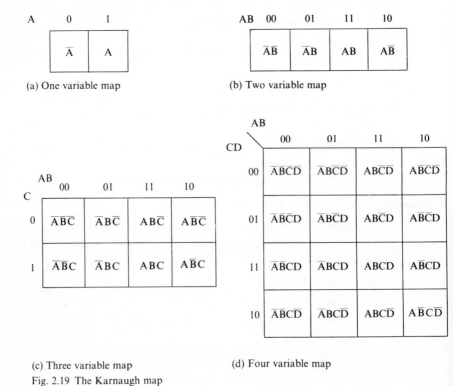

(a) One variable map

(b) Two variable map

(c) Three variable map

(d) Four variable map

Fig. 2.19 The Karnaugh map

Figure 2.19 shows Karnaugh maps for one to four variables. As one and two variable maps represent trivial cases, they will not be considered further. Consider now the three variable map. Figure 2.20 shows the truth table for a

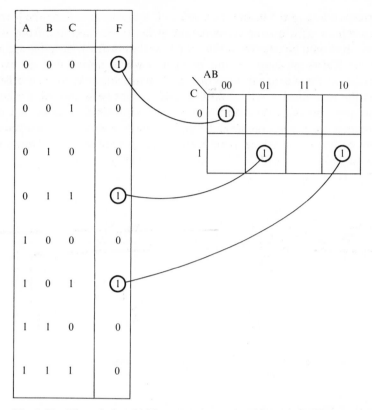

A	B	C	F
0	0	0	①
0	0	1	0
0	1	0	0
0	1	1	①
1	0	0	0
1	0	1	①
1	1	0	0
1	1	1	0

Fig. 2.20   The relationship between the truth table and the Karnaugh map for
$F = \overline{A}\,\overline{B}\,\overline{C} + \overline{A}BC + A\overline{B}C$

three variable function and the corresponding Karnaugh map. Each of the
three ones in the truth table is mapped on to its appropriate square on the
Karnaugh map.

In a three variable Karnaugh map, there are four vertical columns, one for
each of the four possible values of two out of the three variables. For
example, if the three variables are A, B, and C, the four columns represent all
the possible combinations of A and B. Thus, the first (leftmost) column is
labelled 00 and represents the case $A = 0$, $B = 0$. The next column is labelled
01, and represents the case $A = 0$, $B = 1$. The next column is labelled 11 (not
10), and represents the case $A = 1$, $B = 1$. Remember that adjacent columns
differ by only one variable at a time. The fourth column, 10, represents the
case $A = 1$, $B = 0$.

A three variable Karnaugh map has two horizontal rows, the upper row corresponding to $C = 0$, and the lower to $C = 1$. Any square on the Karnaugh map represents a unique combination of the three variables, from $\overline{A}\overline{B}\overline{C}$ to ABC. It should be clear from Fig. 2.20 how the entries in the table are plotted on the Karnaugh map. At this point it is worth noting that no two ones plotted on the Karnaugh map of Fig. 2.20 are adjacent to each other, and that the function $F = \overline{A}\overline{B}\overline{C} + \overline{A}BC + A\overline{B}C$ cannot be simplified. To keep the Karnaugh maps as clear and uncluttered as possible, squares that do not contain a one are left unmarked even though they must, of course, contain a zero. A square containing a one is said to be covered by a one. Now consider the functions $F_1 = A B \overline{C} + ABC$, and $F_2 = AB$ (Fig. 2.21).

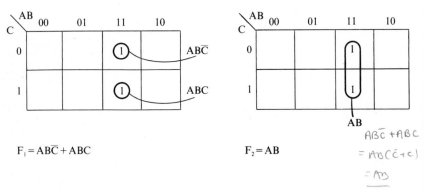

$F_1 = A B \overline{C} + ABC$ $F_2 = AB$

Fig. 2.21 Plotting functions on a Karnaugh map

The Karnaugh map for F_1 has two squares covered corresponding to $AB\overline{C}$ and ABC. The Karnaugh map for F_2 has a group of two squares covered corresponding to the column $A = 1$, $B = 1$. As the function for F_2 does not involve the variable C, a one is entered in the squares for which $A = B = 1$ and $C = 0$, and $A = B = 1$ and $C = 1$.

It is immediately apparent that these two Karnaugh maps are identical, so that $F_1 = F_2$ and $ABC + AB\overline{C} = AB$. From the rules of Boolean algebra $ABC + AB\overline{C} = AB(C + \overline{C}) = AB(1) = AB$.

The first step in simplifying a Boolean expression by means of a Karnaugh map is to plot all the ones in the function's truth table on the Karnaugh map. The next step is to combine adjacent ones into groups of one, two, four, eight, or sixteen. The groups minterms should be as large as possible—a single group of four minterms yields a simpler expression than two groups of two minterms. Finally, the groups are used to form a sum-of-products expression, with each group corresponding to one of the product terms. This process is best demonstrated by means of examples. In what follows, a four-variable map is chosen to illustrate the examples.

Figure 2.22 presents six functions plotted on Karnaugh maps. In these

$$\bar{A}D = \bar{A}D(B+\bar{B})(C+\bar{C})$$
$$= \bar{A}D(BC + \bar{B}C + B\bar{C} + \bar{B}\bar{C})$$
$$= \bar{A}BCD + \bar{A}\bar{B}CD + \bar{A}B\bar{C}D +$$
$$\bar{A}\bar{B}\bar{C}D$$

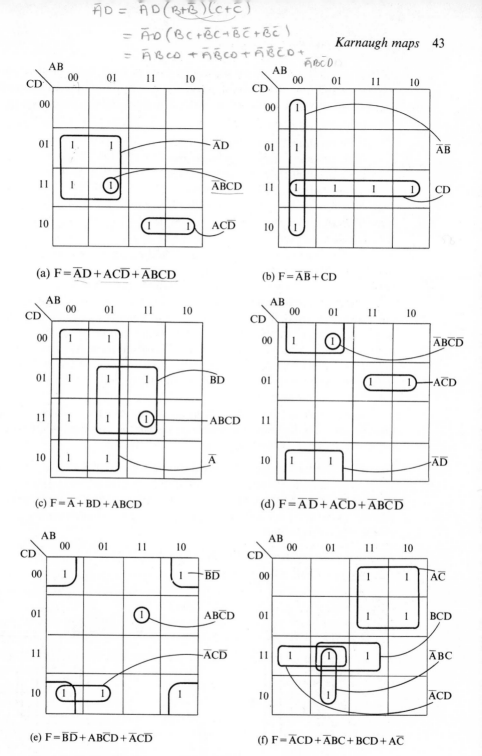

(a) $F = \bar{A}D + AC\bar{D} + \bar{A}BCD$

(b) $F = \bar{A}\bar{B} + CD$

(c) $F = \bar{A} + BD + ABCD$

(d) $F = \bar{A}\bar{D} + A\bar{C}D + \bar{A}B\bar{C}\bar{D}$

(e) $F = \bar{B}\bar{D} + AB\bar{C}D + \bar{A}C\bar{D}$

(f) $F = \bar{A}CD + \bar{A}BC + BCD + A\bar{C}$

Fig. 2.22 Plotting functions on a Karnaugh map

diagrams various sum-of-products expressions have been plotted directly from the equations themselves, rather than from the minterms of the truth table. The following notes should help in understanding these diagrams.

1. For a four variable map:
1 variable product terms cover 8 squares
2 variable product terms cover 4 squares
3 variable product terms cover 2 squares
4 variable product terms cover 1 square

2. A square covered by a one may belong to more than one term in the sum-of-products expression. For example, in Fig. 2.22(b) the minterm $\overline{A}BCD$ belongs to two groups, $\overline{A}B$ and CD. If a 'one' on the Karnaugh map appears in two groups, it is equivalent to adding the corresponding minterm to the overall expression for the function plotted on the map twice. This does not change its value because in Boolean algebra $X + X = X$.

3. The Karnaugh map is not a square or a rectangle as it appears in these diagrams. A Karnaugh map is a torus or doughnut shape. That is, the top edge is adjacent to the bottom edge and, the lefthand edge is adjacent to the righthand edge. For example, in Fig. 2.22(d) the term $\overline{A}\overline{D}$ covers the two minterms $\overline{A}\overline{B}\overline{C}\overline{D}$ and $\overline{A}BC\overline{D}$ at the top, and the two minterms $\overline{A}\overline{B}\overline{C}\overline{D}$ and $\overline{A}B\overline{C}\overline{D}$ at the bottom of the map. Similarly, in Fig. 2.22(e) the term $\overline{B}\overline{D}$ covers all four corners of the map.

4. In order either to read a product term from the map, or to plot a product term on the map, it is necessary to ask the question, what minterms (squares) are covered by this term?

Having shown how terms are plotted on the Karnaugh map, the next step is to apply the map to the simplification of the expressions. This process will be demonstrated in the form of examples. In each case the original function is plotted on the left-hand side of the page, and the re-grouped ones are plotted on the right-hand side.

Example 1 $F = AB + \overline{A}B\overline{C}D + \overline{A}BCD + A\overline{B}\overline{C}\overline{D}$ (Fig 2.23). The simplified function is $F = AB + BD + A\overline{C}\overline{D}$.

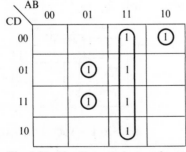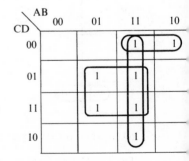

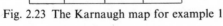
Fig. 2.23 The Karnaugh map for example 1

Example 2 $F = A\overline{C}\overline{D} + \overline{A}\overline{B}C + \overline{A}CD + A\overline{B}D$ (Fig. 2.24). In this case there is only one regrouping possible. The simplified function is $F = \overline{B}D + A\overline{C}\overline{D} + \overline{A}CD + \overline{A}\overline{B}C$.

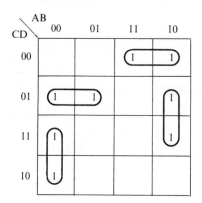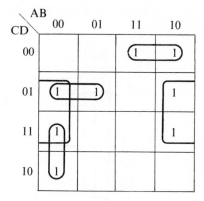

Fig. 2.24 The Karnaugh map for example 2

Example 3 $F = \overline{A}\overline{B}\overline{C}\overline{D} + A\overline{B}\overline{C}\overline{D} + \overline{A}\overline{B}C\overline{D} + A\overline{B}C\overline{D} + \overline{A}BCD + ABCD + \overline{A}B\overline{C}D + AB\overline{C}D$ (Fig. 2.25). The function can be simplified to two product terms with the result that $F = \overline{B}\overline{D} + BD$.

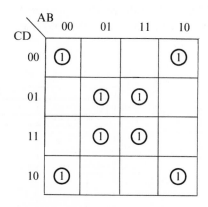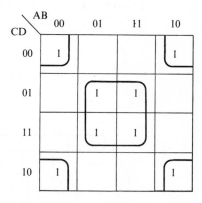

Fig. 2.25 The Karnaugh map for example 3

The application of Karnaugh maps

Apart from the use of Karnaugh maps in the simplification of Boolean expressions, they can be applied to the conversion of sum of products form to the corresponding product of sums form. The first step in this process involves the generation of the complement of the expression.

The example given in Fig. 2.26 shows how the complement of $F = \overline{C}\overline{D} + \overline{A}\overline{B} + A\overline{B} + C\overline{D}$ may be determined. If the squares covered by ones represent F, then the remaining squares covered by zeros represent $\overline{F}$. From the righthand diagram $\overline{F} = BD$.

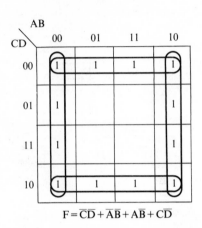
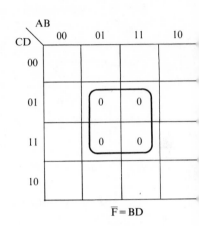

$$F = \overline{C}\overline{D} + \overline{A}\overline{B} + A\overline{B} + C\overline{D}$$

$$\overline{F} = BD$$

Fig. 2.26 Calculating a complement from a Karnaugh map

In order to convert from the sum-of-products form to the product of sums form, it is first necessary to calculate $\overline{F}$ in a sum-of-products form and then to complement this expression to get F in the required product-of-sums form.

Example   Convert $F = ABC + \overline{C}D + \overline{A}BD$ into product-of-sums form (Fig. 2.27). The complement of F may be read from the righthand map as

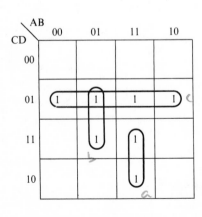
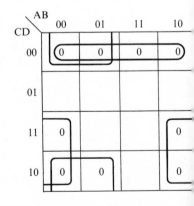

Karnaugh map of F

Karnaugh map of $\overline{F}$

Fig. 2.27

$$F = ABC + \bar{A}BD + \bar{C}D$$

$$\bar{F} = \bar{C}\bar{D} + \bar{B}C + \bar{A}\bar{D}.$$

$$(A + D)\left(BC + C\bar{C} + DB + D\bar{C}\right)$$

So $F = \overline{\bar{C}\bar{D} + \bar{B}C + \bar{A}\bar{D}}$

$$= (C + D)(B + \bar{C})(A + D).$$

$$ABC + AC\bar{C} + ADB + AD\bar{C} +$$
$$BCD + DC\bar{C} + DDB + DD\bar{C}$$

A worked example using the Karnaugh map

Having demonstrated how Karnaugh maps enable Boolean expressions to be simplified, we will now consider an example of their use. A room is protected against fire by means of four sensors. These are a flame detector, a smoke detector, and two high-temperature detectors located at the opposite ends of the room. As such detectors are prone to error or false alarms, a fire alarm is triggered only when two or more of the sensors indicate the presence of a fire simultaneously.

The output of a sensor is a logical one if a fire is detected, otherwise a logical zero. The output of the circuit is to be a logical one whenever two or more inputs are a logical one. The circuit is to be constructed from two-input and three-input NAND gates only.

Table 2.11 is the truth table for this circuit. The inputs from the four sensors are labelled A, B, C, and D. As it is only necessary to detect two or more logical ones on any of the lines, the actual order of A, B, C, and D does not matter. The output of the circuit, F, may be written down from the truth table:

Table 2.11 Truth table for fire detector

Inputs				Output
A	B	C	D	F
0	0	0	0	0
0	0	0	1	0
0	0	1	0	0
0	0	1	1	1
0	1	0	0	0
0	1	0	1	1
0	1	1	0	1
0	1	1	1	1
1	0	0	0	0
1	0	0	1	1
1	0	1	0	1
1	0	1	1	1
1	1	0	0	1
1	1	0	1	1
1	1	1	0	1
1	1	1	1	1

$$F = \bar{A}\bar{B}CD + \bar{A}B\bar{C}D + \bar{A}BC\bar{D} + \bar{A}BCD + A\bar{B}\bar{C}D + A\bar{B}C\bar{D} +$$
$$A\bar{B}CD + AB\bar{C}\bar{D} + AB\bar{C}D + ABC\bar{D} + ABCD.$$

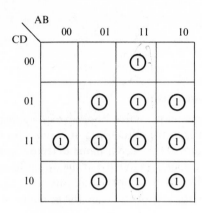

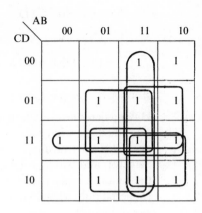

Fig. 2.28(a)   Fig. 2.28(b)

The Karnaugh map of Table 2.11

Plotting these terms on a Karnaugh map we get Fig. 2.28(a). These terms may be formed into six groups of four (Fig. 2.28(b)). Therefore, the simplified sum-of-products form of F is given by:

$$F = AB + AC + AD + BC + BD + CD.$$

In order to convert the expression into NAND logic only form, it is necessary to eliminate the five '+'s.

$$F = \overline{\overline{F}} = \overline{\overline{AB + AC + AD + BC + BD + CD}}$$
$$= \overline{\overline{AB} \cdot \overline{AC} \cdot \overline{AD} \cdot \overline{BC} \cdot \overline{BD} \cdot \overline{CD}}.$$

Although we have realized the expression in NAND logic as required, it calls for a six-input NAND gate. If the expression for F is examined, it can be seen that six terms are NANDed which is the same as ANDing them and then inverting the result. Because of the associative property of Boolean variables we can write $X(YZ) = (XY)Z$, and hence extending this to our equations we get:

$$F = \overline{\overline{AB} \cdot \overline{AC} \cdot \overline{AD} \cdot \overline{BC} \cdot \overline{BD} \cdot \overline{CD}}.$$

Figure 2.29 shows how this expression may be implemented in terms of two- and three-input NAND gates.

This problem could have been attacked in a slightly different way. If the Karnaugh map is examined it is apparent that because most squares are covered by ones, the remaining squares, covered by zeros, give $\overline{F}$ in a moderately simple form (Fig. 2.30).

$$\overline{F} = \overline{A}\overline{B}\overline{D} + \overline{A}\overline{B}C + \overline{A}CD + B\overline{C}D$$

and $F = \overline{\overline{A}\overline{B}\overline{D} + \overline{A}\overline{B}C + \overline{A}CD + B\overline{C}D}$

$$= \overline{\overline{\overline{A}\overline{B}\overline{D}} \cdot \overline{\overline{A}\overline{B}C} \cdot \overline{\overline{A}CD} \cdot \overline{B\overline{C}D}}.$$

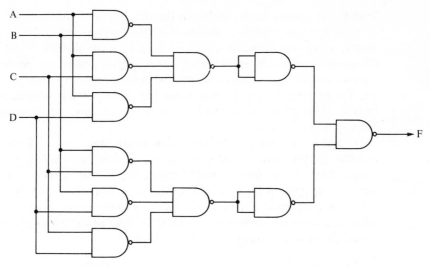

Fig. 2.29 Implementing the fire detection circuit

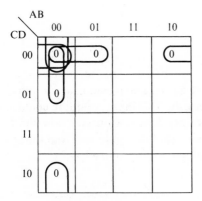

Fig. 2.30 Karnaugh map for $\overline{F}$

I leave it as an exercise to the reader to work out whether this expression can be realized with as few gates as the one above.

Karnaugh maps and don't care conditions

Here we will show how Karnaugh maps can be applied to a class of problems in which the truth table corresponding to a given system is not fully specified.

That is, for certain input conditions the output is undefined.

In all the logic design problems we have encountered so far, a specific output value has been associated with each of the possible input values. Occasionally, a system exists where a certain combination of inputs cannot happen. In such cases, the output may be defined as either true or false. After all, if a particular input is impossible, the corresponding output is meaningless. Or is it? Later we shall see how we can turn these 'meaningless' outputs to good use.

To make the concept of 'impossible input conditions' a little clearer, consider the following example. An air conditioning system has two control inputs. One, C, is from a cold-sensing thermostat, and is true if the temperature is below 55 °F, and false otherwise. The other input, H, is from a hot-sensing thermostat and is true if the temperature is above 70 °F, and false otherwise. As there are two inputs, there are four possible logical conditions as illustrated by the truth table (Table 2.12).

Table 2.12 Thermostat truth table

Inputs		Meaning
C	H	
0	0	Temperature OK
0	1	Too hot
1	0	Too cold
1	1	?

The input condition C = 1, H = 1 has no real meaning as it is impossible to be too hot and too cold simultaneously. This input condition could arise only if one of the thermostats had become faulty. Consider now the following example of an air conditioning unit with four inputs and four outputs. Table 2.13 defines the meaning of the inputs to the controller.

Table 2.13 Controller truth table

Input	Name	Input = 0	Input = 1
H	Hot	temperature < upper limit	temperature > upper limit
C	Cold	temperature > lower limit	temperature < lower limit
W	Wet	humidity < upper limit	humidity > upper limit
D	Dry	humidity > lower limit	humidity < lower limit

The controller has four outputs P, Q, R, and S. When P = 1 a heater is switched on, and when Q = 1 a cooler is switched on. Similarly, a humidifier is switched on by R = 1, and a dehumidifier by S = 1. In each case a logical zero switches off the appropriate device. The relationship between the inputs and outputs is as follows.

If the temperature and humidity are both within limits, switch off the heater and the cooler. The humidifier and dehumidifier are both switched off unless stated otherwise. If the humidity is within limits, switch on the heater if the temperature is too low, and switch on the cooler if the temperature is too high.

If the temperature is within limits, switch on the heater if the humidity is too low, and the cooler if the humidity is too high. If the humidity is high, and the temperature low, switch on the heater. If the humidity is low, and the temperature high, switch on the cooler.

If both the temperature and humidity are high switch on the cooler and dehumidifier. If both the temperature and humidity are too low switch on the heater and humidifier.

The relationship between the inputs and outputs can now be expressed in terms of a truth table (Table 2.14). We can draw Karnaugh maps for P to S, plotting a 0, 1, or X as necessary. Remember that an X corresponds to a don't care condition. Consider P first (Table 2.15).

Table 2.14 Relationship between controller inputs and outputs

Inputs					Outputs			
H	C	W	D	condition	P	Q	R	S
0	0	0	0	OK	0	0	0	0
0	0	0	1	Dry	1	0	0	0
0	0	1	0	Wet	0	1	0	0
0	0	1	1	Impossible	X	X	X	X
0	1	0	0	Cold	1	0	0	0
0	1	0	1	Cold and dry	1	0	1	0
0	1	1	0	Cold and wet	1	0	0	0
0	1	1	1	Impossible	X	X	X	X
1	0	0	0	Hot	0	1	0	0
1	0	0	1	Hot and dry	0	1	0	0
1	0	1	0	Hot and wet	0	1	0	1
1	0	1	1	Impossible	X	X	X	X
1	1	0	0	Impossible	X	X	X	X
1	1	0	1	Impossible	X	X	X	X
1	1	1	0	Impossible	X	X	X	X
1	1	1	1	Impossible	X	X	X	X

Table 2.15 Karnaugh map for P

WD \ HC	00	01	11	10
00		1	X	
01	1	1	X	
11	X	X	X	X
10		1	X	

The don't care conditions are so called because the corresponding input conditions cannot occur. Of course, any real combinatorial digital circuit must have a particular logical output for each of the 2^n inputs. In other words, if an input which is classified as don't care is applied to the circuit, it must produce either a logical one or a zero at the output. We choose the output to be a one or a zero to simplify the design of the circuit. That is, if an X can be used to turn a group of ones into a larger group of ones on a Karnaugh map, it is taken as a logical one. Otherwise it is made a zero. The Karnaugh map below corresponds to output P. Six of the don't care conditions are included within the groupings to get $P = C + \overline{H}D$ (Fig. 2.31(a)).

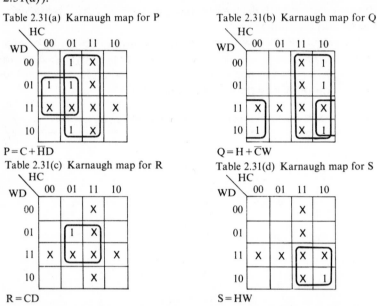

Table 2.31(a) Karnaugh map for P

$P = C + \overline{H}D$

Table 2.31(b) Karnaugh map for Q

$Q = H + \overline{C}W$

Table 2.31(c) Karnaugh map for R

$R = CD$

Table 2.31(d) Karnaugh map for S

$S = HW$

A Karnaugh map may be used to obtain a simplified expression for Q; see Fig. 2.3(b). The Karnaugh maps for R and S are given in Figs 2.31(c),(d).

2.3.2 Special-purpose combinatorial logic elements

So far, we have dealt with the primitive logic elements from which all digital systems can be constructed. As technology has improved, larger and larger numbers of components have been fabricated on single chips of silicon, and more complex circuits produced. It is now possible to obtain chips with several gates connected together in order to perform a particular logic function. Such circuits are called medium scale integration (MSI), in contrast with the gates themselves which fall in the category of small scale integration (SSI). In the 1970s entire systems began to appear on a single chip. The microprocessor is the most spectacular example, and the technology used to make it is called large scale integration (LSI). The 1980s is said to be the era of very large scale integration (VLSI). Interestingly enough, VLSI is not being used primarily to create very powerful computers on a chip, but is applied to the production of exceedingly large memory arrays capable of holding up to 256 kbits of data (i.e. $256 \times 2^{10} = 2^{18} = 262144$ bits).

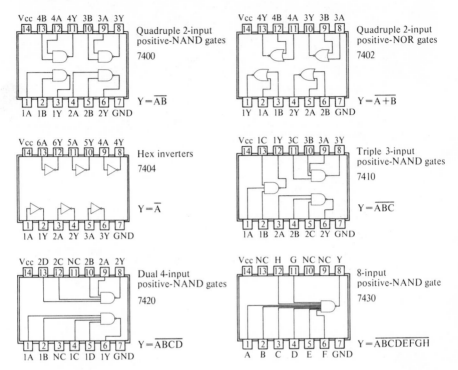

Fig. 2.32 Some basic SSI gates in 14-pin DIL packages

Figure 2.32 illustrates some of the popular SSI gates available in 14 pin DIL (dual-in-line) packages. Dual-in-line simply means that there are two parallel rows of pins. The rows are 0.3 inches apart and the pins are spaced by 0.1 inch. Two pins are needed for the power supply ($V_{cc}= +5.0$ Volts, and ground $= 0$ volts). In each case as many gates of a given type as possible are put in the package. The number of gates is limited only by the number of pins. Figure 2.33 shows this type of integrated circuit together with some larger packages. The physical size of the package does not correspond to the complexity of the device, but rather to the number of external connections (pins).

Figure 2.34 illustrates some of the elementary special-purpose logic elements called AND-OR-INVERT gates. These are still SSI circuits, and implement some frequently appearing logic functions. For example, the 7454 generates $F = \overline{AB + CD + EF + GH}$, the inverse of a sum of products expression. If an equation can be expressed in the form above, it can be generated by a single chip instead of the two or more chips needed if basic gates were used.

16-pin N plastic

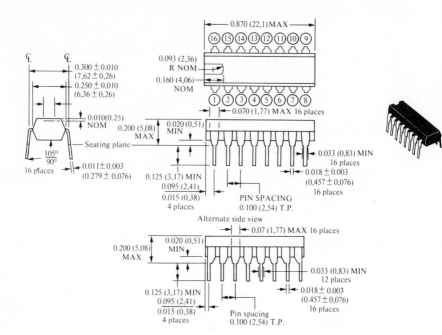

Alternate side view

24-pin N plastic

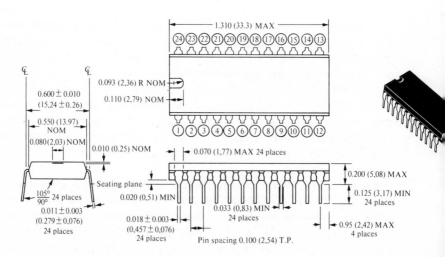

Fig. 2.33 The DIL package

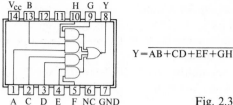

$$Y = \overline{AB + CD + EF + GH}$$

Fig. 2.34 The 7454 AND-OR-INVERT gate

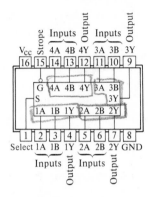

Fig. 2.35 The 74157 quad two-input multiplexer

A particularly common function cropping up regularly in digital design is the multiplexer. We have already encountered a simple 2-input multiplexer in Example 2 on page 23. Figure 2.35 shows the 74157, a quad 2-input multiplexer. This is a 16-pin MSI circuit. Each of the four Y outputs is connected to the corresponding A input pin when SELECT = 0, and to the B input when SELECT = 1. The STROBE input forces all Y outputs into logical zero states whenever STROBE = 1. The use of a multiplexer to switch between two alternative sources of data has already been discussed earlier in the example of the implementation of the conditional branch.

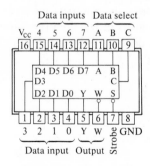

Fig. 2.36 The 74151 one-of-eight multiplexer

Figure 2.36 illustrates a 1-of-8 data multiplexer, the 74151. Here there are 8 inputs, D_0, D_1, D_2, . . ., D_7, an output Y (plus its complement $W = \overline{Y}$), and three data-select inputs, A, B, C. When A, B, C = 0, 0, 0 the output is $Y = D_0$, and when A, B, C = 1, 0, 0 $Y = D_1$, etc. That is, if the binary value of the data select input is i, the output is given by $Y = D_i$. A typical application of this circuit is in the selection of one of a number of logical conditions within a digital system. The eight inputs, D_0 to D_7, are connected to eight points in the system. By applying a suitable code to A, B, C, one of these 8 points can be tested by examining the output at Y.

The inverse function of the multiplexer is the demultiplexer. Figure 2.37(a) illustrates the 74138, a three-line-to-eight-line demultiplexer. Table 2.16 is the truth table for this device.

Table 2.16 Truth table for 74138 demultiplexer

Inputs						Outputs							
Enable			Select										
G_1	G_{2A}	G_{2B}	C	B	A	$\bar{Y}_0$	$\bar{Y}_1$	$\bar{Y}_2$	$\bar{Y}_3$	$\bar{Y}_4$	$\bar{Y}_5$	$\bar{Y}_6$	$\bar{Y}_7$
X	1	1	X	X	X	1	1	1	1	1	1	1	1
0	X	X	X	X	X	1	1	1	1	1	1	1	1
1	0	0	0	0	0	0	1	1	1	1	1	1	1
1	0	0	0	0	1	1	0	1	1	1	1	1	1
1	0	0	0	1	0	1	1	0	1	1	1	1	1
1	0	0	0	1	1	1	1	1	0	1	1	1	1
1	0	0	1	0	0	1	1	1	1	0	1	1	1
1	0	0	1	0	1	1	1	1	1	1	0	1	1
1	0	0	1	1	0	1	1	1	1	1	1	0	1
1	0	0	1	1	1	1	1	1	1	1	1	1	0

The outputs Y_0 to Y_7 are active-low, and remain in a logical one state unless the corresponding input is selected. The device has three enable inputs G_1, G_{2A}, G_{2B}, which must be 1, 0, 0 respectively, for the chip to be selected.

When the chip is selected, one (and only one) of the eight outputs is in a logical zero state. The selected output depends on the three-bit code at the select inputs, A, B, C. One application of this circuit is as a 'device selector'. Suppose there are eight devices, and only one can be active (in use) at a time. If each device is enabled by a logical zero at its input, then the binary code applied to C, B, A, will determine which device is selected. Figure 2.37(b) shows how the 74138 is applied in this way.

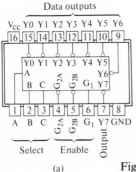

(a)   Fig. 2.37(a) The 74138 three-line-to-eight-line demultiplexer

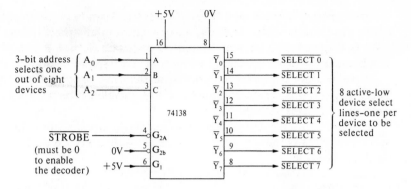

Note Only one of the 8 devices enabled by
SELECT 0 to SELECT 7 can be active
at any instant

Fig. 2.37(b) Applying the 74138 as a device selector

Among the many other special-purpose logic elements are the code-converter, and the arithmetic element. A code-converter transforms one binary code into another. For example, Fig. 2.38 shows how a 7447 BCD-to-

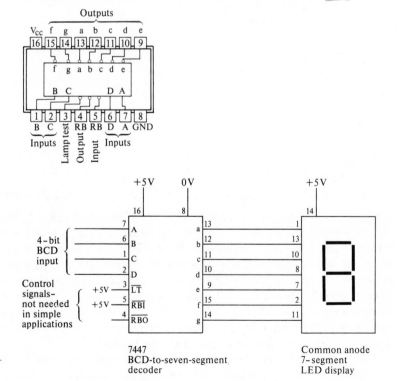

Fig. 2.38 The 7447 BCD-to-seven-segment decoder

seven-segment decoder is used. The ten digits 0 to 9 can be made up of two to seven straight-line segments. This can be seen from any digital watch. The 7447 is designed to convert a 4-bit BCD code (see Section 3.3.9) into the combination of segments needed to form the corresponding decimal digit.

There also are a number of arithmetic elements, ranging from the full adder which forms the sum of three bits, to a complete 8-bit arithmetic unit. Section 3.4.2 deals with the full adder.

In addition to the above combinational logic circuits, there are many sequential circuits implemented as single chips. Section 2.6 deals with the sequential circuit.

2.4 Tri-state logic

The types of logic element introduced at the beginning of this chapter are used to create functional units, where one or more logical outputs are generated from a number of inputs. A computer is made up of the interconnection of such functional units together with the storage elements to be described in Section 2.5. Here we are going to examine a special type of gate (a gate with a tri-state output) which enables the various functional units of a computer to be interconnected.

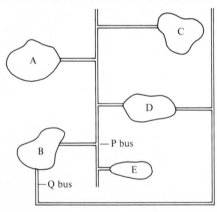

Fig. 2.39 Functional units and buses

Figure 2.39 shows a system composed of five functional units, A, B, C, D and E. These units are linked together by means of two data highways (or buses), P and Q, permitting data to be moved from one unit to another. Buses are not strictly necessary; it is possible to provide direct connections between those parts of a digital system which exchange information. Equally public highways are not necessary; each home could have a private path to all other homes, factories, shops and services with which it needs to communicate. In both these cases the sheer number of interconnections is uneconomic unless there are very few functional units (or homes).

A bus is normally represented diagramatically by a single line (or double line) as in Fig. 2.39. The actual bus is made up of a number of lines, and Fig. 2.40 shows how they are arranged. Networks A and B are able to transmit data to the bus or receive data from it. We are not concerned with the nature of the processes A and B here, we simply wish to show how they communicate with each other. For clarity, the connections to only one line of the bus are shown. Similar arrangements exist for d_1 to d_{m-1}.

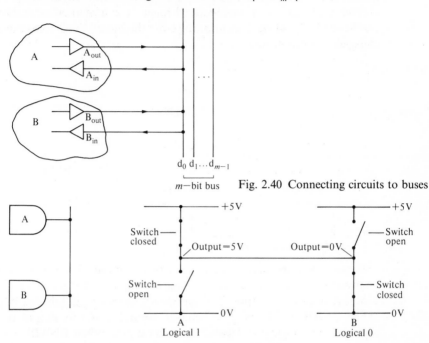

Fig. 2.40 Connecting circuits to buses

Fig. 2.41 The outputs of two gates connected together

Suppose A wishes to send data to B. It puts data on the bus via gate A_{out}, and B receives the data via gate B_{in}. This arrangement is, in fact, unworkable, and a glance at Fig. 2.41 will show why. Each line of the bus has a number of outputs connected to it (from A, B, . . .). Figure 2.41 shows the consequence of connecting together two outputs which happen to be in differing logical states.

Output A is in a logical one state and is pulled up towards +5 V by a switch inside the gate. Similarly, output B is a logical zero state and is pulled down towards 0 V by another switch. These switches are transistors which are either conducting or non-conducting. Because the two outputs are of differing states and are wired together, two problems exist. The first is philosophical. As the logical level along a conductor is constant, because the voltage at all points along the conductor is constant, and yet its ends are connected to different voltages, the logical level on the conductor is undefined and breaks one of the rules of Boolean algebra. That is, there is no such thing as a valid indeterminate state lying between a logical one and a logical zero. Secondly, and more practically, a direct physical path exists between the $+5$ V power supply and ground (0 V). This is a short-circuit and the current flowing through the two output circuits will destroy them.

The difficulty of connecting outputs together is resolved by the tri-state gate. Tri-state logic is not, as its name suggests, an extension of Boolean algebra into ternary or three-valued logic. It is a method of resolving the conflict of Fig. 2.41 by disconnecting from the bus all those gates not actively engaged in transmitting data.

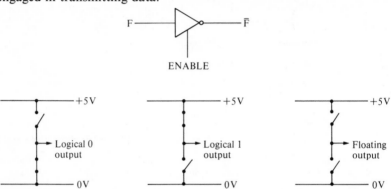

Fig. 2.42 The tri-state output

Figure 2.42 illustrates a gate with a tri-state output. The gate shown here is an inverter (complementer) for the sake of simplicity. In fact, any type of gate can have a tri-state output. This gate has a special input labelled ENABLE. When ENABLE $= 1$, the gate behaves normally, and its output is either a logical 1 or a logical 0 depending on its input. When ENABLE $= 0$, both switches in the output circuit of the gate are open, and the output is physically disconnected from the gate's internal circuitry. If I were to ask what state the output is in when ENABLE $= 0$, the answer should be that the question is meaningless. In fact, because the output of an un-enabled tri-state gate is normally connected to a bus, the logic level at the output terminal is the same as that on the bus to which it is connected. For this reason, the output of a tri-state gate in its 'third state' is said to be 'floating'. It floats up and down with the bus traffic. Table 2.17 is the truth table of an inverter with a tri-state output.

Table 2.17 Truth table for tri-state inverter

ENABLE	A	Output $\bar{A}$	
0	0	X	} Here X represents 'floating'
0	1	X	
1	0	1	
1	1	0	

Figure 2.43 shows how tri-state gates are actually used to implement a bussed structure. The gates shown are called buffers because, when enabled, their outputs are equal to their inputs. They simply serve to connect or

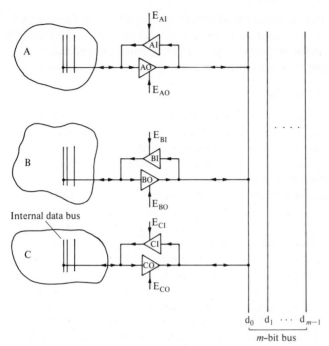

d$_0$ d$_1$ $\cdots$ d$_{m-1}$
m-bit bus

Fig. 2.43 The tri-state gate and the bus

disconnect the networks to the bus. The outputs of networks A, B, and C are placed on the bus by three tri-state buffers AO, BO, and CO, which are enabled by signals E_{AO}, E_{BO}, and E_{CO}, respectively. If any network wishes to put data on to the bus it must set its enable signal (e.g. E_{BO}) to a logical one. Note that it is vital that no more than one of E_{AO}, E_{BO}, and E_{CO} be true at any instant.

Each of the networks receive data from the bus via their own input buffers (AI, BI, and CI). If a network wishes to receive data, it enables its input buffer by E_{AI}, E_{BI}, or E_{CI}, as appropriate. For example, if network C wishes to transmit data to network A, all that is necessary is for E_{CO} and E_{AI} to be set to a logical one simultaneously. All other enable signals remain in a logical zero state for the duration of the information transfer. Note that the input buffers (AI, BI, CI) are not always necessary. If the data flowing from the bus into a network goes into the input of one or more gates, a buffer is not needed. If however, the input data is placed on an internal bus (local to the network) on which other gates may put their output, the buffer is necessary.

In the above description the names of the gates and their control signals have been carefully chosen. AO stands for A_{out}, and AI for A_{in}. This labels the gate and the direction in which it transfers data with respect to the network is serving. Similarly, E_{AO} stand for 'enable gate A out', and E_{AI} for 'enable gate A in'. By choosing consistent and meaningful names, the reading of circuit diagrams and their associated text is made easier.

The details of a bussed system will be elaborated on in Section 2.6.1, and Chapter 4 on the structure of the CPU will make extensive use of buses in its description of how the CPU actually carries out basic computer operations.

2.5 Bistables and registers

The logic circuits we have encountered up to this point have been combinational circuits, in which the output is a function of the inputs only. Circuits whose outputs depend not only on their current inputs, but also on their past inputs, are called sequential circuits. The basic building block of sequential circuits is the flip-flop or bistable.

It is not my intention to deal with sequential circuits at anything other than an introductory level, as their full treatment forms an entire branch of digital engineering. Sequential circuits cannot, however, be omitted from elementary texts on computer hardware because they are needed to implement registers, counters, and shifters, all of which are fundamental to the operation of the central processing unit.

A bistable is so called because, for a given input, its output can remain in one of two stable states indefinitely. That is, for a particular set of inputs, the output may assume either a logical zero or a logical one, the actual value depending on the previous inputs. Such a circuit has the ability to remember its past history. A more detailed discussion of memory elements is given in Chapter 6. A bistable is the smallest possible memory cell and can store only a single bit of information. The term flip-flop, which is synonomous with bistable, is onomatopeic and gives the impression of the circuit going 'flip' into one state and then 'flop' into its complement.

There are two approaches to the description of flip-flops. One is to demonstrate what they do by defining their characteristics as an abstract model and then to point out how they may be designed. The other is to demonstrate how a flip-flop may be implemented with just two gates and then to show how its special properties may be put to work. I intend to follow the latter path.

2.5.1 The RS flip-flop

Figure 2.44 illustrates one of the most complex circuits in this book. Although it involves no more than two simple 2-input NOR gates, its operation is not immediately apparent. This circuit has two inputs, A and B, and two outputs, X and Y. The truth table for the NOR gate is provided alongside Fig. 2.44 for reference.

From the equations governing the gates we can readily write down expressions from X and Y.

(i) $X = \overline{A + Y}$
(ii) $Y = \overline{B + X}$

Truth table for the NOR gate

A	B	$\overline{A+B}$
0	0	1
0	1	0
1	0	0
1	1	0

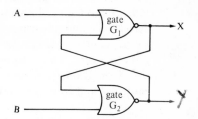

Fig. 2.44 Two cross-coupled NOR gates

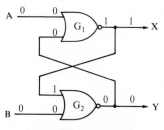

Conventional representation

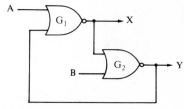

Alternative representation

Fig. 2.45 The operation of Fig. 2.44

If we substitute the value for Y in equation (i), we get:

$$X = \overline{A + \overline{B + X}} = \overline{A} \cdot \overline{\overline{B + X}}$$

$$= \overline{A} \cdot (B + X)$$

$$= \overline{A}B + \overline{A}X.$$

As Boolean alegebra does not define the operations of division or subtraction, we are left with a rather nasty-looking equation in which the output is a function of the output. Perhaps a better approach to understanding this circuit is to assume a value for X and then to see where it leads us.

Figure 2.45 shows this circuit with $X = 1$ and $A = B = 0$. As the inputs to gate G_2 are $X = 1$, $B = 0$, its output, $\overline{X + B}$, must be 0. The inputs to gate G_1 are $Y = 0$ and $A = 0$, so that its output, X, is $\overline{Y + A}$ which is 1. Now note that this situation is self-consistent. The output of gate G_1 is 1, which is fed back to the input of gate G_1 to maintain X at a logical 1 state. That is, the output actually maintains itself. Such a circuit is called cross-coupled because the output is fed back to the input.

If input B to gate G_2 goes high while input A remains low, the output of gate G_2 (i.e. Y) is unaffected because the output of a NOR gate is low if either of its inputs are high. As X is already high, the state of B has no effect on the state of Y.

If now input A goes high while B remains low, the output, X, of gate G_1 must fall to a logical zero state. The inputs to gate G_2 are now both in logical zero states, and its output Y rises to a logical one. However, as Y is fed back to the input of gate G_1, the output X is maintained at a logical zero even if A goes to a zero. Thus, the effect of setting A to a one causes output X to flip over from a one to a zero, and to remain in that state when A returns to a zero. Table 2.18 is the truth table for Fig. 2.44.

Tables 2.18(a), (b) The truth tables corresponding to the circuit of Fig. 2.44

Inputs		Output		Inputs			Output
A	B	X	X^+	R	S	Q	Q^+
0	0	0	0	0	0	0	0
0	0	1	1	0	0	1	1
0	1	0	1	0	1	0	1
0	1	1	1	0	1	1	1
1	0	0	0	1	0	0	0
1	0	1	0	1	0	1	0
1	1	0	0	1	1	0	?
1	1	1	0	1	1	1	?
		Old X	New X			Old Q	New Q

The truth table is interpreted as follows. The output of the circuit is currently X (or Q), and the new inputs to be applied to the input terminals are A, B (or R, S). When these new inputs are applied to the circuit, its output is given by X^+ (or Q^+). For example, if the current output X is 1, and the new values of A and B are A = 1, B = 0, then the new output, X^+, will be 0. This value of X^+ then becomes the next value of X when the next new inputs A and B are applied to the circuit.

Table 2.18(a) corresponds exactly to the two NOR gates of Fig. 2.44, and Table 2.18(b) to the 'idealized' form of this circuit called an RS flip-flop. Figure 2.46 gives the circuit representation of an RS flip-flop. There are two

R   Q

S $\bar{Q}$

Fig. 2.46 The RS flip-flop

differences in these truth tables. The righthand version uses the 'conventional' labelling of an RS flip-flop, with inputs R and S, and an output Q. The other difference is in the last entry of the truth tables for the cases A = B = 1, and R = S = 1. These differences will be dealt with later.

We have already stated that the circuit of Fig. 2.44 has its output defined in terms of itself (i.e. $X = \overline{A}B + \overline{A}X$). The truth table approach gets round this problem by creating a variable, X^+ (or Q^+), where X^+ is the new output corresponding to the old output X, and the current inputs A and B. Similarly, the equation can be re-written as $X^+ = \overline{A}B + \overline{A}X$. The input and output columns of the truth table are now not only separated in space (e.g. input wires on the left and output wires on the right) but also in time. The current output X is combined with inputs A and B to give a new output X^+. The value of X that produced X^+ no longer exists and belongs only to the past.

The labels R and S in the righthand truth table correspond to 'reset' and 'set', respectively. The word 'reset' means 'set to zero' (clear has the same meaning) and 'set' means 'set to one'. The output of all flip-flops is called Q and is a historical convention. Examining the truth table reveals that whenever $R = 1$, the output Q is reset to zero. Similarly, when $S = 1$ the output is set to one. When R and S are both zero, the output does not change. That is, $Q^+ = Q$.

If both R and S are simultaneously high, the output is conceptually undefined (hence the question marks in the truth table), as the output cannot be set and reset at the same time. In the case of the RS flip-flop implemented by two NOR gates, the output X does, in fact, go low when $A = B = 1$. In practice, the user of an RS flip-flop must avoid the condition $R = S = 1$.

The two NOR-gate circuit has two outputs X and Y. An examination of the circuit for all inputs except $A = B = 1$ reveals that X and $\overline{Y}$ are complements. Similarly, all flip-flops have two outputs, Q and its complement $\overline{Q}$.

There are two general ways of presenting the truth table of the RS, or other, flip-flops. The truth tables presented so far are exhaustive in the sense that for each set of possible inputs two lines are needed, one for $Q = 0$ and one for $Q = 1$. An alternative approach is to employ the algebraic value of Q as shown in Table 2.19.

Table 2.19 Truth table for RS flip-flop (alternative form of Table 2.18(b))

Inputs		Output	Description
R	S	Q^+	
0	0	Q	no change
0	1	1	output set
1	0	0	output clear
1	1	X	forbidden

When $R = S = 0$ the new output, Q^+, is simply the old output Q. In other words, the output does not change state. The inputs $R = S = 1$ result in the output $Q^+ = X$. The special symbol 'X' is used in truth tables to indicate an indeterminate (undefined) condition or, as we have already seen, a 'don't care' condition. An 'indeterminate' condition is one whose output cannot be calculated, while a 'don't care' condition is one whose outcome does not matter to the designer.

An important application of RS flip-flops is in the recording of short-lived events. If the Q output of the flip-flop is in a zero state, a logical one pulse at its S input (assuming the R input is zero) will cause Q to be set to a one, and

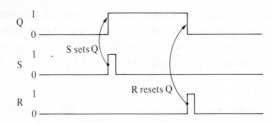

Fig. 2.47 The effect of a pulse on an RS flip-flop

to remain at a one, until the R input resets Q. A pulse and its effect on an RS flip-flop is illustrated in Fig. 2.47.

Consider the following application of RS flip-flops to an indicator circuit. If an aircraft is flown outside its 'performance envelope' no immediate damage may be done, but its structure might be permanently weakened. To keep things simple, we will consider three possible events which are considered harmful and might endanger the aircraft:

1. Exceeding the maximum permissible speed V_{ne}.
2. Extending the flaps above the flap-limiting speed V_{fl}. That is, the flaps must not be lowered if the aircraft is going faster than V_{fl}.
3. Exceeding the maximum acceleration (g-force) G_{max}.

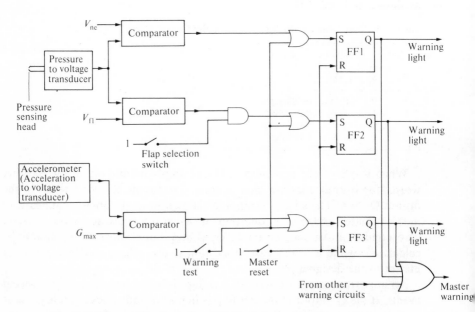

Fig. 2.48 The application of an RS flip-flop to a warning system

into a voltage. The voltages from the transducers are compared with the three thresholds (V_{ne}, V_{fl}, G_{max}) in comparators, whose outputs are true if the threshold is exceeded, otherwise false. In order to detect the extension of flaps above the flap-limiting speed, the output of the comparator is ANDed with a signal from the flap actuator circuits which is true when the flaps are down.

The signals from the comparators are fed, via OR gates, to the S inputs of three RS flip-flops. Initially, on switching on the system, the flip-flops are automatically reset by applying a logical one pulse to all R inputs simultaneously. If at any time one of the S inputs becomes true, the output of that flip-flop is set to a logical one and triggers an alarm. All outputs are ORed together to illuminate a master warning light. This removes the necessity of the pilot having to scan all the warning lights periodically. An additional feature of the circuit is a test facility. When the warning test button is pushed, all warning lights should be illuminated and remain so until the reset button is pressed. This facility tests the correct operation of the system.

The clocked RS flip-flop

The RS flip-flop of Fig. 2.44 responds immediately to its inputs according to its truth table. There are, however, situations when we want the RS flip-flop to ignore its inputs until a suitable time. The circuit of Fig. 2.49 shows how this is accomplished.

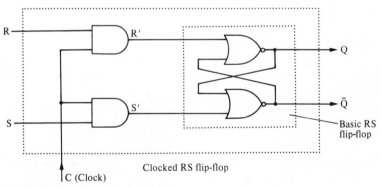

Fig. 2.49 The clocked RS flip-flop

In the inner box lies a normal, unmodified, RS flip-flop. Its inputs R′ and S′ are derived from the inputs R and S by ANDing them with a clock input C. As long as C=0, then inputs to the RS flip-flop, R′ and S′, are forced to remain at zero, no matter what is happening to R and S. While these inputs are zero, the output of the RS flip-flop remains constant. Whenever C=1, R′=R and S′=S, and the flip-flop responds accordingly. The clock input may be thought of as an inhibitor, restraining the flip-flop from acting until the right time. The subject of clocked flip-flops is dealt with in more detail later in this section.

2.5.2 The D flip-flop

Like the RS flip-flop, the D flip-flop has two control inputs, one called D, and the other C. The D input is often referred to as the data input, and C as the clock input. The D flip-flop is, by its nature, a clocked flip-flop and we will call the act of setting the C input high clocking the D flip-flop.

Whenever a D flip-flop is clocked, the value at its D input is transferred to the Q output. The output then remains constant until the next time it is clocked. Some people call the D flip-flop a staticizer because it records the D input and holds it constant. Others call it a delay element because if the D input changes state at time T and it is clocked t seconds later, the output Q does not change state until t seconds after the input. I tend to think of it as a census taker. When it is clocked it takes a census of the input and remembers it until the next census is taken. Table 2.20 is the truth table for a D flip-flop.

Table 2.20 Truth table for a D flip-flop

Inputs		Output			Inputs		Output
C	D	Q	Q⁺		C	D	Q⁺
0	0	0	0		0	0	Q
0	0	1	1	no	0	1	Q
0	1	0	0	change	1	0	0
0	1	1	1	$Q^+ \leftarrow Q$	1	1	1
1	0	0	0				
1	0	1	0	$Q^+ \leftarrow D$		(alternative form)	
1	1	0	1				
1	1	1	1				

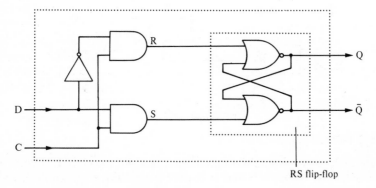

RS flip-flop

Fig. 2.50 The circuit of a D flip-flop

From Fig. 2.50 it can be seen that it is possible to derive a D flip-flop from an RS flip-flop by the addition of a few gates. The effect of the two AND gates is to turn the RS flip-flop into a clocked version. As long as the C input to the AND gates is low, the R and S inputs are clamped at zero and Q cannot change.

When C goes high, the S input is connected to D and the R input to $\overline{D}$. Therefore, (R, S) must either be (0, 1) if D = 1, or (1, 0) if D = 0. Consequently, D = 1 sets the RS flip-flop, and D = 0 clears it.

A typical example of the application of D flip-flops is given in Fig. 2.51. Here an m-bit wide data bus is carrying data from one part of a digital system to another. The data on the bus is constantly changing as different devices use it to transmit their data.

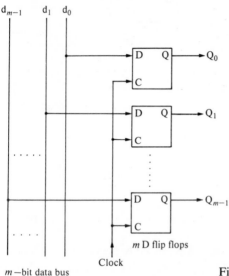

Fig. 2.51 An application of D flip-flops

A set of m D flip-flops have their D inputs connected to the m lines of the bus. The clock inputs of all flip-flops are connected together, allowing them to be clocked simultaneously. As long as C = 0, the flip-flops ignore the data on the bus and their Q outputs remain unchanged. Suppose some device wishes to transfer its data to the flip-flops. It first puts its data on the bus and then the flip-flops are clocked, latching the data into them. When the clock has returned to zero, the data remains frozen in the flip-flops.

2.5.3 Clocked flip-flops

A flip-flop is described in two ways, firstly by its type (RS, D, JK), and secondly by the way in which it is clocked. A digital device, when clocked, responds to its inputs. The whole idea behind clocked circuits is to allow logic elements to respond to their inputs only when they are valid. This point is illustrated in Fig. 2.52.

Imagine that at time $t = 0$, the inputs to processes A and B become valid (i.e. they are the correct inputs to be operated on by the processes). The actual nature of the processes does not matter, what we are concerned with here is the delay between their inputs being valid and their output becoming

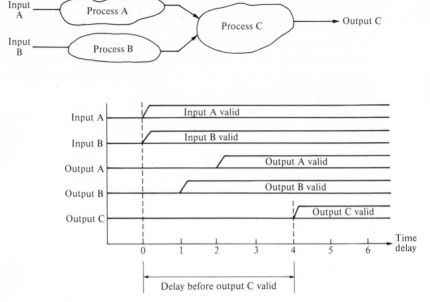

Fig. 2.52 Clocked systems

valid. In Fig. 2.52 process A introduces a two unit delay and process B a one unit delay.

The outputs of processes A and B are fed to process C which has a two unit delay. Clearly, the desired output from C due to inputs A and B is not valid until at least four time units after $t = 0$. The output at C changes several times before it settles down to the intended value. This poses a problem. How does an observer at the output of process C know when to act upon the data from C?

If a D flip-flop is placed at the output of process C, and is clocked say five units of time after $t = 0$, the desired data will be latched into the flip-flop and held constant until the next clock pulse. In a clocked system digital information is held in flip-flops and is operated on by groups of logic elements, analogous to the processes of Fig. 2.43. Between clock pulses the outputs of the flip-flops are processed by the logic elements and the new data values are presented to the inputs of flip-flops.

After a suitable time delay (longer than the time taken for the slowest process to be completed), the flip-flops are clocked. The outputs of the processes are now clocked into the flip-flops and held constant until the next time they are clocked. A clocked system is often called synchronous as all processes are started simultaneously on each new clock pulse. An asynchronous system is one in which the end of one process signals the start of the next. Obviously, an asynchronous system must be faster than the corresponding synchronous system. Asynchronous systems are, however, more complex and difficult to design than synchronous systems.

There are three types of clocked flip-flop:

1. Level-sensitive
2. Edge-sensitive
3. Master–slave

A level-sensitive clock triggers a flip-flop whenever the clock is in a logical one state (some flip-flops are clocked by a zero). The clocked RS flip-flop of Fig. 2.49 is level-sensitive. Unfortunately, a level-sensitive clock can cause problems in certain applications. Consider the circuit of Fig. 2.53. The

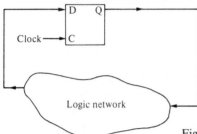

Fig. 2.53 Feedback and the level-sensitive clock

output of a D flip-flop is fed through a logic network and then back to its D input. If we call the output of the flip-flop the current Q, then the current Q is fed through the logic network to generate D. When the flip-flop is clocked, the value of D is transferred to the output to generate the new Q.

Unfortunately, if the clock is level-sensitive, the new Q can rush through the logic network, change D and hence the output. This chain of events will continue in an oscillatory fashion with the 'dog chasing its tail'. To avoid this we need an infinitesimally short clock pulse. As such a thing cannot exist, the edge-sensitive clock has been introduced to solve the feedback problem.

A flip-flop which is said to have an edge-triggered clock, is clocked not by the level of the clock (i.e. high or low), but by the transition of the clock signal from zero-to-one, or one-to-zero. The former case is called a positive or rising-edge sensitive clock, and the latter is called a negative or falling-edge sensitive clock. As the rising (or falling) edge of most pulses has a duration of less than 10 ns, an edge-triggered clock can be regarded as a level-sensitive clock triggered by a pulse of an infinitesimally short duration. For this reason, the problem of Fig. 2.53 ceases to exist; there is insufficient time for the new output to race back to the input within the duration of a single rising edge. A nanosecond (ns) is a thousand millionth (10^{-9}) of a second.

There are some circumstances when edge-triggered flip-flops are unsatisfactory. This is largely due to clock 'skew'. If, in a digital system, a number of edge-triggered flip-flops are clocked by the same edge of a pulse, the exact times at which the individual flip-flops are clocked vary. This variation (clock skew) is very small (several ns), and is due to the different paths by which the clock pulse reaches each flip-flop. Electrical impulses move through circuits at somewhat less than the speed of light which is 30 cm per nanosecond. Unless each flip-flop is located at the same distance from the source of the clock pulse, and unless any additional delays in each path due to other logic elements are identical, the clock pulse will arrive at the flip-flops at differents instants. Suppose that the output of flip-flop A is connected to the input of flip-flop B, and they are nominally clocked together. Ideally, at the moment of clocking, the old output of A is clocked into B. If, by bad design or bad luck, flip-flop A is triggered a few nanoseconds before flip-flop B, B sees the new output from A, not the old output—it is as if A were clocked by a separate and earlier clock. A solution to this problem is provided by the master–slave clocked flip-flop.

The master–slave flip-flop

The master–slave (MS) flip-flop has the external appearance of a single flip-flop, but internally is arranged as two flip-flops operating in series. One of these flip-flops is called the 'master' and the other the 'slave'. On the rising edge of the clock pulse, the input data is latched into the master flip-flop (see Fig. 2.54). At this point the output terminals of the MS flip-flop are not affected and do not change state.

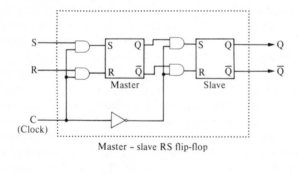

Master – slave RS flip-flop

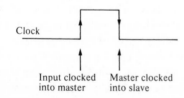

Input clocked   Master clocked
into master   into slave   Fig. 2.54 The master–slave RS flip-flop

On the falling edge of the clock pulse, the data from the master is latched into the slave, and only then may the output terminals change state. This type of flip-flop has its input terminals totally isolated from the output terminals simply because the output of the flip-flop does not change until after the input conditions have been sampled and latched internally. Conceptually, the master–slave flip-flop behaves like an air lock in a submarine or space craft. An air lock exists to transfer people between regions of different pressure (air-to-vacuum or air-to-water) without ever permitting a direct path between the two pressure regions. This is analogous to the flip-flop whose output must not be fed directly back to its input. To operate an air lock in a submarine, a diver in the water opens the air lock, enters and closes the door behind him. He is now isolated from both the water outside and the air inside. When he opens the door into the submarine, he steps inside and closes the air lock door behind him.

In order to understand how the three different types of clocked flip-flop behave, consider Fig. 2.55, where for a given input waveform, the output waveforms for three different types of clocked D flip-flop are presented.

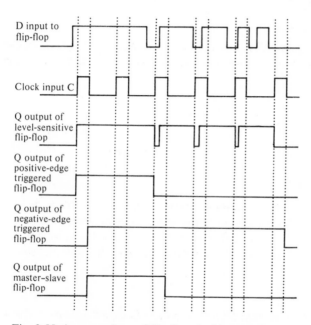

Fig. 2.55 A comparison of flip-flop clocking modes

2.5.4 The JK flip-flop

The JK flip-flop is possibly the most useful of the flip-flops described here because it can be configured, or programmed, to operate in one of two modes. All JK flip-flops are clocked, and the majority of them operate on the master–slave principle. Tables 2.21(a), (b) are truth tables for the JK flip-flop.

For all values of J and K, except J = K = 1, the JK flip-flop behaves exactly like an RS flip-flop with 'J' acting as the 'set' input, and 'K' acting as the 'reset' input. When J and K are both true, the output of the JK flip-flop 'toggles', or changes state, each time the flip-flop is clocked. That is, if Q was a 0 it becomes a 1, and vice versa. It is this property that puts the JK flip-flop

Table 2.21(a) Truth table for
JK flip-flop

Inputs		Output		
J	K	Q	Q⁺	
0	0	0	0	} no change
0	0	1	1	
0	1	0	0	} reset Q
0	1	1	0	
1	0	0	1	} set Q
1	0	1	1	
1	1	0	1	} toggle Q
1	1	1	0	

Table 2.21(b) Alternative form
of truth table

Inputs		Output
J	K	Q⁺
0	0	Q
0	1	0
1	0	1
1	1	$\overline{Q}$

(algebraic form)

at the heart of almost all counter circuits. The operation of counter circuits is dealt with in the next section. The logic symbol for a JK flip-flop is given in Fig. 2.56.

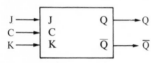

Fig. 2.56 The representation of the JK flip-flop

2.6 Sequential circuits

Just as the logic gate is combined with other gates to form combinational circuits such as adders and multiplexers, flip-flops may be combined together to create a class of circuits called sequential circuits. Here, we are concerned with two particular types of sequential circuits: the shift register and the counter.

The shift register

We have already seen that a collection of m D type flip-flops is able to store an m-bit word. By slightly modifying the circuit of the register we can build a right shift register, a register whereby all the bits may be moved one place right. For example, the binary pattern

01110101

becomes   00111010 when shifted —— place right.

Note that a 'zero' has been shifted in from the left-hand end, and the 'one' at the right-hand end has been lost. I used the expression 'binary pattern' above because, as we shall see later, the byte 01110101 can represent may things. However, when a pattern represents a fixed-point binary number, shifting it one place right has the effect of dividing the number by two.

Figure 2.57 shows how a shift register can be made from a number of D flip-flops. The Q output of each flip-flop is connected to the D input of the flip-flop on its right. All clock inputs are connected together so that all flip-

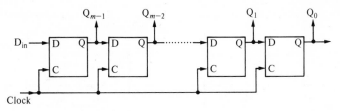

Fig. 2.57 A shift register

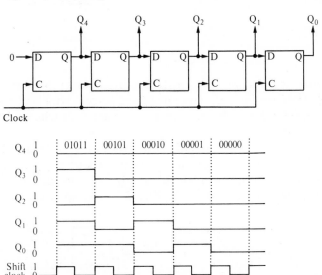

Fig. 2.58 An example of shift register

flops are all clocked simultaneously. When the ith stage is clocked its output, Q_i, takes on the value from the stage on its left, that is, $Q_i \leftarrow Q_{i+1}$. The leftmost stage, Q_{m-1}, has D_{in} shifted into it at each clock pulse. An example of the operation of a 5-bit shift register is given in Fig. 2.58. In this case D_{in} is connected to a logical zero so that zeros are shifted into the left-hand stage, Q_4. It should be obvious that the flip-flops must either be edge-triggered or master–slave flip-flops, otherwise if a level-sensitive flip-flop were used, a Q value at the left-hand end would ripple through all stages as soon as the clock was high.

The output of the right-hand stage, Q_0, consists of a series of five sequential pulses, corresponding to the five bits of the word in the shift register. A shift register is often used to convert a parallel word of m bits into a serial word of m consecutive bits. Such a circuit is called a parallel-to-serial convertor. If the output of an m-bit parallel-to-serial convertor is connected to the D_{in} input of an m-bit shift register, after m clock pulses, the information in the parallel-to-serial convertor has been transferred to the second (right-hand) shift register. This shift register is called a serial-to-

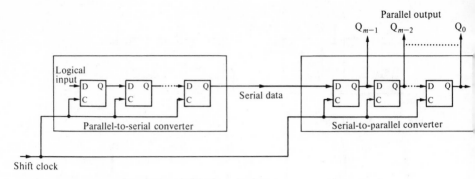

Fig. 2.59 The serial-to-parallel converter

parallel convertor. Figure 2.59 depicts this arrangement. Note that there is almost no difference between a parallel-to-serial convertor and a serial-to-parallel convertor. Many data transmission systems (see Chapter 8) operate on this principle.

The only flaw in our shift register (when operating as a parallel-to-serial convertor) is the lack of any facilities for loading it with m bits of data at one go, rather than by shifting in m bits through D_{in}. A right-shift register with a parallel load capacity is shown in Fig. 2.60. A two-input multiplexer,

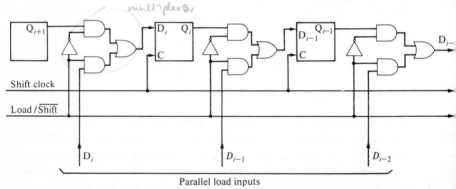

Fig. 2.60 A shift register with a parallel load capability

composed of two AND gates, an OR gate, and an inverter, switches the D input of a flip-flop between the output of the previous stage (shift mode) and the load input (load mode). The control inputs of all multiplexers are connected together, to form the mode control, labelled load/$\overline{\text{shift}}$. This method of labelling a variable means that when the line is active high it is interpreted as executing a load command, and when active low it is interpreted as executing a shift command.

A shift register composed of JK flip-flops is illustrated in Fig. 2.61. I leave it as an exercise to the reader to work out how this arrangement operates. In a later section on computer instructions, it will be seen that there are a

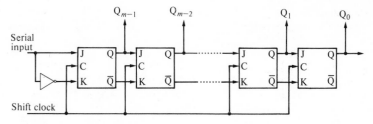

Fig. 2.61 A shift register composed of JK flip-flops

number of different types of shift (circular, arithmetic, logical). In practice, these other types of shift are all derived from the basic shift register described above. Although we have considered the right-shift register, a left-shift register is equally easy to design. The input of the ith stage, D_i, is connected to the output of the $(i-1)$th stage so that, at each clock pulse, $Q_i \leftarrow Q_{i-1}$. In terms of the previous example:

01110101

becomes   11101010.

Counters

A counter is a special type of sequential circuit with a single clock input and a number of outputs. Each time the counter is clocked one or more of the outputs change state. These outputs form a sequence with N unique values. After the Nth value has been observed at the counter's output terminals, the next clock pulse causes the counter to assume the same output as at the start of the sequence. That is, the sequence is cyclic. For example, a counter may display the sequence 01234501234501 . . ., or the sequence 9731097310973 . . .

One of the tools frequently employed to illustrate the operation of sequential circuits is the state diagram. Any system with internal memory (e.g. the flip-flop) and external inputs can be said to be in a state which is a function of its internal and external inputs. A state diagram shows some (or all) of the possible states of a given system. Each of the states is normally represented by a labelled circle. The states are linked by unidirectional lines showing the paths by which one state becomes another state.

Figure 2.62 shows the state diagram of a JK flip-flop. Here, there are only two states, S_1 and S_2. S_1 represents the state $Q = 0$, and S_2 represents the state

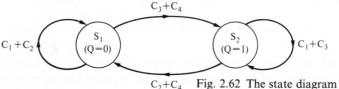

Fig. 2.62 The state diagram of a JK flip-flop

$Q = 1$. The transitions between states are determined by the values of the JK inputs. In Table 2.22, four conditions C_1, C_2, C_3, and C_4 are defined in terms of J and K.

Table 2.22

J	K	Condition
0	0	C_1
0	1	C_2
1	0	C_3
1	1	C_4

The flip-flop changes state on each clock pulse. From Fig. 2.62 it can be seen that conditions C_3 or C_4 cause a transition from state S_1 to state S_2 Similarly, conditions C_2 or C_4 cause a transition from state S_2 to state S_1 Note that condition C_4 causes a change of state from S_1 to S_2 and also from S to S_1. This is, of course, the condition $J = K = 1$. Note also, that some conditions cause a state to change to itself, that is, there is no overall change Thus, conditions C_1 or C_2, when applied to the system in state S_1, have the effect of leaving the system in state S_1.

The state diagram of a three-bit binary counter is given in Fig. 2.63. In this diagram, there is a single path from one state to its neighbour. That is, as the system is clocked, it cycles through the states S_0 to S_7, representing the natural binary numbers 0 to 7. The actual design of counters in general can be quite involved, although the basic principle is to ask 'what input conditions are required by the flip-flops to cause them to change from state S to state S_{i+1}?'

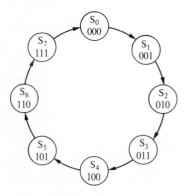

Fig. 2.63 The state diagram of a three-bit counter

The design of an asynchronous binary counter is rather more simple. A three-bit binary counter composed of JK flip-flops is given in Fig. 2.64 together with its timing diagram. The JK inputs to each flip-flop are connected to constant logical one levels. Consequently, whenever a flip-flop is clocked, its output changes state. The flip-flops are arranged so that the Q output of one device triggers the clock input of the next device. The JK flip flops of Fig. 2.64 are MS flip-flops with the output changing on the negative edge of the clock pulse.

Counters find many applications in digital computers. Anticipating Chapter 4, we will find that at the heart of all computers is a 'program counter' or 'instruction counter' which, at any instant, contains the number (i.e. address) of the next instruction to be executed. After each instruction has been executed, the counter is incremented. The program counter is so-called, not because it counts programs, but because it has the circuit, or function, of a counter.

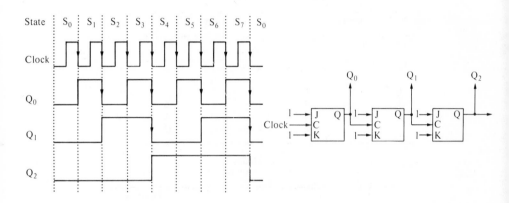

Fig. 2.64 The binary counter

2.6.1 Special-purpose sequential logic elements

Just as the semiconductor manufacturers have provided a range of special-purpose combinational logic elements in single packages, they have done the same with sequential logic elements. If anything, there are more special-purpose sequential logic elements than combinational logic elements. Fig. 2.65 gives an indication of some of the flip-flops available. Flip-flops are the basic building-block of all sequential circuits. These are generally more complex than those presented hitherto in this chapter. Real circuits have to cater for real-world problems. We have already said that the output of a flip-flop is a function of its current inputs and its previous output. What happens when a flip-flop is first switched on? The answer is quite simple. The Q output takes on a random state, assuming no input is being applied that will force Q into a 0 or 1 state.

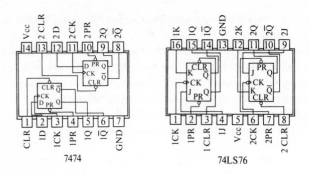

7474   74LS76

74LS74 function table

Inputs				Outputs	
Preset	Clear	Clock	D	Q	$\overline{Q}$
0	1	X	X	1	0
1	0	X	X	0	1
0	0	X	X	1	1
1	1	↑	1	1	0
1	1	↑	0	0	1
1	1	0	X	Q_0	$\overline{Q_0}$

74LS76 function table

Inputs					Outputs	
Preset	Clear	Clock	J	K	Q	$\overline{Q}$
0	1	X	X	X	1	0
1	0	X	X	X	0	1
0	0	X	X	X	1	1
1	1	↓	0	0	Q_0	$\overline{Q_0}$
1	1	↓	1	0	1	0
1	1	↓	0	1	0	1
1	1	↓	1	1	Toggle	Toggle
1	1	1	X	X	Q_0	$\overline{Q_0}$

Fig. 2.65 Two flip-flops available in DIL packages

Random states may be fine at the gaming tables in Monte Carlo; they are
less helpful when the control systems of a nuclear reactor are first energized.
For this reason many flip-flops are provided with special control inputs
which are used to place them in a known state. The 7474, a dual-positive-
edge-triggered D flip-flop illustrated in Fig. 2.65, has two active-low control
inputs—preset and clear (abbreviated $\overline{PR}$ and $\overline{CLR}$). In normal operation
both $\overline{PR}$ and $\overline{CLR}$ remain in logical one states. If $\overline{PR} = 0$ the Q output is set

to a logical one, and if $\overline{\text{CLR}} = 0$ the Q output is cleared to a logical zero. As in the case of the RS flip-flop, the condition $\overline{\text{PR}} = \overline{\text{CLR}} = 0$ should not be allowed to occur. These inputs are unconditional in the sense that they override all activity at the other inputs of this flip-flop. When a digital system is made up from many flip-flops, which must be set or cleared at the application of power, their $\overline{\text{PR}}$ or $\overline{\text{CLR}}$ lines are connected to a common $\overline{\text{RESET}}$ line, and this line is momentarily brought to a logical zero level by a single pulse shortly after the power is switched on.

Flip-flops are found in four general applications: the storage of a single bit (e.g. the carry bit resulting from addition), the storage of an entire word (an accumulator or register), shift registers, and counters. Figure 2.66 illustrates

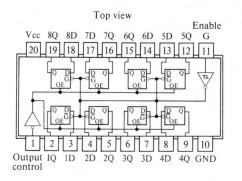

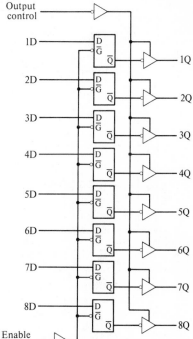

Function table

Output control	ENABLE G	D	Output
0	1	1	1
0	1	0	0
0	0	X	Q_0
1	X	X	floating

Fig. 2.66 The 74LS373 octal register

the 74LS373, an octal D flip-flop. This is available in a 20-pin DIL package with eight inputs, eight outputs, two power supply pins, and two control inputs. The ENABLE input is a level-sensitive clock, which, when high, causes the value at D_i to be transferred to Q_i. All eight clocks are connected together internally so that the ENABLE input clocks each flip-flop simultaneously. This type of circuit may be used to implement the register array shown in Fig. 2.51. The other control input is called $\overline{\text{OUTPUT CONTROL}}$. When $\overline{\text{OUTPUT CONTROL}} = 0$, the flip-flop behaves exactly as we would expect. When $\overline{\text{OUTPUT CONTROL}} = 1$, the eight Q outputs are internally disconnected from the output pins of the device. That is, the 74LS373 has tri-state outputs and $\overline{\text{OUTPUT CONTROL}}$ is used to turn off the chip's output circuits when it is not driving the bus.

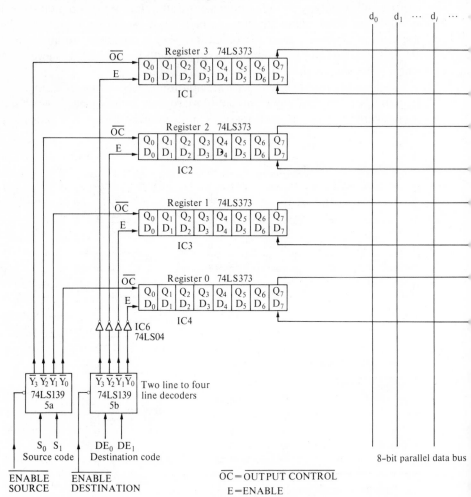

Fig. 2.67 A register array using 74LS373 octal D flip-flops

Figure 2.67 shows how this chip might be used in a computer or some similar digital system. Four 74LS373 eight-bit registers have their inputs and outputs connected to an eight-bit wide bus. Note that both D_i and Q_i of each flip-flop are connected to line i of the bus. One half of a 74LS139 two-line-to-four-line decoder decodes a two-bit binary value into one of four lines each of which is connected to the $\overline{\text{OUTPUT CONTROL}}$ input of one of the four registers. The 74LS139 integrated circuit contains two two-line-to-four-line decoders in a single 16-pin DIL package, and is similar to the 74138 of

Section 2.3.2. The two-bit binary code at the input of IC5a causes one of its output lines to go low and hence forces the corresponding register to put its output on to the data bus. For example, if the code at the input to IC5a is 01, register 1 has its output enabled, and the contents of register 1 are placed on the bus. The outputs of all other registers remain internally disconnected from the bus.

A second, two-line-to-four-line decoder, IC5b, in conjunction with four inverters, converts a two-bit destination code into one of four active-high lines. For each of the four possible codes at the input to IC5b, one of the four lines connected to the ENABLE inputs of the registers goes high, clocking that register.

The input to IC5a is called a source code, and the input to IC5b a destination code. Whenever the two decoders are enabled, the source code selects the register putting data on to the bus, and the destination code selects the register receiving the data. If the contents of register 1 are to be copied into register 3, the source code is set to 01 and the destination code to 11. The two decoders are enabled and the data transfer is made.

The next type of special-purpose sequential circuit is the shift register. Figure 2.68 illustrates 74LS95, a 4-bit parallel-access bidirectional shift register. This figure gives both the pin-out of the device and its internal arrangement. The user accesses the shift register through its pins, and cannot make connections to the internal parts of its circuit. Indeed, its actual internal implementation may differ from the published circuit. As long as it behaves like this circuit, the precise implementation of the logic function does not matter. The 74LS95 is a particularly versatile shift register and has the following functions.

1. *Parallel load*   The four bits of data to be loaded into the shift register are applied to the parallel inputs, the mode control input is set to a logical one, and a clock pulse applied to the clock 2 input. The data is loaded on the falling edge of the clock 2 pulse.

2. *Right-shift*   A shift right is accomplished by setting the mode control input to a logical zero, and applying a pulse to the clock 1 input. The shift takes place on the falling edge of the clock pulse.

3. *Left-shift*   A shift left is accomplished by setting the mode control input to a logical one, and applying a pulse to the clock 2 input. The shift takes place on the falling edge of the clock pulse. A left-shift requires that the output of each flip-flop be connected to the parallel input of the previous flip-flop, and serial data entered at the D input.

The final type of special-purpose sequential circuit to be described here is the counter. There are a large number of counters available, and Fig. 2.69 illustrates a typical counter, the 74177, a four-bit presettable binary counter. The pin-out is given in Fig. 2.69 together with the internal arrangement. Note that in Fig. 2.69 there is a T flip-flop. The T stands for 'toggle', because its

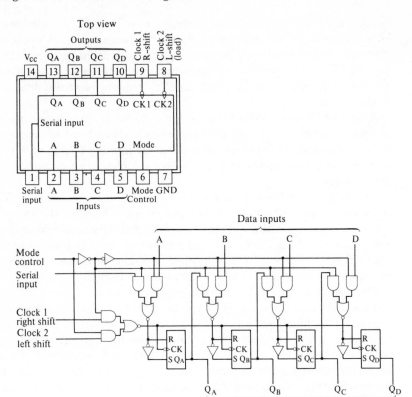

Function table

Inputs								Outputs			
	Clocks			Parallel							
Mode Control	2 (L)	1 (R)	Serial	A	B	C	D	Q_A	Q_B	Q_C	Q_D
1	1	X	X	X	X	X	X	Q_{A0}	Q_{B0}	Q_{C0}	Q_{D0}
1	↓	X	X	a	b	c	d	a	b	c	d
1	↓	X	X	Q_B	Q_C	Q_D	d	Q_{Bn}	Q_{Cn}	Q_{Dn}	d
0	0	1	X	X	X	X	X	Q_{A0}	Q_{A0}	Q_{A0}	Q_{A0}
0	X	↓	1	X	X	X	X	1	Q_{An}	Q_{Bn}	Q_{Cn}
0	X	↓	0	X	X	X	X	0	Q_{An}	Q_{Bn}	Q_{Cn}
↑	0	0	X	X	X	X	X	Q_{A0}	Q_{B0}	Q_{C0}	Q_{D0}
↓	0	0	X	X	X	X	X	Q_{A0}	Q_{B0}	Q_{C0}	Q_{D0}
↓	0	1	X	X	X	X	X	Q_{A0}	Q_{B0}	Q_{C0}	Q_{D0}
↑	1	0	X	X	X	X	X	Q_{A0}	Q_{B0}	Q_{C0}	Q_{D0}
↑	1	1	X	X	X	X	X	Q_{A0}	Q_{B0}	Q_{C0}	Q_{D0}

Fig. 2.68 The 74LS95 shift-register

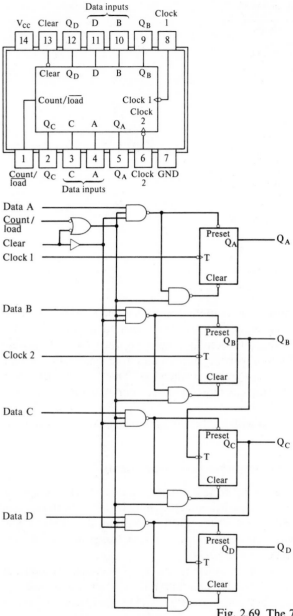

Fig. 2.69 The 74177 4-bit binary counter

output changes state every time it is clocked. The T flip-flop is functionally equivalent to a JK flip-flop with $J = K = 1$.

The counter is arranged as a divide-by-two stage followed by a divide by eight stage. To divide by 16 (i.e. count from 0000 to 1111) it is necessary to connect the output of the first stage (Q_A) to the clock of the succeeding stages

Function table of 74177

Count	Output			
	Q_D	Q_C	Q_B	Q_A
0	0	0	0	0
1	0	0	0	1
2	0	0	1	0
3	0	0	1	1
4	0	1	0	0
5	0	1	0	1
6	0	1	1	0
7	0	1	1	1
8	1	0	0	0
9	1	0	0	1
10	1	0	1	0
11	1	0	1	1
12	1	1	0	0
13	1	1	0	1
14	1	1	1	0
15	1	1	1	1

Note A: Output Q_A connected to clock-2 input.

(clock 2). The count input is applied to clock 1 and on each falling-edge of the clock pulse the contents of the counter are incremented by one. The $\overline{\text{CLEAR}}$ input sets the value of each Q output to zero when $\overline{\text{CLEAR}} = 0$. The $\overline{\text{COUNT/LOAD}}$ input permits normal counting when high, and allows four bits to be loaded into the counter when low. This facility is used to preset the counter so that it counts up from I (rather than 0), where I is the value loaded into it.

We have now dealt with all the circuits needed to design a general-purpose digital computer.

2.7 Some practical considerations in logic design

Any student undertaking an introductory course in logic design, or reading an elementary text on Boolean algebra, may be left with the impression that designing a digital system involves little more than simplifying a few Boolean equations, turning the results into a circuit diagram and then putting it together. In practice this is not so.

In the real world the designer is subject to a number of constraints. The logic elements available to him are not only characterized in terms of Boolean algebra, they have other important properties which cannot be neglected. Moreover, the designer's employer is not interested in just any solution, he is interested in a cheap solution. The blind application of conventional Boolean algebra does not always lead to the most cost-effective solution to a problem. An American astronaut was once asked how it felt to be strapped into his space capsule. He is reported to have replied, 'How would you feel, sitting on top of a million critical components, each supplied by the firm which put in the lowest tender?' In this section we are going to look at some of the characteristics of logic elements that are of greatest interest to the design engineer. This is not intended to be a rigorous approach covering all the practical aspects of digital design. It is a guide to some of the areas of digital design of interest to the engineer.

The electrical characteristics of gates

A glance at a manufacturer's data sheet for even the simplest of logic elements will reveal one or more pages of information. This data sheet is really a set of 'promises' from the manufacturer to the user. The basic parameters of a typical logic element are given in Table 2.23.

Logic elements are produced by a number of different manufacturing processes. One of the basic types of logic element is called TTL, and a particular variant of TTL is called low power Schottky TTL. The actual details of the manufacture and the properties of various logic families is well beyond the scope of this book.

Table 2.23 Sample data for a logic element (low-power Schottky TTL)

Temperature range (commercial)	$= 0\,°C$ to $+70\,°C$			
Temperature range (military)	$= -55\,°C$ to $+125\,°C$			
Operating voltage	$= 5\,V \pm 5\%$			
Maximum ratings				
Storage Temperature	$-65\,°C$ to $+150\,°C$			
Supply voltage	$-0.5\,V$ to $+7\,V$			
DC input current	$-30\,mA$ to $+5.0\,mA$			
DC characteristics				
	Min	*Typ*	*Max*	*Units*
V_{OH} output high voltage	2.7	3.4		Volts
V_{OL} output low voltage			0.4	Volts
V_{IH} input high voltage	2.0			Volts
V_{IL} input low voltage			0.8	Volts
I_{IL} input low current			-0.36	mA
I_{IH} input high current			40	μA
I_{OH} output high current			-400	μA
I_{OL} output high current			$+8$	mA
Switching characteristics				
t_{LH} low-to-high delay	10 ns (max)			
t_{HL} high-to-low delay	12 ns (max)			

The operating temperature range tells the designer how cold or how hot he can let his equipment become without the characteristics of the logic element drifting outside their stated ranges. Considerations of temperature are frequently of little importance to the designers of domestic equipment where the environment is often maintained from approximately 10°C to 25°C. However, the automobile manufacturer may find the thermal behaviour of a logic element one of its most important parameters. He has to sell his car in markets as far apart as Alaska and the Sahara.

The voltage characteristics of a logic element define the worst-case input and output conditions. For example, V_{OL} is the maximum output voltage when the output is in a low level state. If V_{OL} is quoted as 0.4 V, it implies that the output for a logical zero may lie anywhere in the range 0 V to 0.4 V. The low level output will never be greater than 0.4 V unless, of course, the device is faulty.

Similarly, V_{IL} defines the maximum input voltage that an element will reliably recognize as a logical zero. A V_{IL} of 0.8 V means that an input in the range 0 V to 0.8 V is guaranteed to be interpreted as a logical zero. Notice that V_{IL} is quoted as 0.8 V and V_{OL} as 0.4 V. The difference between these two figures is called the 'noise margin' of the device. If we know that an output in a low state will be 0.4 V or less, and that an input will see a voltage of up to 0.8 V as a low state, then up to 0.4 V may be added to the output without any error occurring. The 'additional 0.4 V' allows for noise in the system. Noise is the general term given to all unwanted signals.

Another important set of electrical parameters are those concerning the flow of current between gates. In an ideal world no current would flow between gates. Unfortunately, for the input of a gate to recognize a given logic level it must absorb some current from the gate driving it. That is, from the output to which it is connected. For example, from the Table 2.23 it can be seen that the maximum input current into a gate in a high state, I_{IH}, is 40 μA (40×10^{-6} A).

The maximum current into an output in a logic one statre, I_{OH}, is given as $-400\ \mu$A. The minus sign indicates that current flows out of the gate. Current flows into an output in a logical zero state, and out of an output in a logical one state. A fundamental difference exists between I_{IH} and I_{OH}. While I_{IH} represents the current taken by the input of a gate, I_{OH} represents the maximum current which may be supplied by the output circuit of a gate. The actual output current of a gate will always be a value between 0 and I_{OH} or I_{OL}. When the output of a gate is connected to the input of another gate the output current of one gate must be exactly equal to the input current of the gate to which it is connected. A basic law of electronics states that the current flowing along a given path must be the same at all points along the path. Figure 2.70 illustrates the electrical conditions of a gate with a logical zero output driving two inputs, and the conditions of a gate with a logical one output driving four inputs.

When several inputs are connected to one output, the total current drawn by the inputs must not exceed the maximum current which the output can supply. If there are n inputs, it follows that I_{OH} must be greater than, or equal to nI_{IH} for reliable operation. For the example above, in the high level state one output can supply enough current to drive $400/40 = 10$ inputs. The four basic equations which govern the electrical operation of gates are:

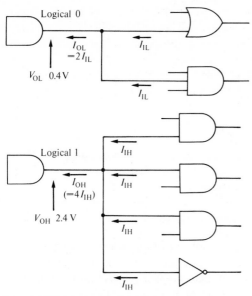

Fig. 2.70 The electrical characteristics of gates in the logical zero (bottom of p. 80) and the logical one states (above)

$$V_{OL} < V_{IL},$$
$$V_{OH} > V_{IH},$$
$I_{OL} > nI_{IL}$ for n inputs connected to one output,
$I_{OH} > nI_{IH}$ for n inputs connected to one output.

Another inportant set of properties of all logic elements is their timing characteristics. Up to now it has been generally assumed that if a number of Boolean conditions are applied to the input terminals of an arrangement of gates, then the correct output (i.e. that determined by the Boolean equations of the gates) will appear instantaneously at the output of the circuit. This is not so. In general, a simple gate has a propagation delay of approximately 10 ns. One nanosecond is an unbelievably short period of time in human terms—but not in electronic terms. This delay is one of the greatest problems designers have to contend with. We have already seen some of the effects of delays in Section 2.5.

Figure 2.71 illustrates the effects of propagation delay on a single inverter. A pulse with sharp (i.e. vertical) rising and falling edges is applied to the input of an inverter. An inverted pulse is produced at its output which is delayed with respect to the input, and its edges are no longer vertical. The time t_{HL} is the time delay between the rising edge of the input pulse and the point at which the output of the gate has reached V_{OL}. Similarly, t_{LH} represents the time between the falling edge of the input and the time at which the output reaches V_{OH}.

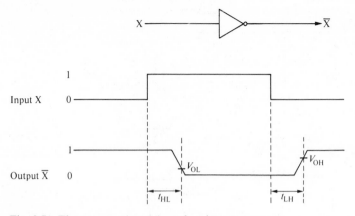

Fig. 2.71 The propagation delay of an inverter

It might be thought that the effect of time delays in the passage of signals through gates simply reduces the speed at which a digital system may operate. Unfortunately, propagation delays have more sinister effects as shown by Fig. 2.72. By the rules of Boolean algebra the output of the AND gate should be permanently zero.

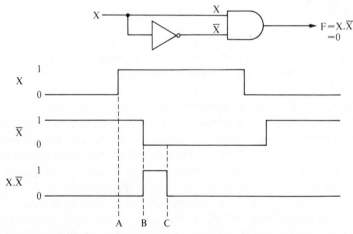

Fig. 2.72 The side effect of propagation delay in a gate

Now examine its timing diagram. At point A the input, X, rises from zero to one. However, the $\overline{X}$ input to the AND gate does not fall to zero for a time which is equal to the propagation delay of the inverter. Consequently, for a short time the inputs of the AND gate are both true, and its output rises to a logical one from points B to C (after its own internal delay). The short pulse at the output of the AND gate is called a glitch, and can be very troublesome in digital systems. There are two solutions to this problem. One is to apply special design techniques to the Boolean logic to remove the glitch. The other is to connect the output to a flip-flop, and to clock the flip-flop after any glitches have died away.

The economic considerations of digital design

Economic considerations in designing digital systems vary widely with the application. For example, an engineer designing an on-board computer in a satellite is concerned largely with optimizing three parameters: weight, realiability, and power consumption. The designer of washing machine controllers may be concerned almost entirely with minimizing the cost of the circuit.

As all but the most trivial of digital circuits require a large number of different types of gate (two-input OR, five-input AND etc.), the designer will look at ways of reducing the number of types of gate in order to minimize the number of integrated circuits required. Sometimes he will sidestep the problem by asking, 'Has any manufacturer produced an integrated circuit with a function close to my requirements?' If the answer is yes, then an off-the-shelf circuit can be used directly, or with a little additional logic. The major semiconductor manufacturers have now produced a wide range of basic building blocks varying from multiplexers through to digital multiplier circuits.

Another approach is to use read-only-memories (ROMs) to implement the circuit as a look-up table. A ROM is a device with n address input lines specifying 2^n unique locations within it. Each location, when accessed, produces an m-bit value on its m output lines. It is called 'read-only' because the output corresponding to a given input cannot be modified (i.e. written into) by the user.

Figure 2.73 shows how a 16×4 ROM implements the multiplier circuit of Fig. 2.17(b). The four address inputs X_1, X_0, Y_1, Y_0 select one of the sixteen possible locations, each containing a four-bit word corresponding to the desired result. The manufacturer of the ROM writes the appropriate output

Input $X_1 X_0 Y_1 Y_0$	Outputs $Z_3 Z_2 Z_1 Z_0$
0000	0000
0001	0000
0010	0000
0011	0000
0100	0000
0101	0001
0110	0010
0111	0011
1000	0000
1001	0010
1010	0100
1011	0110
1100	0000
1101	0011
1110	0110
1111	1001

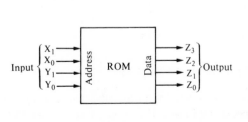

Fig. 2.73 Using a ROM to replace logic elements

into each of the sixteen locations. For example, the location 1011, corresponding to 10×11 ($= 2 \times 3$), has 0110 ($= 6$) written into it. The ROM directly implements not the circuit but the truth table. For each input the corresponding output is stored. This technique does not even require Boolean algebra to simplify the sum-of-products expression derived from the truth table.

Yet another technique open to the designer involves programmable logic. General-purpose logic arrays (collections of different types of gate on a single chip) have been produced. By means of 'blowing' fuses within the chip, the individual gates can be configured in a large number of ways. The digital designer selects the appropriate device from a manufacturer's catalogue and then 'bends' his Boolean equations to fit the type of gates on the chip. He then plugs the chip into a special programming machine which interconnects the gates in the way he wants.

Actually, the interconnections are there already, the programmer does not make new connections, but destroys unwanted connections. Figure 2.74 illustrates this point. At the crosspoints between the vertical and horizontal

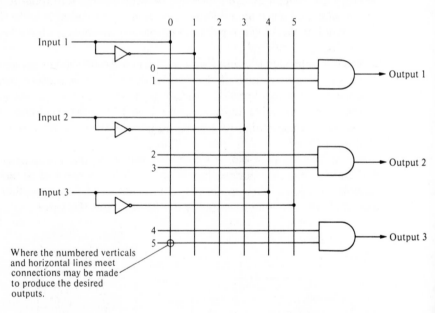

Fig. 2.74 A simplified example of programmable array logic

lines are tiny fuses. If the fuse is left intact an electrical connection exists, linking the vertical and horizontal lines. If a large pulse of current is passed through the fuse during the chip's programming, the link is broken because the fuse melts. The use of programmable logic arrays leads to logic functions being realized with very few integrated circuit packages, greatly reducing the manufacturing costs.

This process can be taken one step further. A large number of gates are fabricated on a chip, but the interconnections between the gates are not made until the last step in the manufacturing process. That is, the manufacturer puts a number of gates on a single chip and allows the customer to specify the actual connections between the gates. Note that the customer may not use all the gates provided. Such a chip is called an uncommitted logic array (ULA), and is cost-effective only for large-scale production, as the cost of setting up the equipment to produce the chips is not small. It is the uncommitted logic array that has enabled Sinclair to produce the ZX80, ZX81, and Spectrum computers with so few parts.

2.8 Computers and reliability

Reliability is one of the major factors in both the selection of components for incorporation in a computer, and in its actual design. The domestic consumer is often not directly conscious of the importance of reliability. When I go into camera shop, the salesman says 'Nice job this, $f1.4$, self-focusing, automatic exposure, motor drive . . .'. I buy it. It breaks down a week later.

If I buy computer equipment for my employer, I don't ask the salesman about irrelevant or frivolous features. Instead, I am concerned about its 'mean time between failure (MTBF)', and its 'mean time to repair (MTTR)'. Professional equipment often has to operate continuously for long periods of time. Sometimes, the failure of such equipment is both expensive and embarrassing. At other times the failure is disastrous. For example, the failure of a computer in a time-sharing bureau leads to a direct loss of income and an additional loss in the form of goodwill. The total failure of a computer operating control rods in an atomic pile is frightening to contemplate. Before we deal with reliability formally, note the word 'total' in the last sentence—later we shall see how systems can be made more reliable by choosing designs which tolerate a partial failure of the system.

There are two widely held personal theories of reliability: one is that demons live in all manufactured devices and that their aim is to cause a breakdown at the worst possible time. The other is that a device is programmed by its manufacturers to fail the moment its guarantee ends. Neither of these theories is entirely true—a device may fail from one of many causes—and it is almost impossible to say when a given device is going to fail. However, when dealing with large numbers of (identical) devices, it is possible to say something about the average device. The reliability of a device is defined as $1 - p$, where p is the probability of its failure in a given time. For example, if there is a one in ten chance of a particular component failing within a year, it may be said to be 90 per cent reliable.

Consider a very large number of components of which, after a time t, N are still working (the rest have failed). The change of N as a function of time is represented by dN/dt, and is negative because N is decreasing. The ratio of the rate of decrease of N to the population of working devices is called the failure rate and is denoted by:

$$L = -\frac{dN}{dt}/N.$$

The failure rate, L, is often expressed in units of failures per cent per 1000 hours, although the period of time varies from application to application. For example if a component is said to exhibit a failure rate of 0.003 per cent per 1000 hours, a batch of 1 000 000 components can be expected to show 30 failures after 1000 hours of use.

From the above expression $dN/N = -Ldt$. Assuming (for the moment) that the failure rate is constant, the expression can be integrated to give:

$$\ln N = -Lt + C \qquad \text{where } C \text{ is a constant of integration}$$

or $\qquad N = Ke^{-Lt}$.

K represents the initial number of components, and is normally written N_0. We now have:

$$N = N_0 e^{-Lt}$$

Incidentally, this equation is also the same equation governing the decay of radioactive material. If we define the term $r(t)$ as N/N_0, that is the current survivors divided by the original population, then we can write:

$$r(t) = e^{-Lt}.$$

The function $r(t)$ is the reliability function and represents the fraction of a batch of components surviving after a time t. The failure rate is simply unity minus the reliability, that is failure rate $= 1 - r(t)$.

A more useful concept than failure rate is mean time between failure, MTBF, because it gives an idea of the expected lifetime of a component. MTBF is defined as

$$\int_0^\infty r(t)dt.$$

Integrating this expression yields MTBF $= m = 1/L$.

Thus, $r(t) = e^{-t/m}$. It should be noted that m is obtained by measurement. That is, the failure rate of a batch of components must be measured by observing their behaviour. Of course, the component you buy may not be a student of statistics, and may therefore fail at the earliest inconvenient moment.

While it is desirable to have components with a large MTBF, it is just as desirable to have components or systems that can be rapidly repaired when they do fail. Another useful parameter is the MTTR (mean time to repair), also called MTRF (mean time to repair a fault). These two parameters can be combined to give the availability or uptime ratio of a system. That is,

$$\text{availability} = \frac{\text{MTBF}}{\text{MTBF} + \text{MTTR}}.$$

We have assumed that the failure rate, L, and therefore m, is a constant. In practice, this is not entirely true. Figure 2.75 shows the classic 'bath-tub' curve of the failure rate of a component as a function of time. The left-hand part of the curve is the 'infant mortality' of the component and corresponds to the initial high failure rate in a batch of components due to manufacturing errors. The flat portion of the curve corresponds to a constant failure rate, and represents the useful life of the batch of components. The rise in failure rate at the end of the batch's life-time corresponds to old age and is due to the wearing out of components.

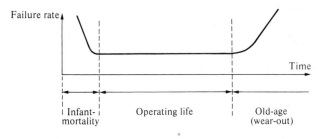

Fig. 2.75 The reliability curve

It is now common for some manufacturers to 'burn-in' their components, before selling them. That is, the components are run, often at a high temperature to accelerate their aging, to get them over the infant mortality region. Components failing during the burn-in period are discarded, and the buyer gets a more reliable component. Of course, components that have been burnt-in are appreciably more expensive than components straight off the production line.

All the above would be useless to computer engineers if it could not be applied to groups of components to enable the designer to determine the overall failure rate of a system made up of many components with known failure rates.

Suppose a system is composed of two components R_1 and R_2. If we know that the reliability of these components is r_1 and r_2, respectively, we can calculate the reliability of the system. For this calculation we will assume that the system, as a whole, fails if either R_1 or R_2 fails.

The reliability of a system made up of components operating in series (i.e. one out, all out) is the product of their individual reliabilities. Thus, the reliability of our two-component system is $r = r_1 \times r_2$. For example, if R_1 is 99 per cent reliable and R_2 is 98 per cent reliable, then the overall reliability is $0.99 \times 0.98 = 0.97$, or 97 per cent. Note that this formula is reassuringly in line with common sense. The overall reliability is dependent on the lowest reliability in the expression—that is, the system is as good as its weakest link.

The reliability of a system made up of links or components operating in series is given in Fig. 2.76.

It is possible to design a system which fails only when more than one component fails. This situation is represented by Fig. 2.77. Such a system involves redundancy or 'back-up'. For example, the parallel modules in Fig. 2.77 may be disk drives in a computer system. Clearly, the whole system fails when all the disk drives have failed.

Fig. 2.76 The reliability of components in series is the product of individual reliabilities. That is, $r = r_1 \cdot r_2 \cdot \ldots \cdot r_n$.

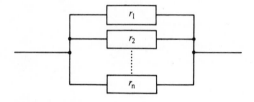

Fig. 2.77 The reliability of components in parallel = 1 − unreliability and is given by $1 - (1 - r_1)(1 - r_2) \ldots (1 - r_n)$

When components are operating in parallel, a failure occurs only when all components fail. If the reliability of the ith component is given by r_i, then its unreliability, or probability of failure, is given by $(1 - r_i)$. If there are n components in parallel, the probability of them all failing together is $(1 - r_1)(1 - r_2) \ldots (1 - r_n)$. Therefore, the reliability of the system is given by

$$1 - \text{system unreliability} = 1 - (1 - r_1)(1 - r_2) \ldots (1 - r_n).$$

Consider now the two components R_1 and R_2 with reliabilities 99 per cent and 98 per cent operating in parallel. The overall system reliability is:

$$1 - (1 - 0.99)(1 - 0.98)$$

$$= 1 - (0.01)(0.02) = 1 - 0.0002$$

$$= 0.9998, \text{ i.e. } 99.98 \text{ per cent.}$$

Notice how parallel components can have a dramatic effect on overall reliability. In practice there are slight penalities to be paid for using parallel systems, as the components, or pathways, linking the parallel modules may themselves fail.

In a real system the reliability can be calculated, and redundancy added, where necessary, to strengthen weak links in the chain. For example, consider the following system illustrated in Fig. 2.78. This system has an

ALU, memory module, three VDUs, three disk controllers, and three disk drives. Table 2.24 gives the reliabilities of the individual components.

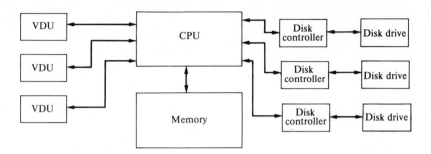

Fig. 2.78 A small computer system

Table 2.24 The reliability of the components in Fig. 2.78

Component	Reliability
VDU	0.98
CPU	0.999
Memory	0.8
Disk controller	0.995
Disk drive	0.8

If it is assumed that the system will still give a reduced, but acceptable, level of service with just a CPU, a memory module, and a single disk controller and associated drive, then Fig. 2.79 shows the system from a reliability point of view. The overall reliability is determined by four groups

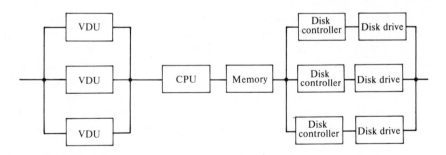

Fig. 2.79 The reliability of the computer in Fig. 2.78

in series: the VDUs, the CPU, the memory, the disk controllers and disk drives. Note that the VDUs are in parallel as a failure occurs only when all three VDUs fail. Similarly, each disk controller or its associated disk drive must fail before the system fails.

The reliability of each of these four links is:

VDUs $1-(1-0.98)(1-0.98)(1-0.98)=1-0.000008=0.999992$
CPU 0.999
Memory 0.8
Disk drive and controller $1-(1-0.995\times0.8)(1-0.995\times0.8)$
$(1-0.995\times0.8)$
$=1-(1-0.796)(1-0.796)(1-0.796)$
$=1-0.008495=0.9915$

The overall system reliability is given by the product of the individual reliabilities of the four links operating in series:

$0.999992\times0.999\times0.8\times0.9915=0.7924\approx79$ per cent.

It should be appreciated that the above result is almost entirely dominated by the low reliability of the memory module. Suppose the manufacturer puts two such modules in parallel. The reliability of the memory would now be $1-(1-0.8)(1-0.8)$, or 0.96, and the reliability of the system $0.9509\approx95$ per cent.

From what I have said above, reliability may look like a science. It is not. It is a black art. The computer designer or any other engineer should not grow too complacent. Reliability calculations are based on two assumptions. The first is that the reliability of a component is constant for most of its life (Fig. 2.75). This ignores new modes of failure in operation. For example, the world's first passenger jet aircraft, the Comet, was designed using reliability theory known at that time. Unfortunately, the theory of metal fatigue was not well understood and cracks developed and spread from the aircraft's square windows. This lead to a disintegration of the fuselage, and a consequent loss of the aircraft.

The second assumption is that the overall reliability can be calculated using the techniques for Fig. 2.75 (parallel and serial networks). This is relatively true for simple systems, but less so for very large systems—an aircraft or a nuclear reactor. When such a large system is analysed, the analysis itself is made by an engineer operating under certain assumptions. Some of these may involve human behaviour. For example, the reliability of a system may depend strongly on its maintenance. If, because of economic pressures, the maintenance is not carried out according to the manufacturer's specifications, the reliability of the system will not match its reliability on paper.

Problems

Logic elements

1. Tabulate the values of the variables, P, Q, R, S, T, and U in Fig. 2.80, for all possible input variables A, B, C, and D.

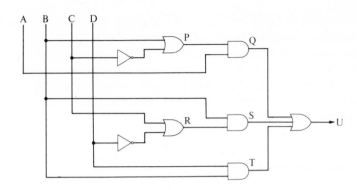

Fig. 2.80

Note The truth table for this question should be in the form given in Table 2.25.

Table 2.25 Truth table for Fig. 2.80

Inputs				Intermediate values					Output
A	B	C	D	$P=B+\bar{C}$	$Q=P\cdot A$	$R=C+\bar{D}$	$S=B\cdot R$	$T=B\cdot D$	$U=Q+S+T$
0	0	0	0	1	0	1	0	0	0
0	0	0	1						
0	0	1	0	·	·	·	·	·	·
0	0	1	1	·	·	·	·	·	·
0	1	0	0	·	·	·	·	·	·
		·							
		·							
		·							
1	1	1	1	1	1	1	1	1	1

2. For the diagram in Question 1 obtain a Boolean expression for the output, U, in terms of the inputs A, B, C, D. This expression need not be simplified.

3. Use a truth table to obtain the relationship between outputs X and Y, and the input variables A, B, and C for the circuit in Fig. 2.81. From the truth

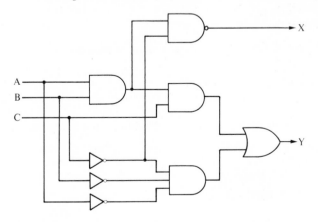

Fig. 2.81

table write down Boolean expressions for X and Y. Derive expressions for X and Y by considering the Boolean equations of the gates.

Demonstrate that the two results (i.e. those derived from the truth table and those derived from the Boolean equations) are equivalent by substituting literals (000, 001, etc.) for A, B, and C in the Boolean equations.

4. Draw logic diagrams using AND, OR, and NOT gates only, to implement the following Boolean expressions.

(a) $F = A\overline{B} + \overline{A}\overline{B}$

(b) $F = (A + B + C)(AB + AC)$

(c) $F = \overline{(\overline{A} + \overline{C})(\overline{A} + B\overline{D})}$

(d) $F = \overline{A} + \overline{C}.A + B\overline{D}$

(e) $F = (A\overline{B} + \overline{A}B + A\overline{C})(\overline{AB} + \overline{A}\overline{B} + A\overline{C})$

Do not simplify the expressions.

Boolean algebra

1. Simplify the following expressions by means of Boolean algebra. That is, do not use Karnaugh maps.

(a) $A\overline{B}\overline{C} + \overline{A}B\overline{C} + \overline{A}\overline{B}\overline{C} + \overline{A}\overline{B}C$

(b) $ABC + \overline{A}BC + A\overline{B}C + A\overline{B}\overline{C} + \overline{A}B\overline{C} + \overline{A}\overline{B}C$

(c) $ABC + A\overline{B}\overline{C} + \overline{A}\overline{B}\overline{C} + \overline{A}\overline{B}C + A\overline{B}C + AB\overline{C} + \overline{A}B\overline{C} + \overline{A}BC$

(d) $(A + B + C)(A + \overline{B} + \overline{C})(A + B + \overline{C})(A + \overline{B} + C)$

(e) $(A\overline{B} + \overline{A}B + A\overline{C})(\overline{A}B + A\overline{B} + A\overline{C})$

(f) $A + \overline{B} + (A + CD)(A + \overline{B}C)$

(g) $\overline{A}B + B\overline{C} + A\overline{B}C + AB\overline{C}D$

(h) $(\overline{A} + B)(A + \overline{B} + C)(A + B + C)(\overline{A} + B + \overline{C})(\overline{A} + \overline{B} + C)$.

2. Use de Morgan's theorem to complement the following expressions. Do not simplify the expressions either before or after you complement them.

(a) $\overline{X}\overline{Y} + XY$

(b) $XYZ + \overline{X}\overline{Y}$

(c) $XYZ + \overline{X}Y$

(d) $WX(\overline{Y}Z + YZ)$

(e) $WX(W\overline{Z} + \overline{Y}Z)$

(f) $XY + \overline{X}\overline{Y}(WZ + \overline{W}Z)$.

3. Convert the following expressions to sum-of-products form.

(a) $(A + B)(\overline{B} + C)(\overline{A} + C)$

(b) $(C + D)(A\overline{B} + AC)(\overline{AC} + B)$

(c) $(A + B + C)(A + CD)(D + F)$.

4. Convert the following expressions to product-of-sums form.

(a) $AB + \overline{A}B + BC$

(b) $AB + \overline{A}C + \overline{B}C$

(c) $\overline{A}B(\overline{CD} + E(B + \overline{C} + D))$

(d) $A\overline{B}\overline{C} + \overline{A}B\overline{C} + \overline{A}\overline{B}C + \overline{A}BC$.

Applying Boolean algebra

1. A circuit has four inputs, P, Q, R, and S, representing the natural binary numbers 0000 = 0, to 1111 = 15. P is the most significant bit. The circuit has one output, X, which is true if the number represented by the input is divisible by three. (Regard zero as being indivisible by three.)

Design a truth table for this circuit, and hence obtain an expression for X in terms of P, Q, R, and S. Give the circuit diagram of an arrangement of AND, OR, and NOT gates to implement this circuit.

Design a second circuit to implement this function using NAND gates only.

2. A logic circuit has two 2-bit natural binary inputs A and B. A is given by A_1, A_0 where A_1 is the most significant bit. Similarly for B. The circuit has three outputs, X, Y, and Z. The relationship between A and B, and X, Y, Z is as follows.

	X	Y	Z
A > B	1	0	0
A < B	0	1	0
A = B	0	0	1

Design a circuit to implement this function.

3. A logic circuit has three inputs A, B, and C where A is the least significant bit. The circuit has eight outputs, Y_0 to Y_7. For any binary code applied to the input terminals (A, B, C), one, and one only, of the outputs goes true—the others remain false. Thus, if C = 1, B = 0, and A = 0 the output Y_4 is true. Design a logic network to implement this circuit. Such a circuit is called a demultiplexer, and has already been met in Chapter 2.

4. A 4-bit binary number is applied to a circuit on four lines A, B, C, and D. The circuit has a single output, F, which is true if the number is in the range three to twelve, inclusive.

Draw a truth table for this problem, and obtain a simplified expression for F in terms of the inputs.

Implement the circuit: (a) in terms of NAND gates only (b) in terms of NOR gates only.

Sequential circuits

1. Assuming that the initial state of the circuit shown in Fig. 2.82 is given by C = 1, D = 1, P = 1, and Q = 0, complete Table 2.26. This question should be attempted by calculating the effect of the new C and D on the inputs to both cross-coupled pairs of NOR gates, and therefore on the outputs P and Q. As P and Q are also inputs to the NOR gates, the change in P and Q should be taken into account when calculating the effect of the next inputs C and D. Remember that the output of a NOR is 1 if both its inputs are 0, and is 0 otherwise.

Table 2.26

C	D	P	Q
1	1	1	0
1	0		
0	0		
1	1		
0	1		
1	1		
0	1		
0	0		
1	0		

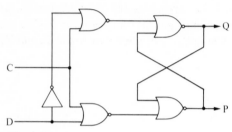

Fig. 2.82

Modify the circuit to provide a new input S which, when 1, will at any time set P to 1 and Q to 0. Provide another input R which will similarly set P to 0 and Q to 1. Note that R and S cannot both be a 1 at the same time, and therefore the condition $R = S = 1$ need not be considered.

2. Investigate the operation of the circuit in Fig. 2.83. Each JK flip-flop is triggered on the falling-edge of its clock input. Give a diagram of the sequence of outputs, Q1 to Q4, as a function of time.

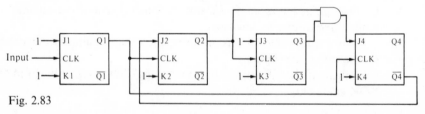

Fig. 2.83

3. Although synchronous counters have not been covered here, their design is not complex. Each flip-flop in the counter is clocked simultaneously. After each clock pulse, the new output is determined by the state of the JK inputs (assuming the use of JK flip-flops) at the time the flip-flop was clocked. For an n-bit counter, the ith output is given by $Q_i \leftarrow J_i$, K_i where $J_i \leftarrow f_a(Q_0, Q_1 \ldots Q_{n-1})$ and $K_i \leftarrow f_b(Q_0, Q_1 \ldots Q_{n-1})$. That is, we use the previous outputs, Q_0, to Q_{n-1}, to generate the values of J and K needed to produce the next outputs. This exercise is carried out for each stage of the counter.

Design a 3-bit binary counter using negative-edge triggered JK flip-flops to produce the following sequence:

Q_2	Q_1	Q_0	
0	0	0	
0	1	0	
0	1	1	basic sequence
0	0	1	
1	0	0	
1	1	0	
0	0	0	sequence repeats
0	1	0	

3 COMPUTER ARITHMETIC

Because of the ease with which binary logic elements are manufactured and because of their remarkably low price, it is inevitable that the binary number system was chosen to represent numerical data within a computer. Before going any further it is worth pointing out that the rules for binary arithmetic are the same as those for decimal arithmetic, only the base or radix has changed.

3.1 Characters, words, and bytes

The smallest quantity of information that can be stored and manipulated inside a computer is the bit. Digital computers store information in their memories in the form of groups of bits called words. The number of bits per word varies from computer to computer. The ICL 1900 series used 24-bit words, the UNIVAC 1100 36-bit words, the PDP-11 16-bit words, and many microprocessors operate with 8-bit words. A group of eight bits has come to be known as a byte. Often a word is spoken of as being 2 or 4 bytes long because its bits can be formed into 2 or 4 groups of eight, respectively. Microprocessors and minicomputers are normally byte-oriented with word-lengths and addresses of 8, 16, or 32 bits. But beware—some computers group bits into sixes and call them bytes.

An n-bit word can have 2^n unique bit patterns. A word can represent many things, there is no intrinsic meaning associated with a pattern of 1s and 0s. The meaning of a particular pattern of bits is the meaning given to it by the programmer. As Humpty Dumpty said to Alice, 'A word means exactly what I choose it to mean, nothing more and nothing less'. The computer itself cannot tell the meaning of the word, but simply treats it in the way the programmer dictates. For example, a programmer could read the name of a person into the computer and then perform an arithmetic operation on the pattern of bits representing the name (say multiply it by two). The computer would happily carry out the operation although the result would be meaningless. If this is not clear, consider the following example. In a Chinese restaurant, 46 represents 'bamboo shoots', and 27 represents 'egg fried rice'. If I were to ask for a portion of 73, I would be most unlikely to get egg fried rice with bamboo shoots!

The following are some entities a word may represent.

1. *An instruction*   An instruction to be performed by the CPU is normally represented by a single word. The relationship between the bit-pattern of the

instruction and what it does is arbitrary and is determined by the designer of the computer.

2. *A numerical quantity*   The word, either alone or as part of a sequence of words, may represent a numerical quantity. The number can be represented in one of many formats: BCD integer, unsigned binary integer, signed binary integer, BCD floating point, binary floating point, complex integer, complex floating point, double precision integer, etc. The meaning of some of these terms and the way in which the computer carries out its operations in the number system represented by the term will be examined later.

3. *A character*   There are many applications of the computer in which text is input and processed, and the results printed. The most obvious and spectacular example of this is the word processor. Programs themselves are in text form when they are first submitted to the computer. The alphanumeric characters (A to Z, a to z, 0 to 9) and the symbols *, $-$, $+$, !, ?, etc. are assigned binary patterns so that they can be stored and manipulated within the computer. Fortunately, one particular code is now in widespread use throughout the computer industry. This is the ASCII code (American Standard Code for Information Interchange), and represents a character by 7 bits, allowing a maximum of $2^7 = 128$ different characters. Of these 128 characters, 96 are the normal printing characters (including both upper and lower cases). The remaining 32 characters are 'non-printing'. These include carriage return, backspace, line feed, etc. Figure 3.1 defines the relationship between the bits of a word and its ASCII equivalent.

Fig. 3.1 The ASCII code

$b_3b_2b_1b_0$	$b_6b_5b_4$	0 000	1 001	2 010	3 011	4 100	5 101	6 110	7 111
0	0000	NUL	DLC	SP	0	@	P	'	p
1	0001	SOH	DC1	!	1	A	Q	a	q
2	0010	STX	DC2	"	2	B	R	b	r
3	0011	ETX	DC3	#	3	C	S	c	s
4	0100	EOT	DC4	$	4	D	T	d	t
5	0101	ENQ	NAK	%	5	E	U	e	u
6	0110	ACK	SYN	&	6	F	V	f	v
7	0111	BEL	ETB	'	7	G	W	g	w
8	1000	BS	CAN	(	8	H	X	h	x
9	1001	HT	EM	)	9	I	Y	i	y
A	1010	LT	SUB	*	:	J	Z	j	z
B	1011	VT	ESC	+	;	K	[	k	{
C	1100	FF	FS	,	<	L	/	l	|
D	1101	CR	GS	-	=	M	]	m	}
E	1110	SO	RS	.	>	N	∧	n	
F	1111	SI	VS	/	?	O	—	o	DEL

<———————> <————————————————————————>
    Control   Printing characters
    characters

To obtain the 7-bit binary code for a character read the most significant three bits in the column in which it appears, and the least significant four bits in the row in which it appears. Thus, the character 'W' is in the 101 column and the 0111 row, so that its ASCII code is 1010111 (or 57 in hexadecimal form). Similarly, the code for carriage return (CR) is 0001101.

3.2 Number bases

We represent numbers in the decimal system by means of positional notation. As each digit moves one place left it is multiplied by ten (the base or radix), and as it moves one place right it is divided by ten. Thus, the 9 in 95 is worth ten times the 9 in 59. If this seems obvious and not worthy of mention consider the Romans. They conquered most of the known world, invented Latin grammar, kept the lions well-fed, had the odd orgy or two, and yet their mathematics was terribly cumbersome. Because they did not use a positional system, each new large number had to have its own special symbol. Their number system was one of 'give and take' so that if $X = 10$ and $I = 1$, then $XI = 11$ $(10 + 1)$ and $IX = 9$ $(10 - 1)$.

A number N when expressed in the base b is written:

$$a_n a_{n-1} a_{n-2} \ldots a_1 a_0 \cdot a_{-1} a_{-2} \ldots a_{-m}$$

and is defined as:

$$N = a_n \times b^n + a_{n-1} \times b^{n-1} + \ldots a_1 \times b^1 + a_0 \times b^0$$
$$+ a_{-1} \times b^{-1} + a_{-2} \times b^{-2} + \ldots + a_{-m} \times b^{-m}$$

$$= \sum_{i=-m}^{n} a_i b^i.$$

For example, the decimal number 1984 is equal to $1 \times 10^3 + 9 \times 10^2 + 8 \times 10 + 4 \times 1$. Similarly, the binary number 10110 is given by $1 \times 2^4 + 0 \times 2^3 + 1 \times 2^2 + 1 \times 2^1 + 0 \times 2^0$, or $16 + 4 + 2 = 22$. Positional notation employs the radix point to separate the integer and fractional parts of the number. The as in the above equation are called digits and may have one of b possible values. Currently, those involved with computers are interested in four bases: decimal, binary, octal, and hexadecimal.

Decimal	$b = 10$	$a = \{0,1,2,3,4,5,6,7,8,9\}$
Binary	$b = 2$	$a = \{0,1\}$
Octal	$b = 8$	$a = \{0,1,2,3,4,5,6,7\}$
Hexadecimal	$b = 16$	$a = \{0,1,2,3,4,5,6,7,8,9,A,B,C,D,E,F\}$

People work in decimal, and computers in binary. We shall see later that the purpose of the octal and hexadecimal systems is as an aid to human memory. It is almost impossible to remember long strings of binary digits. By converting them to the octal or hexadecimal bases (a very easy task) the shorter octal or hexadecimal numbers can be more readily committed to memory. Furthermore, as octal and hexadecimal numbers are more compact than binary numbers (1 octal digit = 3 binary digits and 1 hex digit = 4 binary digits), they are used in computer texts and 'core-dumps'. The latter term refers to a print-out of part of the computer's memory; an operation normally performed as a diagnostic aid when all else has failed. For example, the eight-bit binary number 1000|1001 is equivalent to the hexadecimal number 89. Clearly, 89 is more easy to remember than 10001001.

There are occasions where binary numbers offer people advantages over other forms of representation. Suppose a computer-controlled chemical plant has three heaters, three valves, and two pumps. These are designated H1,H2,H3, V1,V2,V3, and P1 and P2, respectively. An eight-bit word from the computer is fed to an interface unit. This converts the binary ones and zeros into electrical signals which switch on (logical one), or switch off (logical zero), the corresponding device. For example, the binary word 01010011 has the effect shown in Table 3.1 when presented to the control unit.

Table 3.1 Decoding 01010011

Bit	Device	Status
0	H1	off
1	H2	on
0	H3	off
1	V1	on
0	V2	off
0	V3	off
1	P1	on
1	P2	on

By inspecting the binary value of the control word, the status of all devices is immediately apparent. If the output had been represented in decimal (83), hexadecimal (53), or octal (123), the relationship between the number and its intended action would not be so obvious.

3.3 Number base conversion

It is sometimes necessary to convert numbers from one base to another by means of a pencil-and-paper method. This is particularly true when working with microprocessors at the assembly-language or machine-code level. In general, the computer user need not concern himself with the conversion between bases as the computer will have software to convert decimal input into the computer's own internal binary representation of the input. Once the computer has done its job it converts the binary results into decimal form before printing them. A knowledge of the effect of number bases is sometimes quite vital as even the simplest of decimal fractions (say $1/10 = 0.1$) have no exact binary equivalent. Suppose the computer were asked to add 0.1 to itself and stop when the result reached 1. The computer may never stop because 0.1 is not exactly represented by a binary number with the result that the sum of binary representations of 0.1 is never exactly 1. It may be 1.000000000000 or 0.99999999999, which is almost as good as 1, but it is not the same as 1 and a test for equality with 1 will always fail.

3.3.1 Decimal to binary

To convert a decimal integer to binary, divide the number successively by 2 and after each division record the remainder. The process is terminated only when the result of the division is 0 remainder 1. Note that in all the following conversions 'R' is the remainder after a division.

For example, convert 123_{10} to binary form:

$$123 \div 2 \rightarrow 61, \; R = 1$$
$$61 \div 2 \rightarrow 30, \; R = 1$$
$$30 \div 2 \rightarrow 15, \; R = 0$$
$$15 \div 2 \rightarrow 7, \; R = 1$$
$$7 \div 2 \rightarrow 3, \; R = 1$$
$$3 \div 2 \rightarrow 1, \; R = 1$$
$$1 \div 2 \rightarrow 0, \; R = 1.$$

The result is read from the most significant bit (the last remainder) upward to give $123_{10} = 1111011_2$.

3.3.2 Decimal to octal

The process is as above except that division by 8 is used.

For example, 4629_{10}:

$$4629 \div 8 \rightarrow 578, \; R = 5$$
$$578 \div 8 \rightarrow 72, \; R = 2$$
$$72 \div 8 \rightarrow 9, \; R = 0$$
$$9 \div 8 \rightarrow 1, \; R = 1$$
$$1 \div 8 \rightarrow 0, \; R = 1.$$

Therefore, $4629_{10} = 11025_8$.

3.3.3 Decimal to hexadecimal

Conversion is as for binary and octal, but note that the remainder can be in the decimal range 0 to 15 which corresponds to the hexadecimal range 0 to F.

For example, 53241_{10}:

$$53241 \div 16 \rightarrow 3327, \; R = 9$$
$$3327 \div 16 \rightarrow 207, \; R = 15_{10} = F$$
$$207 \div 16 \rightarrow 12, \; R = 15_{10} = F$$
$$12 \div 16 \rightarrow 0, \; R = 12_{10} = C.$$

Therefore, $53241_{10} = CFF9_{16}$.

1.3.4 Binary to decimal

It is possible to convert a binary number to decimal by adding together the requisite powers of two. This technique is suitable for relatively small binary numbers up to about seven or eight bits.

For example, 1010111_2 is represented by:

64 32 16 8 4 2 1
1   0 1 0 1 1 1 = 64 + 16 + 4 + 2 + 1 = 87.

A more methodical technique is based on a recursive algorithm as follows. Take the leftmost non-zero bit, double it and add it to the bit on its right. Now take this result, double it and add it to the next bit on the right. Continue in this way until the least significant bit has been added in. This procedure may be expressed mathematically as:

$$(a_0 + 2(a_1 + 2(a_2 + \ldots))),$$

where the least significant bit of the binary number is a_0.

For example, take 1010111_2.

1 0   1   0   1   1   1
↳2 ⌐→4 ⌐→10 ⌐→20 ⌐→42 ⌐→86
  2⌐ 5⌐ 10⌐ 21⌐ 43⌐ 87

Therefore, $1010111_2 = 87_{10}$.

1.3.5 Octal to decimal

The above procedure may be used with eight replacing two, to give the formula $(a_0 + 8(a_1 + 8(a_2 + \ldots)))$.

For example, take 6437_8.

6   4   3   7
↳48 ⌐→416 ⌐→3352
  52⌐ 419⌐ 3359

Therefore, $6437_8 = 3359_{10}$.

1.3.6 Hexadecimal to decimal

The method is identical to the procedures for binary and octal except that 16 is used as a multiplier.

For example, take $1AC_{16}$.

1 A   C
↳16 ⌐→416
  26⌐ 428

Therefore, $1AC_{16} = 428_{10}$.

1.3.7 Conversions between binary, octal, and hexadecimal

In much of this book, binary numbers will be represented in hexadecimal

form. Although some texts favour octal formats, I find octal numbers il
fitted to the representation of 8 or 16 bit binary values. We shall u
hexadecimal representations of binary numbers simply because of the ea:
with which conversions may be made between binary and hexadecim:
numbers.

Binary to octal

Form the bits into groups of three starting at the binary point and movin
leftwards. Replace each group of three bits with the corresponding octal dig
(0 to 7).

For example, take 11001011101_2.

11	001	011	101
3	1	3	5

Therefore, $11001011101_2 = 3135_8$.

Note how the binary number has been condensed to a more manageab
size.

Binary to hexadecimal

The binary number is now formed into groups of four bits starting from tl
decimal point. Each group is replaced by a hexadecimal digit from 0 to 9, /
B, C, D, E, F.

For example, take 11001011101_2.

110	0101	1101
6	5	D

Therefore, $11001011101_2 = 65D_{16}$.

Octal to binary

This requires the reverse procedure of converting from binary to octal. Eac
octal digit is simply replaced by its three-bit binary equivalent. It is importai
to remember that a (say) 3 must be replaced by 011 and not 11.

For example, take 41357_8.

4	1	3	5	7
100	001	011	101	111

Therefore, $41357_8 = 100001011101111_2$.

Hexadecimal to binary

Each hexadecimal digit is replaced by its four bit binary equivalent.

For example, take $AB4C_{16}$.

A	B	4	C
1010	1011	0100	1100

Therefore, $AB4C_{16} = 1010101101001100_2$.

3.3.8 The conversion of fractions

Binary to decimal

Starting at the rightmost non-zero bit, take that bit and halve it. Now add the result to the next bit on its left. Halve this result and add it to the next bit on the left. Continue until the binary point is reached.

For example, take 0.01101_2.

$$
\begin{array}{ccccccc}
0 & \cdot & 0 & 1 & 1 & 0 & 1 \\
13/32 \leftarrow & & 13/16 \leftarrow & 5/8 \leftarrow & 1/4 \leftarrow & 1/2 \leftarrow \\
& & -13/16 & -13/8 & -5/4 & -1/2
\end{array}
$$

Therefore, $0.01101_2 = 13/32$.

Decimal to binary

The decimal fraction is multiplied by two and the integer part noted. This integer will be either 1 or 0. It is then stripped from the number to leave a fractional part. The new fraction is multiplied by two and the integer part noted. This process is continued as often as necessary. The binary fraction is formed by reading the integer parts from the top to the bottom as illustrated below.

For example, take 0.6875_{10}.

$0.6875 \times 2 = [1].3750$
$0.3750 \times 2 = [0].7500$
$0.7500 \times 2 = [1].5000$
$0.5000 \times 2 = [1].0000$

(handwritten: 0.6875 1.375 0.75 1.5 1.0 / 1 0 1 1)

Therefore, $0.6875_{10} = 0.1011_2$.

Now consider 0.1_{10}.

$0.1000 \times 2 = [0].2000$
$0.2000 \times 2 = [0].4000$
$0.4000 \times 2 = [0].8000$
$0.8000 \times 2 = [1].6000$
$0.6000 \times 2 = [1].2000$
$0.2000 \times 2 = [0].4000$
$0.4000 \times 2 = [0].8000$
$0.8000 \times 2 = [1].6000$
$0.6000 \times 2 = [1].2000$
$0.2000 \times 2 = [0].4000$
$0.4000 \times 2 = [0].8000$
etc.

(handwritten: 0.1 0.2 0.4 0.8 1.6 1.2 0.4 0.8 1.6 1.2 / 0 0 0 1 1 0 0 1 1 / 0.4 et)

Therefore $0.1_{10} = 0.00011001100_2$ etc.

As I pointed out before 0.1 cannot be expressed exactly in terms of binary fractions.

3.3.9 BCD and other codes

Throughout this book a group of binary digits will generally represent one of three things: a numerical quantity, an instruction, or an ASCII character. However, in the world of computing and digital systems there are many different codes, each one best suited to the particular job for which it is designed. A particularly widespread code is BCD or Binary Coded Decimal.

In theory BCD is a case of having your cake and eating it. It has already been stated that computer designers are forced to rely on two-state logic elements on purely economic grounds. This, in turn, leads to the world of binary arithmetic and the consequent problems of converting between binary and decimal representations of numerical quantities. Binary coded decimal numbers accept the inevitability of two-state logic by coding the individual decimal digits into groups of four bits. Table 3.2 shows how the ten digits, 0 to 9, are represented in BCD, and how a decimal number is converted to a BCD form.

Table 3.2 The BCD code

decimal	BCD
0	0000
1	0001
2	0010
3	0011
4	0100
5	0101
6	0110
7	0111
8	1000
9	1001

To convert a decimal number into BCD form simply encode each decimal digit as a 4-bit BCD group. For example:

1942→0001 1001 0100 0010.

Binary codes 1010 to 1111 are redundant and have no meaning as BCD codes

BCD arithmetic is identical to decimal arithmetic and differs only in the way the ten digits are represented. The following example shows how a BCD addition is carried out.

```
  1942 →   0001 1001 0100 0010
+ 2379 → + 0010 0011 0111 1001
  ────            
  4321     0100 0011 0010 0001
```

Although BCD seems a good idea because it makes decimal to binary conversion easy, it suffers from two disadvantages. The first is that BCD arithmetic is more complex than binary arithmetic. This is because the 'binary tables' are exceedingly small and may be implemented in hardware by a few gates. On the other hand, the decimal tables involve all combinations of the digits 0 to 9. With today's digital technology these 'disadvantages' are less evident than in the early days of computer technology where each gate was a large and expensive item. However, once a trend has been started it tends to gain momentum and to continue long after its original driving force has vanished. This is particularly true in the world of computing where, in the early days, one of the main criteria of circuit design was the minimization of the total number of valves or transistors in a circuit. Today, the number of transistors in a circuit is one of the designer's smallest problems.

The major disadvantage of BCD lies in its inefficient storage. As computer owners have to pay for memory modules, it is reasonable to use the smallest memory for a given job. A BCD digit requires four bits of storage but only ten symbols are mapped on to ten of the sixteen possible binary codes. Consequently, the binary codes 1010 to 1111 (10 to 15) are redundant and represent wasted storage. Pure binary numbers require an average of approximately 3.3 bits per decimal digit.

In spite of the disadvantages of BCD, it is frequently found in applications requiring little storage, such as pocket calculators or digital watches. Some microprocessors have special instructions to aid BCD operations, and many interpreters for the language BASIC perform all numeric operations on BCD numbers. There are in fact a number of different ways of representing BCD numbers in addition to the basic BCD code presented above. Each of these codes has special properties making it suitable for a particular application. Other BCD codes are not relevant to this text.

Unweighted codes

The binary code described in Section 3.2 is often called pure binary, natural binary, or 8421 weighted binary. The 8, 4, 2, and 1 represent the weightings of each of the columns in the positional code. There are many other codes, each with its own special properties, where such a weighting does not apply. One form of unweighted code is the Unit Distance Code. Any two binary quantities may be compared in terms of the 'Hamming' distance between them. The Hamming distance between two words is the number of places in which they differ. The examples below should make this clear.

Word 1	00101101	00101101	00101101	00101101
Word 2	00101100	11101100	11101101	00100101
Places different				
Hamming distance	1	3	2	1

In a unit distance code, the distance between consecutive code words is constant. This is not true of natural binary numbers where, for example, 0111 and 1000 are consecutive values but differ by a distance of 4. The most widely encountered unit distance code is the Gray code, the first 16 values of which are given in Table 3.3.

The Gray Code is often associated with optical encoders, a technique for converting the angle of a shaft into a binary value. Figure 3.2 shows an optical encoder using a natural binary code, and Fig. 3.3 shows the same arrangement but with a Gray encoded disk. An optical encoder allows the

Table 3.3 The Gray code

Decimal value	Natural binary value	Gray code
0	0000	0000
1	0001	0001
2	0010	0011
3	0011	0010
4	0100	0110
5	0101	0111
6	0110	0101
7	0111	0100
8	1000	1100
9	1001	1101
10	1010	1111
11	1011	1110
12	1100	1010
13	1101	1011
14	1110	1001
15	1111	1000

Sector	Angle	Binary code
0	0–45	0 0 0
1	45–90	0 0 1
2	90–135	0 1 0
3	135–180	0 1 1
4	180–225	1 0 0
5	225–270	1 0 1
6	270–315	1 1 0
7	315–360	1 1 1

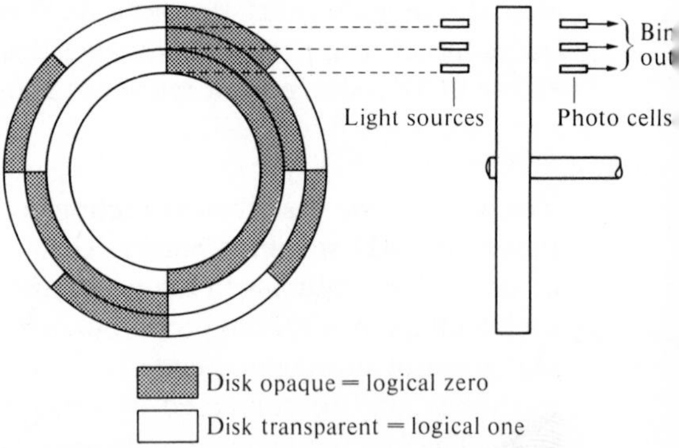

Light sources   Photo cells

Disk opaque = logical zero

Disk transparent = logical one

Fig. 3.2. A natural binary encoded optical encoder

Sector	Angle	Gray code
0	0–45	0 0 0
1	45–90	0 0 1
2	90–135	0 1 1
3	135–180	0 1 0
4	180–225	1 1 0
5	225–270	1 1 1
6	270–315	1 0 1
7	315–360	1 0 0

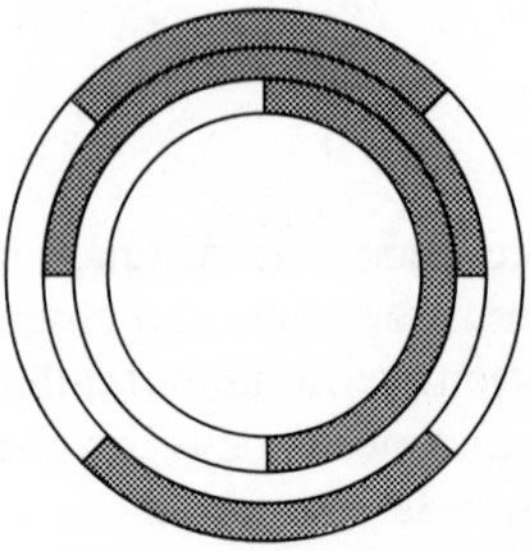

Fig. 3.3. A Gray encoded optical encoder

angular position of a shaft to be determined electronically without any physical connection between the shaft and the measuring equipment. On the end of the shaft is a glass or plastic disk with a number of concentric tracks, one for each of the bits in the code representing the position of the shaft. A four-bit code may be suitable for a wind direction indicator connected to a weather vane, while a ten-bit code may be required to indicate the position of a shaft in a machine. Each of the tracks is divided into a number of sectors which are either opaque or transparent. On one side of the disk are a number of light sources (LEDs or incandescent light-bulbs), one per track. On the other side of the disk are an equal number of photoelectric sensors. Each sensor is situated directly opposite its light source. Thus, for any position of the disk, a particular combination of the photoelectric cells detects a light beam, depending on whether or not there is a transparent sector between the light source and detector.

The problem created by a natural binary code is that between certain sectors two or more bits change state. Unfortunately, as the photoelectric cells cannot be perfectly aligned, when two bits change state one bit must change before the other. Thus, the change from say 001 to 010 may be seen as the sequence 001, 000, 010. Because the least significant bit (LSB) changes before the middle bit, the spurious code '000' is generated momentarily. In some applications this can be very troublesome. From Fig. 3.3 it can be seen that a Gray encoded disk has the property that only one bit at a time changes, solving the problems inherent in the natural binary system. Once the Gray code has been read into a digital system it may be converted into a natural binary code for processing in the normal way.

Error detecting codes (EOCS)

The subject of error detecting codes is large enough to fill a number of text books. Here we shall look only at the simplest of error detecting codes, those using a single parity bit. In any electronic system there are unwanted random signals, collectively called noise, which may interfere with the correct operation of the system. These random signals arise from a variety of causes, ranging from the thermal motion of the electrons in the digital system, to electromagnetic radiation from nearby lightning strikes. The magnitude of these unwanted signals is generally tiny compared with the digital signals inside the computer. The two electrical levels representing the zero and one binary states are so well separated that one level is almost never 'spontaneously' converted into the other level inside a well-constructed computer.

Where digital signals are transmitted over a long distance by cables, their magnitude is diminished, and it is possible for external noise signals to exceed the level of the digital signals and thus corrupt them. This is a familiar situation to most people because those who tune radios or televisions to distant stations know that the sound or picture will be of a lower quality than when a local station is received. Whenever an error occurs in the reception of digital signals it is important for the event to be detected so that a request for retransmission of the corrupted data may be made. This is achieved by transmitting the desired digital information plus one or more check bits whose value is a function of the information bits. Because these check bits convey no new information they are called redundant bits. At the receiving end of a data link the information bits are used to calculate (locally) the check bits. If the received check bits are the same as the locally generated check bits, error-free transmission is assumed, otherwise the receiver must send a message back to the transmitter asking it to repeat the lost data. This topic reappears in Chapter 8.

The idea behind error detecting codes is that an m-bit codeword can convey 2^m unique messages. If r check bits are added to the m message bits to create an n-bit code word, then there are $2^n = 2^{m+r}$ possible code words. Of these code words only 2^m are valid. If a code word is received which is not one of these 2^m values an error may be assumed. The simplest error detecting code involves a single parity bit.

There are two types of parity, even parity and odd parity. We will deal with even parity codes first. An error detecting code with a single even parity check bit chooses the parity bit to make the total number of ones in the word even. Here, the total number of its bits includes the parity bit itself. Thus, if the message is 0101101 the parity bit is chosen to be 0 as there are 4 ones in the word. The code word now becomes 00101101—the parity bit has been appended to the most significant bit position, although in principle there is no reason why the parity bit should be placed at any particular point.

Suppose that the above word is transmitted, and is received as 00101100. The parity of the word calculated at the receiver is odd (there are 3 ones), and an error is assumed to have occurred. We cannot tell from the received word which bit is in error so we cannot correct the error. Note that if there had been two errors, no parity violation would be detected, and the errors would not be flagged. Single parity check bits are helpful where errors are relatively infrequent and tend to occur singly. In a system with odd parity, the parity bit is chosen to make the total number of ones odd. Table 3.4 gives the eight valid code words for a three-bit message, for both even and odd parities. In each case the parity bit is the most significant bit.

Table 3.4 Odd and even parity codes

Message	Code word (even parity)	Code word (odd parity)
000	0000	1000
001	1001	0001
010	1010	0010
011	0011	1011
100	1100	0100
101	0101	1101
110	0110	1110
111	1111	0111

The above ideas can be extended to block- (matrix-) parity error detecting codes. In this case two types of parity are used. If each binary word is written as a column of bits, the parity bit appended to a column is known as a vertical parity bit. If a block of words is made up of a number of columns, a parity word can be formed by calculating the parity across the bits. Each word is composed of, say, four bits: D_0, D_1, D_2, and D_3. Thus, a parity bit for D_0 can be calculated by taking the parity of all D_0s in the block. Parity bits for D_1, D_2, D_3, can be generated in a similar way. This form of parity is called horizontal or longitudinal parity. If a single error occurs in such a block of words, the vertical parity bit will indicate the word in error, and the horizontal parity bit the bit in error. Knowing both the word and the bit in error, it is possible to correct the error.

A simple example of a block error detecting code is given in Table 3.5. Even parity is used, and each column represents a four-bit word—three data bits plus a parity bit. Word 7 is the horizontal parity word formed across the other words.

Table 3.5 Vertical and horizontal parity

Bit	word 1	word 2	word 3	word 4	word 5	word 6	word 7
D_0	0	1	1	0	1	0	1
D_1	1	0	0	1	0	1	1
D_2	1	1	0	1	1	0	0
D_3	0	0	1	0	0	1	0	←vertical parity bits

↑
horizontal parity word

If a single error occurs in the block it is flagged by a parity error in both its column and its row. Consider a single error in the same block of data. The block is transmitted serially, a bit at a time, and the above block appears as the binary sequence

011010101001011010100101011100.

Suppose that the received sequence is

011010101101011010100101011100.

The received sequence can be reformed into words at the receiver as in Table 3.6.

Table 3.6 Detecting a single error

0	1	1	0	1	0	1	√
1	0	1	1	0	1	1	X
1	1	0	1	1	0	0	√
0	0	1	0	0	1	0	√
√	√	X	√	√	√	√	

A tick marks each row or column where the parity is correct, and a cross where it is not. In the above example, the bit in error is detected by the intersection of the row and column in which it creates a parity violation. Thus, although the word 1001 is received incorrectly as 1101 it can be corrected. While the block parity code can detect and correct single errors, it can detect (but not correct) certain combinations of multiple error.

Huffman codes

This short introduction to Huffman codes has been included to show that there is more than one way of 'skinning the cat'. Huffman codes differ from all other encoding techniques found in this book, because they employ a variable-length code word. The idea of a Huffman code is not new. When Samuel Morse devised his famous code he sent his assistant round to the printer's to count the number of letters (i.e. A to Z) in each pigeon hole in which they were stored. As, for example, the letter 'E' appears so frequently in English language text there were many Es. Equally, there were relatively few Qs. So, Samuel Morse created a code whereby frequently used letters had short codes, and infrequently used letters had long codes. For example, the letter E has a morse symbol '.', and the letter Q has the symbol '−−.−'.

A similar arrangement can be extended to binary codes. It must be stated that such codes are applied only to information in which some letters or groups of letters appear more frequently than others. Plain text (e.g. written English) is such a case. To keep things simple, consider the following example. A grocer sells only four items (I did say we were keeping things simple), potatoes, onions, beans, and avocado pears. Being a thoroughly modern grocer, and a computer scientist, he has computerized his business. Every time an item is bought it is encoded in binary form and stored on disk. Because business is brisk and disk space limited, he wishes to code his transactions in such a way as to use the least possible storage. Initially he tried a two-bit binary code (Table 3.7).

Table 3.7 A two-bit binary code

Item	Code
Potatoes	00
Onions	01
Beans	10
Avocado pears	11

If there are n transactions, the total storage required to record them is $2n$ bits. At first sight it would seem that there is no way he can get away with less than two bits to encode each transaction. However, after a little thought, he realizes that the majority of his customers buy potatoes. So he devises the arrangement shown in Table 3.8.

Table 3.8 A Huffman code

Item	% of transactions	Code
Potatoes	75	0
Onions	12.5	10
Beans	6.25	110
Avocado pears	6.25	111

(handwritten annotations: Add up 100%; 0.75 ×1; 0.125 ×2; 0.0625 ×3; 0.0625 ×3)

Now there are four codes of different lengths. One code has a one-bit length, one has a two-bit length, and two have three-bit lengths. After a week's trading, the total storage space occupied will be the number of transactions for each item multiplied by the length of its code. The average code length will be:

$$1 \times \frac{3}{4} + 2 \times \frac{1}{8} + 3 \times \frac{1}{16} + 3 \times \frac{1}{16} = 1\frac{3}{8} = 1.375 \text{ bits/item}$$

(handwritten annotations: 1 bit; 2 bits; 3 bits; 2 → 1.375; (12.5%))

By adopting this code, a Huffman code, the average storage has been reduced from two bits per transaction to 1.375 bits per transaction, a saving of 31.25 per cent. A Huffman code, is often represented in the form of a binary tree, the tree in Fig. 3.4 corresponding to the grocer's example.

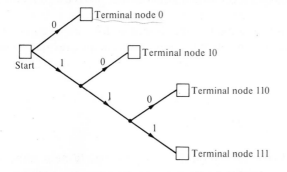

Fig. 3.4. A Huffman code

The diagram is sometimes called a trellis, and is read from left to right. From the left, each of the four terminal nodes (labelled node 0, node 10, etc.) can be reached by following the marked paths. These paths are marked by a 1 or a 0 depending on the bit to be decoded. The example below should clarify things.

The grocer's disk contains the following string of bits, 001100101110. What codes does this string correspond to?

The first (leftmost) bit of the string is 0. From the trellis it can be seen that a first bit 0 leads immediately to a terminal node. Thus, the first code is 0. Similarly, the second code is also zero. The third code begins with a 1 and we must examine another bit to continue. This is also a one, and another bit must be read. The third bit is a zero leading to a terminal node 110. This process can be continued until the string is broken down into the sequence:

0 0 110 0 10 111 0.

3.4 Binary arithmetic

Binary arithmetic follows exactly the same rules as decimal arithmetic. All that needs to be done to work with binary numbers is to learn the 'binary tables'; they are somewhat more easy than their decimal equivalents. Table 3.9 gives the binary tables for addition, subtraction, and multiplication.

Table 3.9 The binary tables

Addition		Subtraction		Multiplication
$0+0=0$		$0-0=0$		$0 \times 0 = 0$
$0+1=1$		$0-1=1$	borrow 1	$0 \times 1 = 0$
$1+0=1$		$1-0=1$		$1 \times 0 = 0$
$1+1=0$	carry 1	$1-1=0$		$1 \times 1 = 1$

A remarkable fact about binary arithmetic is that if we did not worry about the 'carry' in addition, and the 'borrow' in subtraction, then the operations of addition and subtraction would be identical. Such an arithmetic does exist and has some important applications; this is called modulo-two arithmetic.

The addition of n-bit numbers is entirely straightforward, except that when adding the two bits in each column, a carry bit from the previous stage must also be added in.

```
  00110111
+ 01010110
  111  11        ←space for carries
  10001101
```

Subtraction can also be carried out in a conventional fashion, although we shall see later that a computer does not subtract numbers in the way we do because negative numbers are not usually represented in a 'sign plus magnitude' form but by means of their complements.

```
  01010110              86
- 00101010            - 42
  1 1           ←space for borrows   44
  00101100
```

The multiplication of binary numbers can be done by the 'pencil and paper' method of shifting and adding, although in practice the computer uses a somewhat modified technique; see Fig. 3.5.

```
01101          13
×  01010      ×  10
  00000         130
  01101
  00000
  01101
  00000
0010000010
```

Fig. 3.5 An example of binary multiplication

3.4.1 The half adder

Having looked at gates, Boolean algebra and binary arithmetic, we can now consider the design of a circuit to add binary numbers. The most primitive circuit is called the 'half adder' or HA and adds together two bits to give a sum, S, and a carry, C; see Table 3.10.

Table 3.10 Truth table for the half adder

A	B	S	C
0	0	0	0
0	1	1	0
1	0	1	0
1	1	0	1

From this truth table it can be seen that the sum of two bits is their EXCLUSIVE OR so that $S = \overline{A}B + A\overline{B} = A \oplus B$. The carry is given by $C = AB$.

From the earlier section on gates we know that this circuit may be realized in at least three different ways; see Fig. 3.6. This circuit, whatever its implementation, is often represented in many texts by the symbol in Fig. 3.7.

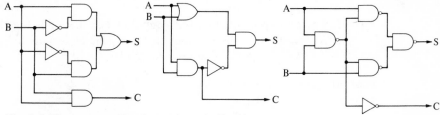

Fig. 3.6 Three ways of implementing a half adder

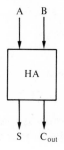

Fig. 3.7 The circuit representation of a half adder

3.4.2 The full adder

Unfortunately, the half adder is of little use as it stands. When two n-bit numbers are added together we have to take account of any carry bits. Adding (say) bits a_i of A and b_i of B together must include provision for adding in the carry bit c_{i-1} from the results of the addition in the column to the right of a_i and b_i. This is represented diagramatically as:

$$a_{n-1} \ldots a_2 a_1 a_0 \qquad a_{n-1} \ldots a_2 a_1 a_0$$
$$+ \, b_{n-1} \ldots b_2 b_1 b_0 \rightarrow b_{n-1} \ldots b_2 b_1 b_0$$
$$+ \, c_{n-2} \ldots c_1 c_0.$$

When people perform an addition they deal with the carry automatically, without thinking about it. More specifically they say, 'If a carry is generated we add it to the next column, if it is not we do nothing'. In human terms 'doing nothing' and 'adding zero' are equivalent. As far as the logic necessary to carry out the addition is concerned, we always add in the carry from the previous stage, where the carry has the value 0 or 1.

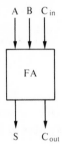

Fig. 3.8 The circuit representation of a full adder

The full adder, represented by the symbol of Fig. 3.8, adds together two bits, plus a carry-in from the previous stage, to generate a sum and a carry-out. Table 3.11 is the truth table for a full adder.

Table 3.11 Truth table from a full adder

C_{in}	A	B	S	C_{out}	
0	0	0	0	0	
0	0	1	1	0	
0	1	0	1	0	same as half adder
0	1	1	0	1	
1	0	0	1	0	
1	0	1	0	1	
1	1	0	0	1	
1	1	1	1	1	

The conventional way of realizing the circuit for a full adder is to connect two half adders in tandem. Conceptually, a full adder requires that the two bits of A and B should be added together and then the carry-in should be added to the result. Figure 3.9 shows a possible representation of the full adder in terms of two half adders.

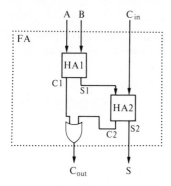

C_{out} S   Fig. 3.9 The representation of a full adder

The sum output of the full adder is given by the sum output of the second half adder, HA2, and the carry-out, C_{out}, is given by ORing the carries from both half adders. To demonstrate that the above circuit does indeed perform the process of full addition a truth table may be used; see Table 3.12

Table 3.12 The truth table for a full adder implemented by two half adders

C_{in}	A	B	S_1	C_1	S_2	C_2	C_{out}
0	0	0	0	0	0	0	0
0	0	1	1	0	1	0	0
0	1	0	1	0	1	0	0
0	1	1	0	1	0	0	1
1	0	0	0	0	1	0	0
1	0	1	1	0	0	1	1
1	1	0	1	0	0	1	1
1	1	1	0	1	1	0	1

                                   ↑   ↑
                               sum   carry out

As the contents of the two columns arrowed are identical with those of the corresponding columns of the truth table for the full adder, we must conclude that our circuit is that of a full adder. In practice the full adder is not often implemented in this way as the propagation path through the two half adders involves six units of delay. An alternative full adder circuit may be derived directly from the equations for the sum and the carry from the truth table. Let the sum be S, the carry-out C_O and the carry-in C.

$$S = \overline{C}\overline{A}B + \overline{C}A\overline{B} + C\overline{A}\overline{B} + CAB$$

$$\text{and } C_O = \overline{C}AB + C\overline{A}B + CA\overline{B} + CAB$$

$$= \overline{C}AB + C\overline{A}B + CA(\overline{B} + B)$$

$$= \overline{C}AB + C\overline{A}B + CA$$

$$= \overline{C}AB + C(\overline{A}B + A) = \overline{C}AB + CB + CA$$
$$= A(\overline{C}B + C) + CB = A(B + C) + CB$$
$$= CA + CB + AB.$$

Note that the value of the carry-out is a majority logic function and is true if two or more of the inputs are true. The circuit diagram of the full adder corresponding to the above equations is given in Fig. 3.10. This circuit contains more gates than the equivalent realization in terms of half adders (12 against 9) but it is faster. The maximum propagation delay is 3 gates in series.

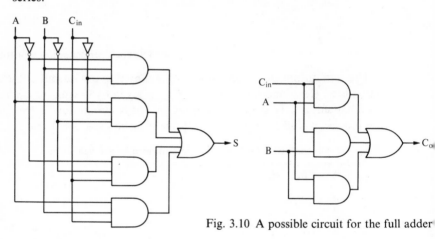

Fig. 3.10 A possible circuit for the full adder

3.4.3 The addition of words

Even a full adder on its own is not a great deal of help, as we frequently wish to add two n-bit numbers together. It is possible to add numbers serially a bit at a time by means of the scheme given in Fig. 3.11. The shift registers containing A and B have their contents shifted into the full adder a bit at a

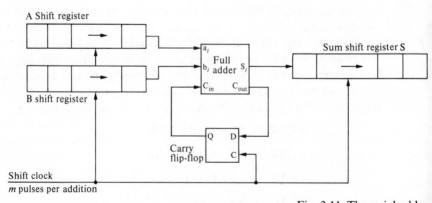

Fig. 3.11 The serial adder

time. The result of each addition is shifted into a result or sum register. A single flip-flop holds the carry bit so that the old carry-out becomes the next carry-in.

After n clock pulses, the sum register, S, contains the sum of A and B. This arrangement is included in some (often older) text books with the comment that 'as it uses only one full adder it is cheaper than a parallel adder using n full adders, although adding only one bit at a time it is slower'. This may have been true in the dark ages but it is not now. With the present ability to put 100 000 or more transistors on a chip, a circuit can be designed to optimize its performance rather than reduce the number of gates. I have included the serial adder here to show the contrast between serial operations (bit by bit) and parallel operations involving all the bits of a word at once. In Chapter 8, we will discover that computers communicate with each other (over long distances) serially, a bit at a time, rather than by parallel transmission, a word at a time.

The more practical form of adder is the parallel adder of Fig. 3.12 which employs n full adders to add two n-bit numbers. The carry-out of each full adder becomes the carry-in of the stage on its left. In a parallel adder the n bits of word A are added to the n bits of word B in one simultaneous operation. The parallel adder is theoretically n times faster than the corresponding serial adder. In practice a real parallel adder is slowed down by the effect of the carry-bit propagation.

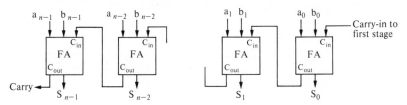

Fig. 3.12 The parallel adder

There are several points worth noting about Fig. 3.12. Firstly, it might be thought that the least-significant stage could be replaced by a half adder as it does not have a carry-in (there is no stage to its right). However, by using a full adder for this stage, the carry-in may be set to zero for normal addition, or it may be set to 1 to generate $A + B + 1$ (the '+' here signifying addition and not logical OR). If B were set to zero, $A + 1$ would be generated and the circuit functions as an incrementer. This facility will prove very useful when we come to complementary arithmetic.

Another feature of this circuit concerns the carry-out from the last (most significant bit) stage. If two n-bit words are added and the result is greater than $111 \ldots 1$, then a carry-out is generated. As the computer cannot store words longer than n-bits, the sum cannot be stored in the memory as a single entity. The final carry-out may be latched into a flip-flop (normally forming part of the computer's processor status register). When addition is performed by software as part of a program it is usual for the programmer to test the carry bit to check if the result has gone out of range.

A final point about the parallel adder concerns the meaning of parallel. It must be apparent that while the first stage can add a_0 and b_0 to get s_0, the second stage must wait for the first stage's carry-out before it can be sure that its own output is valid. In the worst case of $111 \ldots 1 + 1$, the carry must ripple through all the stages. This circuit is parallel in the sense that all the bits of A are added to all the bits of B in a single operation without the need for a number of separate clock cycles. Once the values of A and B have been presented to the inputs of the full adders the system must wait until the circuit has had time to settle down, and for all carries to propagate, before the next operation is started. In many digital systems the clock period is the worst-case settling time required by the slowest circuit in the system. More sophisticated digital systems have a variable clock pulse, with the duration of each pulse tailored to the worst-case delay possible for the current operation being carried out. It is possible to partially reduce the effect of the 'ripple through carry'. Arrangements called 'carry look ahead circuits' can be used to anticipate a carry over group of say four full adders. That is, the carry out to stage $i + 5$ is calculated by examining the inputs to stages $i + 4$, $i + 3$, $i + 2$, and $i + 1$, and the carry in to stage $i + 1$, by means of a special high-speed circuit. This 'anticipated carry' can be fed to the fifth stage to avoid the delay which would be incurred if a ripple-through carry was used. The exact nature of these circuits is beyond the scope of this book.

The full subtractor

Using the techniques we have applied to the full adder it is possible to design a full subtractor in the same way. As the full subtractor is not used widely I leave its design as an exercise for the reader.

3.5 Negative numbers

Any real computer must be able to deal with negative numbers. People do not actually use negative numbers. They use positive numbers (the '5' in -5 is the same as in $+5$), and place a negative sign $(-)$ in front of the number to remind them that it must be treated in a special way when it takes part in arithmetic operations. Thus we have:

$$
\begin{array}{ccc}
8 & & 8 \\
+5 & \text{and} & -5 \\
\hline
13 & & 3
\end{array}
$$

In each case the numbers are the same but the operations we performed on them were different; in the first case we added and in the second case we subtracted. This technique can be extended to computer arithmetic to give the sign and magnitude representation of a negative number.

3.5.1 Sign and magnitude representation

An n-bit word can have 2^n possible different values from 0 to 2^n-1. For example, an eight-bit word can represent the numbers 0, 1, ..., 254, 255. One way of representing a negative number is to take the most significant bit and reserve it to indicate the sign of the number, 0 if it is positive and 1 if it is negative.

For example, in 8 bits we have:

$\underset{\text{sign}}{\underbrace{0}}\ \underset{\text{number}}{\underbrace{0001101}} = +13$ and $\underset{\text{sign}}{\underbrace{1}}\ \underset{\text{number}}{\underbrace{0001101}} = -13$

<table><tr><td>sign</td><td></td><td>sign</td><td></td></tr><tr><td>bit</td><td>number</td><td>bit</td><td>number</td></tr><tr><td></td><td>magnitude</td><td></td><td>magnitude</td></tr></table>

This is a perfectly valid representation of negative numbers, although it is not widely used. The range of a sign-plus-magnitude number in n-bits is given by:

$$-(2^{n-1}-1) \text{ to } +(2^{n-1}-1), \text{ i.e. } -2^{n-1}+1 \text{ to } +2^{n-1}-1$$

All we have done is to take an n-bit number, use one bit to represent the sign and let the remaining $n-1$ bits represent the number. Thus, an eight-bit number can represent from -127 (11111111) to $+127$ (01111111). One of the objections to this system is that it has two values for zero:

$$00000000 = +0 \text{ and } 10000000 = -0.$$

Personally, I do not see this as a particular problem, given the current ability to produce complex digital devices economically. Possibly the sign-and-magnitude notation was abandoned in the earlier days of computers when each and every gate was a precious item. The most widespread reason for rejecting this system is simply that it requires separate adders and subtractors. We shall soon see that other ways of representing negative numbers remove the need for separate adders and subtractors. However, I would emphasize that today the additional cost of a subtractor in a CPU is negligible.

Examples of addition and subtraction in sign and magnitude arithmetic are given below. It must be remembered that the most significant bit is a sign bit and does not take part in the calculation itself. This is in contrast with two's complement arithmetic (see later) in which the sign bit forms an integral part of the number when it is used in calculations.

1.
```
     001011      +01011
   + 001110  →  +01110
   --------      ------
                +11001   →  011001   (as a 6-bit sign and magnitude
                                      number)
```

2.
```
     001011      +01011
   + 100110  →  -00110
   --------      ------
                +00101   →  000101
```

3.   001011   +01011
    + 110110   → − 10110
    ──────   ──────
                    − 01011   → 101011

4.   001011   +01011
    − 001001   → − 01001
    ──────   ──────
                    + 00010   → 000010

3.5.2 Complementary arithmetic

In complementary arithmetic the 'negativeness' of a number is contained within the number itself. Because of this, the concept of signs ('+' and '−') may, effectively, be dispensed with. If we add X to Y the operation is that of addition if X is positive and Y is positive, but if Y is negative the end result is that of subtraction (assuming that Y is represented by its negative form). To demonstrate that there is nothing magical about complementary arithmetic it is worthwhile examining decimal complements.

The 10's complement of an n-digit decimal number, N, is defined as $10^n - N$. The complement may also be calculated by subtracting each of the digits of N from 9 and adding 1 to the result. Consider the 4-digit decimal number 1234. Its ten's complement is:

(a) $10^4 - 1234 = 8766$ or (b)   9999
                                    − 1234
                                    ──────
                              $8765 + 1 = 8766.$

Suppose we were to add this complement to another number (say) 8576. We get:

        8576
    +   8766
    ──────
      17342.

Now let us examine the effect of subtracting 1234 from 8576 by conventional means.

        8576
    −   1234
    ──────
        7342

Notice that the results of the two operations are similar in the least-significant four digits but differ in the fifth digit by 10^4. The reason for this is not hard to find. Consider the subtraction of Y from X. We have $Z = X - Y$. If we perform the subtraction of Y by adding its 10's complement, which is $10^4 - Y$, we get:

$$Z = X + (10^4 - Y) = 10^4 + (X - Y).$$

In other words, we get the desired result, $X - Y$, together with an 'unwanted' digit in the leftmost position. This digit may be discarded.

3.5.3 Two's complement representation

The equivalent of 10's complement in binary arithmetic is 2's complement. To form the 2's complement of an n-bit binary number, N, we evaluate $2^n - N$. For example, in 5 bits, if $N = 00101$ then the two's complement of N is given by $100000 - 00101$.

$$\begin{array}{r} 100000 \\ -\ 00101 \\ \hline 11011 \end{array}$$
OR $\begin{array}{r} 11010 \\ +\ \ \ \ 1 \\ \hline 11011 \end{array}$

11011 Thus, $-N$ is represented by 11011.

If we add this to another binary number we should effect the operation of subtraction.

$$\begin{array}{r} 01100 \\ +\ 11011 \\ \hline 100111 \end{array} \qquad \begin{array}{r} 12 \\ +\ (-5) \\ \hline 7 \end{array}$$

As in the case of the decimal example we get the correct answer, together with the $2^n = 2^5$ term which is discarded. Before continuing further, it is worthwhile examining the effect of adding all the combinations of positive and negative values for a pair of numbers.

Let $X = 01001$ (9) and $Y = 00110$ (6).

$$-X = 100000 - 01001 = 10111$$
$$-Y = 100000 - 00110 = 11010$$

$$\begin{array}{r} +X \\ +Y \\ \hline \end{array} \quad \begin{array}{r} 01001 \\ +\ 00110 \\ \hline 01111 = +15 \end{array} \qquad \begin{array}{r} +X \\ -Y \\ \hline \end{array} \quad \begin{array}{r} 01001 \\ +11010 \\ \hline 100011 = +3 \end{array}$$

$$\begin{array}{r} -X \\ +Y \\ \hline \end{array} \quad \begin{array}{r} 10111 \\ +\ 00110 \\ \hline 11101 = -3 \end{array} \qquad \begin{array}{r} -X \\ -Y \\ \hline \end{array} \quad \begin{array}{r} 10111 \\ +11010 \\ \hline 110001 = -15 \end{array}$$

In the last two cases we should expect -3 and -15. The two's complement value of -3 is $100000 - 00011 = 11101$, and the two's complement value of -15 is $100000 - 01111 = 10001$. The result $-X + Y$ is correct, and is in the two's complement form representing -3. The last result, $-X + -Y$, represents -15, but with the addition of 2^n. In this case, where both numbers are negative, we have $(2^n - X) + (2^n - Y) = 2^n + (2^n - X - Y)$. The first part of our expression is the redundant 2^n and the second part is the two's complement of $-X - Y$. We can now see that the two's complement system works for all possible combinations of positive and negative numbers.

The two's complement system would not be so attractive if it were not for the ease with which two's complements may be formed. Consider the two's complement of N:

$$-N \rightarrow 2^n - N.$$

Suppose we re-arranged the equation by subtracting 1 from the 2^n and adding it to the result.

$$-N \rightarrow (2^n - 1) \quad -N+1$$
$$\rightarrow \underbrace{111 \ldots 1}_{} \; -N+1$$

n places

This operation becomes particularly easy because, if a bit of N is 0, subtracting it from 1 gives 1, and if the bit is 1, subtracting it from 1 gives 0. In other words, $1 - N_i = \overline{N_i}$. That is, to form the two's complement of a number we simply invert the bits and add 1.

For example, in 5 bits $7 = 00111$
$$-7 = \overline{00111} + 1 = 11000 + 1 = 11001.$$

This operation is attractive because it is easy to perform with hardware. To implement an adder/subtractor the logic of Fig. 3.13 is used. This diagram shows how, with the addition of a little extra logic, a parallel binary adder may readily be converted into an adder/subtractor for two's complement numbers.

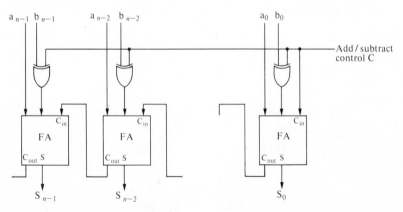

Fig. 3.13 The adder/subtractor

Each of the EXCLUSIVE OR gates has two inputs b_i (where $i = 0$ to $n-1$), and C, a control signal. The output of the EXCLUSIVE OR is $b_i\overline{C} + \overline{b_i}C$. If C is 0 then $\overline{C} = 1$ and the output is b_i. If C is 1 then $\overline{C} = 0$ and the output is $\overline{b_i}$. The n EXCLUSIVE OR's form a chain of programmable invertors, inverting the input if $C=1$ and passing the input unchanged if $C=0$. Note also that the carry-in input to the first full adder is C. When addition is being performed $C=0$ and the carry-in is zero. However, when we perform subtraction $C=1$ so that one is added to the result of the addition. This 'one' is needed to form the two's complement of B; we have already inverted B's bits so that adding the one forms the two's complement of B enabling the subtraction of B from A to take place.

Properties of two's complement numbers

1. The two's complement system is a true complement system in that $+X+(-X)=0$. For example, in 5 bits $+13=01101$ and $-13=10011$. The sum of $+13$ and -13 is:

$$\begin{array}{r} 01101 \\ + 10011 \\ \hline 100000=0. \end{array}$$

2. There is a unique zero $00 \ldots 0$.

3. If the number is positive the most significant bit is 0, and if it is negative the MSB is 1. Thus, the MSB is a sign bit.

4. The range of two's complement numbers in n bits is from -2^{n-1} to $+2^{n-1}-1$. For $n=5$, this range is from -16 to $+15$. Note that the total number of different numbers is 32 (16 negative, zero and 15 positive). What this demonstrates is that a five-bit number can uniquely describe 32 items, and it is up to us whether we choose to call these items the natural binary integers 0 to 31, or the signed numbers -16 to $+15$.

Let us now see what happens if we violate the range of two's complement numbers. Choosing a five-bit representation we know that the range of valid signed numbers is -16 to $+15$. Suppose we first add 5 and 6 and then try 12 and 13.

$$\begin{array}{ll} 5=00101 & 12=01100 \\ +6=00110 & +13=01101 \\ \hline 01011 = 11_{10} & 11001 - 7_{10} \text{ (as a two's comp number)} \end{array}$$

In the first case we get the expected answer of $+11$, but in the second case we get a negative result because the sign bit is '1'. If the answer were regarded as an unsigned binary number it would be $+25$ which is, of course, the correct answer. Once the two's complement system has been chosen to represent signed numbers, all answers must be interpreted in this light.

Similarly, if we add together two negative numbers whose total is less than -16, we also go out of range. For example, $-9=10111$ and $-12=10100$, so that:

$$\begin{array}{rl} -9 & 10111 \\ -12 & +10100 \\ \hline & 101011 \text{ gives a positive result } 01011 = +11_{10}. \end{array}$$

Both of these cases represent arithmetic overflow. An arithmetic overflow occurs in two's complement arithmetic if the result of adding two positive numbers yields a negative result, or if the result of adding two negative numbers yields a positive result. Overflow can be expressed algebraically. If we let a_{n-1} be the sign bit of A, b_{n-1} be the sign bit of B, and s_{n-1} be the sign bit of the sum of A and B, then:

$$V = a_{n-1}b_{n-1}\overline{s_{n-1}} + \overline{a_{n-1}}\,\overline{b_{n-1}}s_{n-1}.$$

That is, if the sign bits of A and B are the same but the sign bit of the result is different, arithmetic overflow has occurred. It is important to note that arithmetic overflow is a consequence of two's complement arithmetic, and should not be confused with carry-out, which is the carry bit generated by the addition of the two most significant bits of the numbers.

An alternative view of two's complement numbers

We have seen that a binary integer, N, lying in the range $0 \leqslant N < 2^{n-1}-1$, is represented in a negative form by the expression $2^n - N$. We have also seen that this expression can be readily evaluated by inverting the bits of N and adding 1 to the result.

Another way of looking at a two's complement number is to regard it as being represented by n bits in the positional notation where the most significant bit has a negative weight. That is:

$$-N = -d_{n-1}2^{n-1} + d_{n-2}2^{n-2} + \ldots + d_0 2^0$$

where $d_{n-1}, d_{n-2}, \ldots, d_0$ are the bits of the two's complement number D. Consider the representation of 14, and the two's complement form of -14, in five bits.

$$+14 = 01110$$

$$-14 = 2^n - N = 2^5 - 14 = 32 - 14 = 18 = 10010$$

or $-14 = \overline{01110} + 1 = 10001 + 1 = 10010.$

This representation of -14 can be regarded as:

$$-1 \times 2^4 + 0 \times 2^3 + 0 \times 2^2 + 1 \times 2^1 + 0 \times 2^0$$

$$= -16 + (0+0+2+0)$$

$$= -16 + 2 = -14.$$

It is possible to prove that a two's complement number is indeed represented in this way. In what follows N represents a positive integer, and D the two's complement form of $-N$. We wish to prove that $-N = D$. That is,

$$-N = -2^{n-1} + \sum_{i=0}^{n-2} d_i 2^i. \tag{1}$$

In terms of the bits of N and D we have:

$$-(N_{n-1}N_{n-2}\ldots N_1N_0) = d_{n-1}d_{n-2}\ldots d_1d_0 = D. \tag{2}$$

The bits of D are formed from the bits of N by inverting and adding 1.

(3) $\overline{N_{n-1}}\,\overline{N_{n-2}}\ldots\overline{N_0} + 1 = d_{n-1}\,d_{n-2}\ldots d_0$

Substituting eqn 3 in eqn 1 to eliminate D we get:

$$-N = -2^{n-1} + \sum_{i=0}^{n-2} \overline{N_i}2^i + 1 \tag{4}$$

But $\overline{N_i} = 1 - N_i$ so that:

$$-N = -2^{n-1} + \sum_{i=0}^{n-2} (1 - N_i)2^i + 1$$

$$= -2^{n-1} + \sum_{i=0}^{n-2} 2^i - \sum_{i=0}^{n-2} N_i 2^i + 1$$

$$= -2^{n-1} + (2^{n-1} - 1) - \sum_{i=0}^{n-2} N_i 2^i + 1$$

$$= -2^{n-1} + (2^{n-1} - 1) + 1 - N$$

$\left(N = \displaystyle\sum_{i=0}^{n-1} N_i 2^i = \sum_{i=0}^{n-2} N_i 2^i \right.$ as the most significant bit of N, N_{n-1}, is zero
for N to be within its stated range.)

$$= -2^{n-1} + 2^{n-1} - N = -N.$$

3.5.4 One's complement representation

An alternative to two's complement arithmetic is one's complement arithmetic where the representation of a negative number, N, in n bits is given by $2^n - N - 1$. This is one less than the corresponding two's complement representation and is formed more simply by inverting the bits of N. For example, for $n = 5$ consider the subtraction of 4 from 9 (Fig. 3.14).

```
+9 = 01001 →     01001
-4 = 00100 → +   11011
                 ───────
                 100100
             +   └──────→1
                 ───────
                 00101
```

Fig. 3.14 Ones complement subtraction

After the answer has been formed the leftmost bit is added to the least significant bit of the result in an arrangement called end-around-carry. The one's complement system is not a true complement as $X + (-X)$ is not zero. Furthermore, there are two representations for zero: 00 . . . 0 and 11 . . . 1. The one's complement system is not as common as the two's complement system for representing signed numbers, but it is found in some computers.

It is instructive to compare the various ways of representing numbers we have encountered so far. Table 3.13 gives the results for $n = 5$ for pure binary numbers, sign and magnitude, one's complement, and two's complement representations.

Table 3.13 The representation of negative numbers

Binary code	Pure binary	Sign and magnitude	One's complement	Two's complement
00000	0	0	0	0
00001	1	1	1	1
00010	2	2	2	2
00011	3	3	3	3
00100	4	4	4	4
00101	5	5	5	5
00110	6	6	6	6
00111	7	7	7	7
01000	8	8	8	8
01001	9	9	9	9
01010	10	10	10	10
01011	11	11	11	11
01100	12	12	12	12
01101	13	13	13	13
01110	14	14	14	14
01111	15	15	15	15
10000	16	−0	−15	−16
10001	17	−1	−14	−15
10010	18	−2	−13	−14
10011	19	−3	−12	−13
10100	20	−4	−11	−12
10101	21	−5	−10	−11
10110	22	−6	−9	−10
10111	23	−7	−8	−9
11000	24	−8	−7	−8
11001	25	−9	−6	−7
11010	26	−10	−5	−6
11011	27	−11	−4	−5
11100	28	−12	−3	−4
11101	29	−13	−2	−3
11110	30	−14	−1	−2
11111	31	−15	−0	−1

3.6 An introduction to computer arithmetic and assembly language programming

Having dealt with addition and subtraction at the hardware level in terms of full adders, it is time to see how these operations are carried out at the software level in terms of assembly language. I do not wish to pre-empt later sections on assembly language, but the following notes should help.

Assembly language is the most primitive language in which programs can be written (forgetting for the moment microprogramming, which is, incidentally, nothing to do with microprocessors). An assembly language uses mnemonics to represent the various operations which may be performed by the computer. For example, ADD = add, SUB = subtract, BRA = branch etc. The mnemonics vary from computer to computer, although many mnemonics are self-evident. Following the mnemonic is often a NAME which refers to a variable. If we write ADD FRED we mean add the number we have called (labelled) FRED to the contents of the accumulator (a special purpose register—see later). FRED refers not to the number but its location in memory. As many computers allow us to specify one name only in an instruction they must have a temporary holding register for all intermediate results. This register is known as the accumulator. Historically because it may be said to accumulate the results. If we had a computer whose instructions could specify three addresses (e.g. ADD NUM1,NUM2,NUM3 which means that NUM1 = NUM2 + NUM3), an accumulator would not be needed. Throughout this book most examples will refer to the 6502 microprocessor. The reasons for this are:

1. It uses an 8-bit data word which is of manageable size for student examples. A short data word does not necessarily restrict the things we can do.

2. Its physical design (architecture) and its assembly language are both easy to use and understand. Furthermore, its architecture is not untypical of the mainstream computer. Some computers are less typical of computers in general and are therefore less well suited to teaching purposes.

3. The 6502 is cheap and is in widespread use. In particular the Apple and BBC computers are based on it, and the AIM 65 microcomputer system is specifically designed to allow the student to input assembly language programs, edit them, assemble them, run them, and then debug them. 'Debug' means 'remove errors from'.

The 6502 has an 8-bit data word and can therefore represent unsigned binary numbers in the range 0 to 255 (i.e. 0 to $2^8 - 1$), and signed two's complement numbers in the range -128 to $+127$.

Suppose we wish to add together the numbers P and Q, and to call the result R. Now P, Q, and R, are names referring to physical locations within the 6502's memory. We use names because we do not want to be bothered with trying to remember addresses. The program to do this is:

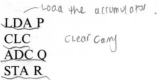

LDA P — load the accumulator.
CLC   Clear Carry
ADC Q
STA R

The first instruction causes the contents of the memory location we have called P to be moved to the accumulator. The mnemonic, 'LDA', means 'load the accumulator'. In a real program it would normally be necessary for the programmer to 'tell' the assembler where the locations P, Q, and R are in the memory. The LDA operation does not affect the number in P. It is a most important rule that unless the contents of a memory location or register are modified by writing a new number into it, they do not change.

The second instruction, CLC, stands for CLear Carry. The carry bit is part of the processor status register (in 6800 terminology it is known as the condition code register) and this instruction clears it (i.e. sets it to zero). If we knew that the carry bit was already zero we could have dispensed with this instruction.

The third instruction, ADC, stands for 'add to accumulator with carry'. The effect of this instruction is to add the contents of memory location Q to the contents of the data already in the accumulator together with the carry bit in the PSW. Many computers have a simple ADD instruction which just adds a number to the accumulator. The 6502 does not. As we have just set the carry bit to 0, we will accomplish the same effect as ADD would have done. Figure 3.15 shows the location of the program and its data in memory.

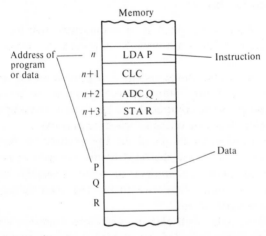

Fig. 3.15 The location of the program and data in memory

The final instruction, STA R, stores the contents of the accumulator in a memory location, which in our case is called R.

There is nothing difficult about this example. The reader may say 'But are we operating with unsigned binary numbers or two's complement numbers?' The answer is that it does not matter. The same addition operation will serve both cases: it is how the programmer deals with the result that matters.

At the end of an arithmetic (and some other types of) operation the CPU updates its processor status register. In the 6502 this register has the form overleaf.

bit	7	6	5	4	3	2	1	0
	N	V		B	D	I	Z	C

Here we are concerned only with bits 0 and 6. These represent Carry and Overflow, respectively. The computer does not know what the programmer is up to. So, at the end of an arithmetic operation it asks:

Was a carry generated (a 1 propagated out of bit 7)?
If I assume the number was in two's complement form, was there an overflow?

It is up to the programmer to use the information in the processor status register according to his application. Consider now the two programs shown in Fig. 3.16.

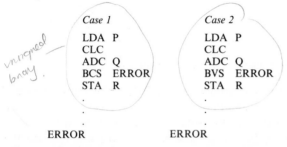

```
Case 1                    Case 2

LDA  P                    LDA  P
CLC                       CLC
ADC  Q                    ADC  Q
BCS  ERROR               BVS  ERROR
STA  R                    STA  R
  .                         .
  .                         .
  .                         .
ERROR                   ERROR
```

Fig. 3.16 Programs for signed and unsigned addition

In Case 1 we have assumed that the arithmetic is unsigned binary. If, after the ADC Q operation, the sum of the two numbers is greater than 255 a one is propagated from the most significant bit position into the carry. The following instruction, BCS, means Branch if Carry Set. Thus, if a carry has been generated the next instruction (STA R) is not executed. Instead a branch or jump is made to the part of the program called 'ERROR'. This part of the program (not shown here) must be designed to deal with the problem. If a branch is not made, the next instruction immediately following the conditional branch is executed.

In Case 2 the arithmetic has been assumed to be in two's complement form. The program is identical to Case 1 except that after the addition we test to see if the overflow bit has been set.

The principal limitation of these examples is that they deal only with eight bit numbers. While I have nothing against small numbers personally, there are times when numbers greater than 255 impinge on my life. In these circumstances I could either throw away the (cheap) 6502 and buy a (more expensive) 16-bit or 32-bit machine, or I could deal with large numbers in chunks of eight bits. Unless speed is of the utmost importance, the latter solution is more feasible (or cost-effective as the jargon goes).

Imagine that I needed to deal with unsigned numbers up to 50 000. The power of 2 that is just greater than 50 000 is $2^{16} = 65\,536$. To create a 16-bit word all I need do is to take two 8-bit words in memory and regard them as a 16-bit entity. Using the previous example with P, Q, and R we can draw a memory map; see Fig. 3.17. A memory map is a diagrammatic representation of the layout of data or instructions in memory.

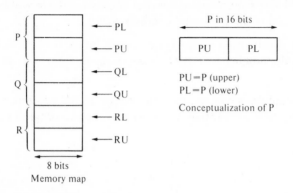

Fig. 3.17 Using 16-bit numbers with an 8-bit computer

Our 16-bit word is now composed of two halves. P is represented by PU (the 8 most significant bits), and PL (the 8 least significant bits). I have drawn the memory map with PL and PU adjacent to each other, although there is no reason why this must be done in practice. To add P and Q to get R we must perform the following operations:

```
   PU PL
+ QU QL
  ─────
   RU RL
```

That is, we add PL to QL to get RL, and then PU to QU to get RU. The only point to note is that when PL is added to QL any carry generated must be added to the (PU + QU) column. In terms of assembly language the program to add P and Q is:

```
LDA     PL
CLC
ADC     QL
STA     RL
LDA     PU
ADC     QU
STA     RU
```

The first four lines are as before. Now, when we come to add PU to QU we do not clear the carry bit so that any carry generated in adding PL and QL is automatically added to PU and QU. This arrangement can be extended to deal with numbers made up of an arbitrary number of bytes. The range of unsigned integers for a given number of bytes is:

Bytes	Range
1	0–255
2	0–65,535
3	0–16,777,215
4	0–4,294,967,295

Subtraction is performed in very much the same way as addition (that is, from the programmer's point of view). To subtract Q from P to get R, the following program is used:

```
LDA P     load P into the accumulator
SEC       set the carry bit
SBC  Q    subtract Q together with the carry bit
STA  R    store the result in R
```

The first thing to notice is that comments have been written alongside the assembly language instructions. A program written in a high level language like PASCAL is often self-documenting because the act of reading it tells the reader what is happening in a clear and unambiguous fashion. Unfortunately, in an assembly language program the morass of detail entirely obscures the point of the program. Consequently, without a copious quantity of comment, the program soon becomes incomprehensible—even to its author.

A second point to consider is that before we performed addition the carry bit was cleared. For subtraction it must be set to 1 by the SEC (set carry) instruction. This operation is very much machine dependent. For example, when performing subtraction with the 6800 (a sister processor of the 6502), the carry bit must be cleared and not set. This demonstrates that operating at the assembly language level requires a most thorough knowledge of the operation of the particular computer being used.

The mnemonic 'SBC' stands for 'subtract with carry'. The carry bit becomes the borrow bit during subtraction. The difference between 'borrow' and 'carry' is one of terminology. In the computer there is just one single-bit register which doesn't care whether people choose to call it a carry- or a borrow-bit.

3.7 Floating-point numbers

Before I go any further I have to admit that floating-point arithmetic is not one of the great fun-subjects of computer science. While, the basic ideas of floating-point arithmetic are perfectly simple, the details of its implementation get rather involved.

We have already demonstrated that to deal with large numbers on a machine having a small word length, we just chain words together. We have not yet looked at binary fractions. A binary (or decimal) fraction presents no problems. Consider the following two calculations.

$$
\begin{array}{r}
7632135 \\
+ \; 1794821 \\
\hline
9426956
\end{array}
\qquad \text{and} \qquad
\begin{array}{r}
763.2135 \\
+ \; 179.4821 \\
\hline
942.6956.
\end{array}
$$

Although the first case (lefthand example) involves integer numbers and th second case fractional numbers, the calculations are entirely identical. Thi principle can be extended to computer arithmetic. All the computer pro grammer has to do is to remember where he has assumed the binary point t lie. All input to the computer is scaled to match this convention and a output is similarly scaled. The internal operations themselves are carried ou as if the numbers were in integer form. This arrangement is called fixed-poin arithmetic. The advantage of the fixed-point representation of numbers i that no specially complex software or hardware is needed to implement it.

A simple example should make the idea of fixed-point arithmetic clearer Consider an eight-bit fixed-point number with the four most significant bit representing the integer part and the four least significant bits representin the fractional part.

Let us see what happens if we wish to add the two numbers 3.625 and 6.5 and print the result. An input program first converts these numbers to binar form.

$3.625 \rightarrow \; 11.101 \rightarrow 0011.1010$ (in 8 bits)

$6.5 \;\; \rightarrow 110.1 \;\;\; \rightarrow 0110.1000$ (in 8 bits)

The computer now regards these numbers as 00111010 and 01101000 respectively. Remember, that the binary point is only imaginary. Thes numbers are added in the nomal way to give:

$$
\begin{array}{r}
00111010 \\
+ \; 01101000 \\
\hline
10100010
\end{array} = 162 \text{ (if considered as unsigned binary)}
$$

The output program now takes the result and splits it into an integer par 1010, and a fractional part .0010, and prints the correct answer 10.125. Not that a fixed-point number may be spread over several words to achieve greater range of values than allowed by a single word.

The fixed-point representation of fractional numbers is very useful in som circumstances, particularly for financial calculations. In these the smalles fractional part may be (say) 0.1 of a penny or 0.001 pound. The larges integer part may be (say) 1 000 000 pounds. To represent such a quantity i (say) BCD a total of $6 \times 4 + 3 \times 4 = 36$ bits are required. In a byte-oriente computer five bytes would be needed for each number.

Fixed point numbers have their limitations. What about the astrophysicis who is examining the behaviour of the sun? She is confronted with quantitie such as the weight of the sun

[199000000000000000000000000000000000 grams]

and the weight of an electron

[0.000000000000000000000000000910956 grams].

If the astrophysicist were to resort to fixed-point arithmetic, she would need to take an extravagantly large number of bytes to represent the numbers. A single byte represents numbers in the range 0 to 256, or approximately 0 to 1/4 thousand. Thus, our physicist would need roughly 14 bytes for the integer part and 12 bytes for the fractional part—a 26 byte (208 bit) number! A clue to a way out of our dilemma is to note that both numbers contain a large number of zeros but few significant digits.

3.7.1 The representation of floating point numbers

Digital computers often represent and store numbers in a floating point format. Just as we represent the number 1234.56 by 0.123456×10^4, the computer handles binary numbers in a similar way. For example, 1101101.1101101 may be represented internally as $0.11011011101101 \times 2^7$ (the 7 is, of course, also stored in a binary format). Floating point notation is sometimes called scientific notation. Before looking at floating point numbers in more detail it is necessary to consider the ideas of range, precision and accuracy which are closely related to the way numbers are represented in floating point format.

Range

The range of a number tells us how big or how small it can be. In the example of the astrophysicist we were dealing with numbers as large as 2×10^{33} to those as small as 9×10^{-28}. This represents a range of approximately 10^{61}, or 61 decades. The range of numbers represented in a digital computer must be sufficient for the vast majority of calculations that are likely to be performed. If the computer is to be employed in a dedicated application where the range of data to be handled is known to be quite small, then the range of valid numbers may be restricted, simplifying the hardware/software requirements.

Precision

The precision of a number is a measure of its exactness and corresponds to the number of significant figures used to represent it. For example, the constant π may be written as 3.142 or 3.141592. The latter case is more precise than the former because it represents π to one part in 10^7 while the former represents π to one part in 10^4.

Accuracy

Accuracy has been included here largely to contrast it with precision, a term often incorrectly thought to mean the same as accuracy. Accuracy is the measure of correctness of a quantity. For example, we can say $\pi = 3.141$ or

$\pi = 3.241592$. We can now see that in the former case we have a low precision number which is more accurate than its higher precision neighbour. In an ideal world accuracy and precision would go hand-in-hand. It is up to the computer programmer to design numerical algorithms which preserve the accuracy that the available precision allows. One of the potential black-spots of computation is calculations of the form:

$$\frac{A+B}{A-B} \quad \text{e.g} \quad \frac{1234.5687 + 1234.5678}{1234.5687 - 1234.5678}$$

When the denominator of the expression is evaluated we are left with 0.0009 a number with only one decimal place of precision. When the calculation is carried out the answer shows eight figures of precision but it may be very inaccurate indeed.

A floating point number is represented in the form:

$$a \times r^e$$

Where a is the mantissa (also called an argument), r is the radix, and e is the exponent or characteristic. The way in which a computer stores floating point numbers is to divide the binary representation into two fields:

exponent	mantissa
e	a

represents $a \times 2^e$.

The base r is understood and need not be stored explicitly by the computer. Throughout the remainder of this section the value of the radix in all floating point numbers is assumed to be two. In some computers the radix of the exponent is octal or hexadecimal, so that the mantissa is multiplied by 8^e or 16^e, respectively.

It is not necessary for a floating point number to occupy a single storage location. Indeed with an eight-bit word, such a representation would be useless. Often a number of words are grouped to form the floating point number. It is worthwhile noting that the division between exponent and mantissa need not fall at a word boundary.

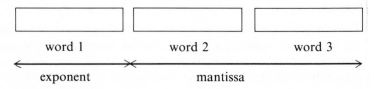

word 1   word 2   word 3

←——————————→|←——————————————————————————→
   exponent   mantissa

3.7.2 The normalization of floating point numbers

By convention the floating point mantissa is always normalized (unless it is equal to zero) so that it is expressed in the form $0.1 \ldots \times 2^e$. For the moment we are considering positive mantissas only. If the result of a calculation were to yield $0.01 \ldots \times 2^e$ the result would be normalized to $0.1 \ldots \times 2^{e-1}$. By normalizing a mantissa the greatest possible advantage is taken of the available precision. It is worth noting here that there is a slight difference between normalized decimal numbers as used by engineers and scientists, and normalized binary numbers. A decimal floating point number is normalized so that its mantissa lies in the range 1.00 . . . 0 to 9.99 . . . 9. A positive floating point normalized binary mantissa is of the form:

$$0.100 \ldots 0 \text{ to } 0.11 \ldots 11.$$

If the floating point mantissa is x, then $\frac{1}{2} \leqslant x < 1$. A special exception has to be made in the case of zero, as this number cannot, of course, be normalized. A negative, two's-complement, floating-point mantissa is stored in the form:

$$1.01 \ldots 1 \text{ to } 1.00 \ldots 0.$$

In this case the negative mantissa, x, is constrained so that $-\frac{1}{2} > x \geqslant -1$. The floating point number is therefore limited to one of three ranges:

$$-1 \leqslant x < -\tfrac{1}{2} \text{ or } x = 0 \text{ or } \tfrac{1}{2} \leqslant x < 1.$$

In a floating point representation of numbers provision must be made for both positive and negative numbers, and positive and negative exponents. For example, in decimal notation this corresponds to:

$$+0.123 \times 10^{12}, \qquad -0.756 \times 10^{9}$$
$$+0.176 \times 10^{-3}, \qquad -0.459 \times 10^{-7}$$

The mantissa of a floating point number is often represented as two's complement number. The exponent, however, is sometimes represented in a biased form. If we take an m-bit exponent, there are 2^m possible unsigned integer values of the exponent from $00 \ldots 0$ to $11 \ldots 1$. Suppose now we re-label these numbers not from 0 to $2^m - 1$, but from -2^{m-1} to $+2^{m-1} - 1$. This is done by subtracting a constant value of 2^{m-1} from each of the numbers. In other words, the biased exponent, b', is defined as $b' = b + 2^{m-1}$, where b is the true exponent. The biased exponent, b', is the internal representation of the exponent. Consider what happens for the case where $m = 4$ (Table 3.14).

The true exponent ranges from -8 to $+7$ allowing us to represent powers of two from 2^{-8} to 2^{+7}. The advantage of this notation is that the most negative exponent is represented by zero. Conveniently, the floating point value of zero is represented by $0.0 \ldots 0 \times 2^l$, where l is the most negative exponent. By selecting the biased exponent system we arrange that zero is represented by a zero mantissa and a zero exponent:

$$0.0 = \boxed{0\ldots0} \boxed{0\ldots0}$$

$$e \qquad m$$

A second advantage of this representation is that the exponents are monotonic in their binary form. That is, increasing the exponent by 1 involves adding one to the binary exponent, and decreasing the exponent by 1 involves subtracting one from the binary exponent. In both cases the binary exponent can be considered as behaving like an unsigned binary number.

Table 3.14 The biased exponent

Binary representation of exponent	True exponent	Biased form
0000	-8	0
0001	-7	1
0010	-6	2
0011	-5	3
0100	-4	4
0101	-3	5
0110	-2	6
0111	-1	7
1000	0	8
1001	1	9
1010	2	10
1011	3	11
1100	4	12
1101	5	13
1110	6	14
1111	7	15

3.7.3 Some typical floating point systems

In order to choose a floating point representation for a given computer, the programmer must select:

1. The number of words used (i.e. total number of bits)
2. The representation of the mantissa (2's complement etc.)
3. The representation of the exponent (biased etc.)
4. The number of bits devoted to the mantissa and exponent
5. The location of the mantissa (exponent first or mantissa first).

Point 4 is worth elaborating on. Once the programmer has decided on the total number of bits in the floating point representation (an integral number of word lengths) he must partition this representation into mantissa and exponent. If he dedicates a large number of bits to the exponent, the result is a floating point number with a very big range. These (exponent) bits have been obtained at the expense of the mantissa which reduces the precision of the floating point number. Conversely, increasing the bits available for the mantissa improves the precision at the expense of the range.

Because of the five points above, the numbers of ways in which a floating point number may be represented is legion, with (almost) no two machines using the same format. Things may be getting better with the introduction of microprocessors; as we shall see later the IEEE has produced a draft specification of a proposed format for floating point numbers. The following examples illustrate the representation found in some computers:

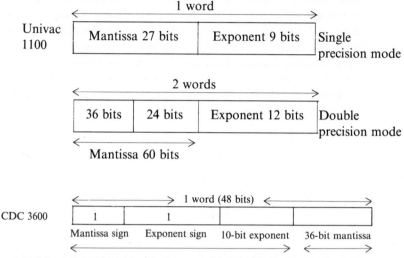

In the Univac single precision mode the range is approximately 10^{-76} to 10^{+76} and the precision amounts to 8 decimal places. In the double precision mode the range is increased to 10^{614} to 10^{-614}, and the precision is equivalent to 18 decimal places. Double precision mode is used in numerical arithmetic where great precision is sometimes necessary. In general, the use of double precision slows the running of a program considerably unless the computer has a special high-speed floating-point unit.

The IEEE floating point format

The Institute of Electronic and Electrical Engineers (IEEE) has produced a standard floating-point format for arithmetic operations in mini- and microcomputers. To cater for a number of different applications, the IEEE has specified three basic formats, called single, double, and quad. Table 3.15 defines the principal features of these three floating point formats.

A floating point number X in single format is normalized so that its mantissa f lies in the range $1 \leqslant f < 2$. This range corresponds to a mantissa with an integer part equal to 1. X is formally defined as:

$$X = (-1)^S \times 2^{E-127} \times (1 + F).$$

Where:

S = sign bit, 0 = positive mantissa, 1 = negative mantissa,
E = eight-bit exponent biased by 127,
F = a 23-bit fractional mantissa (together with an implicit leading 1).

There are two particular points of interest. The first is that a sign and magnitude representation has been adopted for the mantissa. This is represented algebraically by $(-1)^S$, where S is the sign bit. If $S = 0$ we have $(-1)^0$ which is $+1$, and if $S = 1$ we have $(-1)^1$ which is -1.

The second point is that the mantissa is always normalized and lies in the range $1.00 \ldots 0$ to $1.11 \ldots 1$. Note that an IEEE floating point number is normalized differently to the floating point numbers we have encountered earlier. If the mantissa is always normalized, it follows that the leading 1, the integer part, is redundant when the number is stored in memory. If we know that a 1 must be located to the left of the fractional mantissa, there is no need to store it. In this way a bit of storage is saved permitting the precision of the mantissa to be extended by one bit. The format of the number when stored in memory is given below:

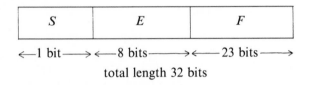

S	E	F

$\leftarrow$—1 bit—$\rightarrow$ $\leftarrow$—8 bits————$\rightarrow$$\leftarrow$— 23 bits —$\rightarrow$

total length 32 bits

As an example of the use of this format consider the representation of the decimal number -2345.125 on a machine having a 16-bit wordlength.

$$-2345.125_{10} = -100100101001.001_2 \qquad (decimal \rightarrow binary)$$
$$= -1.00100101001001_2 \times 2^{11}.$$

The mantissa is negative so the sign bit S is 1.

The exponent is given by $+11 + 127 = 138 = 10001010_2$.

The fractional part is $.00100101001001000000000$ (in 23 bits).

Therefore, the IEEE single format representation of -2345.125 is:

$1\,10001010\,00100101001001000000000.$

This number is stored as two consecutive 16-bit words:

$1\,10001010\,0010010 \qquad 1001001000000000.$

$\uparrow$ $\quad$ E $\qquad$ F
S

In order to minimize storage space, the floating point numbers are packed so that the sign bit, exponent, and mantissa share part of two or more machine words, unless the computer has a 32-bit or longer word-length. When floating point operations are carried out the numbers are first unpacked so that the mantissa is separated from the exponent. For example, the basic single precision format specifies a 23-bit fractional mantissa, giving a 24-bit mantissa. If the processor in which the floating point numbers are being processed has a 16-bit word-length, the unpacked mantissa will occupy 24 bits out of the 32 bits taken up by two words.

If, when a number is unpacked, the number of bits in its exponent and mantissa is allowed to increase to fill the available space, the format is said to be extended. By extending the format in this way the range and precision of the floating point number is considerably increased. In terms of the above example, the 24-bit mantissa takes up two machine words (i.e. 32 bits) and all floating point calculations are done on this 32-bit mantissa. This is particularly helpful when transcendental functions (e.g. $\sin x$, $\cos x$) are evaluated. After a sequence of floating operations have been carried out in the extended format, the floating point number is re-packed and stored in memory in its basic form.

Table 3.15 Basic IEEE floating point formats

Type	Single	Double	Quad
Field width in bits			
S = sign	1	1	1
E = exponent	8	11	15
L = leading bit	1	1	1
F = fraction	23	52	111
Total width	32	64	128
Sign bit	0 = +, 1 = −	0 = +, 1 = −	0 = +, 1 = −
Exponent			
Maximum E	255	2047	32767
Minimum E	0	0	0
Bias	127	1023	16383

Normalized numbers: (all formats)
  Range of exponents (Min $E+1$) to (Max $E-1$)
  Represented number $(-1)^S \times 2^{E-l} \times (L+F)$

A signed zero is represented by the minimum exponent, $L=0$, and $F=0$, for all three formats.

The maximum exponent has a special function and is used to represent signed infinity for all three formats.

Not In

3.7.4 Floating point arithmetic

Unlike integer and fixed point number representations, floating point numbers cannot be added in one simple operation. A moment's thought should demonstrate why this is so. Consider an example in decimal arithmetic. The floating point system used in the following examples will be that described earlier in this section—two's complement mantissa with a biased exponent. Let $A = 12345$ and $B = 567.89$. In floating point form these numbers are represented by:

$$A = 0.12345 \times 10^5 \text{ and } B = 0.56789 \times 10^3$$

If these numbers were to be added by hand, no problems would arise.

```
   12345          A
+   567.89       + B
   12912.89
```

However, as these numbers are held in a normalized floating point format we have the problem below.

$$0.12345 \times 10^5$$
$$+ 0.56789 \times 10^3$$

This addition cannot take place as long as the exponents are different. To perform a floating point addition (or subtraction) the following steps must be carried out.

1. Identify the number with the smaller exponent.
2. Make the smaller exponent equal to the larger exponent by dividing the mantissa of the smaller number by the same factor by which its exponent was increased.
3. Add (or subtract) the mantissas.
4. If necessary, normalize the result (post-normalization).

In the above example we have $A = 0.12345 \times 10^5$ and $B = 0.56789 \times 10^3$. The exponent of B is smaller than that of A which results in B becoming 0.0056789×10^5. We can now add A and B:

$$A = 0.1234500 \times 10^5$$
$$+ B = 0.0056789 \times 10^5$$
$$0.1291289 \times 10^5$$

In this case the result does not need post-normalizing. Note that the answer is expressed to a precision of seven significant figures while A and B are each expressed to a precision of five significant figures.

When people do arithmetic they often resort to what may best be called 'floating precision': if they want greater precision they simply use more digits. Computers use a fixed representation so that the precision may not increase as a result of calculation. Consider the following binary example.

$$A = 0.11001 \times 2^4$$
$$B = 0.10001 \times 2^3.$$

The exponent of B must be increased by 1 and the mantissa of B divided by 2 (i.e. shifted one place right).

$$A = 0.11001 \times 2^4$$
$$B = 0.010001 \times 2^4$$
$$1.000011 \times 2^4$$

The result has overflowed and must be post-normalized by dividing the mantissa by two and incrementing the exponent.

$$A + B = 1.000011 \times 2^4 = 0.1000011 \times 2^5.$$

We have also gained two extra places of precision, forcing us to take some form of action. For example, we can simply truncate the number to get:

$$A + B = 0.10000 \times 2^5.$$

A more formal procedure for the addition of floating point numbers is given in Fig. 3.18 as a flow chart.

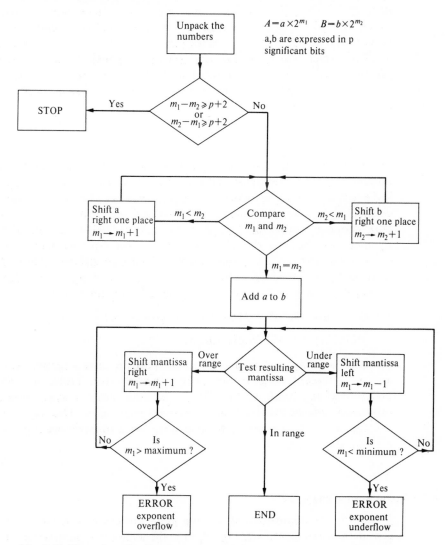

Fig. 3.18 Flow chart for floating point addition

A few points to note about this flow chart are as follows.

1. Because (in many implementations) the exponent shares part of a word with the mantissa it is necessary to separate them before the process of addition can begin. This is called 'unpacking'.

2. If the two exponents differ by more than $p + 1$, where p is the number of significant bits in the mantissa, then the smaller number is too small to affect the larger and hence the result is effectively equal to the larger number, and no further action takes place.

3. During post-normalization the exponent is checked to see if it is less than its minimum possible value, and greater than its maximum possible value. This corresponds to testing for exponent underflow and overflow, respectively. In each of these cases the number is outside the range of numbers which the computer can handle. Exponent underflow would generally lead to the number being made equal to zero, while exponent overflow would result in an error condition and may require the intervention of the operating system.

Rounding and truncation

We have seen that some of the operations involved in floating point arithmetic lead to an increase in the number of bits in the mantissa and that some technique must be invoked to keep the number of bits in the mantissa constant. The simplest technique is truncation and involves nothing more than dropping unwanted bits. For example, 0.1101101 truncated to 4 significant bits becomes 0.1101. A much better technique is rounding. If the value of the lost digits is greater than half the least significant bits of the retained digits, 1 is added to the LSB of the remaining digits. For example, consider rounding to 4 significant bits the following numbers:

$$0.1101101 \rightarrow 0.1101 + 0.0001 = 0.1110 \text{ (round up)}$$

$$0.1101011 \rightarrow 0.1101 \text{ (round down)}$$

Rounding is always preferred to truncation partly because it is more accurate and partly because it gives rise to an unbiased error. Truncation always undervalues the result leading to a systematic error whereas rounding sometimes reduces the result and sometimes increases it. The major disadvantage of rounding is that it requires a further arithmetic operation to be performed on the result.

3.7.5 Some worked examples

Because of the complexity of floating point arithmetic, due largely to the considerable number of steps involved in the addition or subtraction of two numbers, the following fully worked examples have been included.

Question 1

Add together 10.125 and 32.1 using floating point arithmetic with the format below. In each case show how the numbers would be stored in the computer.

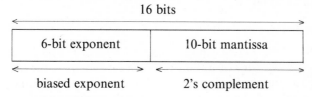

16 bits

6-bit exponent	10-bit mantissa
biased exponent	2's complement

Solution 1

$$10.125 \rightarrow 1010.001_2$$
$$\rightarrow 0.101000100_2 \times 2^4.$$

$$b' = b + 2^5$$
$$b' = 4 + 32$$

The exponent is 4 or, in biased form, $4 + 32 = 36 = 100100$. The floating point representation of 10.125 is:

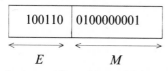

100100	0101000100

$E \qquad\qquad M$

$$32.1 \rightarrow 100000.00011001100 \ldots _2$$
$$\rightarrow 0.100000000110011_2 \times 2^6$$
$$\rightarrow 0.100000001_2 \times 2^6 \text{ after rounding}$$

The exponent is 6 or, in biased form, $6 + 32 = 38$. The floating point representation of 32.1 is:

100110	0100000001

$E \qquad\qquad M$

As these numbers have different exponents the smaller mantissa must be scaled.

$$\begin{array}{cccc} 100100 & 0.101000100 \rightarrow 100110 & 0.00101000100. \\ E & M & E & M \end{array}$$

We can now add the mantissas:
$$\begin{array}{r} 0.00101000100 \\ + 0.100000001 \\ \hline 0.10101001000. \end{array}$$

This result may now be rounded to 10 bits (0.101010010) and our final answer is:

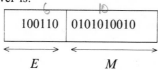

100110	0101010010

$E \qquad\qquad M$

The decimal equivalent of this binary number represents $0.1010100010 \times 2^6 = 101010.010 = 42.25$. Notice that the correct answer is 42.225. The error has been introduced because the mantissa has been restricted to 10 bits.

Question 2

Assuming a 6-bit biased exponent and a 10-bit two's complement mantissa, perform the following operations. In each case compare the calculated result with the true result. During the calculation of the 10-bit mantissa rounding may be employed. During successive floating point operations (i.e. scaling the mantissa) truncation must be used.

(a)	157.3	(b)	157.3	(c)	157.3	(d)	157.3
	+ 257.1		− 12.5		− 142.7		+ 158.3

Solution 2a

$$
\begin{array}{r}
157.3 \\
+\ 257.1 \\
\hline
414.4
\end{array}
$$

Step 1. Convert 157 to binary.

$$
\begin{array}{lll}
157 \div 2 = 78 & R=1 \\
78 \div 2 = 39 & R=0 \\
39 \div 2 = 19 & R=1 \\
19 \div 2 = \ 9 & R=1 \\
9 \div 2 = \ 4 & R=1 \\
4 \div 2 = \ 2 & R=0 \\
2 \div 2 = \ 1 & R=0 \\
1 \div 2 = \ 0 & R=1 \\
\end{array}
$$

Therefore, $157_{10} = 10011101_2$.

Step 2. Convert 0.3 to binary.

$$
\begin{array}{l}
0.3 \times 2 = 0.6 \\
0.6 \times 2 = \overline{1}.2 \\
0.2 \times 2 = \overline{0}.4 \\
0.4 \times 2 = \overline{0}.8 \\
0.8 \times 2 = \overline{1}.6 \\
\end{array}
$$

Therefore, $0.3_{10} = 0.01001 \ldots _2$.

Step 3. Normalize the fixed-point binary number.

$$157.3 = 10011101.01001 \ldots _2$$

$$= 0.1001110101001_2 \times 2^8$$

Step 4. Round the mantissa to ten bits.

0.100111010 <u>1001</u>

greater than $\frac{1}{2}$ LSB of 10 remaining bits

0.100111011 rounded mantissa.

Thus, the floating point representation of 157.3 is 0.100111011×2^8. The exponent is $+8$ (true). In biased form we must add $2^5 (=32)$ to this to get 40. This number would actually be stored as 1010000100111011.

Step 5. Convert 257.1 to a normalized floating point number, rounded to 10 bits.

$257.1_{10} = 0.100000001_2 \times 2^9$.

Step 6. Compare exponents.

0.100111011×2^8

0.100000001×2^9

Step 7. Make the smaller exponent equal to the larger exponent, and shift its mantissa right for each increment of the exponent.

0.0100111011×2^9

0.100000001×2^9

Step 8. Add mantissas.

0.010011101×2^9 Note that the smaller mantissa has
0.100000001×2^9 been truncated to 10 bits
—————————————
0.110011110×2^9

The result is already normalized and needs no further processing. This corresponds to $0.110011110_2 \times 2^9 = 110011110_2 = 414_{10}$, and differs from the exact answer (414.4) by 0.4.

Solution 2b

$$\begin{array}{r} 157.3 \\ - \ \ 12.6 \\ \hline 144.7 \end{array}$$
$= \ 157.3 + (-12.6)$

Step 1. Convert 157.3 to binary.

$157.3_{10} = 0.100111011_2 \times 2^8$ (normalized and rounded).

Step 2. Convert 12.6 to binary.

$12.6_{10} = 1100.10011001100_2$

$= 0.110010011011 \times 2^4$

$= 0.110010011 \times 2^4$ (floating-point rounded binary).

Step 3. Form 2's complement of mantissa.

$0.110010011 \rightarrow 1.001101100$ (invert bits)

$\rightarrow 1.001101101$ (add 1).

Step 4. Equalize exponents.

$$1.\underbrace{001101101}_{S \quad 4} \times 2^4 \rightarrow 1.\underbrace{11110011 0}_{S}(\underbrace{1101}_{4}) \times 2^8$$
$$\rightarrow 1.111100110 \times 2^8.$$

Note 1. When shifting negative numbers right the sign bit is propagated.
Note 2. The bits shifted out have been dropped.

Step 5. Perform addition

$$\begin{array}{r} 0.100111011 \times 2^8 \\ 1.111100110 \times 2^8 \\ \hline 10.100100001 \times 2^8. \end{array}$$

Note. The leftmost 1 in the carry-bit position is the result of two's complement arithmetic and is neglected.

$$\text{Result} = 0.100100001 \times 2^8 = 10010000.1_2 = 144.5_{10}$$

The exact answer is 144.7.

Solution 2c

$$\begin{array}{r} 157.3 \\ - 142.7 \\ \hline 14.6 \end{array}$$

Step 1. Convert 157.3 to binary.

$157.3_{10} = 0.100111011_2 \times 2^8$ (normalized and rounded).

Step 2. Convert 142.7 to binary.

$142.7_{10} = 10001110.1011001_2$

$\qquad = 0.100011101 \times 2^8$ (normalized and rounded).

Step 3. Form 2's complement of the mantissa.

$0.100011101 \rightarrow 1.011100010$ (invert bits)

$\rightarrow 1.011100011$ (add 1).

Step 4. Perform addition.

$$0.100111011 \times 2^8$$
$$\underline{1.011100011 \times 2^8}$$
$$10.000011110 \times 2^8$$

The answer is 0.000011110×2^8.

Step 5. Normalize the result.

$$0.0000011110 \times 2^8 \rightarrow 0.1111000000 \times 2^4$$

$$\rightarrow 15_{10}.$$

The exact answer is 14.6.

Solution 2d

$$157.3$$
$$-\ \underline{158.3}$$
$$-\ 001.0$$

Step 1. $157.3 = 0.100111011 \times 2^8$ (normalized and rounded).

Step 2. $158.3 = 10011110.01001$ (fixed-point binary)

$\qquad\qquad = 0.1001111001001 \times 2^8$ (floating-point binary)

$\qquad\qquad = 0.100111101 \times 2^8$ (floating-point, rounded binary).

Step 3. Form two's complement of mantissa.

$$0.100111101 \rightarrow 1.011000010 \text{ (invert bits)}$$

$$\rightarrow 1.011000011 \text{ (add 1)}.$$

Step 4. perform addition (exponents are the same here).

$$0.100111011 \times 2^8$$
$$\underline{1.011000011 \times 2^8}$$
$$1.111111110 \times 2^8$$

The answer is negative (sign bit $= 1$), but is not normalized.

Step 5. Normalize the result.

$$1.111111110 \times 2^8 \rightarrow 1.000000000 \times 2^0$$

$$\rightarrow -1_{10}$$

Note the operation of the arithmetic shift left:

$$1.111111110 \times 2^8 \rightarrow 1.111111100 \times 2^7$$

$$\rightarrow 1.111111000 \times 2^6$$

$$\text{etc. } \rightarrow 1.111110000 \times 2^5$$

The exact answer is -1.

Problems

Number-base conversion

1. Convert the following decimal numbers into their binary equivalents.

   (a) 15   (b) 42   (c) 235   (d) 4090   (e) 40900

2. Convert the following natural binary numbers to their decimal equivalents.

   (a) 110   (b) 1110110   (c) 110111   (d)11111110111

3. Complete Table 3.16.

Table 3.16

Decimal	Binary	Octal	Hexadecimal
37			
73			
	10101010		
	11011011101		
		42	
		772	
			256
			ABC

4. Convert the following base-five numbers into their base-nine equivalents (for example, $23_5 = 14_9$).

   (a) 24   (b) 144   (d) 1234   (c) 444

Number-base conversion and fractional numbers

1. Convert the following decimal numbers into their binary equivalents. Calculate the answer to five binary places and round the result up or down as necessary.

   (a) 1.5   (b) 1.1   (c) 1/3   (d) 1024.0625   (e) 3.141592

2. Convert the following binary numbers to their decimal equivalents.

   (a) 1.1   (b) 0.0001   (c) 101.101
   (d) 11011.101010   (e) 111.111111   (f) 10.1111101

3. Complete Table 3.17. Calculate all values to four places after the radix point.

Table 3.17

Decimal	Binary	Octal	Hexadecimal
0.37			
0.73			
	11011.011101		
	111.1011		
		0.70	
		1.101	
			2.56
			AB.C

4. Calculate the error (both absolute and as a percentage) if the following decimal fractions are converted to binary fractions, correct to 5 binary places.
Note. Convert the decimal number to six binary digits and then round up the 5th bit if the 6th bit is a 1.

(a) 0.675   (b) 0.42   (c) 0.1975   (d) 0.1   (e) 0.01   (f) 0.001

5. An electronics engineer has invented a new logic device which has three states: -1, 0, $+1$. These states are represented by $\bar{1}$, 0, 1 respectively. This arrangement may be used to form a 'balanced ternary' system with a radix 3, but where the 'trits' represent -1, 0, $+1$ instead of 0, 1, 2. The examples in Table 3.18 illustrate how this system works.

Table 3.18

Ternary	Balanced ternary	Decimal
11	11	4
12	1$\bar{1}\bar{1}$	5
22	10$\bar{1}$	8
1012	111$\bar{1}$	32

Write down the first 15 decimal numbers in the balanced ternary base.

6. The results of an experiment fall in the range -4 to $+9$. A scientist wishes to read the results into a computer and then process them. He decides to use a four-bit binary code to represent each of the possible inputs. Devise a 4-bit code capable of representing numbers in the range -4 to $+9$.

7. Design a natural-binary to Gray-code converter. The circuit has 4 inputs and 4 outputs. For example, the input 1000 results in the output 1100 (see Table 3.3 in Section 3.3.9).

8. Decode the Huffman code below, assuming that the valid codes are P = 0, Q = 10, R = 110, and S = 111. How many bits would be required if P, Q, R, and S had been encoded as 00, 01, 10, and 11, respectively?

000001110111000000101111111101010001111100010

9. Almost all computer hardware courses include a section on number bases and the conversion of numbers between bases. Does the base in which a computer represents numbers really matter to the computer user or even to the student of computer science?

Binary arithmetic

1. Perform the following binary additions.

(a)	10110	(b)	100111	(c)	11011011
	+ 101		111001		10111011
			+ 101101		00101011
					+ 01111111

2. Perform the following octal additions.

(a)	42	(b)	3357	(c)	777	(d)	437
	+ 53		+ 2741		543		426
					+ 420		772
							+ 747

3. Perform the following hexadecimal additions.

(a)	42	(b)	3357	(c)	777	(d)	A BCD
	+ 53		+ 2741		543		F E 1 0
					+ 420		+ 1 2 3A

4. Using 8-bit arithmetic throughout, express the following decimal numbers in 2's complement binary form.

(a) −4 (b) −5 (c) 0 (d) −25 (e) −42 (f) −128 (g) −127
(h) −111

5. Perform the following decimal subtractions in 8-bit 2's complement arithmetic. Note that some of the answers will result in arithmetic overflow. Indicate where overflow has occurred.

(a)	20	(b)	127	(c)	127	(d)	5
	− 5		− 126		− 128		− 20

(e)	69	(f)	− 20	(g)	−127	(h)	− 42
	− 42		−111		− 2		+ 69
							+120

6. Using 2's complement binary arithmetic with a 12-bit word, write down the range of numbers capable of being represented (both in decimal and binary formats) by giving the smallest and largest numbers. What happens when the smallest and largest numbers are:

(a) incremented?   (b) decremented?

7. Distinguish between *overflow* and *carry* when these terms are applied to 2's complement arithmetic on n-bit words.

8. Write down an algebraic expression giving the value of the n-bit integer $N = a_{n-1} a_{n-2} \ldots a_1 a_0$ for the case where N represents a two's complement number.

Hence prove that (in two's complement notation) the representation of a signed binary number in $n+1$ bits may be derived from its representation in n bits by repeating the leftmost bit.

9. Perform the additions below on four bit binary numbers.

(a)	0011	(b)	1111	(c)	0110	(d)	1100
	+1100		+0001		+0111		+1010

In each case, regard the numbers as being (i) unsigned integer, (ii) two's-complement integer, and (iii) sign-and-magnitude integer. Calculate the answer and comment on it where necessary.

10. (a) Write down the largest decimal positive integer in n digits.

(b) Write down the largest binary number in m bits.

(c) It is necessary to represent n-digit decimal numbers in base 2. What is the minimum number (m) of bits needed to represent all possible n-digit decimal numbers? Hint: the largest m-bit binary number should be greater than, or equal to, the largest n-bit decimal number.

11. A 4-bit binary adder adds together two unsigned 4-bit numbers, A and B, to produce a 4-bit sum, S, and a single-bit carry-out C. What is the range of outputs (i.e. largest and smallest values) that the adder is capable of producing? Give your answer in both binary and decimal forms.

An adder is designed to add together two binary coded decimal (BCD) digits to produce a single digit sum and a one-bit carry out. What is the range of valid outputs that this circuit may produce?

The designer of the BCD adder decides to use a pure binary adder to add together two BCD digits as if they were pure 4-bit binary numbers. Under what circumstances does the binary adder give the correct BCD result? Under what circumstances is the result incorrect (i.e. the 4-bit binary result differs from the required BCD result)?

What algorithm may the designer apply to the 4-bit output of the binary adder to convert it to a BCD adder?

12. Design a full subtractor circuit which will subtract bit X together with a borrow-in bit B_i from bit Y to produce a difference bit $D = Y - X - B_i$, and a borrow-out B_o.

Floating-point arithmetic

1. The following floating point format has been designed to give you an 'easy' introduction to the manipulation of floating point numbers. Questions 2 and 3 provide more realistic (and more tedious) examples.

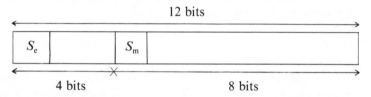

12 bits

4 bits   8 bits

The exponent consists of a 3-bit absolute value plus a sign-bit, S_e. The mantissa consists of a 7-bit absolute value plus a sign-bit, S_m. For example, the binary pattern 110101101000 represents $+0.11010000 \times 2^{-5}$.

Note that the representation of the mantissa is to sign and magnitude and not two's complement. Similarly, the exponent is also represented by the sign and magnitude form rather than the more usual biased form.

For the above format write down the range of numbers capable of being represented. Using this format perform the following operations.

(a)   25   (b)   25   (c)   12.25   (d)   1.125
      $+ 16$ $- 16$ $+ 1.125$ $- 0.625$

2. A computer has a 24-bit word length which, for the purpose of floating-point operations, is divided into an 8-bit biased exponent, and a 16-bit two's complement mantissa. Write down the range of numbers capable of being represented in this format and their precision.

3. For the floating-point format of Question 2, perform the following operations.

(a)   276.123   (b)   276.123   (c) $- 276.123$
      $- 159.014$ $+ 276.123$ $+ 275.123$

(d)   1563.123   (e)   276.123   (f)   276.123
      $-$ 0.042 $+$ 76.123 $-$ 76.123

Use the following assumptions:

(i) The numbers are stored as 24-bit words.
(ii) Floating point operations are carried out on an 18-bit mantissa (2

extra bits in the ALU). That is, the 16-bit mantissa from the memory becomes an 18-bit mantissa while floating point calculations are being carried out.

(iii) During the floating point operations all mantissa bits generated in the 19th position are dropped (i.e. truncation, not rounding).

(iv) The final value has its 18-bit mantissa rounded to 16-bits, and is then packed with the exponent into a 24-bit word, and stored in memory.

In each case, convert the final 24-bit floating point result into a decimal value and compare it with the expected result.

4. The two's complement fractional part of a normalized floating-point number X is constrained to lie within one of the three ranges:

$$-1 \leqslant X < -\tfrac{1}{2}, \qquad X = 0, \text{ or } \qquad \tfrac{1}{2} \leqslant X < 1.$$

Explain why this is so and illustrate your answer with a five-bit mantissa.

4   THE CENTRAL PROCESSING UNIT

The central processing unit (CPU) lies at the heart of a computer system and is responsible for stepping through the instructions of a program in an orderly fashion, executing them, and controlling the operation of the computer's memory and input/output devices.

Before we look at the way in which a CPU works, it is important to understand the relationship between the processor, the memory and the program. Let's take a simple program to calculate the area of a circle and see how the computer deals with it. In what follows the computer is a hypothetical machine devoid of all the nasty complications associated with reality.

We all know that the area of a circle, A, is given by πr^2. When people evaluate the area of a circle they perform all the necessary steps automatically at a subconscious level. However, when they come to write programs they must tell the computer exactly what it should do, step by step. To illustrate this point take a look at '$\pi \times r \times r$'. We write $r \times r$, but we mean a number, which we have given the symbol 'r', multiplied by itself. Fig. 4.1 illustrates the relationship between the program, memory and processor.

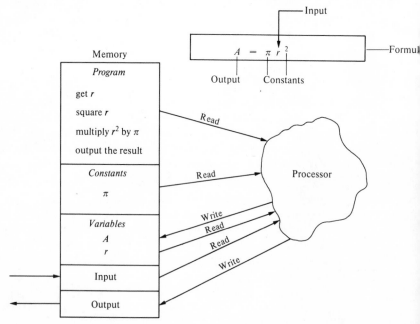

Fig. 4.1 The relationship between the memory, processor, and program

The memory has been divided into five parts: program, constants, variables, input and output. The program is the sequence of operations to be carried out, or executed. The constants (in this case there is only one) are numbers used by the program but which do not change during its execution. In this case π is a constant. The variables represent numbers created and modified by the program. Thus, when the program 'squares *r*' it reads the value of the number in the memory location it has called *r*, squares it, and puts the result back in the same location.

Although the variables are often numerical quantities, there is no reason why this must always be so. For example, the variables used by a word processor are the letters (and other symbols) of the text being processed. It is perfectly possible for the variable to be another program. That is, one program can operate on, or modify, another program. This concept leads to the idea of a self-programming (intelligent?) computer.

Any program must be able to communicate with the outside world, otherwise all its efforts are to no effect. I have labelled two memory locations 'input' and 'output' so that reading from the 'input' causes information to be taken from an input device (say a keyboard) and writing to an 'output' causes information to be moved from the computer to an output device (say a VDU). Regarding input and output as memory locations is not entirely fictional: some computers do indeed perform all input/output transactions via the memory.

The processor may either read data from a memory location or write data to a memory location. Of the five regions of memory described above, three are read-only, one is write-only, and one can be read from or written to. When we come to the processor we will see that keeping track of information in the memory is one of the CPU's most important functions.

4.1 The structure of the CPU

In Fig. 4.2 the block diagram of part of a CPU is given. In this diagram only the address paths are shown for clarity. The address paths are highways along which addresses flow from one part of the CPU to another. An address is the representation of the location of an item of data within the memory. There are two types of information flow in a computer: address and data (strictly speaking, an address is also data but here we take data to mean instructions, constants, and variables).

In order to explain Fig. 4.2 a shorthand called register-transfer language (RTL) is adopted. One or more letters, or letters followed by numerals, denote registers or storage locations. Square brackets denote the contents of the registers they enclose, and a left arrow (←) indicates the transfer of the contents of a register. Thus, the expression

$$[MAR] \leftarrow [PC]$$

means that the contents of the program counter are transferred (i.e. copied into) the memory address register.

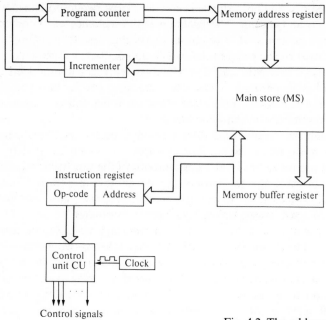

Fig. 4.2 The address paths of the CPU

The name of the program counter (or instruction counter) is somewhat of a misnomer. It does not count programs, or anything else, but contains the address of the next instruction in memory to be executed. It can be said to point to the next instruction to be executed. The execution of an instruction begins with the contents of the program counter being moved to the memory address register. After this, or possibly simultaneously, the contents of the program counter are incremented (increased by 1) and moved back to the program counter. In this way, the program counter is pointing to the next instruction while the current instruction is being executed.

The memory address register (MAR) holds the address of the location in the main store (MS) into which data is being written in a write cycle, or from which data is being read in a read cycle. The MAR now contains a copy of the contents of the PC, so that when a read cycle is performed, the instruction to be executed is read from the memory and transferred to the memory buffer register (MBR). The MBR is a temporary holding place for data received from memory in a read cycle, or for data to be transferred to memory in a write cycle. At this point the MBR contains the binary value of the instruction to be executed.

The instruction is next moved to the instruction register (IR), where it is divided into two fields. A field is part of a word where the bits are grouped together into a logical entity. For example, a person's name is divided into two fields: Christian name and Surname. One field contains the operation code (op-code), or instruction telling the computer which operation is to be carried out. The other field contains an address pointing to the location of the data to be used by the instruction. Sometimes this field is redundant, as not all op-codes refer to a location in memory.

The Control Unit (CU) is the most complex part of the CPU. This takes the op-code from the IR together with a stream of clock pulses and generates a number of signals which control all parts of the CPU. In many computers the time between individual clock pulses is in the range 0.01 to 1 microsecond. It is the control unit that is responsible for moving the contents of the program counter into the MAR, executing a read cycle, and moving the contents of the MBR to the IR.

The above sequence of operations is known as a fetch cycle. All instructions are executed in a two phase operation called a fetch–execute cycle. During the fetch cycle, the instruction is read from memory and decoded by the control unit. The fetch cycle is followed by an execute cycle in which the control unit generates all the signals necessary to execute the instruction. In terms of register-transfer language, the fetch cycle is defined in Table 4.1.

Table 4.1 The fetch cycle

FETCH	[MAR]	←	[PC]
	INCREMENTER	←	[PC]
	[PC]	←	INCREMENTER
	[MBR]	←	[MS[MAR]]
	[IR]	←	[MBR]
	CU	←	[IR(OP-CODE)]

Note that FETCH is a label, and IR(OP-CODE) means the op-code field of the instruction register. The term [MS[MAR]] is read as the 'contents of the Main Store whose address is given by the contents of the MAR'. Sometimes, for convenience, it is helpful to drop the 'MS' because it is understood. Thus, [MS[MAR]] can be written as [[MAR]].

Now that we've sorted out the fetch cycle, let's see what else we need to actually execute instructions. In Fig. 4.3, data paths have been added to our CPU.

The new additions to the CPU are an accumulator, A, and an arithmetic and logical unit, ALU. The accumulator holds temporary and intermediate results during a calculation. The ALU performs all the required operations on the contents of the accumulator together with (if necessary) the contents of the memory buffer register. The output of the ALU is fed back to the accumulator. There are two types of operation carried out by the ALU: arithmetic and logical. The fundamental difference between an arithmetic and a logical operation is that in logical operations a carry is not generated when bit A_i of word A is operated on by bit B_i of B. Table 4.2 gives some typical arithmetic and logical operations.

Having developed our computer a little further, we can now execute an

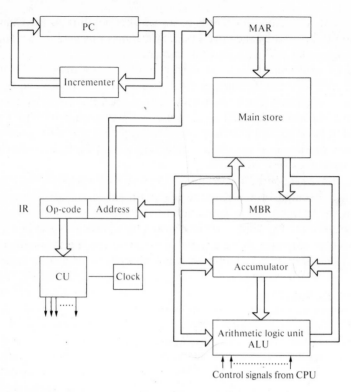

Fig. 4.3 The address- and data-paths of the CPU

Table 4.2 Arithmetic and logical operations

ARITHMETIC	LOGICAL
Addition	OR
Subtraction	NOR
Negation	AND
Multiplication	NAND
Division	NOT
Divide by 2 (shift right)	EOR
Multiply by 2 (shift left)	SHIFT

elementary program. Consider the operation $P = Q + R$. Here, the '+' means arithmetic addition. The program may be written in assembly language as follows:

LDA Q   Load accumulator with the contents of Q.
CLC   Clear the carry bit.
ADC R   Add to the accumulator the contents of R plus the carry bit.
STA P   Store the contents of the accumulator in P.

The way in which the CPU operates can best be seen by examining the execution of the instruction ADC R in terms of register-transfer language (see Table 4.3). This tells us what is actually going on inside the computer.

Table 4.3 ADC R expressed in RTL

FETCH	[MAR]←[PC]	move contents of PC to MAR
	INCREMENTER←[PC]	move contents of PC to incrementer
	[PC]←INCREMENTER	move contents of incrementer to PC
.	[MBR]←[MS[MAR]]	read from the main store
	[IR]←[MBR]	move contents of MBR to IR
	CU←[IR(OP-CODE)]	move opcode from IR to CU
ADC	[MAR]←[IR(ADDRESS)]	move address of operand to MAR
	[MBR]←[MS[MAR]]	read data
	ALU←[MBR], ALU←[A]	perform addition
	[A]←ALU	move output of ALU to accumulator

Where two operations share the same line they are executed simultaneously. Incidentally, the above operations are often referred to as microinstructions. Each assembly level instruction (e.g. LDA, ADC, STA) is executed as a series of microinstructions. In general microinstructions and microprogramming are the province of the computer designer, although some machines are microprogrammable by the user. Section 4.2.1 on the operation of the control unit takes a further look at microinstructions.

So far, we have considered the architecture of a computer capable of executing simple programs in a purely sequential mode—no means yet exists of modifying this sequence of operations. That is, the computer cannot execute either absolute jumps (GOTOs) or conditional jumps. A conditional jump allows high-level constructs such as IF THEN, and ELSE to be implemented. This deficiency is remedied by the arrangement in Fig. 4.4.

Three things have been added to our computer: a carry flip-flop, a processor status register (PSR), and a path between the address field of the instruction register and the program counter. The action of the carry flip-flop is quite straightforward. Whenever an addition or subtraction is performed, the result goes to the accumulator and the carry, or borrow, bit is retained in the carry flip-flop. Similarly, if the contents of the accumulator are moved (shifted) left or right by one bit, the bit that would 'fall off the edge' is transferred to the carry flip-flop. Consequently, the carry bit may be thought of as a one-bit extension of the accumulator.

The processor status register has some of its bits associated with the result of an arithmetic/logical operation. The bits of the PSR of interest here are:

C = Carry Set if a carry was generated in the last operation.

Z = Zero Set if the last operation generated a zero result.

N = Negative Set if the last result generated a negative (in 2's complement terms) result (MSB = 1).

V = Overflow Set if the last operation resulted in an arithmetic overflow (sign bit of result different to sign bit of both operands).

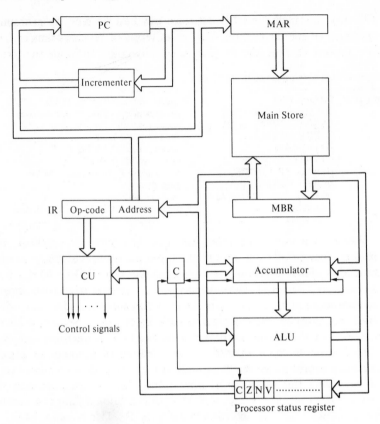

Fig. 4.4 The central processing unit

Some computers (6800, 6809) call their processor status register the condition code register (CCR). The PSR is connected to the control unit, enabling certain types of instruction to interrogate the PSR. There is, of course, no point in carrying out an interrogation unless the results are acted upon.

The final modification to our computer is the addition of a path between the address field of the instruction register and the program counter. It is this feature that enables the computer to respond to the result of its interrogation of the PSR. An instruction can test one or more bits of the PSR and, if the bit is clear, the next instruction is obtained in the normal way. But if the bit is set, the instruction is obtained from the location whose address is in the instruction register. This type of instruction is known as a conditional branch or jump. 'Branch' implies switching between one or more alternatives while 'jump' implies a non-sequential flow of control. Both terms are used in computer science, often interchangeably. In the above example a branch was made if a bit was set, equally a branch can be made if a bit is clear. The way in which conditional branches are actually implemented inside the computer is discussed in Section 4.2 on the Control Unit.

Table 4.4 lists the branch instructions implemented in the 6502 microprocessor.

Table 4.4   6502 microprocessor branch instructions

BCC	Branch on carry clear	branch if $C = 0$
BCS	Branch on carry set	branch if $C = 1$
BEQ	Branch on zero result	branch if $Z = 1$
BNE	Branch on non-zero result	branch if $Z = 0$
BMI	Branch on minus result (2's comp)	branch if $N = 1$
BPL	Branch on positive result (2's comp)	branch if $N = 0$
BVC	Branch on overflow clear (2's comp)	branch if $V = 0$
BVS	Branch on overflow set (2's comp)	branch if $V = 1$

The Motorola 6809 microprocessor (see Section 4.5) has an even larger number of branch instructions. These include additions such as BGT (branch if greater than zero), which causes a branch if $Z + (N \oplus V) = 0$. The difference between this and BPL is that BPL simply causes a branch if the number is zero or apparently positive (i.e. $N = 0$), while BGT requires the number to be greater than zero and will also cause the branch to be taken if the number appears to be negative ($N = 1$) because overflow has occurred and both $N = 1$ and $V = 1$.

The branch operations are written in register-transfer language in an 'if condition then action' format. Below are two examples of conditional branches expressed in terms of RTL.

    BCC   if $[C] = 0$ then $[PC] \leftarrow [IR(ADDRESS)]$
    BEQ   if $[Z] = 1$ then $[PC] \leftarrow [IR(ADDRESS)]$

4.1.1 A programming example

In order to fit together the things we have learned in this section, a programming example on our hypothetical computer should help. Firstly, we need to give the computer an instruction set. With one or two exceptions the instructions in Table 4.5 are those of the 6502 microprocessor. In what follows M and N represent symbolic values.

Instruction 09 (INC M) adds one to the contents of memory location M. In computer science texts 'increment' means increase by one. Similarly, decrement means decrease by one.

The 'branch on zero' and 'branch on not zero' instructions (16 and 17) are dependent on the state of the Z flag from the ALU. The Z flag is set to one if the result of the last operation performed by the ALU yielded a zero value.

In this instruction set there are three operations which cannot be carried out on the present computer. These are IN M, OUT M, and SET M. To implement these instructions we would need data paths from the accumulator to and from our peripherals, and a data path from the address field of the instruction register to the accumulator, respectively.

Table 4.5 Computer instruction set

Instruction	Mnemonic	action
00 M	LDA M	Load accumulator with the contents of memory location M.
01 M	STA M	Store the contents of the accumulator in memory location M.
02 M	IN M	Input a word from device number M into the accumulator
03 M	OUT M	Output the contents of the accumulator to device number M.
04 M	ADC M	Add the contents of M to the accumulator together with the carry bit.
05 M	SUB M	Subtract the contents of M from the accumulator.
06 M	AND M	Logically AND the contents of M with the accumulator. Result remains in accumulator.
07 M	ORA M	Logically OR the contents of M with the accumulator. Result remains in accumulator.
08	COM	Complement the contents of the accumulator.
09	INC M	Increment the contents of memory location M.
10	DEC M	Decrement the contents of memory location M.
11	CLC	Clear carry.
12	SEC	Set carry
13	ROL A	Rotate accumulator left through carry.
14	ROR A	Rotate accumulator right through carry.
15 M	SET M	Put the number M into the accumulator.
16 N	BEQ N	Branch if $[Z]=1$ to location N.
17 N	BNE N	Branch if $[Z]=0$ to location N.
18 N	BCC N	Branch if $[C]=0$ to location N.
19 N	BCS N	Branch if $[C]=1$ to location N.
20 N	JMP N	Unconditional jump to location N.
21	STOP	Stop.

For the purpose of our example we will assume that the input/output device is a VDU and has device number 0. To read data from the VDU's keyboard we execute the instruction IN 0, and to display a number on its screen we execute OUT 0.

The problem we wish to solve is: read a series of numbers which are terminated by a zero, add them together, multiply the result by 10, and print the answer. In a high level language this program may be written as in Table 4.6.

Some people who write programs at the assembly language level first draw a flow chart for their algorithm and then convert it into assembly language; others write the program in a high level language (often Pascal) and then code each of the statements into a number of assembly language operations. Yet others write assembly language directly from the algorithm. These latter people never get their programs right and they fail their exams. A flow chart for this program is given in Fig. 4.5.

Notice that we must multiply a number by 10. As the instruction set lacks

Table 4.6 Program to sum, and multiply by ten

BASIC	Pascal
10 T = 0	Program Sum (Input, Output);
20 INPUT N	Var n, t: Integer;
30 IF N = 0 THEN GOTO 60	BEGIN
40 T = T + N	t: = 0;
50 GOTO 20	read(n)
60 T = T*10	WHILE n < > 0 DO
70 PRINT T	BEGIN
80 STOP	t: = t + n;
	read(n)
	END;
	t: = t*10;
	write(t)
	END

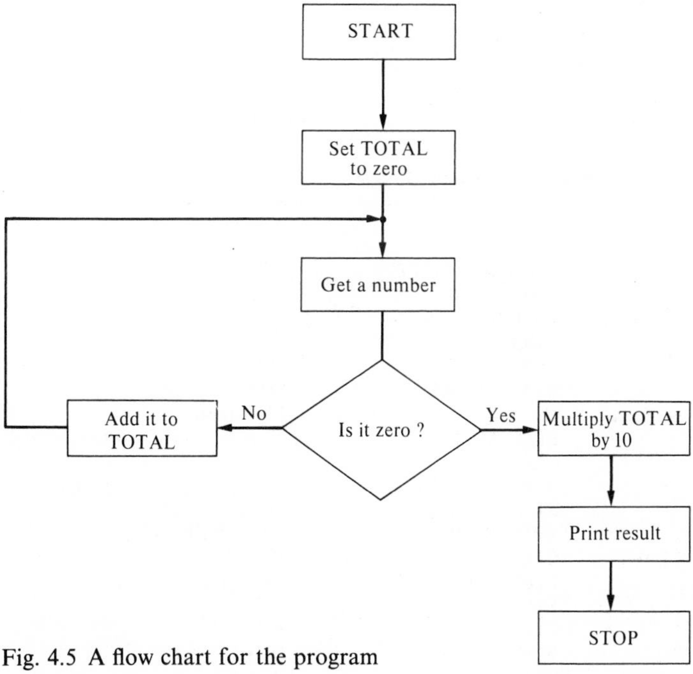

Fig. 4.5 A flow chart for the program

any facilities for direct multiplication we must either resort to repeated addition or write a program to do multiplication. An alternative solution is to note that $10x = (2 \times 2x + x) \times 2$. The flow chart to multiply by 10 involves the steps illustrated in Fig. 4.6. Before we begin to write the program we have to decide where to put it in the computer's memory. For convenience we may assume that the program starts at location 0. We do not know yet how long the program will be, but from the flow chart it should not exceed (say) 20 instructions (the number of boxes multiplied by 2). It should therefore be safe to locate any variables at location 30 onwards.

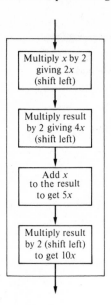

Fig. 4.6 A method of multiplying by ten

Table 4.7 The Assembly Language Program

No.			Comments
1.		NAM EXAMPLE	
2.		ORG 30	
3.	TOTAL	RMB 1	
4.		ORG 0	
5.		SET 0	[A]←0
6.		STA TOTAL	[TOTAL]←[A]
7.	REPEAT	IN 0	[A]←Input
8.		BEQ MULT	IF [Z]=1 THEN [PC]←MULT
9.		CLC	[C]←0
10.		ADC TOTAL	[A]←[A]+[TOTAL]+[C]
11.		STA TOTAL	[TOTAL]←[A]
12.		JMP REPEAT	[PC]←REPEAT
13.	MULT	CLC	[C]←0
14.		LDA TOTAL	[A]←[TOTAL]
15.		ROL A	[A]←[A] * 2
16.		CLC	[C]←0
17.		ROL A	[A]←[A] * 2
18.		CLC	[C]←0
19.		ADC TOTAL	[A]←[A]+[TOTAL]+[C]
20.		ROL A	[A]←[A] * 2
21.		OUT 0	output←[A]
22.		STOP	
23.		END	

The first column (see Table 4.7) containing the numbers 1 to 23 is not part of the program and is merely the line number for later reference. The second column containing TOTAL, REPEAT and MULT is the label field of the program. These three words are labels which may be referred to by the assembly language instructions. For example, BEQ MULT means branch on a zero result to the address of the instruction labelled 'MULT'. Later, when the program is translated into machine code by an assembler, all references to these labels will be translated into the address of the line they label.

At first sight there appear to be some mnemonics and in this program not appearing in the instruction set (lines 1, 2, 3, 4, and 23). These are not assembly language operations but are assembler directives. The final program, when in memory, will be in numeric or machine-code form. The version in Table 4.7 is written in a form suitable for people to read and write, and will eventually be translated into machine code. This is normally done by program called an assembler. It can be done by hand but this is not to be recommended.

The assembler directives tell the assembler things it needs to know about the program. The first assembler directive, NAM names the program (in this case EXAMPLE). The second assembler directive, ORG, sets the origin to 30. That is, any program or data following this statement is to be located at address 30 and successive locations. RMB reserves one or more memory locations for the named value. Thus, 'TOTAL RMB 1' reserves a single location for the item called 'TOTAL'. The second ORG resets the origin to 0 so that the program will be loaded into memory starting at address 0. The final assembler directive, END, tells the assembler that the end of the program has been reached.

When a branch instruction is used, it is accompanied by a label rather than a number. This relieves the programmer of the task of keeping track of addresses. The only other noteworthy point in the program is the use of the CLC instruction before the shifting operations begin. This is because ROL rotates the accumulator left through carry.

That is:

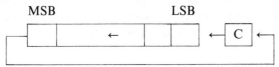

Obviously, the carry bit must be cleared initially, otherwise we may be shifting an erroneous bit into the LSB of the accumulator. For the sake of simplicity, it is assumed that the sum of the numbers will not produce an out-of-range result when multiplied by ten. That is, we do not have to worry about a carry-out being generated from the most significant bit (MSB) position when an ROL is executed.

Once the program has been assembled and placed in the main store of the computer, it can be executed. The layout or memory map of the computer is given by Table 4.8.

Each memory location holds four digits. The first two digits of an instruction define the operation code and the second two point to the memory location accessed by the op-code. Exceptions to this are the IN and

Table 4.8 Memory map of program

Address	Contents	
0	1500	
1	0103	
2	200	
3	1608	
4	11XX	
5	0430	
6	0130	
7	2002	
8	11XX	
9	0030	
10	13XX	
11	11XX	
12	13XX	
13	0430	
14	13XX	
15	0300	
16	21XX	
.	.	
.	.	
.	.	
30		←reserved for TOTAL
.	.	
.	.	
.	.	

OUT operations, in which a peripheral is defined, the SET operation, in which the following two digits are loaded into the accumulator, and instructins like CLC and ROL which do not refer to memory locations. In the latter case **XX** represents a don't care condition—these digits may have any value. In practice they are often set to zero.

4.2 The control unit

The precise way in which a digital computer interprets its machine code instructions is rather complex, and consequently the discussion of the computer's control unit is often left to more advanced courses on computer architecture. Here we are going to look at the execution of a single machine code instruction. The model we use has been stripped of any unnecessary detail to make the basic process easier to understand. There are two radically different approaches to the design of the control unit. The first (Section 4.2.) is to make the control unit itself a 'computer' within a computer, and turn machine-level instructions into a sequence of even more primitive instructions called microinstructions. The alternative approach (Section 4.2.2) is to ask what sequence of logical and arithmetic operations are needed to carry out an instruction, and then to design the appropriate logic circuit to cause this to happen.

4.2.1 Microprogrammed control unit

Before describing the control unit, three terms need defining. These are macrolevel instructions, microlevel instructions and interpretation. The most primitive language of computers is called machine code, and its mnemonic representation is called assembly language. These instructions are also called macroinstructions. Each macroinstruction is effected by means of a number of operations called microinstructions. A microinstruction or micro-operation is the smallest event which can take place in a computer. A micro-operation may consist of clocking a flip-flop or of moving data from one register to another. The process whereby a macroinstruction is executed by means of a series of micro-operations is called interpretation. Note that the use of the prefix 'macro' here is distinct from its use in programming.

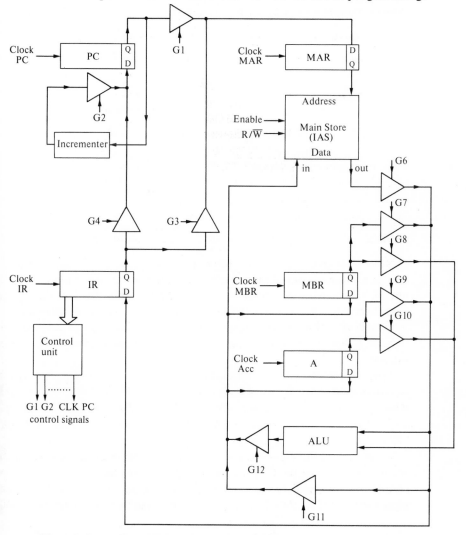

Fig. 4.7 Controlling the data flow within the CPU

Part of the internal structure of a CPU is illustrated in Fig. 4.7. Thi⃞
diagram differs from those of Figs 4.2–4 by showing the mechanism by which⃞
information is moved within the CPU. Each of the registers in Fig. 4.⃞
(program counter, accumulator etc.) is made up of D flip-flops. When th⃞
clock input to a register is pulsed, the data at its input terminals is transferre⃞
to the output terminals and held constant until the register is clocked again⃞
The connections between the registers are by means of *m*-bit wide dat⃞
highways. In Fig. 4.7 only one bit of the data paths is shown, for clarity.

Suppose we wish our computer to perform a fetch–execute cycle where th⃞
op-code is that of addition. We can write down the sequence of operation⃞
not only in terms of register transfer language, but also in terms of th⃞
enabling of gates and the clocking of flip-flops; see Table 4.9.

Table 4.9 The actions necessary to interpret an op-code

Step	Register Transfer Language		Operations required
1	[MAR] ←	[PC]	enable G1, clock MAR
1a	INC ←	[PC]	
2	[PC] ←	INC	enable G2, clock PC
3	[MBR] ←	[MS[MAR]]	enable MS, R/$\overline{\text{W}}$ = 1
			enable G6, enable G11
			clock MBR
4	[IR] ←	[MBR]	enable G7, clock IR
4a	CU ←	[IR(OP-CODE)]	
5	[MAR] ←	[IR(ADDRESS)]	enable G3, clock MAR
6	[MBR] ←	[MS[MAR]]	enable MS, R/$\overline{\text{W}}$ = 1
			enable G6, enable G11,
			clock MBR
7	ALU ←	[MBR]	enable G7
7a	ALU ←	[A]	enable G10
8	[A] ←	ALU	enable G12, clock A

Note 1. Where there is no entry in the third column, that operatio⃞
happens automatically. For example, the output of the program counter i⃞
always connected to the input of the incrementer, and therefore no explici⃞
operation is needed to move the contents of the PC to the incrementer.

Note 2. Any three-state gate not explicitly mentioned is not enabled.

Note 3. Some operations (e.g. steps 7 and 7a) are carried out simulta⃞
neously.

Now imagine that the output of the control unit consists of twelve signal⃞
to enable gates 1 to 12, two signals to control the MS, and five clock signal⃞
which pulse the clock inputs of the PC, MAR, MBR, IR, and A register⃞
Table 4.10 gives the outputs of the control unit as a sequence of binar⃞
values.

If, for each of the eight steps in Table 4.10 the nineteen signals are fed t⃞
the various parts of the CPU in Fig. 4.7 then the fetch/execute cycle will b⃞
carried out. In a real computer there are very many more than 19 contr⃞
signals generated by the CU. A typical value would be in the range 64 to 200

Table 4.10 The control signals required to execute an ADD op-code

Step	\multicolumn{12}{c}{Gate control signals}												\multicolumn{2}{c}{MS control}		\multicolumn{5}{c}{Register clocks}				
	G1	G2	G3	G4	G5	G6	G7	G8	G9	G10	G11	G12	ENABLE	R/W̄	PC	MAR	MBR	A	IR
1	1	0	0	0	0	0	0	0	0	0	0	0	0	X	0	1	0	0	0
2	0	1	0	0	0	0	0	0	0	0	0	0	0	X	1	0	0	0	0
3	0	0	0	0	0	1	0	0	0	0	1	0	1	1	0	0	1	0	0
4	0	0	0	0	0	0	1	0	0	0	0	0	0	X	0	0	0	0	1
5	0	0	1	0	0	0	0	0	0	0	0	0	1	1	0	1	0	0	0
6	0	0	0	0	0	1	0	0	0	1	1	0	0	X	0	0	1	0	0
7	0	0	0	1	0	0	1	0	0	0	0	0	0	X	0	0	0	0	0
8	0	0	0	0	0	0	0	0	0	0	0	1	0	X	0	0	0	1	0

Note MS = Immediate Access Memory = Main Store. When the MS is enabled (i.e. enable = 1), a memory read or write cycle may take place. The R/W̄ (i.e. read/write) signal determines the nature of the memory access when enable = 1. When R/W̄ = 0 the cycle is a write cycle, and when R/W̄ = 1 the cycle is a read cycle. The R/W̄ signal is undefined whenever enable = 0. An X indicates a don't care value.

The eight steps in Table 4.10 represent a microprogram which interprets fetch cycle followed by an **ADD** instruction.

The next step in understanding the operation of the control unit is to s how the microprogram is generated. The microprogram is generated by mechanism similar to the computer itself (wheels within wheels?). F example, instead of a program counter we have a microprogram counter.

The basic structure of a microprogrammed control unit is given in Fig. 4

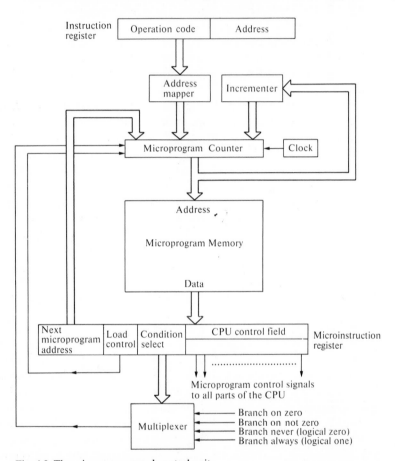

Fig. 4.8 The microprogrammed control unit

Imagine that after power has first been applied to the computer, the conter of the microprogram counter (and the macroprogram counter) are set zero. The microprogram address is applied to the input terminals of microprogram memory. The output of this memory is fed to the micro struction register. Most of the bits in this register control the flow information within the CPU as we have already described.

Three fields of the microinstruction register hold information affecting t operation of the control unit itself. The microprogram counter normally steps through a microprogram sequentially. By loading the contents of the 'next microprogram address' field into the microprogram counter, a jump can be executed to any point in the microprogram memory.

The 'load control' field tells the microprogram counter whether to take its next address from the incrementer, or to get its address from the address mapper (see below), or to use the address in the microinstruction register.

The 'condition select' field implements conditional jumps. If the output of the multiplexer is true, a jump is made to the location of the next microprogram address, otherwise the microprogram continues sequentially. The first two conditions are obtained from the PSW in the CPU. The second two conditions are 'branch never' (continue) and 'branch always' (unconditional jump).

A conditional branch at the macroinstruction level (e.g. BEQ) is interpreted by microinstructions in the following way. The condition select field of the microinstruction selects the appropriate status bit of the PSR to be tested. For example, if the macrolevel instruction is BEQ, the Z bit is selected. The load control field contains the operation 'branch to the address in the microprogram register on selected condition true'. Thus, if the condition is true (i.e. $Z=1$), a jump is made to a point in the microprogram which implements the corresponding jump in the macroprogram. If the selected condition is false (i.e. $Z=0$), the current sequence of microinstructions is terminated by the start of a new fetch–execute cycle.

The first phase of each microprogram executed by the control unit corresponds to a fetch cycle. This ends with the op-code being deposited in the instruction register. The op-code is fed to the address mapper, which is a look-up table containing the starting address of each microprogram for all the possible op-codes executed by the CPU.

The final microinstruction of the fetch cycle causes the microprogram counter to be loaded with the starting address of the microprogram corresponding to the op-code in the instruction register. After this microprogram has been executed, an unconditional jump is made to the start of the microprogram corresponding to the fetch cycle, and the process continues.

The above description of the microprogrammed control unit is, of course, grossly simplified. In practice the microprogram normally includes facilities for dealing with interrupts, the main memory (IAS), and input/output. One of the great advantages of a microprogrammed control unit is that it is possible to alter the content of the microprogram memory (sometimes called the control store) and hence 'roll-your-own machine-level instructions'.

In fact it is perfectly possible to choose a set of microprograms which will execute the machine code of an entirely different computer. In this case the computer is said to emulate another computer. Such a facility is useful if you are changing your old computer to a new one whose own machine code is incompatible with your old programs. This applies to programs which exist in binary (object) form on tape or disk. By writing microprograms (on the new machine) to interpret the machine code of the old machine it is possible to use the old software and still get the advantages of the new machine.

4.2.2 Random logic control units

The type of control unit featured in Section 4.2.1 performs the interpretation of a machine-code instruction by means of a microprogram stored in a read only memory. The complexity of a microprogrammed control unit is no directly related to the complexity of the machine-code instructions interprets, just as the complexity of a computer at the machine-code level not related to the complexity of the high-level language programs being run on it.

When an engineer designs a random logic control unit, he asks 'What sequence of micro-operations is needed to execute each machine-code instruction, and what logic elements do I need to implement them?' In other words, the designer resorts to the Boolean techniques we have already come across in Chapter 2. The word 'random' implies that the arrangement of gates from which the control unit is constructed varies widely from computer to computer. The same microprogrammed control unit can readily be adapted to a host of very different computers with little modification, but the random logic control unit is very much a one-off affair.

Before designing a random logic control unit, let's consider an ultrasimple computer. It is possible to use the CPU structures described earlier in the section. However, by adopting another design I hope to show the reader that the architecture of the CPU is chosen by an engineer and is not some rigid fixed structure. When designing any computer, the engineer has to weigh up the trade-offs between computational power, speed, and cost.

Figure 4.9 presents the structure of a primitive CPU. It is primitive because the number of buses and functional units have been reduced to the bare minimum. This makes the design cheap to produce but reduces its speed. As there is only one bus (the system bus), several micro-operations cannot be performed simultaneously. For example, there is no separate incrementer for the program counter, forcing the ALU to be used to increment the content of the PC. Consequently, the ALU and associated data paths are not available for other operations while the program counter is being incremented.

In Fig. 4.9 a single bus is connected to all registers, the main store, and the ALU, permitting the transfer of only one data word at a time from a source to a destination. This arrangement is almost identical to that of Fig. 2.67.

The main store (MS) gets the address of a memory location to be accessed directly from the MAR, whose output is permanently connected to the address input of the MS. This fixed connection exists because the main store never receives an address input from any source other than the memory address register. A permanent connection is a good thing because it removes the need for bus control circuits.

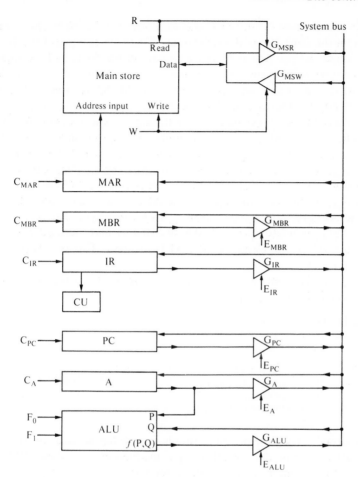

Fig. 4.9 The structure of a primitive CPU

The bidirectional data bus from the main store is connected to the system bus by gates G_{MSR} and G_{MSW}. During a memory write cycle (W true), data is transferred from the system bus to the memory via gate G_{MSW}. In a read cycle (R true) data is transferred from the memory to the system bus via gate G_{MSR}.

The MBR, accumulator, program counter, and instruction register are each arranged in exactly the same way. When one of these registers wishes to place data on the system bus, the appropriate three-state gate is enabled, and when one wishes to receive data from the bus, it is clocked. Note that the instruction register (IR) can receive data from the main store directly, without the data having to pass through the MBR as indicated earlier in this chapter.

The ALU receives data from two sources, the system bus and the accumulator, and places its own output on the system bus. This arrangement raises the question: 'If the ALU gets data from the system bus how can it put data on the same bus at the same time?' There are two possible solutions to this dilemma. The first is to put a register in the ALU to hold input data constant while the system bus is connected to the output of the ALU. That is, the ALU is provided with its own personal 'MBR'. Another solution relies on an effect hitherto considered harmful. This is the propagation delay experienced by digital signals passing through a logic network. When data is presented to the ALU's inputs, it ripples through the gates of the ALU to appear at its output terminals after a delay of the order of 50 ns. Suppose that the contents of the MBR are fed to the ALU by enabling gate G_{MBR}, and that sufficient time has elapsed for the output of the ALU to settle. If now gate G_{MBR} is disabled, the input to the ALU is no longer valid. The output of the ALU cannot change instantly. Consequently, if gate G_A is enabled and the accumulator clocked, the system bus may be used for the data transfer before the output of the ALU changes. This is a sort of digital juggling trick.

The ALU is controlled by a two-bit code, F0,F1, which determines its function as shown in Table 4.11.

Table 4.11 Decoding F0,F1

F1	F0	Function
0	0	add P to Q
0	1	subtract Q from P
1	0	increment Q
1	1	decrement Q

In order to keep the design as simple as possible, we will construct a 3-bit operation-code giving a total of eight instructions; see Table 4.12. In this table M is a memory location within the IAS.

Table 4.12 A primitive instruction set for Fig. 4.9

Op-code	Mnemonic	Operation
000	LDA M	$[A] \leftarrow [M]$
001	STA M	$[M] \leftarrow [A]$
010	ADD M	$[A] \leftarrow [A] + [M]$
011	SUB M	$[A] \leftarrow [A] - [M]$
100	INC M	$[M] \leftarrow [M] + 1$
101	DEC M	$[M] \leftarrow [M] - 1$
110	JMP M	$[PC] \leftarrow M$
111	BEQ M	IF $Z = 1$ THEN $[PC] \leftarrow M$

This is a very primitive instruction set indeed, but it does include many of the types of instruction found in real processors. Having constructed an instruction set, the next step is to define each of the instructions in terms of RTL, and the operations necessary to carry them out on the computer in Fig.

4.9. In Table 4.13 all clock signals are denoted by $C_{register}$, and all bus signals by $E_{source\ of\ data}$. The symbol Z is the 'zero-flag' bit from the PSR which is assumed to be part of the ALU. The first 'operation' to be considered is the instruction: 'fetch'.

Table 4.13 Defining the instruction set of Table 4.12

Instruction	Op-code	Operations (RTL)	Control actions	
Fetch	—	[MAR]←[PC] [IR]←[MS[MAR]] ALU←[PC] [PC]←ALU	$E_{PC}=1$, $R=1$, $E_{PC}=1$, $E_{ALU}=1$,	C_{MAR} C_{IR} F1, F0 = 1, 0 C_{PC}
LDA	000	[MAR]←[IR] [A]←[MS[MAR]]	$E_{IR}=1$, $R=1$,	C_{MAR} C_A
STA	001	[MAR]←[IR] [MS[MAR]]←[A]	$E_{IR}=1$, $E_A=1$,	C_{MAR} W = 1
ADD	010	[MAR]←[IR] [MBR]←[MS[MAR]] ALU←[MBR] [A]←ALU	$E_{IR}=1$, $R=1$, $E_{MBR}=1$, $E_{ALU}=1$,	C_{MAR} C_{MBR} F1, F0 = 0, 0 C_A
SUB	011	[MAR]←[IR] [MBR]←[MS[MAR]] ALU←[MBR] [A]←ALU	$E_{IR}=1$, $R=1$, $E_{MBR}=1$, $E_{ALU}=1$,	C_{MAR} C_{MBR} F1, F0 = 0, 1 C_A
INC	100	[MAR]←[IR] [MBR]←[MS[MAR]] [ALU]←[MBR] [MBR]←ALU [MS[MAR]]←[MBR]	$E_{IR}=1$, $R=1$, $E_{MBR}=1$, $E_{ALU}=1$, $E_{MBR}=1$,	C_{MAR} C_{MBR} F1, F0 = 1, 0 C_{MBR} W = 1
DEC	101	[MAR]←[IR] [MBR]←[MS[MAR]] ALU←[MBR] [MBR]←ALU [MS[MAR]]←[MBR]	$E_{IR}=1$, $R=1$, $E_{MBR}=1$, $E_{ALU}=1$, $E_{MBR}=1$,	C_{MAR} C_{MBR} F1, F0 = 1, 1 C_{MBR} W = 1
JMP	110	[PC]←[IR]	$E_{IR}=1$,	C_{PC}
BEQ	111	IF Z = 1 THEN [PC]←[IR]	IF Z = 1 THEN $E_{IR}=1$, C_{PC}	

From op-code to operation

In order to execute an instruction we have to do two things: convert the three-bit op-code into one of eight possible sequences of action, and cause these actions to take place.

Figure 4.10 shows how the instructions are decoded, and is similar in operation to the three-line-to-eight-line decoder. Figure 4.11 gives the logic diagram of a sequencer. A three-bit binary up-counter, composed of three JK flip-flops, has its outputs connected to eight three-input AND gates to generate eight timing signals T_0 to T_7.

Figure 4.12 illustrates the timing pulses created by this circuit. Note that the timing decoder is similar to the instruction decoder of Fig. 4.10.

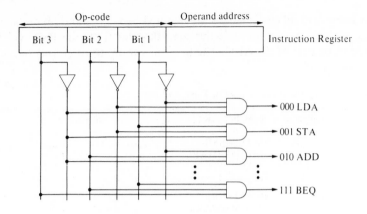

Fig. 4.10 The instruction decoder

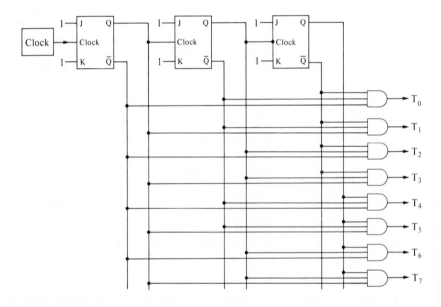

Fig. 4.11 The timing pulse generator

The next step in designing the control unit is to combine the signals from the instruction decoder with the timing signals to generate the actual micro operations. Figure 4.13 shows one possible approach.

For each of the eight machine-level instructions (plus fetch) one of the vertical lines is in a logical one state, enabling the AND gates to which it connected. As the timing signals, T0 to T7, are generated, the outputs of the

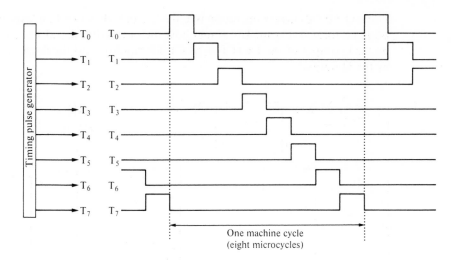

Fig. 4.12 The outputs of the timing pulse generator

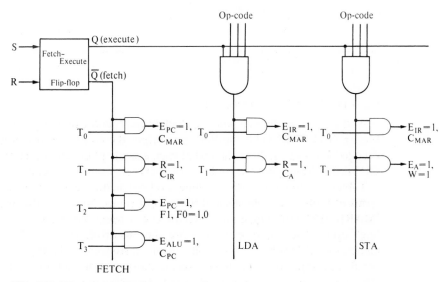

Fig. 4.13 The random logic control unit

AND gates enabled by the current instruction synthesize the control signals of the CPU. The output of each AND gate corresponding to a particular micro-operation (e.g. E_{MAR}) is connected to an OR gate whose output is the actual micro-operation.

As the control unit is always in one of two states (fetch or execute), an RS flip-flop provides a convenient way of switching from one state to another.

When Q=0 the current operation is a 'fetch', and when Q=1 an 'execute' is being performed. Figure 4.14 shows how the instruction decoder is enabled by the Q output of the $\overline{\text{FETCH}}$/EXECUTE flip-flop, and the fetch decoder by the $\overline{\text{Q}}$ output.

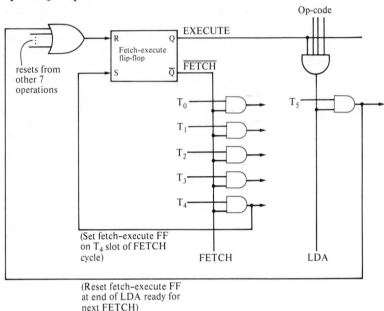

Fig. 4.14 The $\overline{\text{fetch}}$/execute flip-flop

At the end of each fetch phase, a clock pulse from the timing generator sets the $\overline{\text{FETCH}}$/EXECUTE flip-flop, permitting the current instruction to be decoded and executed. At the end of each execute phase, the $\overline{\text{FETCH}}$/EXECUTE flip-flop is cleared, enabling the next fetch phase to begin.

Table 4.14 shows how the machine-level instructions can be represented in terms of both timing signals and micro-operations. Note that the operation [MAR]←[IR] with which most execute cycles begin has been placed in the fetch cycle. The micro-operations are the bus-driver enables, the register clocks, the ALU function select bits, the main store controls (R and W), and the R and S inputs of the fetch–execute flip-flop. For each of the microinstructions we can write down a Boolean expression in terms of the machine-level instruction and the sequence of timing pulses. For example, consider expressions for E_{MBR}, E_{IR}, C_{MAR}.

$$E_{MBR} = ADD.T6 + SUB.T6 + INC.T6 + INC.T8 + DEC.T6 + DEC.T8$$

$$E_{IR} \;\; = Fetch.T4 + \;\; JMP.T5 + BEQ.T5$$

$$C_{MAR} = Fetch.T0 + Fetch.T4$$

Table 4.14 could also be used to implement a microprogrammed control

Table 4.14 The interpretation of machine-code instructions

Instruction	Time	Enables					Clocks						ALU		MS		F/E	FF
		MBR	IR	PC	A	ALU	MAR	MBR	IR	PC	A	ALU	F1	F0	R	W	R̄	S
Fetch	T0	0	0	1	0	0	1	0	0	0	0	0	X	X	0	0	0	0
	T1	0	0	0	0	0	0	1	0	0	0	0	X	X	1	0	0	0
	T2	0	0	1	0	1	0	0	0	1	0	0	1	0	0	0	0	0
	T3	1	0	0	0	0	0	0	1	0	0	0	X	X	0	0	0	0
	T4	0	1	0	0	0	1	0	0	0	0	0	X	X	0	0	0	1
LDA	T5	1	0	0	0	0	0	0	0	0	1	0	X	X	1	0	1	0
STA	T5	0	0	0	1	0	0	0	0	0	0	0	X	X	0	1	1	0
ADD	T5	0	0	0	0	0	0	1	0	0	0	0	X	X	1	0	0	0
	T6	1	0	0	0	0	0	0	0	0	0	0	0	0	0	0	0	0
	T7	0	0	0	0	1	0	0	0	0	1	1	X	X	0	0	1	0
SUB	T5	0	0	0	0	0	0	1	0	0	0	0	X	X	1	0	0	0
	T6	1	0	0	0	0	0	0	0	0	0	0	0	1	0	0	0	0
	T7	0	0	0	0	1	0	0	0	0	1	1	X	X	0	0	1	0
INC	T5	0	0	0	0	0	0	1	0	0	0	0	X	X	1	0	0	0
	T6	1	0	0	0	0	0	0	0	0	0	0	1	0	0	0	0	0
	T7	0	0	0	0	1	0	0	0	0	0	1	X	X	0	0	0	0
	T8	1	0	0	0	0	0	0	0	0	0	0	X	X	0	1	1	0
DEC	T5	0	0	0	0	0	0	1	0	0	0	0	X	X	1	0	0	0
	T6	1	0	0	0	0	0	0	0	0	0	0	1	1	0	0	0	0
	T7	0	0	0	0	1	0	0	0	0	0	1	X	X	0	0	0	0
	T8	1	0	0	0	0	0	0	0	0	0	0	X	X	0	1	1	0
JMP	T5	0	1	0	0	0	0	0	0	1	0	0	X	X	0	0	1	0
BEQ	T5	0	1	0	0	0	0	0	0	Z	0	0	X	X	0	0	1	0

Note. Z = zero flag from PSW

Note also that INC and DEC require nine time slots. To execute these op-codes requires a modification to the timing generator of Fig. 4.1.

unit, in which case the lines of the table represent consecutive words in the control store.

Random logic versus microprogramming

The two approaches to the design of a control unit we have covered are radically different, and any designer has to choose between them. We cannot go into the details of control unit design here, and will therefore point out the most significant features of microprogrammed and random logic control units.

1. Random logic control units are faster than their microprogrammed counterparts. This must always be so because the random logic control unit is optimized for its particular application. Moreover, a microprogrammed control unit is slowed by the need to read a microinstruction from the microprogram memory. Memory accesses are generally slower than basic Boolean operations.

2. Microprogramming offers a flexible design. As the microprogram lives in (read only) memory, it can easily be modified at either the design or the production stage. A random logic control unit is strictly one-off and cannot readily be modified to incorporate new features in the processor (e.g. additional machine-level instructions), and sometimes it is difficult to remove design errors without considerable modification of the hardware.

4.3 The 6502 microprocessor

In the early days of the eight-bit microprocessor there were two very popular devices, the Intel 8080 and the Motorola 6800. Some engineers left Intel to produce an improved vesion of the 8080, called the Z80, and some engineers left Motorola to produce the 6500 series of microprocessors. Any of the above microprocessors could be used as a vehicle to teach computer architecture. The 6502 has been selected here simply because it is relatively easy to understand and is widely used in the low-cost personal computers.

One of the most important differences between microprocessors (micro-processor = a CPU on a chip) and other computers, is that the designers of the microprocessor are subject to two limitations. Firstly, the number of gates that can be put on a single chip is limited by the available technology. Secondly, the number of external connections to the chip is limited to about 40, although chips are now appearing with 48 and 64 pins. While there are some 16-bit microprocessors with very sophisticated architectures, the eight-bit chip lacks complications and frills, making it an ideal introduction to computer architecture.

The simplified internal structure of the 6502 is given in Fig. 4.15. A microprocessor, or any other computer, can be viewed in three different ways. The designer sees the internal architecture; he has created the device

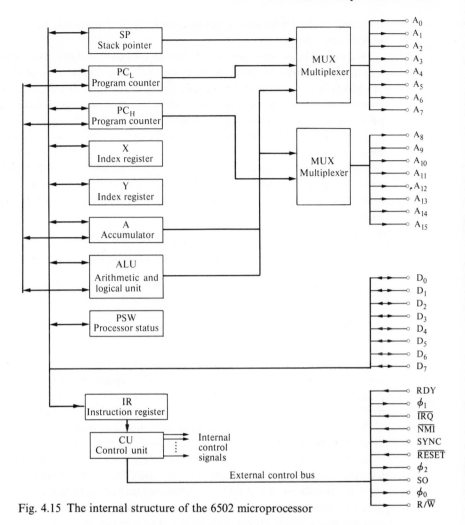

Fig. 4.15 The internal structure of the 6502 microprocessor

and so must have an intimate knowledge of all its aspects, particularly the control unit. The engineer who interfaces the CPU to a system is interested in its electrical properties. He wishes to know about the voltages and currents at each of the pins, the timing requirements and protocols observed by the various signals entering or leaving the chip. The programmer is not interested in such fine detail. He needs a programming model of the machine. That is, he needs to know the instruction set, and the arrangement of the internal registers. The diagram of the 6502 given here is the programmer's model.

In our previous discussion of the CPU we did not look at the length of the data-words. A real computer has a particular data word-length, which is normally the same size as the words stored in the memory locations of the main store. Although the bit is the smallest unit of data stored in a computer, the word is the basic unit of information taking part in all arithmetic and logical operations.

Of course, the programmer would like an effectively infinite word-length to free him from worries about precision in arithmetic operations, or the range of objects he can address with a single word. Unfortunately, the cost of main memory is often the largest component of a computer system, so the programmer's wishes are not fulfilled.

The actual word-length associated with any computer is a compromise between many factors and represents the designer's attempt to satisfy a sector of the computer market. At first sight it might be thought that the minimum word size of a computer must be equal to the number of bits in the op-code field plus the number of bits in the address field of an instruction register. That is,

$$\text{minimum word-length} = \log_2(\text{number of instructions})$$
$$+ \log_2(\text{number of memory locations}).$$

For example, if there are 256 instructions and the largest program to be run is 65 536 locations, then the minimum word-length would be:

$$\log_2(256) + \log_2(65\ 536) = 8 + 16 = 24.$$

Fortunately, at least for the designers of microprocessors, the minimum word-length suggested by the above equation is not necessary. There are two ways of reducing the minimum word-length required by a particular computer. The number of address bits may be reduced by paging. The available memory space is split into a number of units called pages, so that a 65 536 (2^{16}) address memory space is divided into, say, 256 pages of 256 locations. Whenever the computer specifies an address, it needs eight bits to select a location within a page and eight bits to select a particular page. As long as locations within a given page are selected, the CPU is effectively dealing with eight-bit addresses. It should be obvious that this arrangement becomes both complex and time-wasting whenever it is necessary to hop from one page to another many times during the execution of a program.

A second way of reducing the minimum word-length is to store the op-code and address fields of an instruction separately. This approach has been adopted by virtually all eight-bit microprocessors. An eight-bit word-length allows up to 256 different instructions, sufficient for all but the most demanding of applications. During the fetch cycle the operation code is read from the memory and examined. If an address is required by the instruction, two further read operations are carried out, and a 16-bit address formed from two eight-bit words. Consequently we have a 24-bit word-length implemented as three consecutive eight-bit words.

This arrangement has two advantages. Firstly, by using an eight-bit word-length the cost of the system can be greatly reduced, because an eight-bit data highway costs much less than a 24-bit data highway. Furthermore, the number of pins (external connections) of a microprocessor is currently limited to 64, which means that microprocessors cannot have very large word-lengths. Secondly, not all instructions need be a full 24 bits long, so that an eight- or sixteen-bit instruction does not waste valuable memory space. Some instructions, such as LDA, require the address of an operand, while other instructions, such as CLC (clear carry) or INX (increment X register), do not need an address field. These instructions are said to have an inherent addressing mode, as the address of the operand is implicit in the instruction.

The example in Fig. 4.16 should make the above points clearer. The 24-bit computer is forced to use a 24-bit word, even when such a long word is unnecessary, while the 8-bit machine uses 1, 2, or 3 consecutive locations to hold a single instruction. Note that this scheme has a built-in disadvantage—reading three eight-bit words from memory takes longer than reading a single 24-bit word. Earlier, when describing the structure of the CPU it was stated that the contents of the program counter were incremented during an op-code fetch. If a variable-length instruction is used, the first byte of the instruction is examined during the instruction fetch phase, and the program counter incremented by 1, 2, or 3, accordingly.

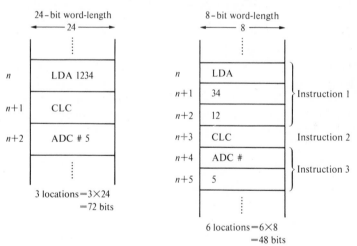

Fig. 4.16 Eight-bit versus 24-bit word-lengths

The registers of the 6502

The 6502 has seven internal (on-chip) registers which may be accessed by the programmer: the accumulator, processor status register (PSR or CCR), program counter (high), program counter (low), X index register, Y index register, and stack pointer (SP). Note that the 16-bit program counter is treated as two eight-bit registers by the internal logic of the 6502. As far as the programmer is concerned there is only one 16-bit program counter.

The 'new' registers of the 6502 are the X and Y registers, and the stack pointer. These registers are very important and are needed to implement special addressing modes. So far we have looked at what computers can do in terms of their operations on data. In the next section we look at the way in which special addressing modes allow tables of data to be speedily accessed, procedures (subroutines) implemented, and programs physically uprooted and relocated in memory without alterations being made to them.

4.3.1 An introduction to the 6502's instruction set

In this section some of the assembly language instructions found on the 6502 are described. My intention is to demonstrate a few of the things a microprocessor can do. The detailed definition of the 6502's instruction set is given in Appendix A2. The actual way in which a processor accesses data (as opposed to what it does with it) is the subject of addressing modes, and is dealt with later in this chapter.

The instruction set of the 6502 is rather primitive and lacks sophisticated operations. A sophisticated machine-level operation would be multiplication, division, floating point arithmetic, or searching a region of memory for a given data value. One of the few eight-bit microprocessors to include relatively sophisticated machine-level operations is the Z80. Of course, any complex operation can be implemented in terms of a sequence of primitive machine code operations, just as a sophisticated computer can be made up of a large number of primitive gates.

There are five classes of machine code instructions: data movement, arithmetic, logical, branch, and control. Data movement involves nothing more complex than moving one item of data from one place to another. It has been reported that 70 per cent of all assembly language instructions in a typical program perform data movement. Some typical 6502 data movement operations are given in Table 4.15.

The X register is a special-purpose register whose function will be revealed

Table 4.15 Some typical 6502 data movement operations

Assembly form	RTL	Description
LDA M	[A]←[M]	Copy the contents of memory location M into the accumulator.
STA M	[M]←[A]	Copy the contents of the accumulator into memory location M
LDX M	[X]←[M]	Copy the contents of memory location M into the X register.
STX M	[M]←[X]	Copy the contents of the X register into memory location M.
TAX	[X]←[A]	Copy the contents of the accumulator into the X register.
TXA	[A]←[M]	Copy the contents of the X register into the accumulator.
PHA		Push A onto the stack—put it in a last-in-first-out queue.
PLA		Pull A off the stack—retrieve it from the last-in-first-out queue.

later. Here, operations like TAX (Transfer Accumulator to X register) illustrate register-to-register data movements as opposed to register-to-memory data movements (or vice versa). Some computers permit memory-to-memory data movements. The operation PHA (push accumulator) puts the contents of the accumulator into a queue. This has the property that items are removed in the reverse order to which they were added to the queue. Such a queue is called a 'stack' and behaves exactly like a pile of letters in an in-tray. New letters are added to the top of the pile, and are also removed from the top of the pile. PLA removes an item of data from the stack and puts it in the accumulator. The applications of the stack are dealt with later in this chapter. Another type of data movement instruction is the 'exchange' which is absent in the 6502. An exchange instruction swaps the contents of two locations. If EXG X,A existed on the 6502 it would have the effect of carrying out [X]←[A] [A]←[X], simultaneously.

Arithmetic operations are those which act on data as if it were a numeric quantity. We have already seen that ADC M adds the contents of memory location M to the contents of the accumulator, and stores the result in the accumulator. Logic operations are those involving Boolean operations on the bits of a word. The instructions listed in Table 4.16 illustrate some of the arithmetic and logical instructions found on the 6502.

Table 4.16 Some typical 6502 arithmetic and logical operations

Assembly form	RTL	Description
ADC M	$[A]←[A]+[M]+[C]$	Add the contents of memory location M to the contents of the accumulator plus the carry bit.
SBC M	$[A]←[A]-[M]-[\bar{C}]$	Subtract the contents of memory location M from the contents of the accumulator together with complement of the carry bit.
CLC	$[C]←0$	Clear the carry bit.
SEC	$[C]←1$	Set the carry bit to 1.
INC M	$[M]←[M]+1$	Add one to the contents of memory location M.
DEC M	$[M]←[M]-1$	Subtract one from the contents of location M.
CMP M	$[A]-[M]$	Compare the contents of the accumulator with the contents of location M.
ASL A ASL M		Shift the contents of the accumulator (or M) one place left. (This corresponds to multiplying the number by 2.)
AND M	$[A]←[A]\cdot[M]$	Form the logical AND between the bits of the accumulator and the contents of M.
ORA M	$[A]←[A]+[M]$	Form the logical OR between the bits of the accumulator and the contents of M.
EOR M	$[A]←[A]⊕[M]$	Form the EXCLUSIVE OR between the bits of the accumulator and the contents of memory location M.
LSR A LSR M		Shift the contents of A or M one place right.

Note that some of the instructions in Table 4.16 act either on the content of a memory location or on the contents of the accumulator. For example LSR M performs a logical shift right on the contents of memory location M while LSR A performs a logical shift right on the contents of the accumulator. Some of the 6502's instructions can be used only on the contents of a memory location. For example, the INC (increment) and DEC (decrement) instructions cannot be applied to the accumulator. This is one of the minor irritations of the 6502. It is possible to create a pseudo (INC A) by the following instructions.

SEC   set carry bit to 1 ([C]←1)
ADC #0   add zero to accumulator plus carry ([A]←[A]+0+[C])

Branch or jump instructions affect the order in which instructions are executed. The 6502 has a jump instruction, JMP M, which causes the processor to execute the instruction at memory location M next. We have already seen that the 6502 has a number of conditional branches which cause the processor to take the branch if the condition is true, and to execute the next instruction in sequence if the condition is false.

The control group of instructions perform special functions (particularly in relation to interrupts and subroutines), and will not be dealt with here.

Applications of some of the 6502's instructions

In order to illustrate the effect of some of the 6502's instructions on actual data, sequences of instructions together with sample data are given in Table 4.17a,b. Three data locations, whose symbolic names are NUM1, NUM2 and NUM3, provide sources and destinations for data taking part in the operations. Some operations are dyadic, operating on NUM1 and NUM2 to produce NUM3, while others are monadic, operating on NUM1 to produce NUM2. Although the actions of all the instructions below are self-evident, Appendix A2 provides the full definition of all the 6502's instructions.

In each of the eight examples the sequence of instructions is provided above a memory map of the data acted on by them. Note that the memory maps are those existing after the instructions have been executed.

Table 4.17(a) Examples of the effects of instructions

1 Addition	2 Subtraction	3 Logical AND	4 Logical OR
LDA NUM1	LDA NUM1	LDA NUM1	LDA NUM1
CLC	SEC	AND NUM2	ORA NUM2
ADC NUM2	SBC NUM2	STA NUM3	STA NUM3
STA NUM3	STA NUM3		

NUM1	01010101	NUM1	01010101	NUM1	01010101	NUM1	01010101
NUM2	00010111	NUM2	00010111	NUM2	00010111	NUM2	00010111
NUM3	01101100	NUM3	00111110	NUM3	00010101	NUM3	01010111

Table 4.17(b) Examples of the effects of instructions

5 Logical EOR	6 Shift left	7 Shift right	8 Rotate left
LDA NUM1	LDA NUM1	LDA NUM1	LDA NUM1
EOR NUM2	ASL A	LSR A	ROL A
STA NUM3	STA NUM2	STA NUM2	STA NUM2

NUM1	01010101	NUM1	01010101	NUM1	01010101	NUM1	01010101
NUM2	00010111	NUM2	10101010	NUM2	00101010	NUM2	1010101C
NUM3	01000010						

In example 8 the 'C' in NUM2 represents the carry bit of the PSW shifted into the LSB position of NUM2.

The 6502, like many other processors, permits certain operations to act on either the contents of the accumulator, or the contents of a memory location. In examples 6 to 8 in Table 4.17, the shifting operations act on the accumulator so that the reader can see the 'before' and 'after' effect, with NUM1 being the data before the operations, and NUM2 the data after them. In many practical programs the shift operations would be applied directly to memory locations—e.g. ASL NUM1.

It is immediately obvious how arithmetic operations may be applied to real applications, as everyone is familiar with numerical calculations in everyday life. The application of logical operations is less obvious. In Chapter 3 we saw how a group of bits can represent the status of devices connected to the computer. The examples provided were pumps, heaters, and valves which were turned on or off by the value of a particular bit in a control word. It is in the manipulation of individual bits within a word that logical operations are needed.

Consider the control of a system having eight single-bit inputs (P,Q,R,S,T,U,V,W), and eight single-bit outputs, (A,B,C,D,E,F,G,H). We are not interested in the details of input/output techniques here, and will assume that the reading of a memory location whose address is 'INPUT' will load the values of P to W into the accumulator. Similarly, writing the contents of the accumulator to memory location 'OUTPUT' has the effect of setting up the eight output bits A to H. The format of the input and output control words is given below.

Input   PQRSTUVW

Output   ABCDEFGH

Suppose that the following control operations must be performed.

IF((P = 1)AND(Q = 0)) OR ((P = 0)AND(S = 1))
THEN
  BEGIN
  C: = 1; E: = 0
  END
ELSE
  BEGIN
  C: = 0; E: = 1
  END;

The above action involves the testing of three bits of INPUT (P, Q, and S), and then setting or clearing two bits of OUTPUT (C and E). An important consideration is that the bits of OUTPUT not involved in the algorithm must not be affected in any way by operations on bits C and E. The sequence of operations listed in Table 4.18 will execute the desired action.

Table 4.18 Using logical operations

	LDA	INPUT	get input status
	AND	# %11000000	mask out all bits but P and Q
	CMP	# %10000000	test for P = 1, Q = 0
	BEQ	TRUE	goto action on test true
	LDA	INPUT	get input status again
	AND	# %10010000	mask out all bits but P and S
	CMP	# %00010000	test for P = 0, S = 1
	BEQ	TRUE	goto action on test true
FALSE	LDA	OUTPUT	get output control word
	AND	# %11011111	clear bit C
	ORA	# %00001000	set bit E
	STA	OUTPUT	set up new output control word
	JMP	EXIT	branch past actions on test true
TRUE	LDA	OUTPUT	get output control word
	AND	# %11110111	clear bit E
	ORA	# %00100000	set bit C
	STA	OUTPUT	set up new output control word
EXIT			continue

The assembly language symbol '%' means that the following number is to be interpreted by the assembler as a binary value. Once more the advantage of programming in binary (in certain circumstances) is self-evident as AND # %11000000 tells the reader much more than the hexadecimal form of the operand: AND #$C0.

The assembly language symbol '#' (pronounced 'hash') tells the assembler that the following value is not the address of a memory location containing the operand, but the actual operand itself. Thus, AND # %11000000 means form the logical AND between the contents of the accumulator and the binary value 11000000. The result is put into the accumulator. The use of the # is called immediate addressing and will be dealt with in more detail later in this chapter.

The operation 'CMP' causes a comparison to be made, and sets the bits of the PSR accordingly. The effect of CMP # %00010000 is to compare the contents of the accumulator with the binary value 0001000. This is done by subtraction (i.e. [A] − 00010000). The result of the subtraction is discarded, leaving the contents of the accumulator unaffected by the operation. Only the bits of the PSR are modified. If the accumulator contains 00010000, the subtraction yields zero, setting the Z (zero) flag of the PSR, and the following operation 'BEQ TRUE' results in a branch to the instruction whose address is labelled 'TRUE'.

The label FALSE is a dummy label, and is not in any way used by the assembly program. It merely serves as a reminder to the programmer of the action to be taken as a result of the test being false. At the end of this sequence is an instruction 'JMP EXIT'. This is equivalent to a 'GOTO' and causes a branch round the action taken if the result of the test were true.

4.4 Addressing modes

The subject of addressing modes is concerned with how the address of an operand is calculated by the CPU. Up to this point we have dealt exclusively with the absolute addressing mode. An absolute address is the actual address of the operand. Thus, LDA 1234 means 'load the accumulator with the contents of memory location 1234'. Some computer manufacturers call this direct addressing.

An eight-bit microprocessor with a 16-bit address bus requires two consecutive memory locations to store an address. To reduce the size of programs some manufacturers have introduced a form of addressing called zero-page addressing. An absolute address of 16 bits is written as XXYY, where the X and Ys represent 4-bit hexadecimal characters. The value of XX lies in the range 00, 01, 02, . . . FE, FF. The first value, 00, is called the zero-page. Suppose a special addressing mode is introduced which assumes that the operand lies in page zero. It follows that it is possible to specify an address only by its location within that page.

For example, LDA 0027 (absolute addressing) may be written LDA 27 (zero-page addressing). This reduces the size of the instruction from three bytes to two, a saving of one byte.

Figure 4.17 shows how both the 6502 and 6800 microprocessors use zero-page addressing to save memory space (a 3 byte instruction becomes a 2 byte

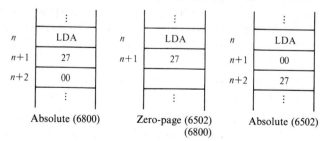

Fig. 4.17 An example of zero-page addressing

instruction). As a consequence of this, programmers tend to dedicate page zero in the 6502 and 6800 to data storage. Note that the 6502 and 6800 store two-byte absolute addresses in different orders. The 6800 stores the high order 8 bits of an address first (the way people write numbers), while the 6502 stores the low order 8 bits first. The 6502 is more efficient than the 6800, and I leave it to the reader to work out why this should be so!

An obvious question should now occur to the reader. How does the CPU know when the zero-page addressing mode is being used? The answer is that there must be two different codes for the instruction LDA; one code indicating absolute addressing and the other zero-page addressing.

Examples

6502 CPU	6800 CPU
LDA absolute = AD	LDA absolute = B6
LDA zero-page = A5	LDA zero-page = 96

The programmer does not usually have to worry about selecting the absolute/zero-page addressing mode. Often the assembler program automatically selects the addressing mode. Thus, LDA 13AE forces the absolute addressing mode, while LDA 67 results in the zero-page addressing mode. Of course, it is possible to use the absolute addressing mode with this address, which would then be stored as 00 and 67.

One of the more recent 8-bit microprocessors, the Motorola 6809, has an interesting approach to zero-page addressing. It has a special page-register which holds the number of the current page. When zero-page addressing is used, the page-address is appended to the operand of the instruction. In this way the memory-saving advantage of the zero-page addressing mode is obtained while allowing the 'zero-page' to be any one of the 256 possible pages. Section 4.5.1 gives further details on the 6809's addressing modes.

4.4.1 Immediate addressing

This mode of addressing (sometimes called literal addressing) is provided on the majority of computers and microprocessors, and allows the programmer to specify a constant. That is, the value following the instruction is not a reference to the address of an operand but the actual operand itself. In some assembly languages the symbol '#' precedes the operand to indicate immediate addressing. Some assemblers use @ for this purpose. Assemblers often differ in the conventions they conform to. The two instructions below show how absolute and immediate addressing modes are represented, respectively.

LDA 1234	means [A]←[1234]	absolute addressing
LDA #24	means [A]←24	immediate addressing

Note 1. In a microprocessor with an 8-bit data word, the immediate addressing mode uses a 2-byte instruction format as an 8-bit accumulator can be loaded only with an 8-bit constant.

Note 2. Remember that symbol # is not part of the instruction. It is a message to the assembler telling it to select that code for 'load accumulator' which uses the immediate addressing mode. In the case of the 6502 this is A9. Do not confuse the symbol # with the symbols $ or %. The $ indicates only that the following number is hexadecimal. The % indicates that the following number is binary. These two symbols are used because most computers cannot deal with subscripts, and the conventional way of labelling the base by a subscript is impractical. For example, LDA #25, LDA #$19, and LDA #%00011001 have identical effects.

Examples of the use of immediate addressing

Immediate addressing is used whenever the value of the operand taking part in an instruction is known at the time the program is written. That is, it is used to handle constants as opposed to variables. It has the advantage that it is faster than absolute addressing because only one memory reference is required by the instruction. When the operation LDA #5 is read from memory in a fetch cycle, the operand, 5, is available immediately without a further memory access to location 5 to read the actual operand. Some of the applications of immediate addressing are given below.

1. As an arithmetic constant.

```
LDA NUM
CLC
ADC  #22
STA   NUM
```

This sequence results in the data in memory location NUM being increased by 22. That is, $[NUM] \leftarrow [NUM] + 22$.

2. In comparisons with a constant. Consider the test on a variable, NUM, to determine whether it lies in the range $7 < NUM < 25$ (Table 4.19).

Table 4.19 Example of immediate addressing

	LDA	NUM	
	CMP	#8	compare it with 8
	BMI	FALSE	if negative NUM $\leqslant$ 7
	CMP	#25	compare it with 25
	BPL	FALSE	if positive NUM $>$ 24
TRUE	...		
FALSE	...		

3. As a method of terminating loop structures. A typical loop structure is illustrated in both BASIC and Pascal in Table 4.20.

The construct in Table 4.20 may readily be translated into 6502 assembly language. The loop counter is stored in memory location 'I' (Table 4.21).

At the end of the loop the counter is incremented in memory by the

Table 4.20 The loop construct

BASIC	Pascal
10 FOR I = 1 TO N	FOR I := 1 TO N DO
.	BEGIN
.	.
.	.
50 NEXT I	.
	END;

Table 4.21 Implementing the loop in assembly language

	LDA	#1	load accumulator with initial value of I
	STA ·	I	set up loop counter
NEXT	...		start of loop
			body of loop
	.	.	
	.	.	
	.	.	
	INC	I	increment counter in memory
	LDA	I	get counter in accumulator
	CMP	#N+1	end of loop test
	BNE	NEXT	if not end then repeat loop

instruction 'INC I' causing the contents of I to be read, incremented and put back in memory. In order to compare I with $N+1$ it must be retrieved from memory by LDA I. Note that the comparison is with $N+1$ because the counter is incremented before it is tested. On the last time round the loop $I = N$ becomes $N+1$ after incrementing, and the branch to NEXT is not taken, allowing the loop to be exited.

The same loop construct can be re-written with the test being made before I is incremented as in Table 4.22. The technique in this Table requires an extra instruction over the former method.

Table 4.22 An alternative form of the loop

	LDA	#1	
	STA	I	
NEXT	...		
	.		
	.		
	.		
	LDA	I	get counter
	CMP	#N	is this the last time round?
	BEQ	EXIT	if so then leave the loop
	INC	I	increment counter in memory
	JMP	NEXT	back to the grindstone
EXIT	...		

In practice these methods of implementing loops are not normally used, because the 6502 and virtually all other processors have one or more special-purpose index registers which can be employed as loop counters. We have already briefly met the X register in the discussion of data movement instructions. The X register of the 6502 is an 8-bit register which can be incremented by INX, and decremented by DEX. The loop can now be re-written in the form given in Table 4.23.

Table 4.23 Using the X register to implement a loop

	LDX	#1	preset counter to 1
NEXT	...		
	.		
	.		
	.		
	INX		increment counter
	CPX	#N+1	Nth time round the loop?
	BNE	NEXT	if not then repeat

This is a more elegant solution than using a memory location as a counter. The process can be taken one step further by counting backwards to zero and using a BNE (branch on not zero) to terminate the loop. This removes the need for an explicit compare instruction. Consider the two examples in Table 4.24.

Table 4.24 Implementing a loop by counting downwards

Pascal	*6502 assembly language*		
FOR I : = 7 DOWN TO 1 DO		LDX #7	set up counter
BEGIN	NEXT	...	
.		.	
.		.	
.		.	
END;		DEX	decrement counter
		BNE NEXT	loop until zero

4.4.2 Indexed addressing

Before defining how indexed addressing works it is worthwhile demonstrating that without it a programmer's life would be very difficult. We know how to add together several numbers. Now imagine adding together one hundred numbers stored in consecutive locations.

```
CLC
LDA NUM1
ADC NUM2
ADC NUM3
        .
        .
        .
ADC NUM99
ADC NUM100
```

Clearly, there has to be a better solution to this problem. One way out of this difficulty is to resort to a self-modifying program. I must point out that the use of self-modifying programs is extremely bad practice and is something that no programmer should ever resort to. It is even worse than using the wrong knife at a banquet.

Table 4.25 gives an example of a self-modifying code.

Table 4.25 The use of self-modifying code

	NAM	SELFMOD	
	NAM	SELFMOD	
COUNT	EQU	$00	
NUM1	EQU	$10	
NUM2	EQU	$11	
	ORG	$0080	
	LDA	#99	[A]←99
	STA	COUNT	[COUNT]←99
	CLC		[C]←0
	LDA	NUM1	[A]←[NUM1]
LOOP	ADC	NUM2	[A]←[A]+[NUM2]+[C]
	INC	LOOP+1	[LOOP+1]←[LOOP+1]+1
	DEC	COUNT	[COUNT]←[COUNT]−1
	BNE	LOOP	IF Z=0 THEN [PC]←LOOP
			(i.e. branch on nonzero to LOOP)

.
.
.

end of program to add 100 numbers

The key to this program is the two instructions 'LOOP ADC NUM2' and 'INC LOOP + 1'. The first instruction adds the contents of memory location NUM2 to the accumulator. The following instruction increments the contents of memory location 'LOOP + 1', that is, the address of the operand NUM2. In this way NUM2 gets added to NUM1 99 times, but on each occasion we have a different 'NUM2' because it has been altered by the operation INC LOOP + 1. Figure 4.18 illustrates the memory map of a system, written in 6502 machine code, which will implement the above pogram.

The program resides at memory locations $0080 to $008E, the cycle counter is located at $0000, and the 100 numbers are stored in the range $0010 to $0073. It should now be clear that the instruction INC LOOP + 1 (E6 88) causes the pointer to NUM2 (initially 11) to be incremented, so that the next number to be added is in location $0012. Note also that the instruction BNE LOOP has a branch address of 'F8'. This will be explained when we come to relative addressing.

There are several arguments against self-modifying code. Self-modifying code cannot (for obvious reasons) be placed in permanent read-only-memory (ROM). More importantly, a bug in a self-modifying program is likely to prove disastrous. If an operation-code is accidentally modified (instead of an operand) the program will almost certainly crash (i.e. run wild). Yet another

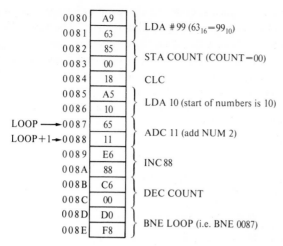

0080	A9	} LDA #99 ($63_{16}=99_{10}$)
0081	63	
0082	85	} STA COUNT (COUNT=00)
0083	00	
0084	18	CLC
0085	A5	} LDA 10 (start of numbers is 10)
0086	10	
LOOP →0087	65	} ADC 11 (add NUM 2)
LOOP+1→0088	11	
0089	E6	} INC 88
008A	88	
008B	C6	} DEC COUNT
008C	00	
008D	D0	} BNE LOOP (i.e. BNE 0087)
008E	F8	

Fig. 4.18 The memory map of a self-modifying program

argument against the use of self-modifying code is its almost total incomprehensibility to the reader. A program relying on self-modifying code is exceedingly difficult for anyone other than its author to follow, and even the author can have difficulties.

Indexed addressing provides a neat solution to the above problem. In indexed addressing the effective address (EA) of an operand is given by the sum of the contents of the index register and the offset in the instruction. The term 'offset' refers to the number following the op-code. Figure 4.19(a) illustrates how the effective address is calculated.

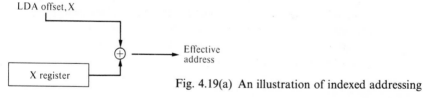

Fig. 4.19(a) An illustration of indexed addressing

Consider the instruction LDA 0025,X where the contents of the X register are 76 (Fig. 4.19(b)). The effective address of the operand is $009B. In terms of register-transfer language the operation LDA OFFSET,X is written: [A]←[OFFSET+[X]].

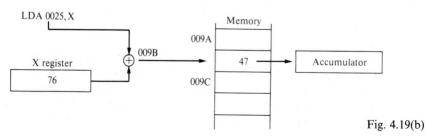

Fig. 4.19(b)

The 6800 CPU has an eight-bit offset and a 16-bit index register, while the 6502 has a 16-bit offset and an eight-bit index register. The 6502 also has a zero-page index mode with an 8-bit offset. The 6502 has two index registers, one called X, and one called Y. This feature is very useful and represents an improvement over the one index register of the 6800. The newer 6809 goes one better and has two 16-bit index registers.

The 6502 has some special instructions which operate directly on the index register. These are listed in Table 4.26.

Table 4.26 Operations which affect the 6502's index registers

CPX	compare the contents of the X register with memory
CPY	compare the contents of the Y register with memory
DEX	decrement the contents of the X register by one
DEY	decrement the contents of the Y register by one
INX	increment the contents of the X register by one
INY	increment the contents of the Y register by one
LDX	load the X index register from memory
LDY	load the Y index register from memory
STX	store the contents of the X register in memory
STY	store the contents of the Y register in memory
TAX	transfer the accumulator to the X register
TAY	transfer the accumulator to the Y register
TXA	transfer the X index register to the accumulator
TYA	transfer the Y index register to the accumulator
TSX	transfer the stack pointer to index register X
TXS	transfer the index register X to the stack pointer

All the operations in this table are symmetric in X and Y except the last two, which apply to the X register only. I regard asymmetric instruction sets as a bad thing because the programmer must remember one set of rules for one register and a different set of rules for the other.

Now that we have defined indexed addressing, let's apply it to the addition of the hundred numbers (Table 4.27).

Table 4.27 Using indexed addressing

	LDX	#0	[X]←0
	CLC		[C]←0
	LDA	NUM1	[A]←[NUM1]
LOOP	ADC	NUM2,X	[A]←[A]+[NUM2+[X]]+[C]
	INX		[X]←[X]+1
	CPX	#99	[X]−99
	BNE	LOOP	IF Z=0 THEN [PC]←LOOP

In this example we add to the contents of the accumulator the contents of the memory location given by NUM2 plus the number in the X register. Initially, [X]=0, so that NUM2 is the first operand. When the loop is repeated a second time, the number in the X register is 1, and the operand at location NUM2+1 (i.e. NUM3) is picked up.

An example of indexed addressing

One of the most common of all calculations (because it crops up in many different areas) is the evaluation of the inner product of two vectors. Suppose A and B are two n-component vectors, the inner product S, of A and B, is given by:

$$S = \sum_{i=1}^{n} a_i b_i = a_1 b_1 + a_2 b_2 + \dots a_n b_n.$$

Consider the case where the components of A and B are 8-bit integers. In what follows we will assume the existence of an operation 'MUL M', which multiplies the contents of the accumulator with the contents of memory location M, and deposits the results in the accumulator. That is, $[A] \leftarrow [A] \times [M]$; see Table 4.27. The 6502, 8080, and Z80 microprocessors do not have a multiplication instruction.

Table 4.27 Using the X register to evaluate an inner product

	NAM	INNER	Name of program
	ORG	$0000	Origin of data
S	RMB	2	Reserve two bytes for the product
VEC1	EQU	$0050	First location in Vector 1
VEC2	EQU	$0100	First location in Vector 2
N	EQU	$20	32 components ($n=32$)
	ORG	$0200	Origin of program
	LDA	#$00	$[A] \leftarrow 0$
	STA	S	$[S] \leftarrow 0$
	STA	S+1	$[S+1] \leftarrow 0$
	LDX	#$00	$[X] \leftarrow 0$
LOOP	LDA	VEC1,X	$[A] \leftarrow [[X]+VEC1]$
	MUL	VEC2,X	$[A] \leftarrow [A]*[[X]+VEC2]$
	CLC		$[C] \leftarrow 0$
	ADC	S+1	$[A] \leftarrow [A]+[S+1]+[C]$
	STA	S+1	$[S+1] \leftarrow [A]$
	LDA	S	$[A] \leftarrow [S]$
	ADC	#$00	$[A] \leftarrow [A]+0+[C]$
	STA	S	$[S] \leftarrow [A]$
	INX		$[X] \leftarrow [X]+1$
	CPX	#N	$[X]-N$
	BNE	LOOP	IF Z=0 THEN $[PC] \leftarrow$ LOOP

There are several points of interest in this program.

1. The result S is a 16-bit value stored in memory locations S and S+1. The least significant byte is in S+1.

2. The origin of the program is $0200. Prefixing a number by a '$' symbol means that the number is in hexadecimal format.

3. 'MUL VEC2,X' puts the result of $a_i b_i$ in the accumulator. The instruction ADC S+1 adds $a_i b_i$ to the current value of the inner product. This operation results in the carry bit being set to 0 or 1. By adding a literal zero to A (ADC #$00), any carry is added in to the most significant byte of S.

4. When using hexadecimal numbers I write four digits if it represents a 16-bit value, and two digits if it represents an 8-bit value. For example, I may write DATA3 EQU $01 or ADDR EQU $0001. As far as the assembler is concerned $01 and $0001 are equivalent. The difference is one of personal style. In a similar way, the instruction LDA #$00 in the above program could have been written in the form LDA #0, as a hexadecimal zero is the same as a decimal zero.

4.4.3 Relative addressing

The relative addressing mode is similar to indexed addressing in the sense that the effective address of an operand is given by the contents of a register plus an offset. As above, the offset is part of the instruction and follows the op-code. In the case of relative addressing the register used to calculate the effective address is the program counter itself. Thus, the location of the operand is specified relative to the current instruction. If we denote relative addressing by means of 'PCR', the operation load accumulator relative is written:

LDA OFFSET,PCR.

The asterisk is often used to represent the current value of the program counter, and some assemblers follow the convention LDA OFFSET,*.

Relative addressing is important because it leads to the idea of position independent code (PIC). That is, the machine-code representation of a program is independent of the actual physical location of the program in memory. This enables programs to be moved about in memory (relocated) without modifications being made to them. For example, 'STA 36,PCR' means store the contents of the accumulator 36 locations on from this instruction. It does not matter where the operation 'STA 36,PCR' lies in memory, because the data associated with it will always be stored in the 36th location following the instruction.

Unfortunately, the majority of 8-bit microprocessors do not have a relative addressing mode for data. However, both the 6502 and 6800 do have a relative addressing mode for branch instructions. The instruction 'BRA *+6' means branch (jump) to the location whose address is six more than the current position. Figure 4.20 illustrates relative addressing in terms of a memory map.

In the assembly language version we write BRA *+6, which means jump to the 6th location from the start of the current instruction (i.e. BRA). In the machine-code form, we see that the offset (i.e. *+6) is stored as 4 and not 6. This is because the program counter is automatically incremented by two after the BRA instruction is read during an instruction fetch. Consequently the stored offset is always two less than that which appears in the assembly language level program.

Both the 6502 and 6800 have a one byte offset with relative addressing. This offset is a signed two's complement number whose range of values is

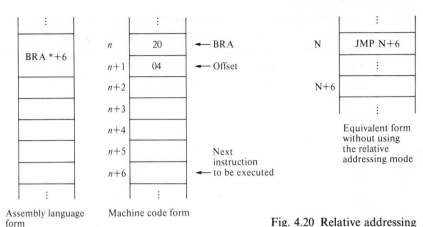

Fig. 4.20 Relative addressing

-128 to $+127$. As 'two' is automatically added to the PC at the start of an instruction, relative branching is possible within the range -126 to $+129$.

Figure 4.20 also illustrates the importance of relative branching. The program containing BRA $*+6$ can be relocated merely by moving it in memory, but the program containing JMP $N+6$ must be modified if it is relocated. It should be noted here that the 6502 (unlike the 6800) does not have an unconditional branch instruction (BRA). All relative branches in the 6502's instruction set are conditional (e.g. BCS, BCC, BEQ, BNE). The following program (Fig. 4.21) uses the instruction BNE LOOP to illustrate relative branching.

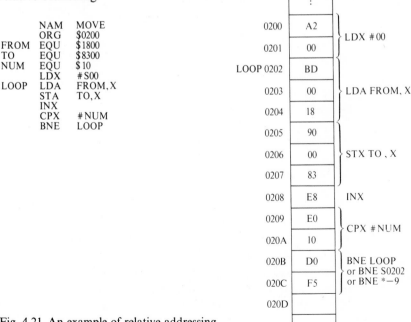

Fig. 4.21 An example of relative addressing

A block of data is to be moved from one region of memory to another. The first location of the block to be moved is 'FROM', and the first location of its destination is 'TO'. The number of words to be moved is given by 'NUM'

The programmer does not normally have to worry about the calculation of relative branch offsets—the assembler performs this process automatically. The instruction 'BNE LOOP' causes a branch, backwards, to instruction 'LDA FROM,X' in the event of the zero bit in the PSR being set. From the memory map, we see that the address of the branch operation is $020B and the address of the operation 'LDA FROM,X' is $0202. We therefore have to branch 9 locations from the start of the 'BNE', or 11 locations from the end of the 'BNE'. As the CPU always increments the PC by 2 at the start of a branch, the stored offset is −11 or −$B. In two's complement form this is $F5.

4.4.4 Indirect addressing

In absolute, or direct addressing, the location of the operand required by an instruction is provided by the address following the op-code. This address is the effective address of the operand. In indirect addressing the effective address of the operand is given by the contents of the memory location pointed at by the address following the op-code. In other words, the instruction provides the address of the address of the data. Figure 4.22 illustrates this concept with the instruction LDA [22]. Square brackets are frequently used to denote the indirect addressing mode.

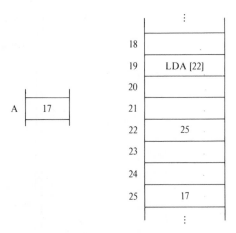

Fig. 4.22 Indirect addressing

The instruction LDA [22] causes the processor to read location 22 to get the address of the operand (i.e. 25). Location 25 contains the number 17 which is the actual value loaded into the accumulator.

Indirect addressing may be thought of as part of a natural progression starting with immediate addressing. Table 4.28 gives the RTL definitions of immediate addressing, absolute addressing, and indirect addressing. I have also included 'indirect indirect addressing' to show that the process can be continued indefinitely.

Table 4.28 Addressing modes

Addressing mode	Assembly language form	RTL form
Immediate	LDA #VALUE	[A]←VALUE
Absolute	LDA ADDRESS	[A]←[ADDRESS]
Indirect	LDA [ADDRESS]	[A]←[[ADDRESS]]
Indirect indirect	LDA [[ADDRESS]]	[A]←[[[ADDRESS]]]

From this definition of indirect addressing it should be apparent that indexed addressing is really a form of indirect addressing, because the index register contains the address of the operand. In fact, indirect addressing is not provided on all microprocessors because it is not absolutely necessary if indexed addressing is available. Of course, indirect addressing gives the programmer an almost unlimited number of index registers. The 6502 has a limited form of indirect addressing which is described in Appendix A2.

Indirect addressing allows the calculation of addresses at run-time during the execution of a program. The program in Table 4.29 shows how indirect addressing is used to add together 100 numbers. Remember that this program cannot be run on a 6502 processor because the general form of indirect addressing is not available.

Table 4.29 An application of indirect addressing

	NAM	EXAMPLE	
	ORG	$0000	data origin
NUMB	RMB	100	reserve 100 locations
POINTER	RMB	1	pointer to location of numbers
	ORG	$0200	origin of program
	LDA	#99	set up counter
	STA	POINTER	pointer points to 100th number
	CLC		clear carry-bit
	LDA	#00	clear total
NEXTONE	ADC	[POINTER]	add in the number pointed at
	DEC	POINTER	decrement the pointer
	BPL	NEXTONE	continue until all added in

This program is intended only to illustrate the application of indirect addressing. I have assumed that the word-length is sufficient to deal with the sum of the numbers without overflow. The only instruction in this program not available on the 6502 is ADC [POINTER].

In this program the variable called POINTER contains the address of the number to be added to the total in the accumulator. Initially, POINTER is set to 99, the address of the last number. After each number is added in by 'ADC [POINTER]', the value of POINTER is decremented by one. When the POINTER reaches zero, the addition is complete. Remember that it is common practice in assembly language programming to count downward, from N to 0, so that a test for zero can be used to terminate the loop.

4.4.5 The stack

A stack is a special type of data structure with the property that items are removed from the stack in the reverse order to which they are entered. For this reason a stack is often called a LIFO (last-in-first-out) queue. Figure 4.23 gives a series of diagrams illustrating the operation of a stack as items are added to it and removed from it.

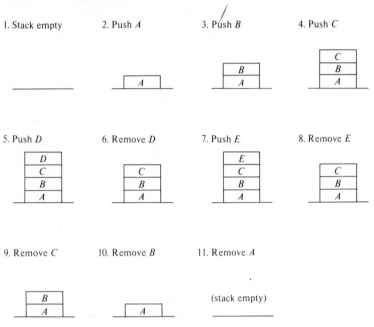

Fig. 4.23 The operation of the stack

It can be seen that the stack expands as items are added to it and contracts as they are removed. Note the stack has only one 'end' and items are always added or removed at this point. This special position is called the top-of-stack (TOS). The next position down is referred to as next-on-stack (NOS). When an item is added to the stack it is said to be 'pushed' on to the stack and when an item is removed from the stack it is said to be 'pulled' off the stack.

The stack is one of the most useful devices to pop-up in computer science and has applications in many different areas. Imagine a computer which is able to move data from memory to the stack (and vice versa), and to perform operations on the top item of the stack (monadic operators) or on the top two items of the stack (dyadic operators). When a dyadic operation takes place (plus, multiply, AND, OR, etc.), the top two items on the stack are removed and the result of the operation takes their place. The example in Table 4.30 illustrates this point by evaluating the expression $(A + B)(C - D)$ on a hypothetical stack-based computer. Figure 4.24 represents the state of

Table 4.30 Operations on a hypothetical stack-based computer

1.	LDA A	get A
2.	PUSH	push it on the stack
3.	LDA B	get B
4.	PUSH	push it on the stack
5.	ADD	pull the top two items off the stack, add them, and push the result
6.	LDA C	get C
7.	PUSH	push it on the stack
8.	LDA D	get D
9.	PUSH	push it on the stack
10.	SUB	pull the top two items off the stack, subtract them, and push the result
11.	MULT	pull the top two items off the stack, multiply them, and push the result

the stack at various stages in this procedure. The number below each diagram in Fig. 4.24 corresponds to the line number in the program in Table 4.30.

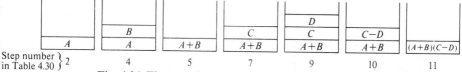

Fig. 4.24 The use of the stack in the evaluation of arithmetic expressions

There are many ways of implementing a stack—some computers have special purpose hardware, while others employ conventional programming techniques to maintain a model of a stack somewhere in the memory. Many of the popular microprocessors use a mixture of the two techniques. They locate their stack in the system memory, but have a special register to keep track of the items being added to, or removed from, the stack. Such a register is called the stack pointer (SP).

The 6502 stack

Most 8-bit microprocessors have a 16-bit stack pointer permitting them to locate their stack anywhere within the normal 64 K memory space. The 6502 has an 8-bit stack pointer limiting the size of its stack to 256 bytes. The region $0100 to $01FF (i.e. page 1) is dedicated to the stack by the 6502 CPU. Consequently, this region of memory should be avoided by the programmer. It is, of course, possible to treat page 1 just like any other region of memory, if the stack mechanism is not being used (an unlikely event).

In some (hardware) stacks, whenever new data is added to the stack, all items already on the stack are pushed down (hence the term push). Similarly, when an item is removed from the stack the NOS becomes TOS and all items are pulled up. When a stack is implemented by a microprocessor, the items on the stack are not moved themselves, but a pointer to the top of the stack is modified as the stack waxes and wanes. In some implementations, the stack pointer points to the next free location on the stack. In others the stack pointer points to the current top of stack. In what follows the 6502 is used as an example.

The assembly language form of the operation to push the accumulator on the stack is PHA. The corresponding mnemonic to pull an item from the stack and put it in the accumulator is PLA. Figure 4.25 illustrates the effect of a PHA and a PLA operation on the 6502's stack. The stack in the 6502 grow

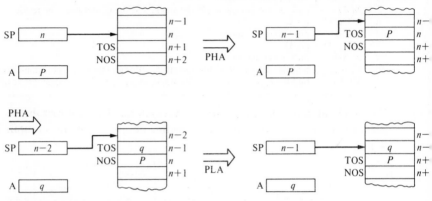

Fig. 4.25 The 6502's stack

'backwards' in memory as items are added to it. That is, if the stack pointer contains $014C and an item is pushed on to the stack, the new value of the stack pointer will be $014B. The way in which the stack grows—towards the 'higher' or 'lower' ends of memory—is entirely irrelevant.

For the 6502, PHA (PUSH) is defined as:

$$[MS[SP]] \leftarrow [A], [SP] \leftarrow [SP] - 1$$

and PLA (PULL) is defined as:

$$[SP] \leftarrow [SP] + 1, [A] \leftarrow [MS[SP]]$$

Note that the stack pointer is decremented after a push and incremented before a pull. This is because it always points to the next free location above the TOS. The notation [MS[SP]] means the contents of memory whose address is given by the contents of the stack pointer. This may be abbreviated to [[SP]] as the MS is understood.

When the stack grows downwards after PLA operations, the items on the stack are not physically deleted, they are still there in the memory until overwritten by a PHA operation.

The stack has many applications in computer science. Some are quite esoteric and involve the manipulation and evaluation of algebraic expressions. Such uses are beyond the scope of this text. The stack has a rather more prosaic use as a temporary data store. Executing a PHA saves the contents of the accumulator on the stack, and executing a PLA returns the contents of the accumulator. This avoids storing data in explicitly named memory locations. The most important applications of the stack from the computer architecture point of view are in the implementation of subroutine (discussed in the following section), and in the implementation of interrupts (Section 5.2). Section 9.2 shows how the stack is used by the operating system to implement multiprogramming, a means of executing two or more programs 'at the same time'.

The stack and subroutines

Suppose a particular sequence of operations is to be performed two or more times during the execution of a program. Writing out the same sequence of assembly-language instructions is both tedious to the programmer and wasteful of memory space. The subroutine provides a solution to this problem. A subroutine is a piece of code which can be called from any point in a program. Here the expression 'calling a subroutine' means that a jump is made to the entry point of the subroutine (i.e. its first executable instruction). After the subroutine has been executed a return must be made to the instruction following the point at which it was called. Figure 4.26 illustrates this concept. In high level languages the subroutine is frequently known as a procedure. The subroutine is to computing what subcontracting is to the building trade.

The key to subroutines is the return mechanism. If the same piece of code can be entered from several points, some mechanism must exist to allow a return to the correct place. The Data General Nova deposits the return address in accumulator A3 (it is a 4-accumulator machine). At the end of the subroutine the programmer simply executes a 'load program counter with the contents of A3' and a return is made. Unfortunately, there is a snag in this arrangement—A3 cannot readily be used by the programmer while a subroutine call is in progress. The contents of A3 may be saved in memory, and A3 made available to the programmer, but this is at the cost of keeping track of the subroutine return address.

A much better way of handling the return addresses of subroutines is to store them on the stack. This is done by most microprocessors and minicomputers in the following way.

1. Subroutine call: push the contents of the PC on the stack; jump to the subroutine.

2. Return from subroutine: pull the return address off the stack and put it in the program counter.

The effect of these operations on the stack is illustrated by Fig. 4.27. For simplicity, return addresses are shown as occupying one location on the stack. As will be explained shortly, the 6502 uses two locations to store a return address. Notice that the stack 'grows' when the subroutine is called and declines after a return. Because the last item stored on the stack is the first item to be removed from it, the stack is well suited to nested subroutines. That is, a subroutine is able to call another subroutine, and this process repeated indefinitely. Actually, it can continue only until all the memory

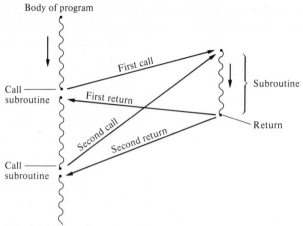

Fig. 4.26 The subroutine call

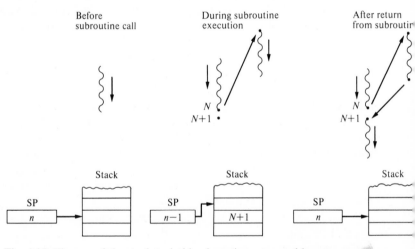

Fig. 4.27 The use of the stack to hold subroutine return addresses

allocated to the stack is exhausted, at which time stack overflow is said to occur. An example of the behaviour of the stack when subroutines are nested is given in Fig. 4.28.

Writing a subroutine in assembly language is simplicity itself. All that needs to be done to turn a block of code into a subroutine is to append the instruction RTS to the end of the block. Suppose it is necessary to divide the eight-bit number in the accumulator by four and add three several times during the course of a program. The subroutine in Table 4.31 will accomplish this.

To call a subroutine in the 6502 it is necessary only to execute the instruction JSR ADDRESS (JSR = jump to subroutine, and ADDRESS

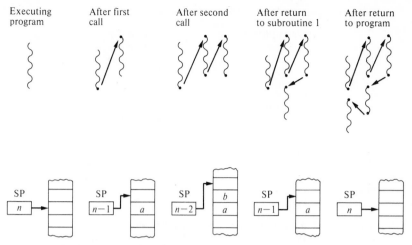

Fig. 4.28 An example of nested subroutines

Table 4.31 An example of a subroutine

DIV4PLUS3	ASR A	shift right (divide by 2)
	ASR A	shift right (divide by 2)
	CLC	clear carry
	ADC #3	add 3
	RTS	return

= actual address of the subroutine's starting point). To call the above subroutine it is necessary to write 'JSR DIV4PLUS3'.

The program in Table 4.32 inputs text from the keyboard of a microcomputer until an '@' is typed. Then the text is printed out. As it would be very tedious to write a subroutine to input a character from the keyboard, a subroutine in the operating system at $E993 is pressed into use to input the data. Similarly a subroutine at $E9BC outputs a single character. When the subroutine at $E993 is called, a return is made with the ASCII code of the key that was pressed stored in the accumulator. Likewise, calling the subroutine at $E9BC causes the character corresponding to the ASCII code of the data in the accumulator to be printed. In the program in Table 4.32 the BUFFER is a region of memory reserved for the data to be stored.

In this example I have adopted the assembler directives associated with a particular 6502-based system rather than those appearing elsewhere in the text. The meaning of these directives should be evident to the reader. In this case an assembly directive (NAM, END) is prefixed by a full-stop. The character '*' corresponds to the program counter, so that '* = 0000' is equivalent to 'ORG 0000'. The line 'BUFFER * = * + 40' means 'call the current location 0000, give it the symbolic name BUFFER, and move the program counter 40 locations onwards'. The instruction CMP #'@ means compare the contents of the accumulator with the byte whose ASCII code

Table 4.32 An example of the use of subroutines

	.NAM PRINTOUT	name the program
	* = $0000	set the origin
BUFFER	* = * + 40	reserve 40 bytes
INPUT	= $E993	defines input routine address
OUTPUT	= $E9BC	defines output routine address
	* = $0200	program origin
	LDX #00	clear index register
NEXTIN	JSR INPUT	get a character
	STA BUFFER,X	store it
	CMP #'@	is it an '@'?
	BEQ PRINT	if it is, print the characters
	INX	point to next place in buffer
	JMP NEXTIN	repeat
PRINT	LDX #00	clear index register
NEXTOUT	LDA BUFFER,X	get a character
	CMP #'@	is it an '@'?
	BEQ DONE	if it is, stop
	JSR OUTPUT	print a character
	INX	point to next place in buffer
	JMP NEXTOUT	repeat
DONE	BRK	halt
	.END	

corresponds to the symbol @. The apostrophe is often used by assemblers to denote that the following character should be replaced by its ASCII value. For example, LDA #'A and LDA #$41 are equivalent.

An interesting aspect of the 6502 is the way in which JSR and RTS are actually implemented. When the instruction JSR ADDRESS is executed, the two-byte address of the last byte of the three-byte JSR instruction is pushed on to the stack, the two-byte operand of JSR is loaded into the program counter, and a jump operation carried out. Note that the address on the stack is not the return address, but the address immediately before it.

When an RTS is encountered at the end of a subroutine, the two-byte address on the top of the stack is pulled and placed in the program counter. The contents of the program counter are then incremented by one so that the PC is now pointing at the start of the next instruction following the 'JSR'.

Subroutines, the stack, and parameter passing

A subroutine exists to carry out some particular function. In order to do this it is almost always necessary to transfer data between the subroutine and the program calling it. The only exception is the use of a subroutine in triggering some event. For example, a subroutine may be designed to ring a bell, or to sound an alarm. Simply calling it causes some pre-determined action to take place, and no communication exists between the subroutine and the program calling it.

Consider now the use of subroutines in inputting or outputting data. Obtaining data from a keyboard (or transferring it to a display device or printer) is a complex operation. Consequently, input (and output) transac tions are often dealt with by subroutines. One popular 6502-based micro-computer has an input subroutine called INALL located at $E993 within its operating system. The word 'INALL' is the symbolic name of the subroutine and is chosen by the computer's designers. It has no other significance.

When the subroutine INALL is invoked by executing the operation JSR INALL (or JSR $E993), a jump to $E993 is made. This address is the entry point to the subroutine, and a jump to $E993 has the effect of reading the keyboard until a key is pressed. When this happens, the corresponding character is displayed on the LED read-out, and a return to the calling point made with the ASCII-code of the character in the accumulator.

In this case there is communication between the subroutine and the calling program. As only a single byte is passed from subroutine to calling program, the accumulator provides a handy vehicle. Note that any data that was in the accumulator before the subroutine is called is lost.

The above method of passing data between subroutine and calling program employs registers to transfer data. In our example, the data was passed in the accumulator. There is no reason why the index registers could not have been used. It is interesting to note that the carry bit of the PSR is often chosen to pass information from a subroutine to its calling program. A single bit may not seem like an awful lot of information. However, problems sometimes happen within the subroutine and the calling program must be informed about them. Suppose a subroutine had been called to input data from a terminal and the terminal was faulty or not switched on. By setting the carry bit before a return from subroutine, the calling program can be told that an error exists. The fragment of a program, listed in Table 4.33, illustrates this point.

Table 4.33 Passing information via the carry bit

	JSR GETDATA	call subroutine and return with data in the accumulator
	BCS ERROR	if carry set something went wrong
	.	
	.	deal with the data
	.	
ERROR		recover from error condition

Apart from destroying old data, passing information via registers has no significant disadvantages. Unfortunately, it is not applicable to situations where larger quantities of data have to be transferred. Suppose a subroutine were written to search a region of memory containing text, for the first occurrence of a given string. In this case the subroutine must be informed of the starting and ending addresses of the region of memory to be searched, and the corresponding starting and ending addresses of the string of characters to be matched. The address map of Fig. 4.29 illustrates this problem.

The information required by the subroutine is the numbers 1000, 1011,

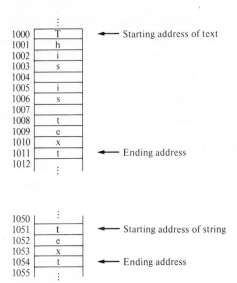

1000	T	← Starting address of text
1001	h	
1002	i	
1003	s	
1004		
1005	i	
1006	s	
1007		
1008	t	
1009	e	
1010	x	
1011	t	← Ending address
1012		

1050		
1051	t	← Starting address of string
1052	e	
1053	x	
1054	t	← Ending address
1055		

Fig. 4.29 Memory map of the string-matching problem

1051, and 1054. That is, four 16-bit addresses. The subroutine must return the value 1008 (the starting-point of the string 'text') to the calling program. Clearly, the information cannot be transferred by means of the 6502's registers.

One possible solution still relying on registers to transfer information between subroutine and calling program, involves passing information by its location rather than its actual value. That is, instead of telling the subroutine the information it needs to know, we can tell it where to find that information. Figure 4.30 shows how the parameters are grouped into a block, and the start of the block passed to the subroutine.

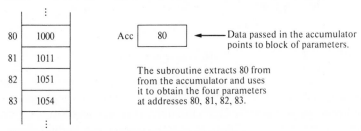

80	1000	Acc [80] ←——— Data passed in the accumulator points to block of parameters.
81	1011	
82	1051	The subroutine extracts 80 from from the accumulator and uses it to obtain the four parameters
83	1054	at addresses 80, 81, 82, 83.

Fig. 4.30 Passing parameters by their address

It is possible to reserve a data area common to both the subroutine and calling program. This removes the problem of passing parameters because the variables required by the subroutine are the same as those in the calling program. Such a solution is not popular, because the subroutine cannot be interrupted and called by another program. Any data stored in explicitly named locations will be corrupted by the interrupting program. Section 5.

deals in detail with the interrupt mechanism and its implementation. For the purposes of this section a brief description of the interrupt will suffice. An interrupt is a method of diverting the processor from its intended course of action, and is employed to deal with input or output transactions (and certain other events) which must be attended to as soon as they occur. Whenever a processor receives an interrupt request from some device, it finishes its current instruction, and then jumps to the program dealing with the cause of the interrupt. After the interrupt has been serviced, a return is made to the point immediately following the last instruction executed before the interrupt was dealt with. The return mechanism of the interrupt is almost identical with that of the subroutine—the return address is saved on the stack.

Suppose a subroutine is interrupted during the course of its execution. If the interrupt-handling routine also wishes to use the subroutine, any data stored in explicitly named memory locations will be overwritten (corrupted) by the re-use of the subroutine. If the data had been stored in registers and the contents of the registers pushed on the stack by the interrupt-handling routine, no data in the subroutine would have been lost by its re-use. After the subroutine has been re-used by the interrupt-handling routine, the contents of the accumulators stored on the stack are restored, and a return from interrupt made with the state of the registers exactly the same as at the instant the interrupt was serviced. An ideal way of passing information between the subroutine and calling program is via the stack. Suppose three parameters, P1, P2, and P3, are needed by the subroutine. The parameters are pushed on the stack immediately before the subroutine call (Table 4.34).

Table 4.34 Passing parameters on the stack

```
LDA    P1
PHA
LDA    P2
PHA
LDA    P3
PHA
JSR    SUB
```

The state of the stack initially, prior to the subroutine call, and immediately after it, is given in Fig. 4.31. Note that the return address takes up two locations on the stack. In the 6502 the stack pointer does not point to the TOS but to the next free location above the TOS. In Fig. 4.31 this is labelled FREE.

On entering the subroutine the data may be retrieved in several ways. One possibility is to transfer the contents of the stack pointer to the index register by means of the instruction TSX. Now parameter P1 can be loaded into the accumulator by 'LDA 5,X'. Similarly, P2 can be loaded by 'LDA 4,X' and P3 by 'LDA 3,X'.

The only difficulty presented by this technique is that after a return from

220   *The central processing unit*

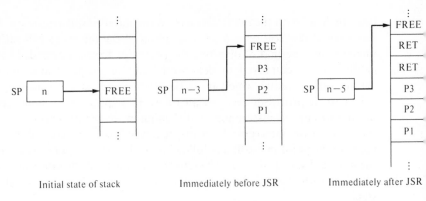

Fig. 4.31 Passing parameters on the stack

the subroutine has been made by an RTS, the contents of the stack pointer
are SP-3, where SP was the value before P1, P2, and P3 were pushed on the
stack. The stack is restored to its initial value by executing three consecutive
(dummy) PLA operations. This process is called 'cleaning up the stack'.

The advantage of using the stack to pass parameters to subroutines is that
the subroutine may be interrupted and then used by the interrupting program
without the parameters being corrupted. As the data is stored on the stack, it
is not overwritten when the subroutine is interrupted because new data is
added at the top of the stack, and then removed after the interrupt has been
serviced.

4.5 The 6809 microprocessor

The Motorola 6809 eight-bit microprocessor is the most advanced device of
its type available today. A significant feature of the 6809 is its wealth of
addressing modes, making the manipulation of data relatively easy. A block
diagram of the internal register structure of the 6809 is given in Fig. 4.32.

The 6809 operates on eight-bit data words and has a 16-bit address bus to
address up to 64 K bytes of memory. From this description the 6809 sounds
virtually the same as the 6502 or the 6800. Unlike the 6502, however, the 6809
has 16-bit address or pointer registers. Furthermore, there are two index
registers (X, Y), and two stack pointers (U, S). Both stack pointers S and U
are available to the programmer. When the CPU itself uses the stack for
interrupt-handling or subroutine return addresses, it uses the S stack pointer.

There are two eight-bit accumulators A and B. A particularly nice feature
of the 6809 is a facility enabling the programmer to treat the two accumulators as a single 16-bit accumulator, the D register. In this way the 6809
behaves as a true 16-bit computer, although it must be admitted that only a
subset of the 6809's data manipulation operations can be applied to the D
register.

A register peculiar to the 6809 is the eight-bit direct page register DP. The

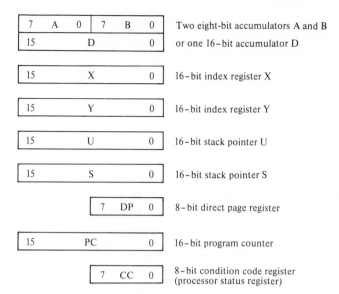

Fig. 4.32 The 6809's internal registers

6502 has 'zero page addressing' and the 6800 has 'direct addressing', both of which allow the first 256 bytes of memory (page zero) to be used with an addressing mode requiring a single eight-bit operand. Clearly, this addressing mode forces the programmer to locate frequently used data in the range $0000–$00FF. There are many occasions when this use of the memory space is inconvenient. The direct page register holds the page (one of 256) which is to be used in conjunction with this form of addressing. Consequently, the 6809 allows the convenience and economy of zero page addressing but gives it greater flexibility by allowing the programmer to select any page as the 'zero' page.

4.5.1 Addressing modes and the 6809

The 6809 has ten addressing modes: inherent, immediate, direct, extended, branch relative, indexed, extended indirect, program-counter relative, indexed indirect, and register. These names are those used by Motorola in their own literature. The operation of these addressing modes is as follows:

Inherent addressing This is not so much an addressing mode as a method of increasing the apparent number of addressing modes for advertising purposes! In inherent (or implied) addressing the address is implied by the instruction itself. For example, 'clear accumulator A' specifies both what is to be done, and the source and destination of the data taking part in the operation. Inherent addressing uses a single byte op-code.

Immediate addressing In this mode the data taking part in an operation immediately follows the op-code. As the 6809 operates with 8- or 16-bit data values, immediate addressing needs a one or two byte operand after the op-code. The examples below make this clear. Note that as the 6809 has two accumulators it is necessary to specify which is being used. Thus, the programmer must write either LDA 1234 or LDB 1234.

LDA #37   [A]←37
LDX #1234   [X]←1234
LDD #1234   [D]←1234, or [A]←12, [B]←34

Extended addressing   In everyone else's terminology this is simply absolute addressing, where the operand following the op-code gives the absolute address of the data to be used in the operation, as in the following examples

LDA   37   [A]←[0037]
LDX 1234   [X]←[1234], [1235]

In order to load a 16-bit value into the X-register, the CPU must fetch two bytes from memory—one from address 1234 and one from address 1235. Note that the 6809 (like the 6800 but unlike the 6502) stores addresses in memory with the most significant byte first (i.e. at the lower address).

Direct addressing   This is entirely analogous to zero-page addressing in the 6502 except that any page can be made the direct page by loading the page number into the 6809's direct page register before using this addressing mode. Consider the following example of direct addressing.

LDA #12   [A] ←12
EXG A,DP   [DP]←[A], [A]←[DP]
LDA 34   [A] ←[1234]

In this example accumulator A is loaded with the immediate value 12. The operation 'EXG A,DP' swaps the contents of accumulator A and the direct page register—there is no 'load DP with an immediate' instruction. The last instruction 'LDA 34' has a single byte operand, so the assembler chooses the direct page addressing mode and the page number '12' is prefixed to the operand '34' to give the required 16-bit address 1234. If we wanted to load A with the contents of 34 instead of 1234, we would write LDA 0034 to suppress the direct addressing mode.

Branch relative addressing   Like the 6502 the 6809 uses relative addressing following branch instructions. The one-byte two's complement operand following a branch is added to the contents of the program counter to give the effective address of the branch. A disadvantage of relative addressing in the 6502 or 6800 is that the branch is restricted to the range of −126 to +129 bytes. The 6809 includes a set of long-branch instructions where the op-code is followed by a two-byte two's complement offset permitting a branching range of −32764 to +32771 bytes from the current value of the program counter.

Program-counter relative addressing   In this mode of addressing (entirely absent in the 6502, 6800, 8080, Z80, etc.) the effective address of an operand is given by the contents of the program counter plus an 8- or 16-bit offset following the instruction. The power of this addressing mode (when coupled with relative branching) is that it leads to entirely position independent code. As all data locations are specified with respect to the program counter, a program and its data area can be moved about in memory without any addresses needing to be changed. This facility is particularly useful when multiprogramming is taking place (Section 9.2). If a new program is stored in memory, other programs may be moved up or down without modification. Two examples of the format and operation of program-counter relative addressing are given in Fig. 4.33.

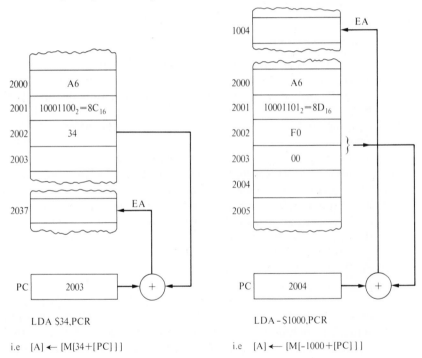

Fig. 4.33 Program-counter relative addressing

In the left-hand case (an eight-bit offset) there are two 8 bit numbers following the op-code. The first, 10001100, is called (by Motorola) the postbyte, and indicates the addressing mode. The 6809 has such a large combination of addressing modes that not all possible op-codes can be accommodated in eight bits. Consequently, a postbyte is necessary to turn the 8 bit instruction into a 16 bit instruction. Further details about the postbyte are given in Table 4.35.

The number (offset) following the post-byte, $34, is added to the contents of the program counter (i.e. $2003) to give an effective address of $2034. Note that in program counter relative addressing, the number in the program counter to be added to the offset is the address of the next instruction to be executed. In the right-hand case the postbyte is 10001101. The least significant bit is set indicating to the CPU that a 16-bit offset is being used. This offset is $-$1000 or, in its two's complement form, $F000. When this is added to the contents of the program counter ($2004), the effective address $1004 is produced.

It must be realized that the numerical calculation of postbytes and offsets is almost never performed by the programmer, but carried out automatically by the assembler. The programmer writes the instruction in symbolic form (e.g. LDA VALUE1, PCR) and the assembler calculates the op-code, the postbyte, and the offset.

Indexed addressing

In indexed addressing the effective address of an operand is obtained by adding an offset following the op-code to the contents of an index register. The 6800 is limited to one 16-bit index register while the 6502 is limited to two eight-bit index registers. The designers of the 6809 went to town on indexing and wiped out the limitations of the 6800 and 6502 with a vengeance.

The 6809 has two 16-bit index registers, X and Y, and employs four variations on indexed addressing. These are: zero-offset indexed, constant-offset indexed, accumulator-offset indexed, and autoincrement (autodecrement) indexed. The first two modes are entirely straightforward. In zero-offset indexed addressing the index register contains the effective address of the operand. This addressing mode was included because it was observed that the most common indexed addressing form used by the 6800 programmer was LDA 00,X. By dropping the zero offset a byte is saved (cf. zero-page addressing).

In constant offset indexed addressing a 5, 8, or 16-bit signed offset is added to any of the four pointer registers to generate an effective address. The actual type of indexing is determined by the post-byte following the op-code as discussed earlier. In fact, when a 5-bit signed offset is used, the offset itself forms part of the post-byte. A 5-bit signed offset may sound odd, but Motorola has determined that in many applications of the index register an offset in the range $-$16 to $+$15 is sufficient.

When an eight-bit signed offset is required, the single-byte offset following the post-byte provides an indexing range of $-$128 to $+$127. A 16-bit signed offset is provided by two bytes following the postbyte to give an indexing range of $-$32 768 to $+$32 767.

An important feature of the 6809 is accumulator-offset indexed addressing in which the contents of an accumulator are added to a pointer register to give the effective address of the operand. The eight-bit accumulator A or B can be used, or a 16-bit offset may be created by using the D register. As in the above indexed addressing modes, the 6809 assumes the offset in the accumulator to be a signed value. This addressing mode is useful because it allows the generation of variable offsets calculated at run-time. In the other indexed addressing modes the offset is a constant defined by the programmer when the program is written.

When stepping through the data in a table by means of indexed addressing, the index register is incremented by the programmer after each indexed operation. In the autoincrement indexed addressing mode the contents of the index register are automatically incremented each time this mode is used. It is also possible to use an autoincrementing by two mode, so that we can step through tables of 16-bit words. Besides the autoincrementing mode, the 6809 has an autodecrement by one or two mode. It should be noted that autoincrementing takes place after an indexed operation. The 6809 assembler indicates autoincrementing/autodecrementing by a $+/-$, and autoincrementing/autodecrementing by two by $++/--$, respectively.

The action of autoincrementing by one, and autodecrementing by two is illustrated below. I have selected operations involving accumulators A and B, and index registers X and Y, in order to show the versatility of the 6809.

$$
\begin{array}{ll}
\text{LDA ,X}+ & [A] \leftarrow [[X]] \\
 & [X] \leftarrow [X]+1 \\
\text{LDD ,} --\text{Y} & [Y] \leftarrow [Y]-2 \\
 & [D] \leftarrow [[Y]]
\end{array}
$$

It has already been stated that the wealth of indexed addressing modes provided by the 6809 requires an additional byte (called the postbyte) to qualify the op-code. Table 4.35 illustrates how the eight bits of the postbyte determine the mode of the indexed addressing operation.

Indirect addressing   In indirect addressing the effective address of the operand is found at the location specified by the instruction. There is, of course, no reason why indirect addressing cannot be used in conjunction with other addressing modes such as indexing. Indeed, indirect addressing can be applied to all the 6809's indexed modes with the exception of autoincrementing/autodecrementing by one. Bit 4 of the postbyte selects the indirect addressing modes. When clear the address of the operand is given by EA, as in the table above. When set indirect addressing is selected and the address of the operand is given by [EA]. That is, the operand is the contents of the location, whose effective address is calculated according to the particular indexed mode selected. For example, if the index register contains 5, the operation 'LDA 7,X', results in the contents of memory location 12 being deposited in the accumulator. If the operation had been LDA [7,X], the contents of memory location 12 would be used to provide the address of the data which is to be loaded into the accumulator.

Table 4.35 The postbyte following a 6809 indexed operation

Postbyte bit								Effective address
7	6	5	4	3	2	1	0	
0	R	R	X	X	X	X	X	EA = [R] + 5-bit offset
1	R	R	0	0	0	0	0	EA = [R], [R]←[R] + 1
1	R	R	I	0	0	0	1	EA = [R], [R]←[R] + 2
1	R	R	0	0	0	1	0	[R] = [R] − 1, EA = [R]
1	R	R	I	0	0	1	1	[R] = [R] − 2, EA = [R]
1	R	R	I	0	1	0	0	EA = [R]
1	R	R	I	0	1	0	1	EA = [R] + [A]
1	R	R	I	0	1	1	0	EA = [R] + [B]
1	R	R	I	1	0	0	0	EA = [R] + 8-bit offset
1	R	R	I	1	0	0	1	EA = [R] + 16-bit offset
1	R	R	I	1	0	1	1	EA = [R] + [D]
1	I	X	I	1	1	0	0	[PC] + 8-bit offset
1	I	X	I	1	1	0	1	EA = [PC] + 16-bit offset
1	X	X	1	1	1	1	1	EA = [16-bit unsigned offset]

I = indirect bit (when set indicates indirect addressing). X = don't care (may be 0 or 1) except in the case of the 5-bit offset where the X's define the value of the offset. Bits 5 and 6 of the postbyte are the two register select bits and define the register acting as the index register in the generation of an effective address. Bit 6, bit 5 = 0,0→R = X register. Bit 6, bit 5 = 0,1→R = Y register. Bit 6, bit 5 = 1,0→R = U register. Bit 6, bit 5 = 1,1→R = S register.

Indirect addressing is indicated by enclosing the operand of an instruction in square brackets. The three examples below illustrate this point.

Assembly language form	Register transfer language form
LDA [25]	[A]←[[25]]
LDA [10,X]	[A]←[[X] + 10]]
LDA [25,PCR]	[A[←[[PC] + 25]]

Register addressing   Register addressing is really a form of inherent addressing except that two registers are used with data being moved (or exchanged) between them. A postbyte follows a register transfer or exchange. The four most significant bits of the postbyte specify the source register and the least significant bits specify the destination register.

Highlights of the 6809's instruction set

This book is not intended to provide a course in comparative microprocessor architectures. I have chosen to illustrate the structure of a processor with the 6502. As this is now a rather dated processor this section includes details on the more recent 6809 which has a similar architecture and instruction set, but with more internal registers and addressing modes. There is little point in presenting the full instruction set of the 6809. However, it is worthwhile describing some of the 6809's instructions which differ from those of the 6502. As the 6809 has more registers than the 6502, it is necessary to distinguish between registers in many instructions. This is particularly true because there are two accumulators (A and B), two index registers (X and Y) and two stack pointers (U and S). Whenever the two accumulators are used as a single 16-bit register, it is referred to as the D register.

Data movement

LEA (load effective address) is a very powerful instruction and involves an operation on one of the 16-bit pointer registers. Its general form is:

LEAP OFFSET, Q

where P is one of: X, Y, S, and U; Q is one of: X, Y, S, U, and PC; and OFFSET is a signed offset.

The effect of 'LEAP OFFSET, Q' is [P]←OFFSET+[Q].

The LEA instruction replaces several instructions found on the 6502 or 6800. For example, 'LEAX − 1,X' is equivalent to DEX, and 'LEAX 1,X' is equivalent to INX. The operation 'LEAY 50,X' has the effect of transferring the contents of register X, plus 50, to register Y.

PSH (push registers on to the stack) behaves like the 6502's PHA but with two exceptions. As there are two stacks, the instruction must be written as PSHS or PSHU. This instruction is able to push any combination of registers on the stack at one go (with the exception of the stack pointer being used). For example, 'PSHS X,Y,A' has the effect of pushing the X, Y, and A registers on the stack. This is very useful in subroutine entries where it is often convenient to save registers before executing the subroutine and then to restore them before the return from subroutine. The inverse function to PSH is PUL. Note that the operation PULS PC (pull program counter off the system stack) has the same effect as RTS.

TFR (transfer register to register) copies the contents of one register into another. One of the accumulators can be copied into the other by 'TFR A,B' (or TFR B,A), or the contents of a 16-bit register copied into another 16-bit register. The operation 'TFR X,Y' copies the contents of X into Y, and has the same effect as 'LEAY 0,X'. The operation 'TFR X,PC' has the effect of transferring the contents of the X register to the program counter, and hence forcing a jump to the address in the X register.

EXG (exchange register contents) has the effect of swapping the contents of two registers. As the exchange operation is symmetric, the assembly forms 'EXG A,B' and 'EXG B,A' are equivalent.

Arithmetic and logical instructions

The arithmetic and logical instructions of the 6809 are very similar to those of the 6502 with a few exceptions. Some useful additions to the 6502's repertoire are as follows.

ABX (add the contents of accumulator B to the contents of the X index register) is very useful because it allows arithmetic operations to be performed on the contents of the index register.

ADD (add the contents of accumulator A, B, or D to the contents of a memory location) is equivalent to the 6502 sequence CLC, ADC. Because the A and B accumulators can be combined to form a single 16-bit accumulator, D, the effect of ADD M is to add the contents of memory locations M and M + 1 to the contents of D. Consider the following sequence of operations:

    LDD P
    ADD Q
    STD   R

These have the effect of adding the 16-bit values P and Q and depositing the result in R.

CLR (CLeaR accumulator or memory) has the effect of setting the contents of an accumulator (CLRA or CLRB), or a memory location, to zero.

COM (COMplement the contents of an accumulator, or a memory location) has the effect of forming a one's complement. For example, COMA has the effect of complementing or inverting all the bits of A.

DEC (DECrement the contents of an accumulator or memory location) has the effect of subtracting one from the relevant word. The 6502 has this instruction in its memory reference form, but not an accumulator equivalent (i.e. DECA). The 6809 also has the corresponding INC (increment) instruction.

NEG (NEGate the contents of an accumulator or a memory location) has the effect of forming the two's complement of the selected word.

SEX (Sign EXtend accumulator B into acumulator A) transforms an 8-bit two's complement number in accumulator B, into a 16-bit two's complement number in accumulator D. The effect of SEX is to fill accumulator A with eight copies of bit 7 (the MSB) of accumulator B.

An example of a 6809 program

It is almost impossible to demonstrate the power of the 6809 over the 6502 by writing just one short program. In any case we have not defined the meaning of power. Do we mean speed, physical size of the object program (number of bytes of machine code), or elegance (ease of writing and understanding an assembly language program)? As a matter of fact, the 6809 shows improvements over the 6502 under all the three above headings.

The following program implements the type of text matching algorithm described in the section on parameter passing. A region of memory contains a line of text whose starting address is $2000. The line is terminated by a carriage return, whose ASCII code is $0D. A text string is stored in a buffer at location $0080 onwards, and is also terminated by a carriage return. The program is to be written in the form of a subroutine, and the address of the first character in the line matching the first character of the string placed on the user stack before the return. If the match is unsuccessful, the null address, 0000, is pushed on the stack.

In what follows the line of text will be referred to as 'line', and the text string as 'text'. The problem can be solved by sliding the string along the line until each character of the string matches with the corresponding character of the line; see Tables 4.36(a),(b)

Table 4.36(a) Matching two strings

| THIS THAT THEN THE OTHER | line |
| THEN THE | string |

THIS THAT THEN THE OTHER	Step	Matches	
THEN THE	1	2	
THEN THE	2	0	
THEN THE	3	0	
THEN THE	4	0	
THEN THE	5	0	
THEN THE	6	2	
THEN THE	7	0	
THEN THE	8	0	
THEN THE	9	1	
THEN THE	10	0	
THEN THE	11	8	(All match)

Table 4.36(b) 6809 program

1.	LINE	EQU	$2000	starting point of line of text
2.	STRING	EQU	$0080	starting point of string
3.	CRET	EQU	$0D	carriage return = CRET = end-of-line
4.		LDX	#LINE	X points to the line of text
5.		LDY	#STRING	Y points to the string
6.	NEXT	LDA	,X+	get a character from the line
7.		CMPA	#CRET	test for end-of-line (eol)
8.		BEQ	FAIL1	if eol then fail
9.		CMPA	,Y	compare with first character of string
10.		BNE	NEXT	if no match look at next char in line
11.		PSHS	X,Y	push both pointers on the stack
12.		LEAY	1,Y	point at 2nd character in string
13.	REPEAT	LDB	,Y+	get a character from string
14.		CMPB	#CRET	test for end of string
15.		BEQ	SUCCESS	if end of string then successful match
16.		LDA	,X+	get a character from line
17.		CMPA	#CRET	test for eol
18.		BEQ	FAIL	if we find an eol in a submatch abandon all hope
19.		CMPA	−1,Y	compare characters
20.		BEQ	REPEAT	if same continue submatching
21.		PULS	X,Y	if different restore X and Y
22.		BRA	NEXT	try next character in line
23.	FAIL	PULS	X,Y	restore the stack
24.	FAIL1	LDX	#$0000	clear X register
25.		PSHU	X	push on user stack for failure
26.		RTS		return
27.	SUCCESS	PULS	X,Y	restore the stack
28.		LEAX	−1,X	undo autoincrement of line pointer
29.		PSHU	X	push pointer to start of match on stack
30.		RTS		return

The following notes provide further details on some of the 6809's instructions.

1. All references to the accumulators end in either A or B to distinguish between them.

2. The push and pull instructions must define which of the two stacks they are using (e.g. PSHS or PSHU). The 6809 push/pull is able to push or pull any group of registers on or off the stack.

3. In line 12 of the above program the X register is incremented by 'LEAY 1,Y'. Similarly, in line 28 the operation 'LEAX −1,X' decrements the X register. Note that the offset is a signed value.

Problems

These three questions are intended for those with an Aim 65 microcomputer. They can be adapted to suit after 6502-based microcomputers.

An introduction to the Aim 65

1. Use the Aim 65 to store numbers in memory and to read them back. Note, the numbers must be in hexadecimal format, expressed as two hexadecimal characters per byte. Each byte may range from $00 to $FF. Do not confuse the letter O with the number 0 (zero). Store your numbers in locations $0000 onwards. For example, entering the two hexadecimal characters A5 results in 10100101 being stored in the memory. Remember that an address requires 4 hexadecimal digits because the 6502 has a 16-bit address bus.

2. The program in Table 4.37 will add the contents of memory locations 0000 and 0001 together, and deposit the results in location 0002.

Table 4.37

Address	Data	
0000	XX	
0001	XX	
0002	ZZ	
.	.	
.	.	
.	.	
0080	A5 |	Load A with the contents of 0000
0081	00 |	
0082	18	Clear the carry bit
0083	65	Add the contents of 0001 to A
0084	01	plus the carry bit
0085	85 |	Deposit the result in 0002
0086	02 |	
0087	00	BRK ('break' or return to operating system)

Use the 'M' function to enter this program in memory. Provide your own data for XX and YY. Run the program using the 'G' function after you have first set the program counter to $0080 by the '*' function. Use the 'M' function to examine the result in location 0002. Run the program first with simple numbers (say 04 and 07) and then try more difficult numbers (say AB and CD).

3. Investigate the operation of the instructions listed in Table 4.38, using Question 2 as a model.

Table 4.38

Mnemonic	Operation	Op-Code	Operation (RTL)
ADC MM	add with carry	65	$[A] \leftarrow [A] + [MM] + [C]$
AND MM	logical AND	25	$[A] \leftarrow [A] \cdot [MM]$
ASL MM	arithmetic shift left	06	
LSR MM	logical shift right	46	
SBC MM	subtract with borrow	E5	$[A] \leftarrow [A] - [MM] - [\overline{C}]$
CLC	clear carry	18	$[C] \leftarrow 0$
SEC	set carry	38	$[C] \leftarrow 1$
LDA MM	load accumulator	A5	$[A] \leftarrow [MM]$
STA MM	store accumulator	85	$[MM] \leftarrow [A]$

Addressing modes

1. For the memory map below evaluate the following expressions, where [N] means the contents of memory location N. For example, $[3] = 4$.

(a) $[7]$

(b) $[[4]]$

(c) $[[[0]]]$

(d) $[2 + 10]$

(e) $[[9] + 2]$

(f) $[[9] + [2]]$

(g) $[[5] + [13] + 2*[14]]$

(h) $[0]*3 + [1]*4$

(i) $[9]*[10]$

00	12
01	17
02	7
03	4
04	8
05	4
06	4
07	7
08	0
09	5
10	12
11	7
12	6
13	3
14	2

2. Draw the block diagram of a CPU with a stack pointer and two index registers. Show the buses along which information may flow between the various parts of the CPU.

3. For the block diagram of Question 2 use register transfer language to illustrate the sequence of operations carried out during the execution of the following operations:

(i)	PSH	push accumulator onto the stack
(ii)	PLA	pull accumulator off the stack
(iii)	LDA OFFSET, X	load accumulator indexed
(iv)	STA, Y − −	store accumulator indexed (autodecrementing-by-two mode)
(v)	ADD [OFFSET, X]	add to the contents of the accumulator the contents of the memory location whose indirect address is indexed.

4. If you were designing a computer and were drawing up a list of conditional branches (e.g. BEQ, BCC, BOV etc.), what new types of conditional branch would you like to include?

5. Some computers have the following form of indexed addressing:

$$\text{LDA OFFSET, R1,R2}$$

where R1 and R2 are internal registers.

The effect of this instruction is $[A] \leftarrow [OFFSET + [R1] + [R2]]$, so that the sum of the contents of both R1 and R2 are used to generate an effective address. How do you think that this instruction would be used?

6.

X   12

30	19
31	46
32	31

46	32

For the above memory map give the contents of the accumulator after each of the following instructions has been executed. The instructions are not meant to represent any real machine, but the conventions are those used in the text. All values are decimal.

(a) LDA 31   (b) LDA 32   (c) LDA 19,X
(d) LDA [46]   (e) LDA 34,X   (f) LDA [34,X]

7. Many computers have an instruction JMP OFFSET,X, which is an indexed jump. Indicate how this instruction may be used.

8. Modify the CPU structure of Fig. 4.7 to include provision for a stack mechanism, with an internal stack pointer and an external stack (i.e. stack in IAS as in the case of the 6502 etc.). Show the data and address paths and indicate any additional three-state gates required.

9. For your answer to Question 7, write a register transfer language program to illustrate the operation PSH (push accumulator). Then produce a table of control signals to effect this operation, in the style of Table 4.10.

Assembly language examples

1. Write a program in both mnemonic and hexadecimal form to add two 16-bit unsigned binary integers together. The numbers to be added, P and Q, are stored as follows:

Address

Address		
0080	12	P = $1234
0081	34	
0082	AB	Q = $ABCD
0083	CD	
0084		R
0085		

Notes

(a) Start your program at memory location $0000.

(b) The operation codes for ADC, CLC, LDA, STA are 6D, 18, AD, 8D respectively and require (where applicable) a 16-bit absolute address. For the 6502 microprocessor, the address is stored with the least significant byte first (i.e. at the lower address).

After writing the program, show the state of the program counter, accumulator, processor status word, and memory locations 0080 to 0085 after each instruction is executed.

2. Write a program to subtract two 16-bit unsigned binary integers. Use the same format and values as in Question 1 (i.e. R = Q − P).

3. Write a program to multiply two eight-bit unsigned binary integers together. The multiplier is to be stored in location $0040, the multiplicand in $0041, and the 16-bit result in $0042 and $0043. The multiplication is to be carried out by means of repeated additions.

The numbers to be multiplied may be input from the keyboard by the subroutine RBYTE at $E3FD. This subroutine inputs two hexadecimal characters and returns with them in the accumulator.

The number in the accumulator may be printed as two hexadecimal characters by calling the subroutine NUMA at $EA46. To print a carriage return and newline call the subroutine CRLOW at $EA13.

Note that calling a subroutine may result in the contents of the A, X, and Y registers being modified. For example, calling CRLOW has the effect of destroying the contents of the accumulator prior to the call. If this is to be avoided, the contents of the accumulator may be saved before the call, and restored after it. Below are two ways of avoiding the corruption of the contents of the accumulator by its use in a subroutine.

Method 1	Method 2
STA TEMP	PHA
JSR $EA13	JSR $EA13
LDA TEMP	PLA

Using the index register

1. Write an assembly language program to input text from the keyboard (use subroutine INALL at $E993) and store the characters in consecutive memory locations starting at $0200. The loading process is to be terminated when a full stop is entered. The ASCII code for a full stop is $2E. When a full stop has been entered, a new line is to be output (use CRLOW at $EA13) and the stored text printed. (To print a character use OUTALL at $E9BC.) Locate the program at memory location $0040. After you have run the program examine memory locations $0200 onwards to verify that they contain the characters you entered. Modify your program to output the stored data in the reverse order to which it was entered.

2. Write a program to input a sequence of bytes (use RBYTE at $E3FD) and store them sequentially starting at $0200. The sequence is to be terminated by 00. Print the even numbers in the sequence using NUMA at $EA46. To do this it will be necessary to test each number—if it is even print it, otherwise skip to the next number. To test for even/odd, shift the least significant bit into the carry flip-flop.

3. A sequence of 8-bit unsigned integers is stored in ascending order in memory locations $0000 to $000F. Another number is stored at $0020 and is to be inserted in the correct place in this sequence, which will then occupy locations from $0000 to $0010. Write a program to do this and test it using your own data. Locate your program at $0080 onwards.

4. Write a program to read a line of text, terminated by a full stop, and to count the number of vowels. For example, inputting the line 'LIFE THE UNIVERSE AND EVERYTHING' results in the output:

```
A  = 1
E  = 6
I  = 3
O  = 0
U  = 1.
```

The following subroutines will be useful:

CRLOW $EA13   output carriage return and newline
INALL $E993   input an ASCII character into the accumulator
OUTALL $E9BC   output the ASCII character in the accumulator
                  to the printer

The ASCII code of a space is $20, and of a '=' $3D. As the subroutine OUTALL outputs the contents of the accumulator in the form of the corresponding ASCII character, it is necessary to convert numeric values into their ACSCII equivalent before they are printed. Assume that there will be no more than 9 of any one vowel in a sentence. What modification to the numeric-to-ASCII conversion process is needed to handle integers greater than nine?

5 INPUT/OUTPUT

So far we have examined the internal structure and operation of the digital computer. However, if a computer is to be of value to people it must have some way of communicating with them. After all, there's no point in creating a super computer the size of a shoe box which can solve the ultimate question of life, the universe, and everything, if it cannot tell us the answer.

Computer input/output (I/O) is quite a complex subject and is best subdivided into the three following areas.

1. The strategy by which information (data) is moved into and out of the computer.

2. The hardware which actually moves the data.

3. The input/output devices themselves which convert data into 'useful manifestations' or vice versa. I use the term 'useful manifestations', because data may be converted into an almost infinite number of forms, from a close approximation to human speech to a signal which opens or closes a valve in a chemical factory. Input/output devices are frequently called 'peripherals'.

The difference between these areas is readily illustrated by means of examples. Consider first a small computer connected to a visual display unit (VDU or, in US terminology, a CRT terminal). The data is moved into or out of the computer by programmed data transfers. Whenever the computer has data for the VDU, an instruction in the program writes data into the output port which communicates with the VDU. Similarly, when the computer requires data, an instruction reads data from the input port. The term port indicates an interface between the computer and an external I/O device. Programmed data transfer or programmed I/O represents the strategy.

To keep things simple, let's just consider data output from the computer. When the computer sends a word to the output port, the output port transmits that data to the VDU. The output port is normally a sophisticated integrated circuit whose complexity may even approach that of the CPU itself. Such a 'semi-intelligent' device relieves the computer of the tedious task of actually communicating with the VDU directly, and frees it to do useful calculations. In practice, the connection between a computer and a VDU almost always consists of a 'twisted-pair' (two parallel wires twisted at regular intervals). As the data written into the output port by the CPU is in parallel form (say eight bits), the output port must serialize the data and transmit it—a bit at a time—over the twisted pair to the VDU. Moreover, the output port must supply 'start' and 'stop' bits to enable the VDU to synchronize itself with the stream of bits from the computer. Section 8.1 deals in more detail with serial data transmission. Thus, the output port is the device which is actually responsible for moving the data between the processor and the peripheral.

The VDU is the output device proper. It accepts serial data from the computer, reconstitutes it into a parallel form and uses the information to select a character from a table of symbols. The symbols are then displayed on a television-style (raster-scan) screen. Sometimes the transmitted character is a control symbol (e.g. carriage return, line-feed, back-space) which affects the format (layout) of the display rather than adding a new character to it. Figure 5.1 illustrates the relationship between the concepts expressed in the above example.

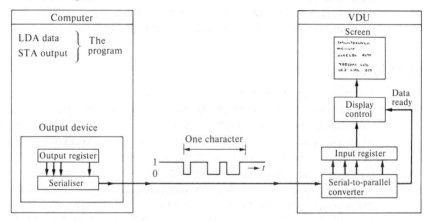

Fig. 5.1 The relationship between the CPU and VDU

As another example, consider the writing of a block of data to a disk. In this case it is often unpractical to use programmed data transfers (which are either too slow or waste valuable computing time). The output strategy most frequently resorted to is direct memory access (DMA), in which the data is transferred from the computer's main memory to a peripheral (or vice versa) without passing through the CPU's registers. The CPU simply tells the DMA hardware to move a block of data and the DMA hardware gets on with the task, allowing the CPU to continue its main function of information processing.

The DMA hardware is called a DMA controller (DMAC) and is responsible for actually moving the data between the memory and the peripheral. It must provide addresses for the source or destination of data in the RAM, and signal to the peripheral that data is needed or is ready. Furthermore, the DMAC must grab the computer's internal data and address buses for the duration of a data transfer. This must be done while avoiding a conflict with the CPU for the possession of the buses. In this example the peripheral is a disk drive—a complex mixture of electronics and high-precision mechanical engineering designed to store data by locally affecting the magnetic properties of the surface of a disk rotating at a high speed.

Input/output strategies

There are four basic ways of carrying out I/O operations.

1. Programmed I/O
2. Interrupt-driven I/O
3. Direct memory access
4. Channel I/O

In this section we examine the operation of each of these modes of I/O. W are not concerned here with the details of the hardware needed to implemen these strategies, nor are we interested in the periphals themselves. Befor dealing with these strategies, the topic of 'handshaking' will be introduced a it is fundamental to all exchanges of information.

Handshaking

Irrespective of the strategy by which data is moved between the processc and peripheral, all data transfers fall into one of two classes: open-ended c closed-loop. In an open-ended I/O transaction the data to be output is sex on its way and its safe reception assumed. This corresponds to the basic lev of service offered by the Post Office. A letter is written and dropped into post-box. The sender believes that after a reasonable delay it will be received

In most systems, both human and computer, open-ended data transfe are perfectly satisfactory. The probability of data getting lost or corrupted very small, and its loss may not be of any importance. If Aunt Mabel doesn get a birthday card the world does not come to an end. Consider now th following exchange of information.

Approach control: 'Golf Zulu Victor Cleared to Teesside for straight i approach Runway 23 Wind 270 degrees 10 knots QF 1019 Report field in sight.'

Aircraft   'Runway 23 QFE 1019 Golf Zulu Victor'

In this case the loss or corruption of information is potentially disastrou and the open-ended transfer of data abandoned in favour of a closed-loo system. The aircraft acknowledges the receipt of the message and reads bac any crucial data. In data transmission systems (see Chapter 8) data integrit is not achieved by repeating a message but by some form of error detectin code.

In a closed-loop data transfer between a computer and peripheral, th transmitter (i.e. originator of the data), first makes the data available, an then asserts a signal, DAV (data valid) to indicate that the data is valid. Th device receiving the data sees that DAV has been asserted, indicating tha new data is ready, and reads the data off the data bus. The receiver in tur asserts a signal called DAC (data accepted) which is a reply to th transmitter, indicating the satisfactory reception of the data. The transmitte then de-asserts DAV. This whole process is known as handshaking. Apart from indicating the receipt of data it also caters for slow peripherals, because the transfer is held up until the device indicates its readiness by asserting DAC. Figure 5.2 illustrates handshaking.

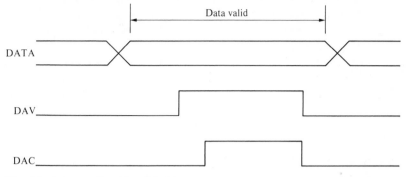

Fig. 5.2 An example of handshaking

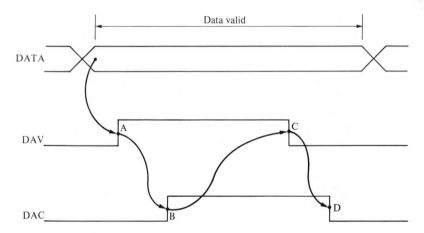

Fig. 5.3 Fully-interlocked handshaking

Figure 5.3 shows how the handshaking process may be taken a step further in which the acknowledgement is acknowledged. This is called a fully-interlocked data transfer. At point A the transmitter asserts DAV indicating the availability of data. At B the receiver asserts DAC indicating that DAV has been observed and the data accepted. So far this is the same procedure as in Fig. 5.2. The transmitter sees that DAC is true and de-asserts DAV indicating that data is no longer valid and that it is acknowledging that the receiver has accepted the data. Finally, at D the receiver de-asserts DAC to complete the cycle, and to indicate that it has seen the transmitter's acknowledgement of its receipt of data.

In many real systems employing closed-loop data transfers, the entire

handshaking process is automatic in the sense that it is carried out by special
purpose hardware. The computer itself does not get involved in the process.
Only if something goes wrong does the processor take part in the handshaking.

In any data transfer involving handshaking, a problem arises when the
transmitter asserts DAV, and DAC is not asserted in turn. In a reasonable
system a timer is started when DAV is asserted and if DAC is not asserted
after a given time has passed, the operation is aborted. When this happens an
interrupt (see next section) is generated, forcing the computer to take action.
In an unreasonable system the noncompletion of a handshake causes the
transmitter to wait for DAC forever. The system is then said to hang up.

5.1 Programmed I/O

In programmed I/O an instruction in the program initiates the data transfer.
Some microprocessors (e.g. Intel 8080) have explicit I/O instructions. For
example, executing an 'OUT 123' with the 8080 causes the contents of its
accumulator to be placed on the data bus, the number 123 to be placed on the
eight least significant bits of the address bus, and a pulse to be generated on
the system's $\overline{\text{IOW}}$ (input/output write) line. Each of the peripherals in a given
system monitors the address lines. To be more precise, it is the I/O port
connected to the peripherals that actually perform this function. When an
I/O port sees its own address, together with a read or write signal to a port, it
acts on that signal.

Some microprocessors (notably the 6800, 6809, and 6502) lack any form of
I/O instruction. If these devices are to use programmed I/O they must resort
to memory-mapped I/O. That is, some part of the normal memory space of
the CPU is dedicated to I/O operations. This means that an I/O port is
arranged to look like a normal memory location. A disadvantage of this
system is that part of the memory space available to programs and data is
lost to the I/O system.

Consider a 6502 microprocessor with an output port located at $8000
connected to a VDU. In other words, storing a word in memory location
$8000 has the effect of sending it to the VDU. As far as the processor is
concerned, it is merely storing a word in memory. A program at $0200 sends
128 characters (starting at $1000) to the VDU. The system and its memory
map is given in Fig. 5.4.

The program in Table 5.1 will output the data.

The numbers in the right-hand column give the time to execute each
instruction in microseconds, assuming a clock rate of 1 MHz. To output the
128 words takes approximately $128 \times (4+4+2+2+2) = 1792$ μs. This is a
little under two thousandths of a second.

Although this program should theoretically work, it is unsuited to almost
all real situations involving programmed output. Most peripherals connected

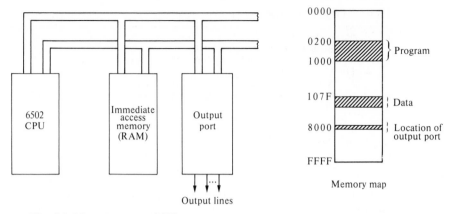

Fig. 5.4 Memory-mapped I/O

Table 5.1 Programmed output

Instructions		Cycles
LDX #00	[X]←0	
LOOP LDA $1000,X	[A]←[[X] + 1000] get data	(4)
STA $8000	[8000]←[A] output the data	(4)
INX	[X]←[X] + 1	(2)
CPX #$80	[X] − 80 test for end	(2)
BNE LOOP	IF Z = 0 THEN [PC]←LOOP	(2)

to an output port are relatively slow, and data output at this rate would simply be lost. Some peripherals are, however, able to deal with short bursts of high-speed data because they hold data in a buffer (a short-term memory arranged as a first-in-first-out queue) while they are slowly processing it.

A solution to the problem of mis-match in speed between computer and peripheral is found by asking the peripheral if it is ready for data, and not sending data to it until it is ready to receive it. Almost all memory mapped I/O ports occupy two or more memory locations. One location is reserved for the actual data to be input or output, and one holds the status word associated with the port. For example, let $8000 be the location to which data is sent, and $8001 the location of the status word. Suppose that bit 0 of the status is a 1 if the port is ready for data, and a 0 if it is busy. The program listed in Table 5.2 will deal with this situation.

This program is identical to the previous example except for lines 3 to 7 inclusive. In line 3 the data to be output is temporarily pushed on to the stack. This is because we wish to use the accumulator and must therefore save its contents. In line 4 the status word of the peripheral is read, and in line 6 a branch is made back to line 4 if the output port is busy. When the port becomes free the branch is not taken, the data is retrieved from the stack in line 7, and the program continues as before.

The action of lines 4, 5, and 6 is called a polling loop. The output device is

Table 5.2 Programmed output and the polling-loop

1.		LDX	#00	[X]←0
2.	LOOP	LDA	$1000,X	[A]←[[X] + 1000]
3.		PHA		[[SP]]←[A], [SP]←[SP] − 1 (save A on stack)
4.	WAIT	LDA	$8001	[A]←[8001]
5.		AND	#1	[A]←[A].00000001 (mask out all but LSB)
6.		BEQ	WAIT	IF Z = 1 THEN [PC]←WAIT
7.		PLA		[SP]←[SP] + 1, [A]←[[SP]] (pull A off stack)
8.		STA	$8000	[8000]←[A]
9.		INX		[X]←[X] + 1
10.		CPX	#$80	[X] − 80
11.		BNE	LOOP	IF Z = 0 THEN [PC]←LOOP

continually polled (questioned) until it indicates it is free, allowing the program to continue. A typical low-cost printer operates at 30 characters-second, or approximately 1 character per 33 000 μs. As the polling loop takes 7 μs, the loop is executed 4 700 times per character. The computer is being operated in a grossly inefficient mode. This is not always a bad thing. A small microprocessor-based computer (e.g. Pet, Apple, Aim 65) often has 'nothing better to do' while data is being input or output. On the other hand, a mainframe computer working in a multiprogramming environment can attend to someone else's program during the time the I/O port is busy. In this case a better I/O strategy is to ignore the peripheral until it is ready for a data transfer and then let the peripheral ask the CPU for attention. Such a strategy is called interrupt-driven I/O.

5.2 Interrupt-driven I/O

A computer executes instructions sequentially unless a jump or a branch is made. There is an important exception to this rule called an interrupt. An interrupt is an event which forces the CPU to modify the sequence of actions which would have occurred if the interrupt had not taken place. Here we deal entirely with hardware interrupts and omit the software interrupt which is essentially, a programmed call (or jump) to the operating system.

Most microprocessors have one or more input lines called interrupt request inputs. In the 6502 this line is designated $\overline{\text{IRQ}}$ (pronounced 'not interrupt request'). The bar above the 'IRQ' signifies that a low level (logical zero) on the line requests the interrupt. Note that the word 'request' carries with it the implication that the interrupt request may or may not be granted. In the 6502's processor-status word, bit 2 is an interrupt flag bit which, when set, causes interrupt requests to be ignored.

When the 6502's $\overline{\text{IRQ}}$ line goes low, and assuming the interrupt mask bit of the PSW is clear, the following sequence of events takes place. Firstly, the CPU is allowed to finish its current instruction. All 8-bit microprocessors and many larger computers cannot be stopped in mid-instruction. The individual machine code instructions are indivisible and must always be executed to completion. Secondly, the contents of the program counter, and the program status word are pushed on to the stack. Thirdly, the interrupt mask bit of the PSW is set to stop (disable) further interrupts. Finally, the program counter is loaded with the contents of memory locations $FFFE and $FFFF ($FFFF holds the most significant byte of the address and $FFFE the LSB).

The CPU now executes the interrupt-handling routine pointed at by the contents of $FFFE and $FFFF. At the end of this routine an RTI (Return from interrupt) instruction is executed which takes the contents of the registers saved on the stack and returns them to the CPU's registers, so that the CPU continues as if the interrupt had never happened. I like to think of an interrupt as a subroutine which is jammed or forced into a program by an external event ($\overline{IRQ}$ going low). Figure 5.5 illustrates the action of an

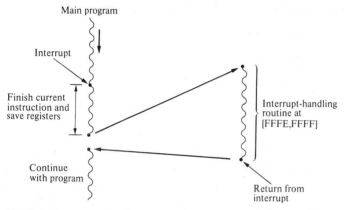

Fig. 5.5 The sequence of events taking place during an interrupt

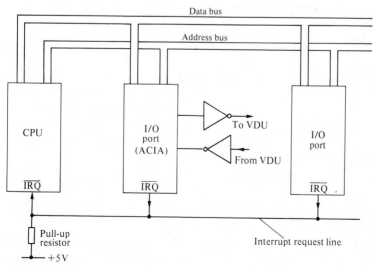

Fig. 5.6 Interrupt-handling logic in a 6502 system

interrupt in a 6502 system. An example of the hardware required t
implement interrupt-driven I/O in a 6502 system is given in Fig. 5.6. Here th
$\overline{\text{IRQ}}$ input to the CPU is pulled up to a logical one state by a resistor. Whe
any I/O device generates an interrupt, it pulls the $\overline{\text{IRQ}}$ line down to a logica
zero. Note the simplicity of Fig. 5.6—very few components are needed t
implement interrupt-driven I/O in a small microprocessor system. Thi
arrangement is analogous to the communications cord in a train. When it i
pulled, the driver knows only that his attention is requested. He does not ye
know who pulled the cord.

Interrupt-driven I/O requires a more complex program than programme
I/O. This is because the information transfer takes place not when th
programmer wants or expects it, but when the data is available. A fragmer
of a typical interrupt-driven output routine listed in Table 5.3.

Table 5.3   Dealing with interrupt-driven output

LDX POINTER	[X]←[POINTER]
LDA BUFFER,X	[A]←[BUFFER + [X]]
STA $8000	[8000]←[A]
INX	[X]←[X] + 1
STX POINTER	[POINTER]←[X]
RTI	return from interrupt

Each time the interrupt-handling routine is called, data is obtained from
buffer and passed to the memory-mapped output port at $8000. In a rea
system some check would be needed to test for the end of the buffer.

Although the basic idea of interrupts is common to most computers, ther
are considerable variations in the precise nature of the interrupt-handlin
structure from computer to computer. Listed below are some of thes
variations.

Interrupt acknowledge   When a peripheral generates an interrupt it
sometimes helpful if the computer signals to the peripheral that the interrup
has been detected, and is being acted upon. This facility is particularly usefu
with vectored interrupts (see below), where the acknowledgement can b
arranged to supply the CPU with details of which particular interrup
handling routine is to be used. Some microprocessors (e.g. the 8080) have a
explicit interrupt acknowledge mechanism, whereas others (e.g. 6800, 650:
do not. It is, of course, possible to derive a pseudo-interrupt acknowledge fc
the 6502. I have said that the 6502 responds to an interrupt by loading th
program counter with the contents of locations $FFFE and $FFFF. B
trapping (i.e. detecting) a read to these locations, we can provide an interrup
acknowledge.

Nonmaskable interrupt   Some microprocessors (e.g. 6502, 6800, Z80) have
nonmaskable interrupt ($\overline{\text{NMI}}$) input. This behaves like the $\overline{\text{IRQ}}$, except tha
it cannot be masked (turned off or disabled) by setting a bit in the processo

status word. This type of interrupt is often found in two particular applications. Firstly, where the interrupt is caused by an event which must not be missed. Typically, this is due to an interruption of the power supply. When this happens the system still functions for a few milliseconds on energy stored in capacitors (energy storage devices found in all power supplies). A nonmaskable interrupt generated at the first sign of a power loss is arranged to shut down the computer in an orderly fashion, so that it may be restarted later with little loss of data and no corruption (accidental overwriting) of disk files.

A second application of nonmaskable interrupts is in real-time systems. Suppose that in a complex chemical process the temperature and pressure at various points must be measured periodically. If this is not done by polling each of these points on a programmed basis, a stream of regularly spaced NMIs will do the trick. At each NMI the contents of a register are updated and, if a suitable span of time has elapsed, the readings are taken. The time represented by the contents of the register effectively maintains a copy of the time-of-day.

Prioritized interrupts   Some computers have several interrupt request lines. A few of these lines are connected to peripherals requiring immediate attention (e.g. a disk drive) while others are connected to peripherals requiring less urgent attention (e.g. a VDU). If the disk drive is not attended to (serviced) when its data is available, the data will soon be lost. The data is lost because it is replaced by new data. In such circumstances it is reasonable to assign a priority to each of the interrupt request lines. For example, a processor may be provided with eight interrupt request lines from $\overline{IRQ0}$ first (most important), to $\overline{IRQ7}$ last. If an interrupt is caused by $\overline{IRQ3}$, and no other interrupts are pending, it will be serviced. If $\overline{IRQ0}$ to $\overline{IRQ2}$ are activated they will interrupt the interrupt and be serviced. However, interrupts generated by $\overline{IRQ4}$ to $\overline{IRQ7}$ will be stored pending the completion of $\overline{IRQ3}$. Note that the NMI is really a special type of high-priority interrupt which must always be serviced immediately.

Polled interrupts   The 6502 has a single $\overline{IRQ}$ line, and all peripherals capable of generating an interrupt have their $\overline{IRQ}$ output pin connected to the CPU's $\overline{IRQ}$ line. Consequently, when a peripheral generates an interrupt by pulling $\overline{IRQ}$ low, the CPU cannot immediately determine which peripheral was responsible. One way out of this difficulty is to poll each of the peripherals' status registers. This is, of course, done within the interrupt-handling routine. Most peripherals have a status register containing one or more interrupt request flag bits. If a peripheral caused the interrupt, its interrupt flag bit will be set. As the programmer chooses the order in which the peripherals are polled following an interrupt, a limited measure of prioritization is built into the polling process. Polling can be very inefficient if there are many devices capable of causing an interrupt. It is a well-known law of the universe that when searching through a pile of magazines for a particular issue, the desired issue is always at the opposite end to the point at which the search was started. Likewise, the device that generated the interrupt is the last device to be polled.

Vectored interrupts   In a vectored interrupt, the interrupting device itself provides some means of identifying its associated interrupt-handling routine. This removes the need for polling. In a typical arrangement, a peripheral generates an interrupt by pulling $\overline{IRQ}$ low, and the CPU acknowledges it by putting a signal (a logical one or a logical zero pulse) on the interrupt acknowledge line. When the peripheral sees the acknowledgement, it puts an address on the low-order bits of the address bus. The processor can then identify the source of the interrupt by reading the response of the interrupting device. In this way the CPU can load the program counter with (say) the contents of one of eight different locations allowing eight separate interrupt-handling routines, one for each peripheral.

Interrupts considered harmful   Each aspect of life can be divided into one of two categories: a good thing or a bad thing. There are those who are firmly convinced that interrupts are a bad thing. A single peripheral generating the occasional interrupt causes few headaches. But imagine a system with many peripherals, all generating their interrupts asynchronously (i.e. at random). The entire system no longer behaves in a deterministic way but becomes stochastic (nondeterministic) and is best described by the mathematics of random processes. This system is analogous to a large group of people in a bar—there is always someone who never seems to get served.

5.3 Direct memory access

Direct memory access (DMA) is a technique whereby data is moved between the CPU's immediate access store and a peripheral, without the direct intervention of the CPU. This form of data transfer is the fastest possible and, as it carries no CPU overhead, leaves the CPU free to do useful work. As in most walks of life, if something is worth having, it is expensive. DMA is no exception to this rule, because it is quite complex to implement and requires a relatively large amount of hardware. Figure 5.7 illustrates the operation of DMA.

During normal operation of the computer, bus switch 1 is closed, and bus switches 2 and 3 are open. The CPU controls the buses, providing an address on the address bus and reading data from memory or writing data to memory via the data bus. When a DMA transfer takes place, bus switch 1 is opened and switches 2 and 3 closed. The DMA controller (DMAC) provides an address to the address bus and hence to the IAS. At the same time it provides a DMA grant (DMAG) signal to the peripheral which is then able to write to, or read from, the IAS directly. When the DMA operation has been completed, the DMAC hands back control of the bus to the CPU.

A real DMA controller is a very complex device. It has several internal registers—at least one to hold the current address and one to hold the

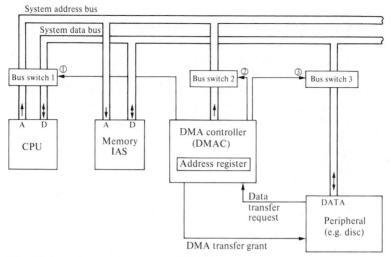

Fig. 5.7 Input/output by means of DMA

number of words to be transferred. Many DMACs are able to deal with several peripherals, which means that their registers must be duplicated. DMA normally operates in one of two modes: burst mode or cycle-stealing mode. In the burst mode the DMA controller seizes the system bus for the duration of the data transfer operation (or at least for the transfer of a large number of words). This allows data to be moved into memory as fast as the weakest link in the chain: memory-bus-peripheral will permit. Unfortunately, in the burst mode the CPU is effectively halted because it cannot use the buses.

In the cycle-stealing mode, DMA operations are interleaved with the normal memory accesses of the computer. As the computer does not require access to the system buses for 100 per cent of the time, DMA can take place when they are free. In many microprocessor systems, this 'free time' occurs while the CPU is busy generating an address ready for a memory read or write cycle. Figure 5.8 illustrates cycle-stealing.

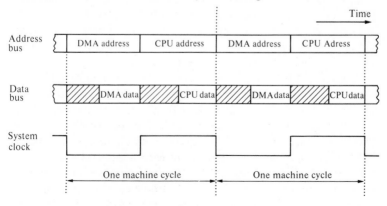

Note The shaded region indicates invalid data

Fig. 5.8 DMA by cycle-stealing

When the system clock is low, the CPU does not need the use of the buses, so the DMAC grabs them and carries out a data transfer. When the clock goes high the CPU carries out its normal memory access cycle. This form of DMA is said to be transparent because the computer does not 'see' it. That is, the transfer is invisible to the computer and no processing time is lost. A DMA operation is initiated by the CPU writing a start address and the number of words to be transferred into the DMAC's registers. When the DMA operation has been completed, the DMAC generates an interrupt indicating to the CPU that the data transfer is over, and that a new one may be initiated or results of the current transfer made use of. The majority of small microprocessor systems do not make use of DMA facilities.

5.4 Channel I/O

As computers have become more and more powerful, and an increasing number of input-output devices attached to them, even DMA has proved insufficient to cope with the volume of I/O traffic. When people become overloaded, they delegate responsibility for certain tasks to other people. Computers have been forced to do the same and have given the job of dealing with large quantities of I/O to other computers.

Channel I/O is effected by placing a small computer between the main computer and its peripherals. This small computer is frequently called a front-end processor (FEP), because it processes the data being input to, or output from, the main processor. It is interesting to note that as mainframe computers get more powerful, so do their FEPs. I have even heard people boast about the power of their mainframes by quoting the type of computer used as an FEP. The implication is, if that's the power of the FEP, just imagine what the mainframe can do.

The FEP is known by other names. IBM uses the term 'channels' to describe the streams of data handled by the FEP, and CDC have renamed the FEPs 'peripheral processing units' (PPUs). Because of the widespread influence of IBM, the concept of I/O channels is now standard throughout the computer industry. Note that 'FEP' or 'PPU' denotes what the I/O system is, while 'channel' describes the facility it provides.

When an FEP handles a mainframe's I/O transactions, two types of I/O need be considered. There is the I/O as seen by the mainframe, and the I/O as seen by the FEP. The FEP deals with the peripherals themselves and may employ any of the techniques described earlier (polled, interrupt-driven, DMA) to actually move the data between itself and a peripheral. Clearly, the FEP must know the characteristics of each peripheral it services.

Input/output operations as seen by the mainframe are very simple. It no longer has to be aware of the characteristics of each peripheral. All the processor has to do is send a single command, a channel control word

(CCW), to the FEP. Such a command may include the following information. 'Read 256 bytes of data into my memory starting at location \$002F00. Get the data from channel B, device number 4.' Once this command has been issued, the mainframe can deal with another program while the FEP is getting on with its task. When the FEP has finished, it interrupts the mainframe and returns a status word indicating the success, or otherwise, of the data transfer.

The last few years have seen the rise of a new factor in the treatment of I/O. This is the so-called intelligent peripheral. Once upon a time, peripherals were all different in the way they were interfaced to a computer. Each peripheral required a particular sequence of signals to be exchanged between it and the processor to ensure an orderly flow of data. This sequence varied widely from peripheral to peripheral. Today microprocessors are being embedded in all but the most primitive of peripherals. This means that the microprocessor can deal with some of the complexities of interfacing, with the result that peripherals can now be bought with standard interfaces. One such example is the IEEE-488 bus. Any device sold as being compatible with the IEEE-488 bus can be connected to all other devices displaying the same compatibility. This allows new devices to be plugged into systems without any changes in hardware, and few (if any) changes in software.

5.5 Input/output devices

So far we have examined how information in digital form is read by a computer, processed in the way dictated by a program, and then output in digital form. We have not yet considered how information is converted between real-world form and digital form.

In the first part of this section the two most frequently encountered computer interfaces are described. These are the VDU, and the printer. As microprocessor systems are now being 'hooked up' to a wide variety of interfaces, from speech synthesizers to robots, a short section is devoted to the direct control of electronic devices, and the conversion of information between analogue and digital form.

5.5.1 The VDU

The VDU has now become the principal input/output device for the majority of microcomputer (not to mention minicomputer and mainframe) systems. This is because it is an almost entirely electronic device and is cheap to produce, whereas all teletypes and printers are electromechanical devices, and are inherently more expensive. A VDU can logically be separated into two parts: an input device (the keyboard), and an output device (the display). Note that the terms 'input' and 'output' refer here to the device as seen from the CPU. That is, a keyboard provides an output which in turn becomes the CPU's input.

The keyboard

A keyboard is composed of two parts, a set of keys which detect the pressure of a finger, and an encoder which converts the output of a key into a unique binary code representing that key.

The keyswitch which detects the pressure of a finger (a 'keystroke'), is normally a mechanical device. A typical keyswitch contains a plunger which is moved by a finger against the pressure of a spring. At the end of its travel the plunger forces two wires together, making a circuit. Note that the output of this device is inherently binary (two-state). Between the plunger and wires is a small stainless steel 'snap-disk' which when bowed downwards by the plunger produces an audible click. A similar click is made when the plunger is released. In this way the act of depressing a keyswitch has a positive feel because of its tactile feedback. In fact, one of the differences between cheap and 'professional' keyboards is the presence, or otherwise, of this feedback.

Another form of mechanical switch has a plunger with a small magnet embedded in one end. As this magnet is pushed downwards, it approaches two gold-plated iron contacts in a glass tube (a reed relay). These contacts become magnetized by the field from the magnet, attract each other, and close the circuit. Although the mechanical switch has excellent ergonomic properties, it has rather less good electrical properties. In particular, the contacts get dirty and make intermittent contact, or they tend to bounce when brought together, producing a series of pulses rather than a single, clean make.

Three alternative forms of switch are: the Hall-effect switch, the elastometric switch, and the capacitive switch. The Hall-effect switch consists of a magnet which is pushed against the force of a spring towards a Hall cell. The Hall cell is a semiconductor device through which a steady current flows. When a magnetic field is applied at right angles to the current, a voltage is produced across the terminals of the cell at right angles to both the magnetic field and the current flow. Figure 5.9 illustrates the operation of such a switch. This type of switch does not suffer from contact bounce, but is relatively expensive.

The capacitive switch relies on the change in capacitive coupling between two metallic contacts when a finger is pressed against them. The great advantage of a capacitive-switch keyboard is its extremely low cost and small size—it is often nothing more than a printed-circuit board, the contacts are simply etched on the surface. Unfortunately, this form of keyboard has no

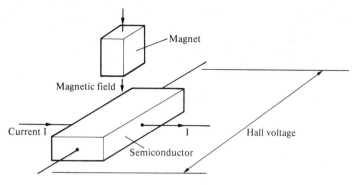

Fig. 5.9 The Hall-effect switch

tactile feedback and is rather unpleasant to use. Some designers get round the lack of tactile feedback by providing audio feedback. Each time a keystroke is made, a short audio bleep is sounded from a loudspeaker. The capacitive switch is found in some very low-cost personal computers, television 'touch-sensitive' tuners, and in professional equipment which must be hermetically sealed for operation in hazardous environments.

Keyboards relying on elastometric techniques employ certain types of material which change their electrical resistance when subjected to pressure. When a finger is pressed against the material, the drop in its electrical resistance is detected by a suitable interface. As above, this type of switch lacks any tactile feedback and its feel is said to be 'mushy and ill-defined'.

Because of the influence of the typewriter, the layout of most electronic keyboards closely follows that of the QWERTY keyboard. QWERTY is not a mnemonic; it is the order of letters on the back row of characters (from left to right) on a typewriter. Some keyboards have a separate numeric keypad containing the digits 0–9, decimal point, and some cursor control characters (backspace, line-feed, carriage-return, etc.).

In order to reduce the total number of keys, and hence the size and cost of the keyboard, many of the keys have two or even three different functions. This is achieved by the introduction of two special keys, shift and control, whose purpose is to modify the meaning of the other keys. The shift key behaves in a fashion entirely analogous to the corresponding key on a typewriter and either converts a lower case character into its upper case equivalent, or selects between one of two alternative symbols (e.g. ':' or '*'). The action of the control key is to permit the normal alphanumeric keys to be used to generate the non-printing ASCII control characters. In Fig. 3.1 the first two columns depict the control characters. The control characters are normally intended for the control of a data-link between a computer and a remote device.

The conversion of a keystroke into its ASCII-encoded equivalent is frequently performed by a special-purpose LSI chip called a keyboard encoder. The ideas behind such a chip are illustrated in Fig. 5.10. An eight-bit

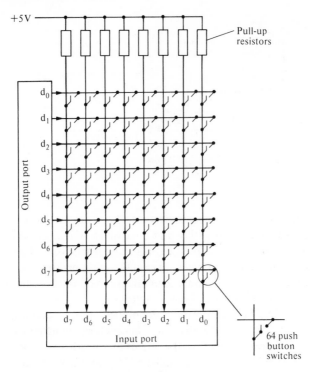

Fig. 5.10 The keyboard encoder

output port has a wire connected to each of its output lines. These wires run
horizontally in Fig. 5.10. Similarly, an eight-bit input port has eight wires
connected to it, and these run vertically in Fig. 5.10. At each of the $8 \times 8 = 64$
cross-points is a keyswitch which, when depressed, makes a connection
between the vertical line and the corresponding horizontal line. As long as no
key is pressed, there is no connection between any vertical and any horizontal
line.

The input lines are each terminated in a resistor connected to $+5$ volts, so
that these lines are 'pulled up' to a logical one. That is, if a byte were read
from the input port, it would be 11111111. Suppose now the output port puts
the binary word 11111110 on to its eight output lines. This situation is
illustrated in Fig. 5.11. If the CPU reads from its input port with, say, the top
right hand key pressed, it will see 11111110. If the next key to the left is
pressed it will see 11111101. Clearly, pressing a key on the topmost row, will
cause a zero to be read into the vertical position corresponding to that key.
Pressing a key in any other row has no effect on the data read.

The CPU next outputs the byte 11111101 and reads the input lines to
interrogate the second row of keys. This process is continued cyclically with
the CPU outputting 11111011 to 01111111, as the zero is shifted one place
left each time. In this way all eight rows are interrogated one by one. This

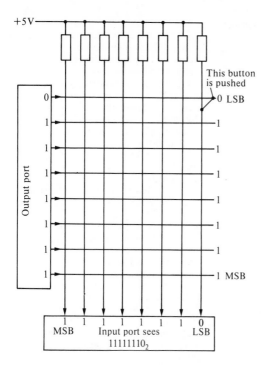

Fig. 5.11 The state of the keyboard with one key pressed

action is rather similar to the operation of coincident current core memories described in Section 6.3. The assembly-language program listed in Table 5.4 gives an idea of the software necessary to operate the keyboard.

The display

The exact details of a display system are well beyond the scope of this book. However, it is possible to give an outline of the way in which a raster-scan display works.

At the heart of most display systems is the cathode-ray tube (CRT), which is operated in one of two modes: point-plotting or raster-scan. A block diagram of the display part of a point-plotting display is given in Fig. 5.12. When the temperature of the cathode of a CRT is raised to about 600 °C by a heating element, it gives off negatively charged electrons. The sides of the far end of the CRT are coated with a conductive material connected to a very high positive voltage with respect to the cathode. This voltage is normally in the range 3 000 to 20 000 volts. At this potential the electrons are accelerated down the CRT to strike its front surface (face) with considerable kinetic energy. The face is coated with a phosphor which glows when bombarded by high-energy electrons. As the stream of electrons is focussed into a narrow beam, a small, bright spot is created on the front of the screen.

In front of the cathode is a fine wire mesh, called the grid, which when

Table 5.4 Reading the keyboard encoder

```
            ORG  $0200          origin of program in memory
XLINES      EQU  $8000          output port for horizontal lines
YLINES      EQU  $8001          input port for vertical lines
XVAL        RMB  1              temporary storage location
XCOUNT      RMB  1              current X value (output lines)
YCOUNT      RMB  1              current Y value (input lines)
START       CLR  XCOUNT         clear horizontal counter
            LDA  #%11111110     set up initial value to strobe the X lines
            STA  XVAL           save the initial value
LOOP        LDA  XVAL           get current value of X output
            STA  XLINES         put it out on the horizontal lines
            LDA  YLINES         get Y input
            CMP  #%11111111     see if a key has been pressed in this row
            BNE  LOOP1          if key pressed then decode it
            INC  XCOUNT         increment X cycle counter
            SEC                 set the carry bit (we need to shift in ones)
            ROL  XVAL           rotate the X output left in memory
            BCS  LOOP           if one in carry not last cycle
            JMP  START          if last cycle then start again
            *now we must encode the character into a 6-bit value
LOOP1       CLR  YCOUNT         YLINES must be compressed into a 3-bit value
LOOP2       CMP  #%11111110     is its value zero?
            BEQ  LOOP3          if so no more processing
            SEC                 set carry
            ROR  A              shift Y value right
            INC  YCOUNT         bump up Y cycle counter
            JMP  LOOP2          repeat
LOOP3       CLC                 clear carry
            LDA  XCOUNT         get the X cycle counter
            ASL  A              shift it three places left
            ASL  A              second shift
            ASL  A              third shift
            ORA  YCOUNT         combine (merge) it with the Y cycle count.
            RTS                 return with value of key in accumulator
```

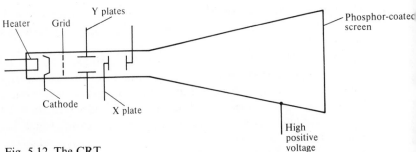

Fig. 5.12 The CRT

negatively charged repels electrons from the cathode, and hence reduces the intensity of the spot. The beam passes between two pairs of plates, one in the X plane and one in the Y plane. By putting an electrostatic charge on these plates, the beam can be deflected to any point on the face of the tube. Modern VDUs and televisions operate on a slightly different principle. They deflect the beam magnetically by passing a current through a pair of coils oriented a right-angles to each other, outside the CRT. It is easier to deflect a beam of electrons through a wide angle magnetically than electrostatically.

Two binary inputs are applied to two *n*-bit digital-to-analogue converters which transform the binary number into a voltage proportional to its digital value. The analogue voltages are conveyed, via amplifiers, to the X and Y deflection plates (or deflection coils). Thus, the binary inputs directly determine the X and Y co-ordinates of the spot on the screen. An additional input is applied to the grid to turn on, or turn off (blank), the beam. To operate this type of display, a table of X, Y values is maintained in the computer's IAS, and pairs of values are fed to two output ports sequentially. The ports are connected to two digital to analogue converters which provide the voltages needed to deflect the beam. The points are plotted rapidly to avoid flicker, as the image soon fades. It is necessary to display all points about 50 times a second.

An alternative form of display operates in a raster-scan mode (a raster is the path of the beam over the surface of the screen), in which the beam of electrons is periodically swept across the screen, line by line, so that the entire surface of the display is covered. In this mode the CRT controller does not have to specify explicit X and Y coordinates of the point it wishes to plot. Instead, the CRT controller brightens up the display, to produce a dot, when the beam is at the appropriate X, Y location. The detailed operation of a raster-scan display, which forms the principle of the television picture, is as follows.

A linearly rising sawtooth voltage is applied to the X deflection circuits of the CRT (see Fig. 5.12). This causes the beam of electrons to trace out a horizontal line across the display. In a television the intensity of the beam is modulated by the received signal to form the picture. In a VDU the beam is switched fully on or fully off to generate a pattern of dots. When the beam reaches the right hand edge of the display it is turned off and rapidly returned to its horizontal starting position (flyback), ready for the next scan. While the beam is scanning in the horizontal plane it is also scanned in the vertical plane, at a much lower rate. In this way each horizontal scan (a line) falls below the preceding scan. In the UK there are 50 vertical scans a second and each vertical scan (called a field) is composed of $312\frac{1}{2}$ lines. A frame is made up of two consecutive fields containing $312\frac{1}{2}$ odd numbered lines and $312\frac{1}{2}$ even numbered lines. The total number of lines per frame is $2 \times 312\frac{1}{2} = 625$.

The reason for displaying odd numbered and even numbered lines in consecutive fields is due to the difficulty of scanning all 625 lines in one fiftieth of a second. Such an arrangement is called interlacing. Interlacing is used in some VDUs to give 625 lines of vertical resolution, but many VDUs do not employ interlacing and are left with $312\frac{1}{2}$ pairs of lines. We will soon see that the number of lines displayed affects the number of rows of characters that can be fitted on to a screen.

A VDU screen is divided into a matrix of rows and columns, defining the display format. Typical VDU formats are 80×24, 40×24, 64×16, and

32 × 16. The first figure in each pair gives the number of columns per line, and the second figure the number of rows per frame. Figure 5.13 gives the format of a typical display. Each character is displayed as a 5 × 7 dot-matrix, called a font, within a block of 6 dots by 8 lines.

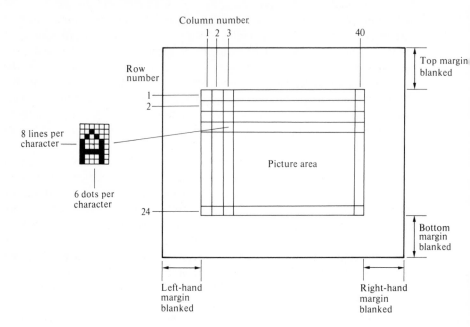

Fig. 5.13 The format of a raster-scan display

The block diagram of a simple 40 column by 24 row display generator is given in Fig. 5.14. The output of this circuit is called 'composite video' and is fed to the video circuits of a normal TV. In other words, this block diagram represents the additional logic needed to enable a TV to display digital data. The key to the operation of the circuit is a clock generator, which provides pulses at a rate of 5.76 MHz. This frequency is called 'the dot clock' and is the rate at which successive dots are displayed. The dot clock is divided by six to produce a character clock at 0.960 MHz or 960 kHz. The divisor is six because there are five dots per character plus a blanked dot space between adjacent characters.

The character clock (i.e. one pulse per character) is divided by 60 to get 60 character positions, or time slots, per line. Only 40 characters are to be displayed, the remaining 20 time slots form the left and right hand margins of the display, and allow time for the flyback. After dividing the character clock by 60, a frequency of 960 kHz/60 (i.e. 16 kHz) is obtained. This is the line rate and is also used to generate a line synchronizing signal called the line sync. It is this synchronizing signal that 'tells' the TV when to start a new line. The line clock is then divided by 10 to give 10 vertical lines per row of characters.

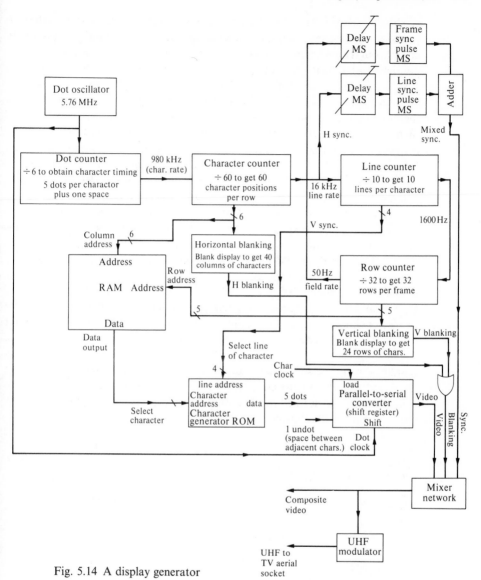

Fig. 5.14 A display generator

Seven lines are needed to build the character, and three lines to form a space between adjacent rows of characters.

The output of the line counter, $16\,\text{kHz}/10 = 1.6\,\text{kHz}$, is divided by 32 to give 32 row slots per field. Of these 32 slots only 24 display characters, the remaining eight form the top and bottom margins. The output of the row counter is $1.6\,\text{kHz}/32 = 50\,\text{Hz}$, which is the field rate found in the UK. The field rate is also used to generate field sync pulses to keep the TV display in step with the display generator.

Having set up the dividers, or 'timing chain', it is a simple matter to generate the display itself. As the character and row counters sequentially step through all $40 \times 24 = 960$ character positions, the binary outputs of these counters interrogate a block of random-access memory to produce an ASCII-encoded word for each character position. That is, the row and column counts act as address inputs to the memory, and the data from the memory represents the code of the character to be displayed. This block of memory may be part of the VDU circuitry or it may be part of the CPU's own IAS. The latter case is true of many of the small personal computers (Apple, Pet, ZX81). The output of the random-access memory is fed to the address input of a special-purpose read only memory (ROM) called a 'character generator', which converts the character code into the actual pattern of dots forming that character. The ROM has an additional address input which selects one of the seven lines of the character currently being displayed. This address comes from the divide-by-10 line counter.

The output of the ROM consists of a 5-bit word forming one of the seven lines of the character. The bits are zero for a blank dot and one for a displayed dot, and are fed to a six-bit shift register (one bit is permanently set to 0 to give the intercharacter spacing). The shift register is loaded by the character clock at the start of each new character, and the dots are shifted out by the dot clock. These dots are then fed to the circuits which generate the signal to be fed to the TV receiver. Other parts of the circuit are the display blanking, which sets the video output to zero when characters are not being displayed, and the mixing circuitry, which combines the video signal with the synchronizing (sync) pulses. The output waveform is called the composite video signal, and is illustrated in Fig. 5.15.

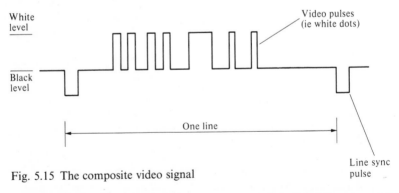

Fig. 5.15 The composite video signal

If the display generator above is to be turned into a VDU, some additional circuitry is needed to write characters into the RAM, sometimes called video RAM or display memory. Counters, either in hardware or software, are also needed to keep track of where the next character is to go. Special arrangements are necessary to cater for control characters. For example, when a carriage return is received by the VDU, it does not display it, but uses it to reset to zero the column position counter. Similarly, a new line simply increments the row position counter.

Virtually all VDUs have a cursor. A cursor is a special symbol (sometimes flashing) displayed on the screen to indicate the position into which the next character is to go. To generate a cursor the contents of the display generator's row and column counters are compared with the pointers to the next free position on the screen. When the two values are equal, the beam of the CRT must be at the position of the next free character and may therefore be turned on to produce a cursor.

The above description of a VDU is, of necessity, rudimentary, with much fine detail omitted. However most VDUs do operate on these principles. Today, much of the logic of a display generator is available on a single integrated circuit costing a few pounds. In general, the cost of VDUs is dropping as their internal circuitry uses fewer and fewer components.

5.5.2 The printer

The printer produces a permanent 'hard-copy' output from a computer by converting digital information into marks on paper. Because printers rely on precisely-machined, moving mechanical parts, they tend to be more expensive than purely electronic VDUs and are often less reliable. Moreover, the range of prices for printers is much greater than that for VDUs. A low cost printer of the type used with the ZX81 costs about £50, while a high-volume line printer may cost more than £10 000.

There is a very wide variety of printer types and mechanisms, each being a particular trade-off between cost, speed, reliability, and quality of printing. However, all printers must perform the same basic functions. These are:

1. Move the paper to a given line
2. Move the 'print-head' to a given point along a line
3. Select a character to be printed
4. Make a mark on the paper corresponding to that character

The first and last points are relatively easy to explain, so they will be dealt with first. Depending on the application, paper is available in single sheet, continuous roll, or fan-fold form. The feed mechanism of printers is not radically different from that of typewriters. The paper may be moved by friction feed, in which the paper is trapped between a roller driven by a motor and pressure rollers, which apply pressure to the surface of the paper. As the roller (or platen) moves, the paper is dragged along with it. Figure 5.16(a) shows the operation of a friction feed drive. Such a drive is not perfect and may allow paper to slip, or at least prevent the precise alignment of the paper. An alternative paper-feeding mechanism is the tractor- or sprocket-feed (Figure 5.16(b)). Here a number of conical pins form a ring round the ends of the platen. The edges of the paper (invariably fan-fold paper) are perforated

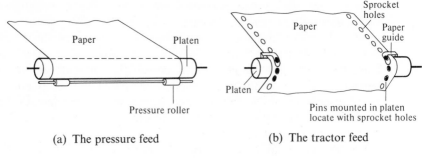

(a) The pressure feed   (b) The tractor feed

Fig. 5.16 Mechanisms for feeding the paper through a printer

with holes on the same pitch (spacing) as the pins. The pins fit through the holes and, as the platen rotates, the paper is accurately and precisely pulled through the printer.

Making a mark on paper is intimately connected with the way a character is formed, but a number of fundamental principles can be identified. The most widespread method of marking paper is based on the impact of a hard object against an ink-coated ribbon, which is then forced on to the paper to make a mark in the shape of the object. This is how most office typewriters operate. Printers are often referred to by the way in which the mark on the paper is made. Popular arrangements using impact printing are the golf-ball, the cylinder, the daisy-wheel, the line-printer, and the drum printer.

Another technique involves special paper, coated with a material which turns black (or blue) when heated to about 110 °C. Such printers are called thermal printers and form a character by heating a particular combination of dots within a matrix of, typically, 7 by 5 points (like the VDU). Thermal printers are often very cheap (until you think about the cost of the special paper), and are relatively silent in operation. Another mechanism involves paper coloured black but surfaced with a thin film of shiny aluminium. If a needle electrode is applied to the surface, and a large current passed through it, the aluminium film is locally vapourized to reveal the dark coating underneath.

One of the more recent methods of printing involves spraying a fine jet of ink at the paper. As this technique also includes the way in which the character is selected and formed, it will be dealt with in more detail later.

The mechanism which actually prints the character is called the print head. There are two classes of print head, the single print head and the multiple print head, found in line printers. In a typewriter the print head is fixed and the paper and platen move as each new character is printed. This is unsuitable for high-speed printing as the platen and paper have a high mass and hence a high inertia. As the mass of the print head is very much less than that of the platen, most printers are arranged so that the paper stays where it is and the print head moves along the line. One way of moving the print head is to attach it to a nut on a threaded rod (the lead screw). At the end of the rod is a stepping motor, which can rotate the rod through a fixed angle at a time. Each time the rod rotates the print head is moved left or right (depending on the direction of rotation). In another arrangement the print head is connected to a belt, moved by the same technique as the paper itself. The belt passes between two rollers, one of which moves freely and one of which is controlled by a stepping motor.

As the way in which the character is formed is so fundamental to the type of printer, a number of printer types are described as follows.

The dot-matrix printer

A dot-matrix printer forms individual characters from a matrix of dots in much the same way as a VDU forms its characters. The dots are formed by a number of wires (called needles) pressing an inked ribbon on to the paper, or the needles may be used with spark erosion techniques, or may be replaced by heating elements in a thermal printer. Dot-matrix printers have relatively few moving parts and are moderately cheap. Most printers found in personal computer systems employ dot matrix techniques and cost in the range £100 to £600. Figure 5.17 illustrates the operation of a dot-matrix print head.

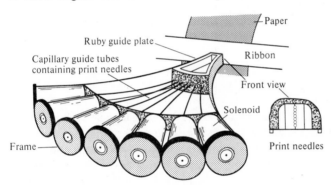

Fig. 5.17 The dot-matrix print head

Seven solenoids individually control seven wires. The solenoid is a coil which, when energized by a current, creates a strong magnetic field inside it. Because the wires are made of iron they can be moved in or out of the solenoid by passing a current through it. The seven wires are brought together by a ruby guide-plate to form a column of seven dots. By energizing a particular combination of solenoids, that group of needles is propelled towards the ribbon producing a pattern of dots on the paper. After each column of dots has been printed, the head is moved one dot position to print another column. After five (or seven) columns have been printed a complete character has been formed.

Because the character is made up of small dots, it is possible to program the dot matrix printer for any character set, and some printers also allow the use of dot graphics. Unfortunately, the print quality of a dot matrix printer is unacceptably poor in business applications where image is everything. Some dot matrix printers do produce a moderately high-quality output by slightly overlapping the dots to give the appearance of a continuous character.

The cylinder and golf-ball printers

Figure 5.18 illustrates the operation of the cylinder print head, and the golf ball. The operation of both these print heads is very similar. The cylinder print head is found in teletype machines and is a metallic cylinder with four

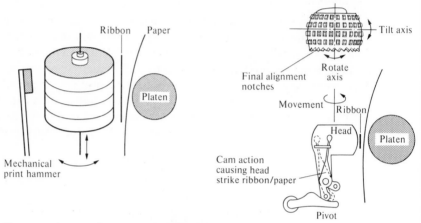

Fig. 5.18 The cylinder and golf-ball print heads

rows of sixteen symbols embossed around it. The ribbon and paper are positioned immediately in front of the cylinder, and the hammer is located behind it. The cylinder is rotated about its vertical axis and is moved up or down until the desired symbol is positioned next to the ribbon. A hammer, driven by a solenoid, then strikes the back of the cylinder, forcing the symbol at the front on to the paper through the ribbon.

The golf-ball head was originally used in IBM electric typewriters, but is now appearing in a wider range of printers. Characters are embossed on the surface of a metallic sphere. For a given volume the sphere has more usable space than the cylinder. The golf-ball rotates in the same way as a cylinder, but is tilted rather than moved up or down to access different rows of characters. Unlike the cylinder, the golf-ball is propelled towards the ribbon and the paper by a cam mechanism, rather than by a hammer striking it at the back.

Although there is no conceptual difference between the cylinder and the golf-ball, the cylinder mechanism currently in use provides only the lower-case 64 character subset of the ASCII code. The golf-ball provides both upper and lower case characters and is interchangeable. This means that by changing golf-balls different type faces may be obtained. The golf-ball printer is said to produce 'correspondence quality' printing.

The daisy-wheel printer

Like its namesake, the daisy-wheel printer has a disk with a large number of slender 'petals' arranged around its periphery. At the end of each of these 'petals' or spokes is an embossed character. The wheel is made of plastic or metal and is very light-weight, giving it a low inertia. A typical daisy wheel has 96 spokes, corresponding to the upper- and lower-case subsets of the ASCII code. Figure 5.19 illustrates the daisy-wheel.

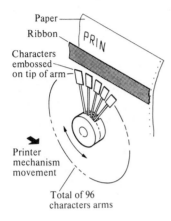

Fig. 5.19 The daisy-wheel printer

The daisy-wheel rotates in the vertical plane, at high speed, in front of the ribbon. As the wheel rotates, each of the characters passes between a solenoid-driven hammer and the ribbon. When the desired character is at a print position, the solenoid is energized and the hammer forces the spoke against the ribbon to mark the paper. It should be appreciated that a considerable amount of (microprocessor controlled) electronics is needed to carry out the complex timing required by a daisy-wheel printer. Some printers even control the amount of current in the solenoid (and hence the force of the hammer) according to the size of the character. This gives each character a uniform density. Some impact printers put so much force into a full-stop that a tiny hole is made in the paper! Daisy-wheel printers are often found in word processors because of their high quality printing.

The line printer

A line printer is so-called because it prints a whole line of text at one go, rather than by printing characters sequentially. Line printers are expensive, often produce low quality output, and are geared to high-volume, high-speed printing. One of the common forms of line printer, the drum printer, is illustrated in Fig. 5.20.

In front of the ribbon is a drum extending along the entire width of the paper. Along the circumference of the drum is embossed the character set to be printed. This character set is repeated, once for each of the character positions, along the drum. A typical line printer has 132 character positions

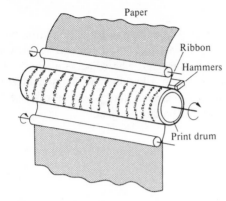

Fig. 5.20 The drum printer

and a set of 64 characters. Consequently, there are $132 \times 64 = 9448$ characters embossed on the drum. As the drum rotates, the rings of characters pass over each of the 132 print positions, and a complete set of characters passes each printing point once per revolution. Unlike some other printers, a mark is made on the paper by a hammer hitting the paper and driving it into the head through the ribbon. By timing the point at which a hammer is energized, any particular character may be printed. As there is one hammer per character position, a whole line may be printed during the course of a single revolution of the drum.

Suppose the line to be printed contains the single word ALAN, and that in each ring of characters the first character is A followed by B etc. The paper is assumed to have been advanced to the current line by a tractor mechanism. As the drum rotates, a timing signal is generated and sent to the electronics controlling the hammers. When a synchronizing pulse is produced by the first letter (i.e. A), hammers one and three are energized and the pattern A A is printed. After the drum has stepped to its twelfth position, the second hammer is energized and the line now contains ALA . Another two steps of the drum and the fourth hammer is energized to generate the finished line ALAN. After the drum has completed a full revolution, the paper is advanced one line and the sequence repeated.

A drum printer operates in the speed range of 100–400 lines per minute. As there are up to 132 hammers striking the paper in a very short time, the drum printer is a fairly noisy machine. In fact, it is possible to create a sequence of characters that will play a tune on the line printer. It is also a very good way of annoying the computer room operators.

The chain or belt printer is another realization of a line printer and is illustrated in Fig. 5.21. A continuous belt is made up of links, each containing an embossed character. The belt rotates in the horizontal plane, and the ribbon is positioned between the belt and the paper. A number of hammers (one per character position) are located behind the belt. As the appropriate character moves in front of a hammer, the hammer is energized and the character forced on to the paper through the ribbon.

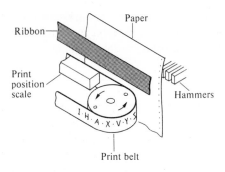

Fig. 5.21 The belt printer

The ink-jet printer

The ink-jet printer is an unusual type of printer owing more to the CRT for its operation than the impact printer. The basic features of an ink-jet printer are illustrated in Fig. 5.22. A fine jet of ink is emitted from a tiny nozzle to create a high-speed stream of ink drops. The nozzle is vibrated ultrasonically so that the ink stream is broken up into individual drops. As each drop leaves the nozzle it is given an electrical charge, so that the stream of drops can be deflected electrostatically, just like the beam of electrons in a CRT. By moving the beam, characters can be written on to the surface of the paper. The paper is arranged to be off the central axis of the beam, so that when the beam in undeflected, the ink drops do not strike the paper and are collected in a reservoir for reuse.

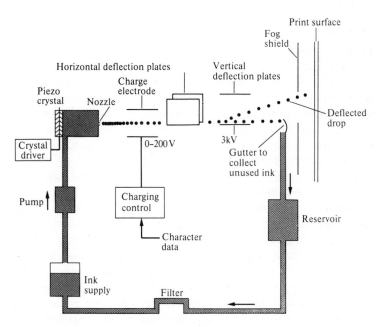

Fig. 5.22 The ink-jet printer

Ink-jet printers are high speed devices and are silent in operation. They are still very expensive and suffered a number of 'teething problems' during their development. In particular, they were prone to the clogging of the nozzle.

5.5.3 User-oriented interfaces

So far we have described the conventional computer input/output devices: the keyboard, VDU, and printer. There is, however, an immense range of other input/output devices, each designed for some specific application. For example, a cartographer uses a digitizer to enter a map into a computer, and a graph-plotter to draw the map after it has been processed. On the other hand, an automatic baggage-handling system at an airport may get its input in the form of human speech (a varying air pressure) and use its output to control the hydraulic devices needed to move the baggage from one conveyor to another.

As the topic of special-purpose input/output devices can be expanded without limit, we will give only a broad overview here. There are two fundamental classes of I/O device: digital and analogue. Devices whose inputs or outputs can be directly represented in a binary form are classified as digital devices (including those already discussed). Devices whose inputs or outputs are in the form of a continuously varying signal, which may have an infinite number of values, are classified as analogue devices. For example, the microphone, loudspeaker, and thermometer are all intrinsically analogue devices.

Digital input

All that is needed to implement digital input is some form of switch to select between a logical one and a logical zero. The electronic aspect of most mechanical switches is utterly trivial; two conductors are either pushed together to make a circuit, or pushed apart to break it. Conventional toggle switches, push buttons and rotary switches (found on volume controls in some radios and televisions) are part of everyday life. We have already come across some of the many forms of switch in Section 5.5.1. While many switches are in full view some are kept hidden.

Consider the humble limit switch, designed to detect the extreme motion of a moving device. If the control electronics of an elevator fail and the winding gear attempts to pull the carriage up beyond the highest floor the possibility of an accident exists. If a switch connected to a lever is mounted above the normal upper limit of the carriage, any unwanted upward movement will push the lever, close a circuit, and enable the safety devices to take over.

Another form of mechanical switch is illustrated in Fig. 5.23. It is often necessary to know whether the pressure of fluid or gas in a pipe is above or below a given value. The fluid is allowed to come into contact with a thin, flexible diaphram which is bowed outwards by the pressure. Clearly, the degree of movement by the diaphram is a function of the pressure of the

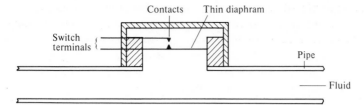

Fig. 5.23 The pressure-sensitive switch

fluid. By attaching a contact to the diaphram, a fixed contact closes the circuit when the pressure is sufficiently high. In addition to the purely mechanical switch there are two-state switches that respond to other stimuli such as light or heat. All the above digital inputs force the computer to take some action when a particular event takes place—the opening or closing of the switch.

Digital output

The output of all digital computers is one or more binary values, each represented as signals in the range 0 to 0.4 volts for a logical zero, and 2.8 to 5 volts for a logical one. The simplest way of exploiting these signals to turn on (or off) some device, is to use a relay. Figure 5.24 shows the

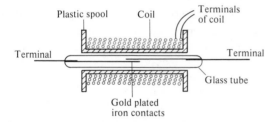

Fig. 5.24 The relay

construction of a typical reed relay. When a current passes through the coil, a magnetic field is induced in the iron core. At a sufficiently high value the magnetic field is strong enough to attract a piece of iron, whose movement opens (or breaks) a contact. The coil can be connected directly between the output of the computer and ground. An output of 0.4 volts is too low to energize the coil, while an output of 2.8 volts is enough to operate the switch. In a real system some additional electronics would probably be needed to boost the output of the computer to a sufficient level, as all but the smallest relays require moderately large currents to energize the coil. The relay performs exactly the same function as a mechanical switch, and therefore anything that can be operated by a human pushing a button or throwing a switch can also be done by a computer.

Analogue input

It is often said that we live in an analogue world, where the vast majority of measurable quantities have an infinite number of values within a given range. The temperature of a room is an analogue quantity because it changes from one value to another by going through an infinite number of infinitesimal increments on its way. Similarly, air pressure, speed, sound intensity, weight, and time, are all analogue quantities. Figure 5.25 illustrates a varying analogue value as a function of time.

Fig. 5.25 An analogue quantity as a function of time

At first sight it might appear that the analogue and digital worlds are mutually incompatible. Fortunately there exists a gateway between the analogue and digital worlds called quantization. The fact that an analogue quantity can have an infinite range of values is irrelevant. If somebody says he will arrive at 9.0 a.m., he is not telling the truth: 9.0 a.m. exists for an infinitesimally short period, so no event can be said to take place at 9.0 a.m. Of course, what he really means is that he will arrive at 9.0 a.m. plus or minus an unspecified amount of time. In other words, if we measure an analogue quantity and specify it to a precision sufficient for our purposes, the error between the actual analogue value and its measured value is unimportant. Once the analogue value has been measured, it exists in a numeric form which can be transformed into a binary value and fed into a computer.

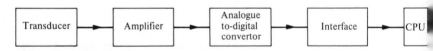

Fig. 5.26 Reading analogue quantities

Figure 5.26 illustrates the equipment necessary to convert an analogue quantity into a digital value. The transducer is a device which converts an analogue quantity (temperature, pressure etc.) into an electrical signal whose level is a well-defined function of the property being measured. The output of most transducers is very small and must be increased to a suitable level by an amplifier. The output from the amplifier is then converted into digital form by an analogue-to-digital converter (ADC). The operation of an ADC is not particularly complex but, because it cannot be explained without a knowledge of electronics, is beyond the scope of this book. The output of the ADC is often in binary form and is fed in to the computer by means of a normal digital interface.

Consider a system to read the temperature of the air. The transducer may operate in one of several ways, all of which involve some change in the electrical properties of matter with a change in temperature. Suppose the transducer generates an output from 0 volts to 1 volt as the temperature varies from $-10\,°C$ to $+40\,°C$. The output of the transducer is connected to an eight-bit analogue-to-digital converter producing an output of $FF for an input of 1 volt. Therefore, the 50 degree range, $-10\,°C$ to $+40\,°C$, generates a binary output in the range 00000000 to 11111111. Each bit of the output corresponds to $50/256 = 0.2\,°C$. This figure is known as the resolution of the converter, and is the smallest change in temperature that can reliably be detected.

Because analogue quantities are continuous, there is always an error equal to the difference between the actual signal being measured and its quantized value. This error is less than, or equal to, the resolution of the converter. At least in theory—all ADCs have small imperfections called nonlinearities and do not behave perfectly. Usually the error inherent in the ADC is less than one half of the least significant bit. When designing an analogue input for a computer, it is necessary to choose an ADC with the required resolution. This is easier to say than to do. Eight-bit single-chip ADCs cost very little. As the resolution is increased the price goes up exponentially.

Having quantized a signal in value, it must also be quantized in time. It is impossible to sample a varying analogue signal continuously. In any case, it takes several microseconds for a typical microprocessor to read an input. So how often do we have to sample a signal? The answer can be found from everyday experience. A television picture appears to be moving, yet it is (like a cine film) made up of a sequence of still pictures. Clearly, viewing a rapid sequence of stills (i.e. samples) gives the impression of continuous motion. Now consider sampling the temperature of a swimming pool. As such a large body of water has a high thermal inertia its temperature changes very slowly, so that a sample taken every few minutes would probably be adequate. These two examples demonstrate that the rate at which an analogue quantity must be sampled is related to the rate at which it is changing.

There is a theorem stating that a signal can be completely reconstructed if it is sampled at more than twice the frequency of the maximum frequency component in the signal. If speech is being sampled for processing by a computer, and the maximum frequency component in the speech signal is 3000 Hz, then it must be sampled at least 6000 times a second. This is the theoretical minimum, and a higher sampling rate (say 10 000 Hz) would be needed in a real system. This corresponds to a sample every 0.1 ms (i.e. 100 µs). Once a signal has been sampled and input to a computer, it can be processed digitially in the same way as any other numerical value.

Analogue output

Generating an analogue signal from a sequence of digital values is considerably easier (and cheaper) than the reverse process. Digital-to-analogue converters are readily available as single chips which produce a voltage a their terminals proportional to the binary value of the digital input.

A digital-to-analogue converter (DAC) can be used to generate a tim varying signal such as speech or music.

6 COMPUTER MEMORY

Memory can be defined as the long- or short-term change in one or more of the physical properties of matter caused by some event. That is, after the event has taken place, the change remains. For example, ice forms on a pond during a spell of cold weather, and lingers when the weather gets warmer. The water remembers that it has been cold. Without memory humans would not be able to follow a film, because anything that happened prior to the current point in time would have vanished. As the film is watched, the optical signal from the eye causes actual changes within the brain—the event has passed but its effect lingers. The film itself is a memory. The photons of light once produced by a scene alter the chemical structure of a thin coating of silver halides on a sheet of plastic. Both human memory and photographic film share a property called forgetfulness. The human memory may gradually fade unless it is refreshed (by repetition or a reminder). Even colour film slowly fades when exposed to bright sunlight. At least one type of computer memory also forgets its stored data unless it is periodically reminded.

A computer needs memory for two reasons. Firstly, the whole concept of the stored program (von Neumann) computer is founded on the sequential execution of a number of operations. Clearly, the program must be stored (remembered) if the individual instructions are to be carried out sequentially. A memory would not be necessary if all instructions were executed simultaneously. Furthermore, as the results of these instructions yield temporary or intermediate results, some memory is needed to hold them. Secondly, computers normally execute many different programs and those not currently being used must be stored somewhere. In addition to programs there are often large quantities of data to be retained until needed.

As much of computer technology (e.g. the CPU) is associated with binary arithmetic and Boolean algebra, it is reasonable to expect computer memories to follow this trend. Most memory systems store information in binary form by exploiting some two-valued property of the storage medium. Humans sometimes do this in non-computer applications. For example, consider the proverbial knot in a piece of string. The information is stored as one bit; knot or no-knot. I've always wondered why people don't tie different types of knot and thereby increase the information-carrying capacity of the piece of string.

The most important requirement of a binary memory element is that two stable (at least over a short period of time) states exist, and that these states are separated by an energy barrier. If there were no energy barrier separating the states it would be possible for a binary value to change its state at the least provocation. In the case of our piece of string, it requires a considerable energy input either to tie a knot or to untie it.

There are many ways of storing binary information and each technique has its advantages and disadvantages (cost, speed, power consumption, size etc.). Among the most popular forms of storage are the following.

Electrical with feedback. An electronic switch is held in a given logical state because its output is fed back to its input, holding it in a fixed state. A flip-flop or bistable is such a memory element.

Electrical with a stored charge. An electrical charge (a surfeit or deficit of electrons) is stored on a conductor which is electrically insulated from its surroundings to stop the charge draining away.

Magnetic. Individual atoms have a magnetic field caused by the spin of electrons. The spin has one of two values (up or down), creating two possible magnetic states. As the orientation of the spin of the electrons in most matter is random (due to the much stronger thermal vibrations of the atoms), there is no overall magnetic effect. However, a class of materials exhibit ferromagnetism, where the interactions between the spins of adjacent electrons cause them to align themselves parallel with one another. Under these circumstances, the bulk material may be magnetized. As we can magnetize material with its electron spins in one of two states, and detect these states, magnetic materials may be used in computer memories.

Structural. By modifying the structure of some object we can obtain a very large number of possible states. In practice, real systems use the 'there/not-there' principle in which holes are made or not made in paper. This (rapidly disappearing) form of memory is found in punched cards and paper tape. The gramophone record is a structural memory which stores analogue information by deforming the spiral groove cut into the surface of a plastic disk. At any instant the analogue information is a function of the depth of the deformation in the side of the groove.

Spatial. Superman has a neat trick enabling him to see into the past. He just zooms away from earth at a speed faster than light and then simply views the past event from its light, which has been streaming away from the earth at a constant speed of $300\,000$ km sec^{-1}. The memory of the event is represented by a stream of photons moving in space. Early computers converted information into sound pulses travelling down delay lines filled with mercury. When the train of pulses reaches one end, it is recirculated back to the other. This type of memory is called a delay-line memory, and is no longer found in digital computers. The magnetic bubble memory of Section 6.5 is a modern form of spatial memory.

Memory technology

As there are many different types of memory device, each with its own chracteristics, a vocabulary must be devised to describe them. Below are a few of the terms found most frequently in literature dealing with memory technology.

Memory cell. A memory cell is the smallest unit of information storage.

and can hold a single logical zero or logical one. Memory cells are often grouped together to form words. The location of each cell in the memory is specified by its address.

Access time. The access time is one of the most important parameters of any memory component, and is the time taken to read data from a given memory location, measured from the start of a read cycle. The access time is made up of two parts: the time taken to locate the required memory cell and the time taken for the data to become available from the memory cell. Because many semiconductor memories have identical read and write access times, the access time is normally taken to mean the read or write access time. This is not true of all forms of memory because some devices have quite different read and write access times. Some memories are also specified in terms of cycle time. This is the time which must elapse between two successive read or write accesses. Access time and cycle time are often identical. However this is not true for either semiconductor dynamic memories or ferrite cores.

Random-access. When I first came across this term I naively thought it meant that a memory cell was selected at random and that if it was not the desired cell another random access was made. This is not so. When a memory is configured so that the access time of any cell within it is constant (or effectively constant) and is independent of the actual location of the cell, the memory is then said to be random-access memory (RAM). That is, the access time of random-access memory is constant and does not depend on the location of the data being accessed. In practice, this means that the CPU does not have to worry about the time taken to read a word from memory because all read cycles have the same duration. If a memory is random-access for the purpose of read cycles, it is invariably random-access for the purpose of write cycles. It is unfortunate that the term RAM is often employed to describe read–write memory (as opposed to read-only-memory) where data may be read from the memory or written into it. This usage is incorrect, because random access indicates only the property of constant access time, and has nothing to do with the memory's ability to modify (i.e. write) its data. Another term for random-access is immediate-access. In everyday life the closest analogue of random-access memory is the dialled telephone system. The time taken to connect with (access) any subscriber is constant and independent of their physical location.

Serial-access. In a serial-access memory, the time taken to access data is dependent on the physical location of the data within the memory, and can vary over a wide range for any given system. Usually, the data moves past some read/write device so that in accessing any given memory cell, the waiting time depends on the time taken for the memory cells to move to the read-write device. Examples of serial-access memories are magnetic-tape transports, disk drives, shift registers and magnetic-bubble memories. Serial access is also referred to as sequential access.

Volatile memory. Volatile memory loses its contents when the source of power is removed. This term applies to most types of semiconductor memory where data is stored as a charge on a capacitor or as the state of a transistor (on or off) in a bistable circuit.

Read-only memory (ROM). Read-only memory can have its contents read but not (under normal operating conditions) modified. True read-only memories are, by defintion, nonvolatile. Read-only memory is frequently used to hold operating systems, interpreters, assemblers, and other system software in small microprocessor systems.

Static memory. Once data has been written into a static memory cell, it remains there until it is either altered by overwriting it with new data or by removing the source of power if the memory is volatile. Static semiconductor memory cells usually employ cross-coupled transistors (i.e. a flip-flop) to hold the data.

Dynamic memory. In a dynamic memory the data is stored in the form of a charge on the interelectrode capacitance of a field-effect transistor. Because the capacitor is not perfect the charge gradually leaks away, discharging the capacitor and losing the data. Whenever dynamic memories are used (they are much cheaper than static memories) some additional circuitry is needed to restore periodically (every 2 ms) the charge on the capacitors in an operation known as memory refreshing.

6.1 Semiconductor memory

Semiconductor random-access memory is fabricated on silicon chips in an identical process to that by which microprocessors and other similar digital devices are manufactured. Were it not for the availability of low-cost semiconductor memory, the microprocessor revolution would have been seriously delayed if microprocessors were constrained to use the ferrite-core memory of mainframes.

The principle features of semiconductor memory are its low cost, high density (bits per chip), and ease of use. There are two major classes of semiconductor memory: static and dynamic.

Static semiconductor memory

Static semiconductor memory is easiest to use from the designer's or engineer's point of view, and is generally found in small and medium-size memories. Large memories use dynamic memory because of its lower cost. A typical semiconductor memory chip, the 6116 16 K CMOS RAM is illustrated in Fig. 6.1. The abbreviation CMOS represents the technology used to manufacture it (cf. TTL), and the '16 K' denotes the capacity of the memory in bits. All semiconductor memories are specified in terms of their capacity (1 K, 4 K, 16 K, 64 K, or 256 K bits), and their organization. Some memories are bit-organized, so that a 16 K chip is arranged as 16 K locations of one bit

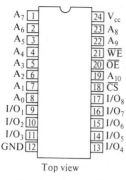

Top view

I/O₁=input/output 1 etc

Fig. 6.1 The 6116 2 K × 8 RAM

Others are nybble-organized with, for example, a 4 K chip arranged as 1024 locations, each containing 4 bits. The 6116 is byte-organized as 2 K words of 8 bits. Such 'byte-wide' chips are suited to small memories in microprocessor systems where one or two chips may be sufficient for the processor's read-write memory. The next generation of chips with a capacity of 256 K are now beginning to appear.

Figure 6.1 illustrates the pin-out of the 6116. It has 24 pins, of which eleven are the address inputs needed to select one of $2^{11} = 2048$ unique locations. There are eight data lines which supply data from the 6116 during a CPU read cycle, and receive data from the processor during a CPU write cycle. The electrical power is fed to the chip via two pins. Finally there are three control pins:

$\overline{CS}$ — chip select

$R/\overline{W}$ — read/write

$\overline{OE}$ — output enable.

In order for the chip to take part in a read or write operation the $\overline{CS}$ pin must be in a logical zero state. Whenever $\overline{CS}$ is high, the memory component 'ignores' any activity at its other pins. This allows several 6116s to share the data bus as long as only one 6116 is enabled at a time. The $R/\overline{W}$ input determines whether the chip is storing the data at its eight data pins ($R/\overline{W} = 0$), or is transferring data to these pins ($R/\overline{W} = 1$). The $\overline{OE}$ pin is used to turn on the chip's three state bus drivers during a write cycle.

Data is stored in this and other static RAM chips in flip-flops, each composed of four transistors. Figure 6.2 shows the internal arrangement of this type of chip. It is fortunate that all the address decoding and read/write electronics is located on the chip, greatly simplifying the design of the memory system. Figure 6.3 shows how the 6116 is connected to a 6502 CPU. As this memory component responds to 2 K locations out of the CPU's 64 K memory space, it is necessary to map the 6116's memory space on to the CPU's. That is, the chip must be made to respond only to addresses falling in one of the CPU's 32 blocks of 2 K. In Fig. 6.3 a few gates decode the CPU's

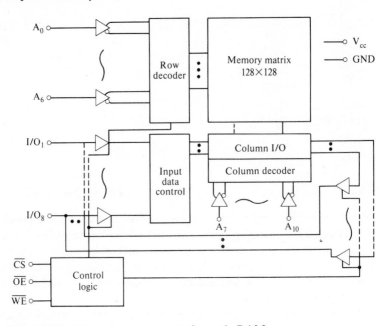

Fig. 6.2 The internal arrangement of a static RAM

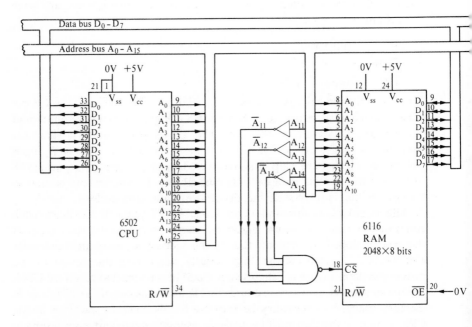

Fig. 6.3 Connecting the 6116 static RAM to a 6502 CPU

five higher order address bits, A_{11} to A_{15}, to provide a $\overline{CS}$ input for the 6116.

Whenever $A_{15}=1$, $A_{14}=0$, $A_{13}=1$, $A_{12}=0$, $A_{11}=0$, the chip is selected by an address in the range A000 to A7FF. That is, the address bus contains the bit pattern 10100XXXXXXXXXXX, where the Xs represent the state of A_0 to A_{10}. This is not intended to be an excursion into memory design but an illustration of the ease of the use of memory chips. Apart from a few simple gates, only the appropriate connections between the 6502 and 6116 are required.

One of the parameters of a memory chip of most interest to the designer is the timing diagram. This is a 'cause and effect' diagram and illustrates the sequence of actions which take place during a read or write cycle. The designer is concerned with the relationship between information on the address and data buses, and the control inputs. Figure 6.4(a) shows the simplified timing diagram of a memory chip during a read cycle.

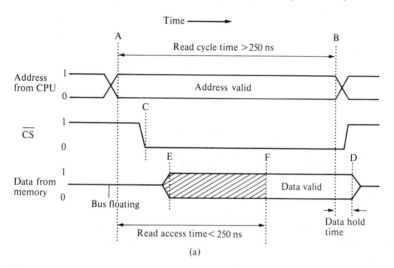

Fig. 6.4(a) the read-cycle timing diagram of a static RAM

In Fig. 6.4(a) the timing diagram of the address bus appears as two parallel lines crossing over at points A and B. The use of two parallel lines is a convention and means that some eleven address lines may be in a logical zero state and some in a logical one state. It is not the actual logical state of the address lines that is of interest, but the time at which the contents of the address bus become stable for the duration of the current memory access cycle.

At point A in Fig. 6.4(a) the contents of the address bus have fully changed from their previous value and are now stable. This point is taken as a reference for some of the memory's timing parameters. Because logic transitions are never instantaneous, it is usual to show all changes of state by a sloping line.

Between points A and B the address bus contains the address of the memory location currently being read from. During this time the address from the CPU must not change. The time between A and B is the minimum cycle time of the memory. A quoted value of 250 ns means that another memory access cannot begin until at least 250 ns after the current cycle. The $R/\overline{W}$ line must be at a logical one state for the duration of the entire read cycle.

Consider now the operation of the chip in a read cycle. The higher-order address lines are decoded and used to select the chip as in Fig. 6.3. At point C the chip select input, $\overline{CS}$, goes low. This has the effect of turning on the three state bus driver outputs connected to the data pins. Up to point E the contents of the data bus are represented by a single line midway between the two logic levels. This convention indicates that the data bus is floating, and is disconnected from the data output circuits of the memory.

When the three-state output circuits are turned on by $\overline{CS}$ going low at point E, the data bus stops floating and data appears at the output terminals. Unfortunately, sufficient time has not yet elapsed for the addressed memory word to be located and its contents retrieved. Consequently, the contents of the data bus between points E and F are not valid and cannot be used. At point F the data is valid and the time between points A and F is called the read access time of the chip.

At the end of the read cycle designated by point B, the contents of the address bus begin to change. Because of propagation delays in the chip, the data at the output pins does not change until some guaranteed minimum time has elapsed. This is called the data hold time, and is the duration between points B and D. The above description is a rather simplified description of a read cycle.

The write cycle is similar to the read cycle except that $R/\overline{W}$ must be in a logical zero state, and data placed on the chip's data input lines by the CPU. Figure 6.4(b) shows the simplified write-cycle timing diagram of a typical semiconductor static RAM.

Dynamic memory

Dynamic random-access read–write memory or, more simply, dynamic memory, is the most compact and lowest-cost form of semiconductor memory available today. Currently, the industry-standard dynamic RAM chip has a capacity of $64\,K \times 1$ bits, and $256\,K \times 1$ bit chips are now in production. Not only is the dynamic RAM denser and cheaper than its static counterpart, it also consumes less electrical power. What then is the difference between static RAM and dynamic RAM? The classical answer to this question is 'Static RAM works and dynamic RAM doesn't'. Behind this remark lies the fact that dynamic memory systems, unlike static memories, need a considerable amount of circuitry to control them. Moreover, the operation of this control circuitry is quite critical.

The static RAM stores data in the form of the state of two cross-coupled

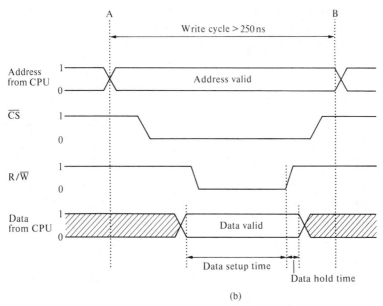

Fig. 6.4(b) The write-cycle timing diagram of a static RAM

transistors acting as an RS flip-flop. One of the transistors in the pair is 'on' and the other is 'off'. The typical static memory chip requires an additional two transistors per flip-flop making a total of four transistors per bit of stored information.

The dynamic memory manages to store one bit of information in a single-transistor memory cell. Consequently, for a given number of transistors per chip, a dynamic memory can store four times as much data as its static counterpart. The data in a dynamic memory cell is stored as an electrical charge on one of the terminals of a field-effect transistor. The effect of the charge is to modify the flow of current between the other two terminals of the transistor. A dynamic memory chip contains all the electronics needed to access a given cell, to write a logical one or a logical zero to it in a write cycle, and to read its contents in a read cycle.

Unfortunately, the charge on the transistor in a memory cell gradually leaks away and the transistor 'forgets' its data. Most dynamic memories are guaranteed to retain data for a period of 2 ms (i.e. 2000 μs) after it has been written. In order to retain data for longer than 2 ms, the dynamic memory requires that the data be rewritten into every cell periodically. This operation is called 'refreshing' and is largely responsible for the difficulty in using dynamic memory. In practice, simply accessing a memory cell refreshes it and, as we shall soon see, it is possible to refresh a group of 128 or 256 cells at a time.

Figure 6.5 illustrates the arrangement of a typical 64K × 1 dynamic

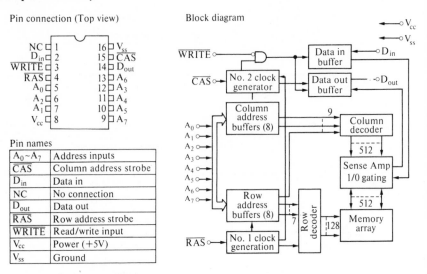

Fig. 6.5 The internal organization of a 64 K dynamic RAM

memory chip. This device is available in a 16-pin DIL package. By putting
the 64 K RAM in a 16-pin package the semiconductor manufacturers have
created another problem for the designer. A 64 K memory space is spanned
by 16 address lines ($2^{16} = 64$ K), so that a 16-pin package is clearly unable to
cater for the address inputs, data lines, power supply pins, and control lines.
The apparent lack of pins is overcome by multiplexing the address bus—the
address is fed into the chip as two 8-bit bytes. This increases further the
difficulty of using dynamic RAM. As this memory component contains only
a single bit in each of its 64 K addressable locations, eight of these chips must
be used to construct an eight-bit wide memory module.

The simplified timing diagram of a dynamic RAM read cycle is given in
Fig. 6.6. From Fig. 6.5 it can be seen that internally the RAM is organized as
four arrays of 128×128 memory cells. The cells are accessed by specifying
the row and the column of a given cell.

The read cycle starts with the 8-bit row address of the current memory
location being applied to the address inputs of the RAM. The $\overline{RAS}$
(row address strobe) of the chip is then brought to a logical zero state and
the row address latched into flip-flops inside the chip. The next step is to
apply the 8-bit column address to the chip and then bring the
column address strobe ($\overline{CAS}$) low. The data in the cell accessed by the 16-bit
address then appears on the data-output line after a delay of typically
150–300 ns from the point at which $\overline{RAS}$ went low.

A write cycle is essentially similar to a read cycle except that the write input
must go low before $\overline{CAS}$ goes low, and the data to be stored in the addressed
cell must be applied to the data-in line.

There are several ways of performing the refresh operation, but one of the

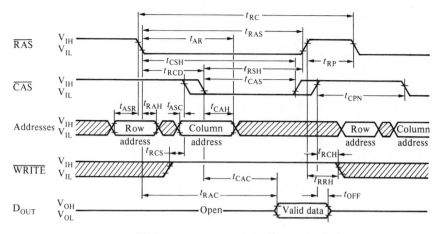

Fig. 6.6 The read-cycle timing diagram of a 64 K dynamic RAM

simplest is known as a $\overline{\text{RAS}}$-only refresh cycle and is illustrated in Fig. 6.7. The row-refresh address is applied to the address input of the chip, and the $\overline{\text{RAS}}$ input brought low for a specified period. After each refresh operation, the row-refresh address is incremented by one, so that all 128 rows are eventually refreshed. The refresh address must be supplied by logic external to the chip. Some of the latest 64 K dynamic chips have internal refresh cycle counters.

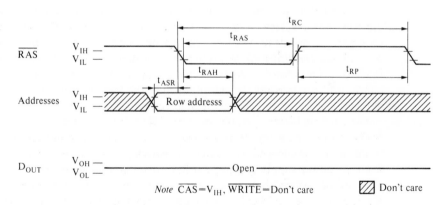

Fig. 6.7 The RAS-only refresh cycle

Unlike the static RAM, which has an access time equal to its cycle time, the dynamic RAM has a cycle time longer than its access time. This is because certain internal operations must take place before another access can begin. A typical chip has an access time of 150 ns and a cycle time of 300 ns.

An indication of the logic needed to control a dynamic memory is given in Fig. 6.8. The dynamic memory control must carry out the address multiplex-

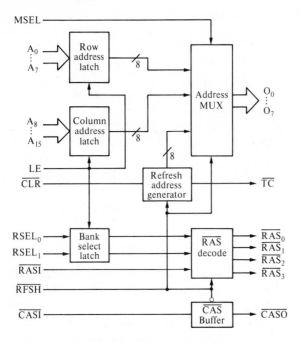

Am 2964B Dynamic memory controller

Fig. 6.8 Controlling the dynamic memory

ing and generate the necessary $\overline{\text{RAS}}$ and $\overline{\text{CAS}}$ signals. It must also perform 128 row refresh cycles every 2 ms. To do this it has to send a refresh request to the CPU and await a refresh grant from the CPU. When the refresh is granted, the controller sends a row refresh address to the memory and forces $\overline{\text{RAS}}$ low. The refresh address counter is automatically incremented. Fortunately, it is now possible to obtain much of the logic needed to implement a dynamic memory controller on a single chip.

The semiconductor dynamic memory suffers from two weaknesses peculiar to this type of memory. When a memory cell is accessed and the interelectrode capacitor charged, the dynamic memory draws a very heavy current from the power supply causing a voltage drop along the power supply lines. This can be reduced by careful layout of the circuit of the memory system. Another weakness of the dynamic memory is its sensitivity to alpha particles. The chip is encapsulated in a plastic or ceramic material which may contain tiny amounts of radioactive material. One of the products of radioactive decay is the alpha-particle (helium nucleus) which is highly ionizing and has the effect of corrupting data in cells through which it passes. The number of alpha particles can be reduced by careful quality control in selecting the encapsulating material, but never reduced to zero.

In most of the personal computers an occasional corrupted bit is an irritation, in professional systems the consequences may be more severe. The practical solution to this problem lies in error correcting codes. A 16-bit data word has five bits appended to it to create a 21-bit code-word. If, when the code word is read back from the dynamic RAM, a bit is in error, it is possible to calculate which bit it was and therefore correct the error.

As dynamic RAM is more difficult to use than static RAM it tends to be found in minicomputers and mainframes. However, in the last few years dynamic RAM has been adopted by the manufacturers of many of the personal computers. Only microprocessor systems with very small memories (typically less than 16 K bytes) appear to be using static RAM. A few larger microprocessor systems do employ the more expensive static memory because of its greater reliability than the dynamic RAM. One of the popular 8-bit microprocessors, the Z80, has been specifically designed to facilitate interfacing to dynamic memory. The Z80 periodically puts out an 8-bit refresh address.

Other types of semiconductor memory

ROM. Semiconductor technology is eminently well suited to the production of high-density low-cost read-only memories. There are several types of ROM; mask-programmed, PROM, EPROM, and EAROM being the most frequently encountered types. In general, semiconductor ROM, unless stated otherwise, is of the mask-programmed type, and is programmed during the manufacture of the chip. The mask-programmed ROM is available in sizes from 8 K to 256 K bits organized as 1 K × 8 and 32 K × 8, respectively, in 24 or 28 pin DIL packages. The application of ROM is even easier than semiconductor static RAM. As the ROM is never written to, a ROM chip requires nothing more than the address of the location to be accessed, and a chip select (or chip enable) signal to operate the output circuits of the chip's data bus. Figure 6.9 gives the pinout of a typical ROM, and shows how it is connected to a processor's address and data buses.

As much as any other component the ROM has been responsible for the growth in personal and other similar low-cost computers. A typical operating system and BASIC interpreter requires approximately 8 K to 16 K bytes of memory, and is therefore able to fit into (typically) two or four 32 Kbit ROMs. Without such large ROMs, system software would have to be stored on floppy disks (usually £300 or more for a disk drive and its associated power supply and controller), or on low-cost, slow, and unreliable domestic cassette tapes. Although ROMs cannot be reprogrammed or modified, it is not excessively expensive to remove the ROMs containing the system software of a computer, and to replace them with an updated version.

Another application of the ROM is in dedicated microprocessor-based controllers. When a microcomputer is assigned to a particular fixed task, say an ignition control system in an automobile, the software is fixed for the lifetime of the device. A ROM provides the most cost-effective way of storing this form of software.

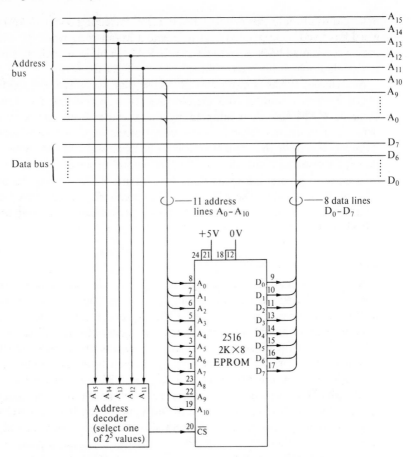

Fig. 6.9 The pinout and application of a semiconductor ROM

EPROM. The EPROM is an erasable programmable read-only memory. It shares some of the basic features of the mask-programmed ROM and many EPROMs can even be plugged into a socket designed for a mask-programmed ROM. The EPROM can be programmed by the user by means of a special programming machine costing from a hundred dollars upwards. Data is stored in an EPROM in the form of electrostatic charges on highly insulated conductors. The charges can remain for periods in excess of ten years without leaking away.

The EPROM costs several times as much as a mask-programmed ROM of the same density, but has the advantage that small-scale productions of microprocessor systems with their operating systems in EPROM are feasible. Although ROMs are very cheap, the manufacturer normally charges several thousand pounds for setting up the mask. The EPROM can be used several times because the data stored in it can be erased by illuminating the silicon chip with ultraviolet light. The silicon chip is located in a DIL package under a quartz window which is transparent to UV light. The UV light causes the stored charge to drain away through the insulator.

As EPROMs can be programmed, erased, and reprogrammed, they are suitable for both small-scale projects and for development work in laboratories. Once a program has been written and debugged in EPROM it can later be committed to mask-programmed ROM if necessary. A mistake in EPROM costs less than the same mistake in mask-programmed ROM.

EAROM. A recent development of the EPROM is the electrically alterable ROM. This variant of EPROM can be programmed and erased electrically. Consequently it can be programmd in situ and does not have to be removed and placed under a UV light. The reader might be forgiven for asking what the difference between a read–write RAM and an EAROM is. The EAROM is nonvolatile, unlike the typical semiconductor RAM. Unfortunately, it is much more expensive than semiconductor RAM, often requires nonstandard sources of power, and has a relatively long access time. The EAROM is found in special applications where data must be retained when the power is off. A typical application is in a radio receiver which can store a number of different frequencies and recall them when the power is reapplied.

PROM. The PROM (programmable read only memory) can be programmed by the user just like the EPROM. However, the PROM is programmed by fusing tiny metallic links in the chip by passing such a large current through them that they melt. A continuous link represents a logical one, and a broken (fused) link a logical zero. Clearly, a PROM can be programmed once and once only. Because of the way it is made, the PROM has a very low access time (50 ns), and is largely used as a logic element rather than as a means of storing a program.

Pseudo-ROM. Until recently the majority of LSI chips including the 6502 were fabricated by an NMOS process. These chips require a current in the range of several tens to several hundred milliamps for normal operation. Another process for the manufacture of LSI chips is called CMOS and produces chips with a very much lower power consumption. Although CMOS technology has been around for some time, the cost of CMOS was prohibitively high for all but special-purpose devices until the 1980s. When CMOS memories are not being accessed, their current consumption is so tiny that a small battery producing approximately 2.8 V is sufficient to supply enough current to retain the stored data while the mains power is disconnected. Such memory is strictly a read–write memory, but because it is effectively nonvolatile, has some of the characteristics of ROM.

6.2 Ferrite-core memory

Ferrite-core memories belong to the adolescence of the computer industry. In the very early days of computing immediately after the second world war, all manner of weird and wonderful devices were used to store digital data. For example, in 1949 Williams employed a cathode ray tube to store data in the form of an electrostatic charge on the face of the tube at a density of up to ten bits per square centimetre. In 1953 the ferrite core was first introduced in the MIT Whirlwind computer. The ferrite core is a small toroid of magnetic material (i.e. shaped like a Polo mint) which stores data in the form of a clockwise or anticlockwise internal magnetic field.

Until a few years ago, the size, cost and speed of ferrite cores made them the logical choice as the basis of the computer's main immediate access store. As semiconductor memory continues to plummet in price while offering higher densities (bits per chip), greater speeds (lower access times), and a much reduced power consumption, the ferrite core is fast becoming obsolete. As ferrite cores are nonvolatile and consume no power when they are not being accessed (unlike semiconductor memory), there are still a few areas where their use continues. With the advent of CMOS semiconductor memory and its tiny current consumption, even these applications of ferrite core will soon disappear. Having said this, I should point out that ferrite-core memories are still popular in certain industrial applications because they are regarded as being more robust than other types of memory and are therefore better suited to harsh environments. Plated-wire memory, a more modern offshoot of core memory, has now largely replaced ferrite-core memory.

There are three reasons why the principles of ferrite-core memories are taught today. Firstly, they illustrate very well the two-state nature of digital devices. Secondly, and more cynically, their operations can readily be explained in a few pages and the question 'Explain the basic principles of a ferrite-core memory' helps to fill in a gap in all elementary computer science exams. Unfortunately, it is almost impossible to teach the fundamentals of semiconductor memory in a 'few pages' because the operation of semiconductors is exceedingly complex and requires a considerable knowledge of the electronic properties of matter. Thirdly, the basic principles of ferrite-core memory may be extended to disk and tape units which still reign supreme in the province of backing storage.

A ferrite core or toroid is a small ring-shaped piece of magnetic material with a diameter normally in the range 0.01 to 0.07 mm. When magnetized, the field inside the core lies in the plane of the core and runs clockwise or anticlockwise as shown in Fig. 6.10.

In order to use ferrite cores in a practical memory two things are necessary. It must be possible to magnetize a core in a required state to store data, and it must be possible to determine the direction of a core's magnetization to read (retrieve) the data.

Magnetic field clockwise   Magnetic field anti-clockwise
   (logical state 0)   (logical state 1)   Fig. 6.10 The ferrite core

Storing data in a core is not difficult and relies on the fact that a wire carrying a current *I* generates a vector magnetic field, *H*, in the surrounding space. Figure 6.11 shows a wire carrying a current *I* passing through a ferrite core.

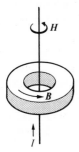

Fig. 6.11 The relationship between *I*, *H*, and *B*.

The current *I* creates a magnetic field of intensity *H* around the wire, where *H* is proportional to *I*. Inside the core a magnetic field, *B*, is produced by the combined effects of the external field, *H*, and the internal magnetization of the core material. A graph of the relationship between the internal magnetic field intensity *B* and the external magnetic field intensity *H* for a square-loop ferrite material is given in Fig. 6.12. The curve is called a hysteresis loop.

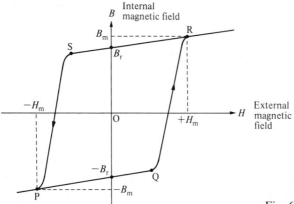

Fig. 6.12 The hysteresis curve

Before considering the implications of a hysteresis curve, it is helpful to examine the nature of ferromagnetic materials. It has already been stated that the origin of magnetism lies in the motion of electrons in their orbits. In most matter the magnetic effects of electron spin are entirely overcome by the stronger force generated by the thermal vibration of the atoms, which has the effect of stopping any magnetic interaction between adjacent atoms. In ferromagnetic materials such as iron and some of its compounds, there is a strong interaction between electron spins, resulting in the alignment of electrons over a region of the material called a domain. These domains range from one micrometre to several centimetres in size. Because the electron spins are aligned within a domain, the domain exhibits a very strong spontaneous magnetization, and behaves like a tiny magnet. However, within a large piece of ferromagnetic material, the individual domains have their magnetic axes arranged at random. Because of this there is no overall magnetic field in the bulk material. We will now describe the hysteresis curve and then relate it to the above model of ferromagnetism.

Suppose that the external field is zero. That is, $H=0$ because $I=0$. There are two possible values of B, $+B_r$ representing a logical state one, and $-B_r$ representing a state zero. The suffix r in B_r stands for remnant, and refers to the magnetism remaining in the core when the external field is zero. Like the flip-flop, the ferrite core has two stable states and can remain in either of the states indefinitely. Unlike the flip-flop, the ferrite core is a nonvolatile store and requires no power source to retain data.

Assume that initially the core is magnetized in a logical zero state. If a negative external field is applied (i.e. negative I, therefore negative H), the value of B goes slightly more negative than $-B_r$ and we move towards point P in Fig. 6.12. If H is now reduced to zero the remnant magnetization returns to $-B_r$. In other words, there is no net change in the state of the core.

Now consider applying a small positive value of H. We move along the curve towards Q. If the external magnetization is reduced we move back to $-B_r$. However, if H is increased beyond $+H_m$, the magnetization of the core 'flips over' at Q, and we end up at R. Now, when we reduce H to zero, we return to $+B_r$ and not $-B_r$. That is, if the core is initially in a negative state, increasing the external magnetization beyond H_m causes the core to assume a positive state. A magnetic field of less than H_m is insufficient to change the core's state.

Similarly, if the core is in a one state ($+B_r$), a positive value of H has little effect, but a negative value of H less than $-H_m$ will switch the core to a zero state ($-B_r$).

The switching of a core from one state to another is done by applying a pulse with a magnitude greater than I_m to a wire passing through the core. A current pulse of $+I_m$ will always force a core into a logical one state, and a pulse of $-I_m$ will force it into a logical zero state.

The hysteresis curve can readily be explained in terms of the behaviour of domains. Figure 6.13 shows a region of a ferromagnetic material at three stages. At stage (a) the magnetic material is said to be in its virgin state with the domains oriented at random, and has no net magnetization. This corresponds to the origin of the hysteresis curve, where $H=0$, and $B=0$.

At stage (b) an external magnetic field has been applied and some of the domains have rotated their magnetic axes to line up with the external field. As the external field is increased, more and more domains flip over, and there comes a point where the domains already aligned with the external field reinforce it, causing yet more domains to flip over. This process soon develops into an avalanche as the internal field rapidly builds up, and all

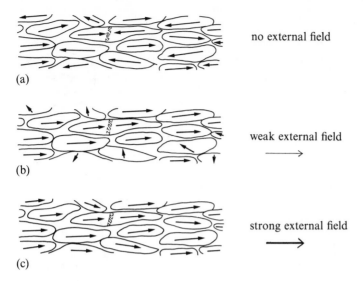

(a)

no external field

(b)

weak external field
$\longrightarrow$

(c)

strong external field
$\longrightarrow$

Fig. 6.13 The magnetization of a ferromagnetic material. (a) Virgin state of magnetization–net overall magnetization is zero, (b) domain rotations under the influence of a
magnetic field; 50% magnetized in the field direction ($\rightarrow$), (c) 100% magnetization in
the direction of the field (saturation).

domains are aligned with the external field. At this point (stage (c)) the bulk
material is fully magnetized and is said to be saturated.

The hysteresis curve of Fig. 6.12 is also called a *B–H* curve, and differs
from one magnetic material to another. In general, the best *B–H* curve for
the purpose of storing data is square, and the transition from one state to
another (i.e. from $-B_r$ to $+B_r$) takes place for an infinitesimally small
change in *H*. Such a magnetic material is said to have a square-loop *B–H*
characteristic. Magnetic materials displaying strong hysteresis effects are
called 'hard', while those displaying little or no hysteresis are called 'soft'.

Having magnetized a core, it is necessary to determine its state in order to
find out whether it was storing a logical one or zero. Unfortunately, it is
effectively impossible to determine directly which state a core is in. However,
we can determine the state indirectly.

Consider a second wire passing through the core called a sense wire, so
called because it senses the core's state. When a current pulse of $-I_m$ is
applied to the core, one of two things may happen. If the core was originally
in a zero state ($-B_r$), it will remain in that state. If, however, the core was in a
one state ($+B_r$), it will be switched to a zero state by the pulse. Figure 6.14
shows the effect of these two operations on the voltage induced into the sense
line.

In Case 1 the core does not change state and the voltage on the sense line
consists of two small pulses (the differential of the switching pulse). In Case 2
there is a much larger pulse on the sense line caused by the change in

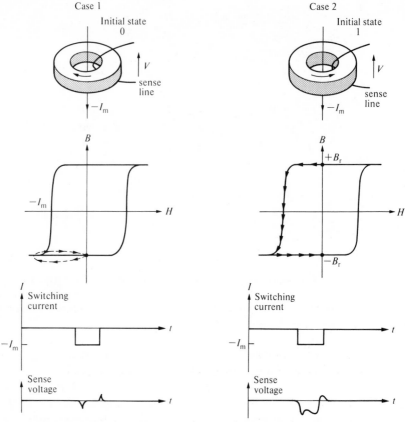

Fig. 6.14 Reading the ferrite core

magnetic flux as the core changes state. The two hysteresis diagrams in Fig. 6.14 illustrate the paths taken by the cores in these two cases.

It should be apparent that the effect of reading a core is to destroy its data. For this reason ferrite cores are said to be destructive readout (DRO) devices. After a read cycle has taken place all cores which have been interrogated are left to a zero state so that a read cycle must be followed by a write cycle to restore the data. For this reason, the read access time of a ferrite core is less than its cycle time, because a new access cannot begin until after the data has been rewritten following a read operation.

The core memory plane

So far we have looked at the characteristics of a single core representing one memory cell. In a practical arrangement of a ferrite core memory n words by m bits must be catered for. One of the many possible systems is illustrated in Fig. 6.15.

The key to the operation of memory planes is the coincident-current selection technique. The current needed to switch a core is at least I_m, and

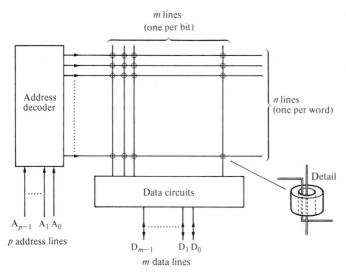

Fig. 6.15 The two-dimensional (2-D) core store

may be provided by a single pulse on one wire or as a number of pulses on separate wires. That is, two wires each carrying $I_m/2$ will do as well as one wire carrying I_m. Consider now the writing of data into the ith word of the array. The address decoder uses the p-bit word address to select one of the n word lines ($n = 2^p$). If a pulse of $-I_m$ is applied to the ith word line (horizontally), all m cores threading that line are forced into a zero state.

To write a logical one into the ith word, a current pulse of $+I_m/2$ is applied to the appropriate word line. This current is, of course, not enough to alter the magnetization of the cores alone. If a pulse of $+I_m/2$ is applied to one of the m data lines, the total current flowing through the core threaded by that word and data line is now $+I_m$, sufficient to switch it into a logical one state. It should now be clear why this is called a coincident-current selection technique.

Figure 6.16 illustrates how a 4 word by 4-bit memory writes the data value 0101 into word 01. If the cores in word 01 have all been set to a zero state by a pulse of $-I_m$, the two cores in heavy shading will be switched to a logical one state, because only these two cores have a total current of $+I_m$ flowing through them. All other cores in the plane have either no current, or $+I_m/2$ flowing through them which is not enough to make them change state.

A read cycle is executed by applying a pulse of $-I_m$ to the appropriate word line. The data lines now serve as sense lines and detect whether the core was in a zero or a one state. Figure 6.17 shows how the data in the above example is read.

Once more it should be noted that the read cycle has destroyed the data and a write cycle is needed to restore it so that the access time of a ferrite core is shorter than the cycle time. The cycle time is the minimum time which must elapse between two consecutive read accesses of the core store.

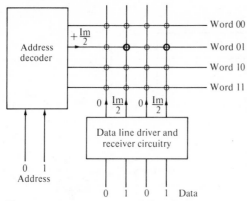

Fig. 6.16 An example of the 2-D core store in a write cycle. Data 0101 is written into word 01 by applying a current pulse of $+I_m/2$ to the word line corresponding to address 01, and current pulses of 0, $I_m/2$, 0, and $I_m/2$, respectively, to the four data lines.

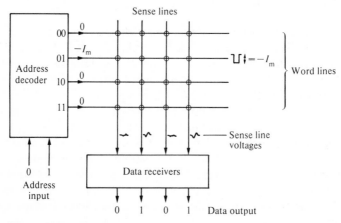

Fig. 6.17 Reading the 2-D core memory. A current pulse of $-I_m$ is applied to word line 01 forcing all four cores threaded by this line into a logical zero state. The cores are read by sensing the voltage on the four data lines.

6.3 Thin-film memory

Thin-film memory is a logical extension of ferrite core memory in which the ferrite core is replaced by either a thin film of magnetic material, or a coating of magnetic material along a conductor. The latter arrangement is called a plated-wire memory.

Two disadvantages of ferrite-core memory have led to the search for a better alternative. These are the relatively slow switching speed of the core (typically 1 μs to less than 50 ns), and the manufacturing difficulties of threading them.

Very thin films of nickel–iron are deposited on an inert substrate. These films, having a thickness of approximately 1 μm, exhibit two important magnetic properties. They do not have the same domain structure as ferrite materials, and the switching of the direction of magnetization takes place at the molecular level rather than by the rotation of the individual domains. For all practical purposes the thin film behaves like a single domain.

The other property of interest is its magnetic anisotropy. Unlike many ferrite materials whose magnetic properties are largely independent of the direction of the applied external field, the thin film exhibits different magnetic properties according to the orientation of the field. Anisotropy is a characteristic of many materials—wood is easier to chop along the grain than across it.

When the film is first laid down on the substrate, the deposition is done in the presence of a steady external field. This has the effect of creating two magnetic axes in the film. One axis is called the easy direction and lies in the direction of the external field present during the film's manufacture. The thin-film displays a square-loop B–H characteristic in the easy axis, very much like the ferrite core.

The other axis, the hard axis of magnetization, perpendicular to the easy axis, has a nearly linear B–H relationship. That is, the internal field intensity, B, is proportional to the external field intensity H, and little hysteresis is exhibited.

The reader can best understand what follows if he regards a thin film as behaving almost like a ferrite-core store. The major difference between the thin film and the ferrite core is that the core is a two-state device, and the thin film a four-state device. Two of the thin film's states are stable corresponding to a logical one or zero, and two are unstable and cannot be maintained in the absence of an external field. Think of the thin film as a coin which, when dropped, can land in one of three ways: heads or tails (the stable states), and on its edge (the unstable state).

Figure 6.18(a) shows two thin films in the absence of an external magnetic field. One is in a logical zero state, and the other in a logical one state. In Fig. 6.18(b) an external field has been applied parallel to the hard axis, causing the field in the thin film to be rotated as shown. The internal field is the vector sum of the fields in the hard and easy axes. If the external field is reduced to zero, the magnetization of the film returns (or relaxes) to its initial state as in Fig. 6.18(a).

If the external field in the hard direction is increased to the level in Fig. 6.18(c), the magnetization of the film aligns itself parallel to the hard direction. Note that both samples are now in neither a logical one nor a logical zero state. Once the film is in this state a small magnetic field parallel to the easy axis will determine the state of the film when the field in the hard direction is removed. This is analogous to a coin balanced on its edge; it needs only a very small force to topple it in one direction or the other.

Figure 6.19 shows how a 2-dimensional, word-organized thin-film store is

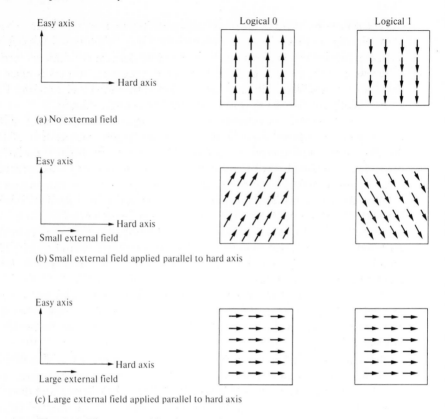

Fig. 6.18 The easy and hard magnetic axes

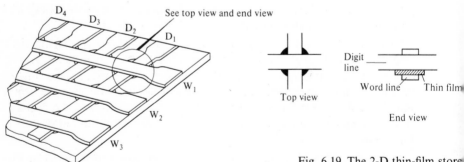

Fig. 6.19 The 2-D thin-film store

constructed. Digit lines run parallel to the hard axis of magnetization of the thin films. Perpendicular to the digit lines run the word lines, arranged as hairpin loops running across over digit lines and then back under them.

To read data from a film, a word current is passed down a word line to create a magnetic field along the hard axis of the films. This causes all the thin films traversed by the selected word line to rotate their internal field through

90 degrees from their stable axis. The rotating magnetic field causes a voltage to be induced in each of the digit lines passing over the film. The direction of rotation determines the polarity of the induced voltage, and hence indicates whether the film was in a zero state or a one state.

Data is written into the bits of a word by applying a word pulse to force the films representing the bits of the chosen word to be magnetized along the hard axis. Then a current is applied to the digit lines to produce magnetic fields either up or down the easy axis. When the word current is removed, the magnetization of the films rotate clockwise or anticlockwise into the easy axis. The direction of rotation is determined by the polarity of the current in the digit lines.

The thin-film store may be operated in either a destructive readout mode like ferrite cores, or in a nondestructive readout (NDRO) mode. If the word current is sufficient to rotate the magnetization fully through 90 degrees, the readout is destructive. If the word current is carefully controlled so that the rotation is through less than 90 degrees, the sense of the core can still be determined by the induced voltage in the digit line. When the word current is removed, the internal magnetization relaxes to its undisturbed easy state.

Unfortunately, when operating in a NDRO mode, the word current must be carefully controlled. Too little and the field is not rotated sufficiently to induce a high enough voltage in the digit line for reliable detection. Too much and the magnetization will be rotated through 90 degrees, and the stored data lost.

The planar thin-film store described above suffers from poor coupling between the sense line and the magnetic films. Figure 6.20 shows an alternative arrangement in which the digit lines are actually coated with the thin film. The so-called plated-wire store operates in exactly the same way as a planar thin-film store but is easier to produce. Because of the excellent coupling between the digit line and the thin film, the signal induced in the digit line is 100 times greater than the corresponding signal in a planar store, for the same word-drive current. The speed of a real thin-film store is

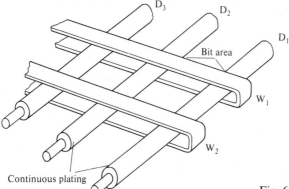

Fig. 6.20 The plated-wire store

determined not by the thin-film itself but by the associated electronics. Plated-wire stores are available with 250 ns cycle times and have replaced ferrite core stores in many mainframes. Plated-wire store is often found in on-board computers in spacecraft and satellites where their nonvolatility, zeropower consumption when not in use, and insensitivity to the effects of radiation are important characteristics.

6.4 Memory hierarchy

In any real computer system there are many ways of storing information. For example, there are the internal registers within the CPU itself—the accumulators, stack pointers, index registers and program counter. Then there is immediate access store (main memory, core store or RAM). Even this is sometimes partitioned into a high-speed cache memory and a slower core store. The cache memory will be discussed in Section 9.3. Next we have disk stores followed by tape transports. If all these devices store data, why do we need so many of them?

The answer to this question is the same as to that of the question 'Why do I travel by rail instead of air?' As in every aspect of life, economics play a dominant role. The characteristics a computer designer would like to see in a memory device are often mutually exclusive. The ideal memory has the following characteristics.

1. High speed. Its access time should be very low, preferably 2 ns, or less.
2. Small size. It should be physically small. One thousand megabytes per cubic centimetre is ideal.
3. Low power consumption. The entire memory system should run off a watch battery for ten years.
4. Highly robust. The memory should not be prone to errors—a logical one spontaneously turning into a logical zero or vice versa. It should also be able to work at temperatures of $-60°C$ or at $200°C$. (The military are very keen on this.)
5. Low cost. The memory should cost nothing and should be given away free with software.

Now let us look at the characteristics of real memory devices.

Internal CPU memory. Registers in CPUs have very low access times as they are built with the same technology as the CPU itself. They are very expensive and consume much power. This frequently limits the number of internal registers and 'scratchpad' memory within the CPU itself. This is especially true when the CPU is fabricated on a silicon chip, although the number of registers which can be included on a chip has increased dramatically in recent years.

Immediate-access store. This memory holds the programs and data during their execution, and is relatively fast (50 ns–1 µs). It is normally implemented as semiconductor storage or ferrite-core storage (plated wire memories are a variation on ferrite-core store). This memory is costly, consumes relatively high power and is physically bulky.

Magnetic disk. The magnetic disk can store large quantities of data in a small space and has a very low cost per bit. Unfortunately it is a serial access device and its access time (although fast in human terms) is orders of magnitude slower than immediate-access store. A typical disk drive can store 300 megabytes and has an access time of 25 ms.

Magnetic tape. Magnetic tape is an exceedingly cheap serial access device and can store up to 46 megabytes on a tape costing only £6. Unfortunately, its average access time is abysmally long.

By combining all these types of memory in a single computer system, the computer engineer can get the best of all worlds and build a relatively low-cost memory system with a speed performance only a few percent lower than that of a large immediate access memory. The key to computer memory design is having the right data in the right place at the right time. A very large computer system may have thousands of programs and millions of data files, but only a few programs and files are required by the CPU at any one time. By designing an operating system which tries to move data from disks and tapes into the immediate access store so that the CPU always (or nearly always) finds the data it wants in the IAS, the system has the speed of a giant high-speed store at a tiny fraction of the cost. Such an arrangement is called a virtual memory because the memory appears to the CPU as (say) a 1000 megabyte IAS, when in reality there may be a real IAS of only one megabyte and 1000 megabytes of disk storage. Section 9.3 provides further details on virtual memory systems.

Backing stores

We have already seen that a computer's memory is partitioned into a high-speed, high-cost, low-capacity, immediate access store and a low-speed, low-cost, high-capacity backing store. Today the term 'backing store' is synonymous with tape transports and disk drives, although magnetic bubble memories may get a look-in in the near future, and some form of optical memory (e.g. Video disk) may be lurking round the corner.

6.4.1 Magnetic recording

The operation of both disk drives and tape units is virtually the same: one records data on a flat platter coated with a magnetic material, while the other records data on a thin band of flexible plastic coated with magnetic material. Figure 6.21 illustrates this process.

The write head (or record head) used to write data consists of a ring of high-permeability soft magnetic material with a coil wound round it. High-permeability means that the material offers a low resistance to a magnetic

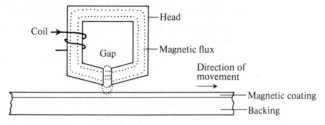

Fig. 6.21 The read/write head

field. Notice the similarity between a write head and a ferrite core with a write line passing through it. The material of the write head does not have the same square-loop hysteresis property of the ferrite core, and does not exhibit residual or remnant magnetization. A very important feature of the write head is a tiny air-gap in the ring. When a current flows in the coil a magnetic flux is created within the core. This flux flows round the core, but when it encounters the air gap, it spreads out as illustrated in Fig. 6.22.

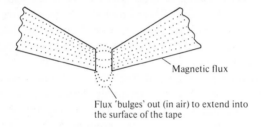

Flux 'bulges' out (in air) to extend into
the surface of the tape   Fig. 6.22 The head–air gap

The magnetic field created round the gap passes through the magnetic material coating the backing. If this field is strong enough, it causes the magnetic particles (domains) within the coating to become aligned with the field. As the magnetic surface is moving, a continuous strip of surface is magnetized. If the direction of the current is changed, the field reverses and the magnetic particles in the coating are magnetized in the opposite direction.

A read head is essentially the same as a write head (sometimes the same head serves as both read and write head). When the magnetized material moves past the gap in the read head, a magnetic flux is induced in the head. This flux, in turn, induces a voltage across the terminals of the coil. The voltage is proportional to the rate of change of the flux, not to the absolute value of the magnetic flux itself. Figure 6.23 shows the waveforms associated with writing and reading. The voltage from the read head is given by:

$$V = K \frac{d\Phi}{dt}.$$

K is a constant depending on the physical parameters of the system, and Φ is the field produced by the tape. Note that the differential of a constant is zero, so that only transitions of magnetic flux can be detected. The output from a

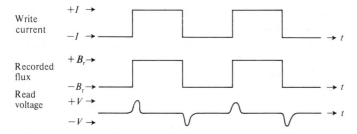

Fig. 6.23 Read/write waveforms

region of tape with a constant magnetization is zero. This makes it difficult to record digital data directly on tape or disk as we shall soon see.

Data encoding techniques

Having described the basic process by which information is recorded on a magnetic medium, we are going to look at some of the ways in which the digital data is encoded before it is recorded. All magnetic backing stores record data serially, a bit at a time, along the path described by the motion of the magnetic medium under the write head. Tape transports record a number of parallel tracks simultaneously across the width of the tape. However, the data recorded along each track is recorded serially.

It is not possible to transmit the logical ones and zeros to be recorded directly to the write head. A process called encoding or modulation must first be used to transform the data pattern into a suitable format. Similarly, when the information is read back from the tape it must be decoded or demodulated to extract the original digital data. The actual encoding/decoding process chosen is a compromise between the desire to pack as many bits of data as possible into a given surface area while preserving the reliability of the system and keeping its complexity within reasonable bounds.

When various encoding techniques are compared, the comparison is done on the basis of a number of properties associated with all recording methods. Interestingly, these are roughly the same criteria involved in the selection of a system for transmitting digital data over long distances. In what follows the term 'flux reversal' is used frequently. It indicates a change of state in the recorded magnetic field in the coating of the tape or disk. Simply reversing the direction of the current in the write head causes a flux reversal.

1. *Efficiency*. The storage efficiency of any code is defined as the number of stored bits per flux reversal, and is expressed as a percentage. The maximum value is 100 per cent and corresponds to one bit per flux reversal.

2. *Intersymbol correlation*. The symbols representing the data to be sorted should be as unlike each other as possible. By doing this we make it easy to distinguish between the symbols even if they are badly distorted due to defects in the recording/playback process. In a two-valued digital system, the

symbols should be identical but of opposite sign (i.e. inverted). This is defined as 100 per cent correlation.

3. *Bandwidth.* The bandwidth occupied by a signal is a measure of its rate of change. According to mathematical theory, any waveform can be expressed as an infinite series of sine waves with frequencies of f, $2f$, $3f$, ... , etc. The bandwidth occupied by a signal is the range of frequencies over which it extends. Bandwidth is measured in units called Hertz (Hz) which correspond to the old 'cycles per second'. For example, the telephone has a bandwidth of 300 Hz to 3000 Hz. Frequencies above and below these limits are not transmitted. As real human speech has a wider bandwidth, the telephone distorts it by cutting off low and high frequencies. Consequently, the quality of telephone speech is rather poor. In engineering terms very low and very high frequencies are difficult to handle. A code with a narrow bandwidth is preferable to one with a wide bandwidth. In particular, very low frequencies approaching DC (direct current or zero frequency) should be avoided.

4. *Self clocking.* The encoded data must ultimately be decoded and separated into individual bits. A code which provides a method of splitting the bits off from one another is called self-clocking and is highly desirable.

5. *Complexity.* The simpler the encoding and decoding processes are the less they cost. Because the recording and playback processes involve time-varying analogue signals, the precision and tolerance of the circuitry should not be so great that its cost is prohibitive. Although the signals involved in digital recording are nominally digital (i.e. two-state), in practice the signal read off the tape or disk has all the properties of an analogue signal.

6. *Noise immunity.* An ideal code should have the largest immunity to extraneous signals. In magnetic recording systems noise is caused by imperfections in the magnetic coating leading to 'drop-outs' and 'drop-ins'. A drop-out is a loss of signal caused by missing magnetic material, and a drop-in is a noise-pulse. Another source of noise is cross-talk which is the signal picked up from adjacent tracks.

In what follows the characteristics of a number of possible encoding/decoding techniques are presented. The list is by no means exhaustive but does include those found in many tape-transports and disk drives.

Return-to-zero

In its pure form return-to-zero (RZ) recording requires that the surface be unmagnetized for a logical zero, and magnetized by a short pulse for a logical one. Unfortunately, because no signal is applied to the write head during a zero, any logical ones already on the tape are not erased or overwritten. A modification of RZ recording is return-to-bias (RB) recording, where a logical zero is recorded by saturating the magnetic coating in one direction, and a logical one by saturating it in the opposite direction by a short pulse of the opposite polarity.

Figure 6.24 illustrates RB reading. The actual pulse width used depends on the characteristics of the head and the tape. A wide pulse reduces the maximum packing density of the recorded data and is wasteful of tape, while a very narrow pulse may be difficult to detect.

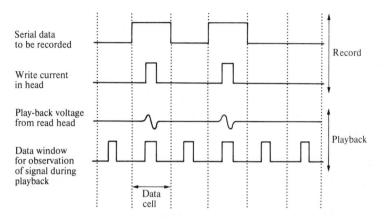

Fig. 6.24 Return-to-bias recording

To read information from the tape a data window (i.e. the time at which the output from the tape is sampled) is generated and the output of the read head examined during the window. Unfortunately, a sequence of zeros generates no output from the tape, and there is no simple way of making sure that the data window falls exactly in the middle of a data cell. For this reason return-to-bias is said to be non-self-clocking. The efficiency of RB recording is 50 per cent, the correlation fair, but the noise sensitivity poor. A low-frequency response is needed to handle the signal from the tape. For all these reasons, RB recording is not popular and is seldom employed.

Nonreturn-to-zero

One of the most widely used data encoding techniques is called modified nonreturn-to-zero or NRZ1. Each time a logical one is to be recorded, the current flowing in the head is reversed. When reading data each change in flux is interpreted as a logical one. Figure 6.25 illustrates NRZ1 recording. This requires a maximum of one flux transition per bit of stored data, and represents the optimum packing density of 100 per cent. NRZ1 has a poor correlation, requires a low frequency bandwidth, and has fair sensitivity to noise. The greatest drawback of NRZ1 is that it is not self-clocking.

Phase encoding

The majority of high-density magnetic tape transports employ phase encoding or Manchester encoding to record data. At the centre of each and every bit cell is a flux transition: a low-to-high indicates a logical one, and a high-to-low a logical zero. As there is always a transition at the centre of each data

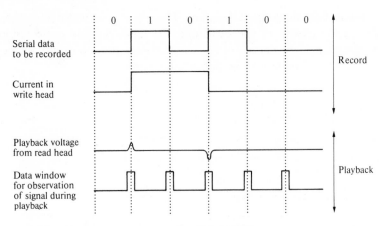

Fig. 6.25 Nonreturn-to-zero 1 recording (NRZ1)

cell, a clock signal can be derived from the recorded data, and therefore the encoding technique is self-clocking. A stream of alternate zeros and ones requires one flux transition per bit, while a stream of ones or zeros requires two flux changes per bit. Figure 6.26 illustrates phase encoding. Phase encoding has a low efficiency (50 per cent) because a maximum of two transitions per bit are required. The correlation is 100 per cent because there is a maximum difference between ones and zeros. The bandwidth requirements are good because there is no low frequency component in the recorded signal. However, as there are two flux transitions per bit, the maximum recorded frequency is twice that of NRZ1 at an equivalent bit density. The circuit complexity is greater than that of NRZ1, although suitable encoder/decoders are available as single chips. Finally, phase encoding has a good immunity to noise. Because of these attributes phase encoding is also widely used in digital data transmission systems.

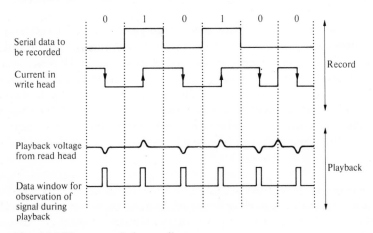

Fig. 6.26 Phase-encoded recording

Frequency modulation

Frequency modulation (FM) is widely used to encode data in floppy disk systems. Like PE, this encoding technique is self-clocking. The encoded waveform is created by marking the boundary of each data cell with a clock pulse. A pulse is then placed at the centre of a cell to denote a logical one, otherwise the cell is left empty. Figure 6.27 shows the clock pulses, data pulses, and combined clock and data pulse waveform. This waveform is then

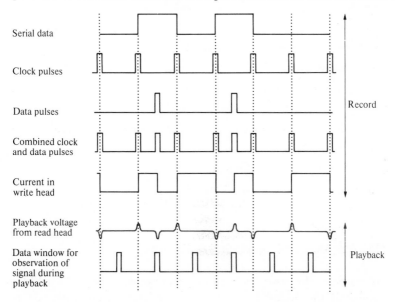

Fig. 6.27 Frequency modulation

used to record the information by reversing the current flowing in the write head (and therefore the flux) at each pulse. FM recording is identical to PE in all its properties except that a one or zero is recorded by the presence or absence of a transition at the centre of a cell rather than by the direction of the transition. Frequency modulation is somewhat a misnomer. True frequency modulation is described in Section 8.1 when dealing with data transmission.

Modified frequency modulation

Modified frequency modulation (MFM) is rapidly replacing FM as the standard for the recording of data on floppy disks. In fact, the terms FM and MFM are little used outside technical literature. FM is generally referred to as single density recording and MFM as double density recording because it is able to store twice the amount of data for a given surface area. This is because MFM is 100 per cent efficient and needs only one flux transition per bit.

Figure 6.28 shows how an MFM signal is encoded. As in FM, a data pulse

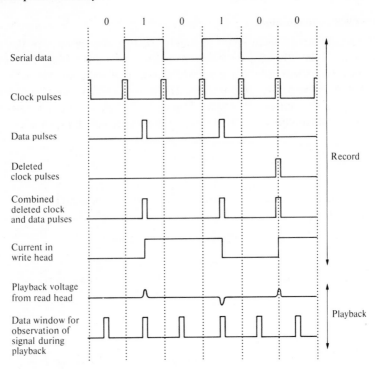

Fig. 6.28 Modified frequency modulation (MFM)

is placed at the centre of each cell containing a one. Unlike FM the clock pulses at the boundary of the cells are deleted, but with one exception. Whenever two zeros are to be recorded in succession, a clock pulse is placed between them. MFM has similar properties to FM and PE, although its correlation is lower. Because the maximum gap between flux transitions is no more than $2T$, where T is the width of a data cell, MFM is self-clocking. Although it is the most complex of the codes described so far, there are a number of chips designed to encode and decode it. Some chips will deal with FM and MFM, so that both systems may be used to record and play back data without modification of the hardware. This allows disks to be transferred from one system to another.

Group codes

One of the most recently introduced encoding techniques found in both magnetic-disk and tape-backing stores is the group code. All other arrangements assign a particular waveform to each bit. This proves incompatible with some of the requirements of an optimum code in terms of bandwidth, intersymbol correlation, and flux density. A group code takes n bits to represent an m-bit code. Thus, although there are 2^n possible waveforms, only 2^m are used to represent valid data values. This means that waveforms with poor characteristics can be removed from the code. For example, the 4/5 group code below uses five bits to represent the 16 possible values of a 4-bit code. The algorithm which maps the data values into the 5-bit code to be recorded avoids the occurence of more than two zeros in succession. This guarantees at least one flux change per three recorded bits, making the code self-clocking.

Data to be encoded	GCR 4/5 code to be recorded
0000	11001
0001	11011
0010	10010
0011	10011
0100	11101
0101	10101
0110	10110
0111	10111
1000	11010
1001	01001
1010	01010
1011	01011
1100	11110
1101	01101
1110	01110
1111	01111

6.4.2 The disk drive

A disk is a flat, circular, rigid sheet of aluminium coated with a thin layer of magnetic material. The disk rotates continually about its central axis in much the same way as an audio disk rotates in a record player. Information is stored along concentric tracks round the disk, and a read/write head is positioned above the track currently being written to, or read from. Here we shall consider only the movable-head disk, where one head can move from one track to another rather like the tone-arm of a record player. Figure 6.29 illustrates the operation of such a disk drive. A major difference between the audio and magnetic disks is that the groove on the audio disk is physically cut into its surface. The tracks on a magnetic disk are simply the circular path traced out by the motion of the disk under the read/write head. As a current is passed through the head it writes data along the track. Similarly, when reading data, the head is moved to the required track and the motion of the magnetized surface induces a tiny voltage in the coil of the read head.

A precision servo-mechanism called an actuator moves the head horizontally from track to track. Remember the difference between the magnetic disk and the audio record: in the former the tracks are concentric and it is necessary for the head to step from track to track, in the latter a spiral groove

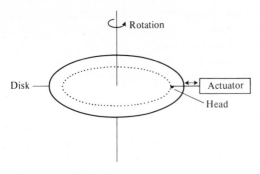

Fig. 6.29 The magnetic disk

is cut into the surface of the disk and the stylus gradually moves towards the centre as the disk rotates.

The characteristics of disk drives vary from manufacturer to manufacturer and are continually being improved on. A typical disk drive has 200 tracks per inch, stores data at a density of 2200 bits per inch, and rotates at 2400 rpm. The storage capacity of disk drives is expressed in megabytes, and ranges from 2 to 1000 Mbytes.

Disk drives are very expensive items, and in some installations their cost may exceed that of the CPU and IAS. The cost of a disk drive (several thousand pounds) lies in its complex and precise mechanical structure. For this reason manufacturers have reduced the effective cost of disk drives by stacking the disks and using more than one head. Figure 6.30 illustrates this arrangement.

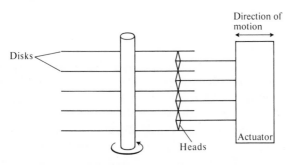

Fig. 6.30 The multidisk drive

Typically there are 11 disks with 22 surfaces, of which 20 are used for storing data (the top- and bottom-most surfaces are not used). The 20 heads move together and are driven by a common actuator. The motion of the heads describes a cylinder. That is, the corresponding tracks on each of the surfaces are collectively known as a cylinder.

The heads themselves are quite complex. They must not only have the correct electrical and magnetic properties (the air-gap in the read/write head may be only 50 μm wide), but the correct mechanical properties. If the head were actually in physical contact with the disk surface, the abrasive magnetic coating would soon wear it out as its velocity over the surface of the disk is of the order of 100 km/hour. The head is mounted in a holder called a 'slipper' which is positioned above the disk at about 0.5–2.5 micron from the surface. Such a level of precision is not possible by current techniques of purely mechanical positioning. However, by giving the slippers some of the properties of an aerofoil (an aeroplane's wings) they float in the moving layer of air just above the surface of the disk. When an object moves, the layer of air (boundary layer) at its surface moves with it. At some distance from the surface the air is still. Consequently there exists a velocity gradient between the surface and the still air. At a certain point above the disk's surface, the velocity of the air flowing over the head generates enough lift to match the pressure of the spring pushing the head towards the disk. At this point, the head is in equilibrium and floats above the disk. Modern slippers fly at below 0.5 micron and have longitudinal grooves cut in them to dump some of the lift. The precision of a modern slipper is so great that the acid in a fingerprint caused by careless handling can destroy its aerodynamic contour.

Occasionally, the head does hit the surface and is said to crash. This usually damages part of a track and this track must be labelled 'bad' and the lost data rewritten from (hopefully) a back-up copy of the file.

The tracks are subdivided into units called sectors and the sectors are themselves divided into blocks of data (Fig. 6.31).

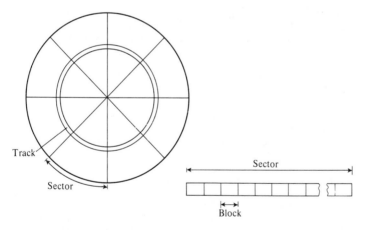

Fig. 6.31 The format of data on the disk

Normally, the disk controller (i.e. the electronic system that controls the operation of a disk drive) specifies a track and sector and either reads its contents into a buffer (i.e. temporary store) or writes the contents of the buffer to the disk. The ability to step to a given track leads to disks being regarded as random-access devices by some, although strictly speaking disk drives are sequential-access devices because it is necessary to wait until the desired sector moves under the head before it can be read. A tape unit is never regarded as a random-access device because of its slowness.

The user of a disk drive is often most interested in three parameters: the total capacity of the system, the rate at which data is written to or read from the disk, and its average access time. Typical storage capacities range from $\colon$ to 200 megabytes, data rates are usually several megabytes per second, and average access times range from 20 ms to 60 ms. The average access time is composed of three parts: the time required to step to the desired track (seek time), the time taken for the disk to rotate so that the sector to be read is under the head (latency), and the time taken to actually read the data. In practice, the reading time is often left out of published access times.

The average time to step from track to track is quite difficult to obtain because the head does not always step at constant velocity and consider ations such as head settling time need to be taken into account. The head settling time is the time taken for the head to stop bouncing after it has been loaded (pushed against the surface of the disk), and refers to floppy-disk drives (see later). Moreover, the average number of steps per access depends very much on the arrangement of the data, and on what happens to the head between successive accesses. If the head is 'parked' at the periphery of the disk, it must move further on average than if it is parked at the centre of the tracks. In the absence of any other information, a crude estimate of the average stepping time is half the number of tracks multiplied by the time taken to step from one track to the adjacent track. The average time for a given sector to move to a head (rotational latency) is easier to calculate. It is simply one half of a period of revolution. For a disk operating at 3600 r.p.m. it is:

$$\tfrac{1}{2} \times \frac{60}{3600} = \frac{1}{120} \text{ s}$$

$$= 8.33 \text{ ms}$$

A worked example on the operation of a disk drive is given later in this section.

A short glossary of disk-drive terminology

There is insufficient space in this introductory text to cover all the various aspects of disk drives in any detail, so the following glossary is provided to help the reader:

Moving-head disk. A single read/write head scans the surface of a disk by stepping from track to track. This is the type of disk drive already covered and should be contrasted with the fixed-head disk drive described below.

Fixed-head disk. A separate read/write head is employed for each track. The heads are permanently positioned over the tracks and the unit is normally pressurized with an inert gas to keep out dust. Such an arrangement is found where a very low access time is required because, of course, the access time is equal to the rotational delay period.

Exchangeable disk pack. Some moving-head disk drives are sealed and the disks themselves cannot be taken out. Others have exchangeable disk packs so that the disks may be removed and replaced.

Hard-sectored disk. Hard-sectored disks have a physical means of identifying the beginning of the sectors forming a track. Typically, these take the form of holes or slots in the disk which may be detected optically.

Soft-sectored disk. A soft-sectored disk is formatted before any data can be written on it. This involves writing the track and sector number of each sector on to the disk. Soft-sectored disks allow more flexibility in that various sector sizes may be created under software control. Hard-sectored disks are more efficient because no space is wasted labelling the start of a sector. Figure 6.34 in the following section provides an example of a soft-sectored floppy disk.

The floppy-disk drive

The floppy-disk drive bears the same relationship to the hard-disk drives previously described as a microlight does to a jumbo jet. This is not intended to be a disparaging comparison because the floppy-disk brings to the microcomputer the ability to create, manipulate, store and retrieve files at a reasonable price.

The floppy-disk drive was developed by IBM in the late 1960s as a low-cost alternative to the conventional disk drive. The standard floppy disk is made of plastic coated with a magnetic material, and is enclosed in an 8-inch square protective envelope. The floppy disk is a removable medium, and can be transported from one system to another. Figure 6.32 shows the arrangement of the floppy disk, with a central hub aperture, a cut-out to allow the head to access the disk, and an index hole. The floppy disk is so called because the sheet of plastic of which it is composed is very thin and is therefore not rigid.

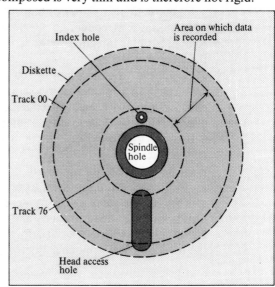

Magnetic media concealed by protective wrapper

Magnetic media visible through holes in protective wrapper

Fig. 6.32 The floppy disk

A floppy disk can readily be bent and (probably) destroyed. They should therefore be handled with great care.

The disk drive is invariably mounted so that its mouth is at the front of the equipment in which it is located. This contrasts with the traditional hard disk drive which is a large item and stands alone from the computer; the floppy disk drive is normally contained within the computer console. The mouth which receives the floppy disk is covered by a flap which is opened to insert the disk and then closed to clamp it in place. A tapered drive hub fits through the central hole in the disk. The disk is clamped in place by a second spring loaded hub forced against the opposition surface of the disk.

The disk rotates at 360 r.p.m., or about one tenth the speed of a hard disk drive. This simplifies the drive mechanism and reduces the frictional heating of the disk in its envelope, but at the cost of increasing the rotational latency (delay period) to 166 ms.

A small hole is cut in the disk to provide a method of detecting the start of a track. Whenever the hole passes between a light source on one side of the disk and a photoelectric detector on the other, an electrical pulse is generated. This informs the disk controller that the start of a track has been located. This hole is called the index. A hard-sectored disk has 26 holes spaced round the circumference because the start of each sector must be indicated by a pulse.

The read/write head of a floppy disk is moved to the desired track by a stepping mechanism which we shall describe shortly. The head is positioned over the disk and is able to access its surface through a cut-out in the cardboard envelope. During a read or write access, the head is loaded by applying a pressure pad to the back of the disk and pushing it against the head. Figure 6.33 shows this arrangement. Note that the head comes into intimate contact with the disk and does not fly above it.

Figure 6.33 also shows how the head-positioning mechanism works. A stepper motor is connected to a lead screw which rotates as the motor rotates. A nut is threaded on the screw and attached to the head carriage. As the screw rotates, the nut moves in or out carrying the head assembly with it. The motor is a stepping motor which, unlike conventional motors, does not rotate smoothly but moves in a jerky fashion a few degrees at a time. Short electrical pulses are applied to the motor causing it to step a precise number of degrees, moving the head assembly to the selected track.

Because the floppy-disk drive is a relatively low-precision device and makes extensive use of low-cost plastic parts, the track-to-track spacing is much greater than that found in hard disks. An 8-inch floppy disk has 77 tracks at a density of 48 tracks per inch. The tracks are divided into 26 sectors and the overall capacity of the standard 8 inch floppy-disk is 300 Kbytes. This is the formatted capacity—and represents the data available to users. It does not include data which performs house-keeping tasks such as labelling the track and sector number of each sector stored on the disk. The worker

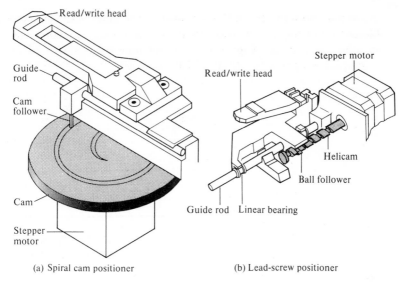

(a) Spiral cam positioner   (b) Lead-screw positioner

Fig. 6.33 The head positioning mechanism

example at the end of this section indicates that the physical capacity is closer to 500 Kbytes. In hard disk terms this capacity is tiny indeed. But in terms of the capacity of typical microcomputers it is large enough for most applications—especially when it is remembered that the floppy disk costs only a few pounds.

A recent variation on the floppy disk is the mini floppy disk. This is almost identical to the floppy disk except that it is $5\frac{1}{4}$ inches square, has a capacity of 80-640 Kbytes, and a disk drive costing under half the price of a standard floppy-disk drive. The 'minifloppy' is found largely in personal microprocessor systems, while the standard 8-inch floppy is used in professional equipment, particularly word processors.

The amount of data stored on both standard and minifloppy disks has greatly increased in recent years. The standard technique of recording data on disk is called single-density recording and employs frequency modulation (FM). Many systems now use MFM, or double density, to increase the capacity. Another way of increasing the capacity is to use two heads, one on either side of the disk. As the manufacturing precision has increased, some disk-drives have halved the track spacing, thereby doubling the total capacity. All these measures combined yield an eightfold increase in capacity. Unfortunately, it has also made it more difficult to transfer programs between computers because there are now two recording methods (single or double density), single or double-sided disks, and two different track densities.

The recording format

IBM provided not only the floppy-disk drive they also created a de facto recording standard, the IBM 3740 format. The major semiconductor manu-facturers have made a number of single-chip floppy-disk controllers imple-menting this format. Figure 6.34 shows how data is written on a disk formatted according to the IBM 3740 standard.

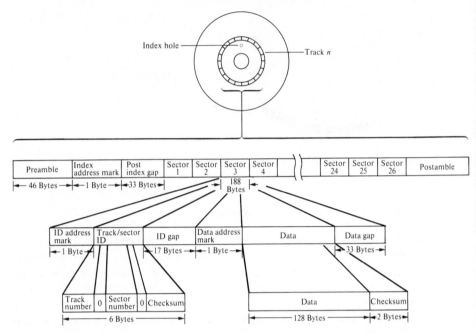

Fig. 6.34 The IBM 3740 floppy-disk format. The format is 'soft' sectored, meaning that data written in the track controls the organization of information on each track. Each of the 77 data tracks on the floppy disk contains data, address and control fields grouped together to form sectors. Each sector contains a sequence of fields, identical to those of the other sectors, which are further broken down into individual data bytes. One complete track is shown in this illustration. The index hole provides the only hardware synchronization in this format.

The Winchester disk drive

One of the growth areas of computer technology in the early 1980s is in compact, low-cost, hard-disk drives for use in minicomputers and high-performance microprocessor systems. Such disk drives are generally called Winchester disks. The term 'Winchester' is generic and describes a wide range of small disk drives—there appears to be no single feature that makes a system a Winchester. The term is associated with IBM and is said to be related to the Winchester rifle by some, and to the town of Winchester by others.

As the recording density has increased and the intertrack spacing reduced, it has become more and more necessary to find ways of making sure that a head flies exactly over the track it is accessing. This has lead to increasingly complex head positioning mechanisms and their associated electronics. Winchester technology solves the problem of head tracking by making the disks, read/write heads, and positioner, an integral unit. The disks cannot be changed so the problem of trying to follow a track on a disk written by another unit does not arise. Because the 'head disk assembly' requires no head alignment, the track spacing can be reduced and the storage density increased.

The Winchester disk drive is a sealed chassis which stops the entry of dirt and dust. Most drives have a small hole in the unit protected by an air filter to equalize internal and external air pressures. As the disk rotates in a clean environment, the flying height of the head can be reduced, and the recording density increased.

Unlike conventional hard disk drives, it is not necessary to retract the heads beyond the outer rim of the disks when the unit is not in use. As the heads fly only when the disks are rotating, and are not retracted when the disk is stationary, it is necessary to make a portion of the surface of the disks available to the heads as a 'landing area'. That is, the heads are permitted to land on (come in contact with) a part of the disk where the data is not stored. In order to make this possible it is necessary to lubricate the surface of the disk. A consequence of this arrangement is that the disks must be brought up to speed (and stopped) as quickly as possible to reduce the time for which the heads are in contact with the disks.

Some, but not all, Winchester disk drives use a rotary head positioner to move the read/write heads rather than the linear (in and out) positioners found on conventional hard disk drives. Figure 6.35 shows how a voice-coil actuator rotates an arm about a pivot, causing the head assembly to track over the surface of the disks. A voice-coil is so called because it works like a loudspeaker. A current is passed through a coil positioned within a strong

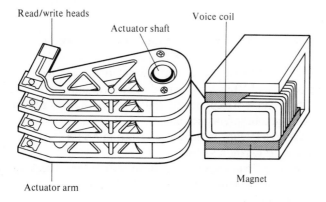

Fig. 6.35 The Winchester head-assembly positioning mechanism

magnetic field provided by permanent magnet. The current in the coil generates a magnetic field, causing the coil to be attracted to, or repulsed by, the fixed magnet, moving the pivoted arm. This represents just one of the many head-assembly actuators currently in use.

Winchester technology was originally applied to 14-inch disks. It has been extended to 8-inch disks, and the $5\frac{1}{4}$ inch mini-Winchester is now available. A mini-Winchester costs as little as £500 and can store ten megabytes. There are a vast number of Winchester disk drives on the market, each with its own particular parameters. However, the typical rotational speed is 3600 r.p.m., the data transfer rate 5 Mbits-sec, the capacity 10 Mbytes, and the access time 30 ms. It is not unreasonable to believe that the floppy-disk drive will come under ever-increasing pressure from the Winchester.

A worked example

An 8-inch floppy disk drive uses two-sided disks, and records data on 77 tracks per side. Each track has 26 sectors, and holds 128 bytes of data. The disk rotates at 360 r.p.m., the seek time is 10 ms track-to-track, the head settling time is 10 ms, and the head-load time is 200 ms. From the above information calculate:

1. The total capacity of the floppy disk in bytes.
2. The average rotational latency.
3. The average time to locate a given sector assuming that the head is initially parked at track 0, and is in an unloaded state. The head is loaded after the required track has been located.
4. The time taken to read a single sector once it has been located.
5. The average rate at which data is moved from the disk to the processor during the reading of a sector. This should be expressed in bits per second.
6. Estimate the packing density of the disk in terms of bits per inch around a track located at 3 inches from the centre.

Solution

1. Total capacity = sides × tracks × sectors × bytes per sector
   $$= 2 \times 77 \times 26 \times 128$$
   $$= 512\,512 \text{ bytes (approximately } \tfrac{1}{2} \text{ megabyte)}.$$
2. Average rotational latency = $\frac{1}{2}$ period of revolution.
   360 r.p.m. corresponds to 360/6 = 6 revolutions per second.
   One revolution = $\frac{1}{6}$ second.
   Average latency is therefore $\frac{1}{12}$ second = 83.3 ms.
3. Average time to locate a sector
   = latency + head load time + head setting time + seek time
   = 83.3 ms + 200 ms + 10 ms + 77/2 × 10 ms
   = 678.3 ms.
4. In one revolution (1/6 second) 26 sectors pass under the head. Therefore, time to read one sector is 1/6 × 1/26 = 6.41 ms.

5. During the reading of a sector, 128 bytes are read in 6.41 ms. The average data rate is the number of bits read divided by the time taken = $(128 \times 8)/0.00641 = 159\,750$ bits per second.

6. Packing density = total number of bits divided by track length
$$= 26 \times 128 \times 8/(2 \times 3.142 \times 3)$$
$$= 1412.3 \text{ bits per inch}$$

6.4.3 The tape transport

In a tape storage system, information is recorded on a thin strip of polyester tape coated with a magnetic material. The tape is $\frac{1}{2}$ inch wide and is stored in (typically) 10.5 inch reels of 2400 feet. A tape drive (or tape transport) for digital data is not greatly different from a high-quality domestic reel-to-reel recorder. The possible arrangement of a digital tape deck is given in Fig. 6.36.

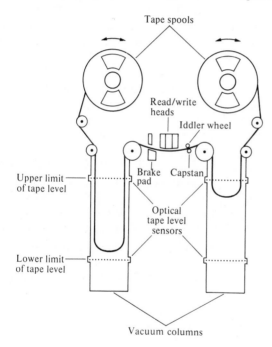

Fig. 6.36 The tape transport

The basic function of a tape transport is to move tape at a constant speed past a read/write head. When searching for a particular block of data the tape is moved at a relatively high speed and stopped when the start of the block is found. Because of their inertia, the tape spools cannot be halted instantaneously. Consequently, if a simple tape transport were used, the tape would be broken, or at least stretched, every time it were stopped. In high-quality tape transports the movement of the tape past the heads is decoupled from the motion of the give-out and take-up spools. How this is actually achieved is described shortly.

Tape is pulled past the read/write head(s) by a capstan and idler-wheel arrangement. The capstan is a cylinder (or tube) of precisely machined and polished hard metal rotating at a constant speed. The tape passes the capstan and is pushed against it by an idler-wheel (or pinch roller). The friction between the capstan, tape and idler causes the tape to be pulled. The idler wheel rotates because of the motion of the tape against it—it is not driven by any mechanism itself. When the tape is stopped, a solenoid pulls the idler wheel away from the tape. Brake pads are also applied to the tape to stop it.

The tape between capstans and spools hangs in a loop in the two vacuum columns below each of the tape spools. By sucking air out of the bottom of the column, the tape loop is kept hanging down. At the top and bottom of the vacuum columns photo-electric sensors are located to detect the presence or absence of the tape loop. By using these sensors to control the speed of the spool motors, the length of the loop in the vacuum column can be kept approximately constant. For example, if the left-hand reel is paying out tape too fast, the loop grows downwards. When it reaches the lower sensors the motion of the left-hand spool is slowed down and the loop starts to shorten.

The purpose of the vacuum columns is to allow the almost instantaneous stopping of the tape as it moves past the tape heads. When the idler wheel disengages from the capstan, the tape brakes are applied and the spool motors stopped. The tape under the heads stops, but the spools momentarily continue either to pay out tape or take it up. This simply leads to one of the tape loops growing and the other shrinking. Vacuum column buffers have their disadvantages. A power failure can lead to tape spillages when the power is reapplied. They also consume considerable power and are regarded as being error-prone. They cannot be used in aircraft because of the low ambient air pressure. The vacuum system sucks dust from the air and deposits it where it is least wanted—on the tape. Finally, the constant hiss of the air into the vacuum columns sometimes annoys the operators.

Early tape transports used tension arms to buffer the tape—a technique still widely found on domestic tape decks. Figure 6.37 illustrates the tension-arm, which takes up slack tape or pays out tape when the tape tension

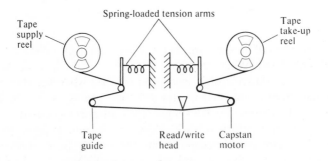

Fig. 6.37 The tension-arm tape buffer

increases. This arrangement proves satisfactory for low to medium tape speeds up to 45 in sec^{-1}.

The tension-arm has been developed to allow tape speeds of 75 in sec^{-1} in an arrangement called the 'floating shuttle' and is illustrated in Fig. 6.38. It was observed that the tension-arms tend to work in unison, with one taking up slack and the other paying out tape. By combining the two loops in a freely moving shuttle, an improved performance is possible because the shuttle can be kept light (15 grams). The shuttle is a small block with two pulleys around which are routed the take-up and pay-out loops from the reels. A sophisticated motor control system is needed to keep the shuttle within two or three inches of its centre position.

Tape unit parameters vary widely in terms of both tape speed and recording format. Typical speeds vary from 0.3 to 6.0 m/s^{-1}. The details of a popular recording format (nine-track phase-encoded data) are given in Fig. 6.39.

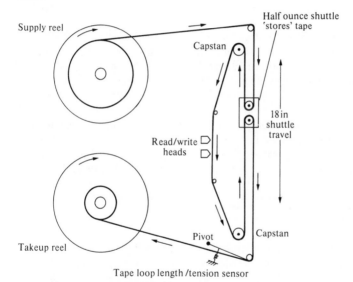

Fig. 6.38 The floating shuttle

The read/write heads have nine tracks, of which eight record a byte at a time across the width of the tape. The ninth track contains an odd parity bit. That is, if the nine tracks are considered to form a column of data, the bit in the parity track is chosen to make the total number of ones in the column odd. This helps to detect errors because if a column with an even number of ones is found at least one error must have occurred.

Data is recorded in blocks as it is impossible to read a single byte at a time by starting and stopping the tapes. Between the blocks is an interblock gap (typically about 20 mm) giving the tape time to stop after a read/write operation and to accelerate to normal speed before the next operation. Each

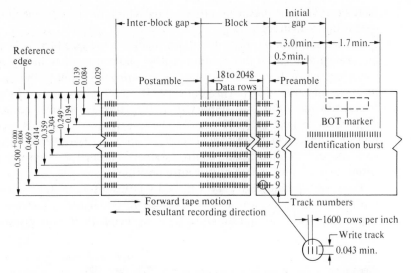

Fig. 6.39 The format of data on a tape. *The nine-track phase-encoded* format does not utilize the CRC and LRC characters for error checking. Each data block is preceded by 40 all-zero bytes followed by a single all-ones byte (preamble) and is terminated by a single all-one byte followed by 40 all-zeros bytes (postamble). The preamble synchronizes the read detection circuits so that ones and zeros are correctly identified in the data bytes which follow. The symmetry of preamble and postamble permits reading in either direction. At the load point (beginning of tape) an 'identification burst' consisting of 1600 flux reversals per inch, is written in the parity track. Odd character parity is specified. The Tape Mark consists of 64 to 256 flux reversals at 3200 flux changes per inch in tracks 1, 2, P, 5, 7, 8. The remaining tracks are DC erased.

Note 1. Tape is shown with magnetic surface towards observer, read-write head on same side.
Note 2. All dimensions are given in inches.
Note 3. Track positional tolerances are ± 0.003 in.

block is preceded by a preamble and followed by a postamble. These are used to synchronize the electronics during a read operation. By making the preamble and postamble symmetric it is possible to read the tape in either direction.

Tapes have markers at their ends to indicate the physical start and end of the tape. The markers take the form of a piece of metallic foil attached to the tape, or small holes. There are also software markers recorded on the tape, BOT (beginning of tape) and EOT (end of tape).

The parameters of a UNIVAC 16 tape transport are given below:

Data rate (bytes/sec)	96,000	
Density (bits/inch)	1,600	(63 bits mm^{-1})
Tape speed (inches/sec)	125	(3.2 m s^{-1})
Interblock gap (inches)	0.75	(19 mm)
Interblock gap time (ms)	12	
Rewind time (minutes)	2	

The streaming tape drive

The types of tape transport we have already discussed are the classic backing stores of mini- and mainframe-computers. Their parameters, performance, and cost belong to the world of the mainframe. By the early 1970s tape transports were using recording densities of 250 bytes mm^{-1}, speeds of $5 \, m \, s^{-1}$, a 8 mm interrecord gap, and were able to start and stop within 1 ms.

Today low-cost, high-performance microcomputers are freely available with Winchester hard disks providing the high-speed backing store. As Winchesters have fixed media it is necessary to find some way of transferring programs between computers, and preserving the contents of the Winchester in the event of a system failure leading to the corruption of part of the surface of the disk. The floppy-disk provides a convenient way of transporting programs, but is not as well suited to the role of a back-up store.

The solution to this problem is provided in the shape of the streaming-tape drive, a low-cost tape transport designed to provide back-up facilities for Winchesters. The cost of a high-performance tape transport lies in the mechanism needed to stop and start the tape quickly. This has been abandoned in the tape streamer, resulting in a mechanism small enough to fit in the same space as an 8-inch disk drive.

The tape streamer cannot stop and start the tape within an interblock gap. Figure 6.40 shows how a tape is nominally stopped at the end of a block but overshoots it because of the lack of any sophisticated tape buffering

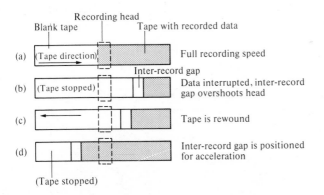

Fig. 6.40 Re-positioning the tape in a streamer. Streaming-tape repositioning is necessary due to the inability of streaming mechanism to stop within a narrow inter-record gap when the data stream is interrupted. When tape is moving at full speed (a), the interruption of data causes the tape to slow, but not sharply enough to stop the tape with the inter-record gap underneath the head (b). The tape is then rewound (c), until the inter-record gap is positioned far enough behind the head (d) to allow acceleration to full speed when the data stream is resumed. Buffering mechanisms in start/stop drives make repositioning unnecessary, and thus improve performance in applications in which the data stream is frequently interrupted.

mechanism. The tape must then be rewound and positioned before the interblock gap so that when the tape is re-started it will come up to speed by the time the next block is passing the read/write head. This process takes approximately one second and is a thousand times slower than a vacuum-buffered tape transport.

The inability to stop and start on an interblock gap is not as bad as it sounds. The tape streamer is frequently used to store large blocks of data from the disk and therefore runs continuously, rather than by skipping from one data block to another. Some of the latest tape streamers solve the stop-start problem by providing a 'massless buffer'. As the cost of semiconductor memory is now so low, it is possible to read a large chunk of data from the tape into memory local to the streamer. The host computer then reads data not from the tape directly, but from the semiconductor memory. In this way it is possible to skip almost instantaneously from block to block, because the data is now held in random-access memory.

Some manufacturers have pressed the ordinary domestic video cassette recorder (VCR) into service as a tape streamer. The VCR is not only remarkably cheap, it can record as much as 100 Mbytes on a single video cassette. Because the VCR was never designed to store digital data reliably, it is necessary to record each data block six or more times for added security.

Tape cassettes and cartridges

The digital cassette recorder is the most inexpensive form of magnetic tape transport, and is comparable in size with the domestic cassette player. The cassettes themselves are identical to those used to record music except that they are made to a much higher standard, and are free from imperfections such as drop-out. Figure 6.41 shows the structure of a cassette drive which

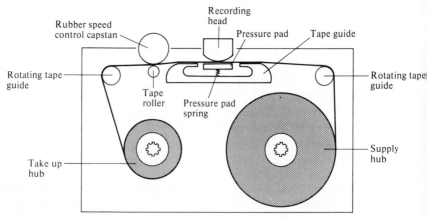

Fig. 6.41 The cassette drive uses two motors to turn the reels and maintain tape tension. Speed is controlled by pulling the tape between the tape roller and a rubber speed-control capstan. Tape wear is constant, but the cassette drive is the least expensive type of tape drive, and cassettes are inexpensive and readily obtainable.

hardly differs from the domestic version. Indeed, the only major difference is that all the controls are operated electronically by solenoids instead of the piano-key controls found on some domestic units.

A typical cassette recorder, the TEAC MT-2, records digital data at a density of 1600 bpi (bits per inch). Note that a cassette drive records data along one track serially, unlike the nine-track reel-to-reel tape transport. The data is phase encoded. In fact, the MT-2 has a two-track head, but the tracks are not used concurrently. They merely double the effective length of the tape by allowing one head to access the upper surface, and one head the lower. The tape moves at 15 inches per second in the read or write modes, and data is transferred at $24\,\text{Kbits}\,\text{sec}^{-1}$. The total capacity of the cassette is 760 Kbytes. The major parameters of the MT-2 are given in Table 6.1.

Table 6.1 Details of the TEAC MT-2 cassette transport

Parameter	Value
Data format	1600 b.p.i., phase encoded
Tape speed (read/write)	15 i.p.s.
(fast forward)	45 i.p.s.
(rewind)	74 i.p.s.
Start distance (15 i.p.s.)	0.4 inches
(45 i.p.s.)	2.4 inches
Start time (15 i.p.s.)	40 ms
(45 i.p.s.)	80 ms
Stop distance (15 i.p.s.)	0.11 inches
(45 i.p.s.)	1.8 inches
Stop time (15 i.p.s.)	40 ms
(45 i.p.s.)	80 ms
Data transfer rate	24 Kbits per second
Recording density	1600 b.p.i.
MTBF	1000 hours
Commands	Write a block
	Write tape mark
	Erase
	Read one block
	Skip one block
	Reverse one block
	Set load point
	Rewind start
	Search tape mark
	High speed search

The read–write head has a dual gap allowing simultaneous reading and writing. This permits the recorded data to be read back immediately after it has been recorded, and any record errors detected. If an error is found, the writing of the current block may be aborted, the tape backed-up, and the block rewritten.

The price of the cassette drive falls somewhere in between that of the $5\frac{1}{4}$ inch and the 8-inch floppy-disk drive. The main applications of the cassette are the exchange of data between computers, numerical control and data logging. Data logging is the term used to describe a system dedicated to the gathering of information. For example, a cassette mechanism and a microprocessor system can be encapsulated in a small sealed unit, and left at the side of a busy road to record the timing and density of traffic. After several days, an engineer will come and unlock the box, replace the cassette, and take away the old cassette for analysis, usually on a minicomputer.

The cartridge is merely an up-market version of the cassette. A typical cartridge uses $\frac{1}{4}$-inch magnetic tape, holds ten times as much data as a cassette, and generally exceeds the performance of a cassette drive in all respects.

The audio cassette recorder and data storage

Almost all the low-cost personal microcomputers are able to read data from, and write data to, an unmodified domestic cassette recorder. These cassette recorders cannot handle digital data as such, because they are designed to process speech and music signals rather than digital waveforms. This difficulty is bypassed by converting digital signals into two tones (constant frequencies). For example, a logical zero may be recorded as a tone at 1200 Hz, and a logical one as a tone at 2400 Hz. Unfortunately, this inefficient process, coupled with the lower performance of many cheap cassette recorders, leads to data rates in the range of 300 to 2400 bits per second, corresponding to practical data rates of roughly 30 to 240 bytes per second. The above process is called frequency modulation (not to be confused with digital FM) and is described in Section 8.1.

6.5 Magnetic-bubble memory

The magnetic-bubble memory is a small, high-density, serial-access backing store with a very low latency. When I first encountered magnetic-bubble memories in the late 1960s, I was told that they represented the future form of backing store. In the early 1980s the bubble memory is still awaiting its call to fame. Although they are now in commercial production and are very useful in a few applications, they have not caught on to any extent. In fact, some semiconductor companies have stopped producing them. The magnetic-bubble memory has been squeezed from two sides—there has been a steady reduction in the cost and size of disk drives, while at the same time there has been an even more dramatic drop in the price of semiconductor random-access memory, together with a massive increase in the number of bits per chip.

The discovery of magnetic-bubble technology is associated with Andrew Boback at Bell Labs in 1967. Magnetic bubbles are cylindrical domains within a thin layer of a special magnetic material. The most common material used to create magnetic-bubble devices is gadolinium gallium garnet (GGG). Like the thin films we have discussed earlier, GGG exhibits uniaxial magnetic anisotropy, and is easier to magnetize in one plane than another. A thin film of GGG has its easy axis oriented perpendicular to its plane. Figure 6.42 shows the structure of a sheet of GGG under the effect of varying degrees of external magnetization.

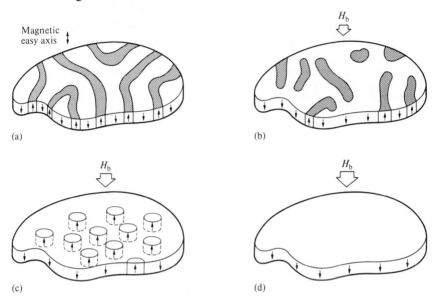

Fig. 6.42 Magnetic bubbles

In Fig. 6.42(a) there is no external field and the domains are arranged at random in a striped or serpentine fashion. If a bias field, H_b, is applied at right angles to the film, in the plane of easy magnetization, the domains not magnetized in the same direction as the external field begin to shrink. The magnetization of the bulk material is parallel to the external field and is in the down direction. The magnetization of the antiparallel domains is said to be in the up direction. Figure 6.42(b) shows the effect of small values of H_b.

As the external field is increased (Fig. 6.42(c)), the irregularly shaped islands of up magnetization shrink further and become bubble shaped when 'viewed' from above. The bubbles are very small, ranging from 100 μm to 0.01 μm. Typical bubbles have a diameter of approximately 10 μm. If the external magnetic field is increased to the point illustrated in Fig. 6.42(d), the bubbles become unstable and disappear.

Because a bubble is inherently two-state (there or not-there) it can be used to represent binary data. Typical devices store 1 Mbit. All that is needed is a method of generating bubbles at will, detecting them, addressing them, and removing (annihilating) them.

The bubbles are very mobile under the influence of a magnetic field in the plane of the material. Although the bubbles move laterally through the film, there is no actual physical movement involved, it is the orientation of the atoms in the crystal that changes.

Once the GGG film has been deposited on some inert substrate, a layer of silicon dioxide is placed on top to provide a carrier for the next layer, and to act as a barrier between layers. On top of the silicon dioxide is deposited a layer of an alloy of copper and aluminium. This layer is deposited by photolithographic techniques to produce the structures which generate, transfer, replicate, detect, and annihilate the bubbles. On top of this is a second silicon dioxide layer, followed by a permalloy layer also deposited by photolithography. Permalloy is a magnetic material which reacts with the magnetic bubbles. A magnetic bubble memory is sandwiched between two permanent magnets to generate the constant (static) field, H_b, needed to maintain the bubbles.

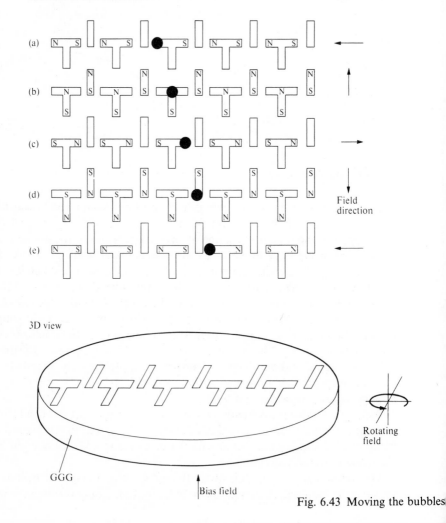

Fig. 6.43 Moving the bubbles

Figure 6.43 shows how the permalloy patterns deposited on the surface of the film are used to guide the movement of bubbles through the film. In this diagram we are looking down on the film. The permalloy patterns take the form of rows of 'T' and 'I' bars. If a magnetic field, H_p, is applied in the plane of the film, the permalloy Ts and Is are magnetized. Note that the polarizing field, H_p, is at right angles to the bias field, H_b, which serves only to maintain the bubbles. H_p is a variable (rotating) field, and serves to move the bubbles through the film.

In Fig. 6.43(a) the direction of magnetization is along the top of the Ts from right to left, causing the top of the Ts to be magnetized and to behave as if they were tiny bar magnets. The North pole is at the left of the T. Remember that the bubbles are really columns of magnetization with their poles at the top and bottom. Suppose that the bubbles have their South poles at the top. Initially the magnetic bubble in Fig. 6.43(a) is attracted to the North pole of a T. As everyone knows 'Like poles attract; unlike poles repel'.

The in-plane magnetic field, H_p, is rotated 90 degrees clockwise to produce the situation of Fig. 6.43(b). Here the vertical sections of the Ts and Is are magnetized. The base of the I to the left of the bubble's former position becomes a South pole, repelling the bubble. The centre of the T becomes a North pole attracting it. Consequently, it moves to the centre of the T.

In Fig. 6.43(c) the magnetic field has been rotated a further 90 degrees clockwise and the magnetization of the Ts and Is is that of Fig. 6.43(a), but with North and South reversed.

A further 90 degree rotation of H_p produces the situation shown in Fig. 6.43(d). The bubble is repelled by the South pole of its T, and attracted to the North pole of the I to its right. The bubble leaves the T and moves to the I. The bubble has now moved from a T to an I, representing a small step for bubblekind, but a giant leap for memory technology.

In Fig. 6.43(e) the field has rotated through a further 90 degrees (360 in total). The magnetization of the Ts and Is is now identical to the starting position of Fig. 6.43(a). The bubble leaves the I and is attracted to the North Pole of the T to its right. The bubble has now moved from one T to the next T.

The structure of Fig. 6.43 behaves like a shift register, with one full rotation of the in-plane magnetic field corresponding to a clock pulse in a conventional shift register built from flip-flops.

Continuing the analogy with the shift register, data is shifted into the least significant position of the shift register on each clock pulse. In magnetic-bubble memory terms, a bubble is created at the entry to a row of Ts and Is for a logical one, or not created for a logical zero. The bubble is created by passing a current pulse through a tiny conducting loop in the copper–aluminium layer. This generates a magnetic field in the easy direction of magnetization, reversing the bulk magnetization of the film to create a bubble. If a sufficiently large current is passed through the loop in such a direction as to enhance the bias field, H_b, the bubble is destroyed.

The detection mechanism for magnetic bubbles is given in Fig. 6.44. A series of chevron elements have the effect of stretching a bubble into a rod shape, increasing the intensity of the bubble's external magnetic field. The effect of the bubble's field on the chevrons is to alter their electrical resistance to a current flowing through them, and hence permit the detection of a bubble by measuring the resistance of the chevrons.

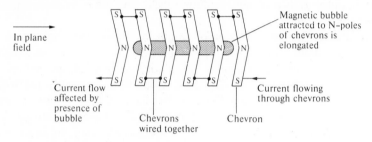

Fig. 6.44 The bubble detector

We have now described how the bubbles are created, shifted, detected, and destroyed. The actual details of a real magnetic-bubble memory module are fairly complex, particularly its physical construction, the electronics needed to generate its in-plane rotating magnetic field and its generation/detection circuitry. Figure 6.45 shows the construction of a typical magnetic-bubble memory module.

The major difference between a real magnetic-bubble memory and the above description is in the arrangement of the shift register. A single large loop would result in a very long access time, and any fault in the loop would render the entire chip useless. Figure 6.46 illustrates the major–minor loop organization of a typical device. A number of minor loops (say 128 each containing 513 bits) store the data. Data is transferred to the desired minor loop via the major loop linking all minor loops with the bubble generate/detect circuitry. Modern devices have access times of approximately 4 ms, transfer rates of 0.1 Mbits per second, and capacities of 1 Mbits.

Problems

1. A dynamic RAM chip costs $3 and is organized as 65536×1 bits. A memory composed of 0.5 megaword is to be built with these chips. If each word of the memory is 48 bits wide, how many chips are required? What will the cost of the memory be, if the cost of the other components is estimated to be 20 per cent of the cost of the memory chips themselves? Note that one megaword is 2^{20} words.

2. A magnetic tape has a packing density of 800 characters per inch, an interblock gap of $\frac{1}{2}$ inch, and is filled with records. Each contains 400

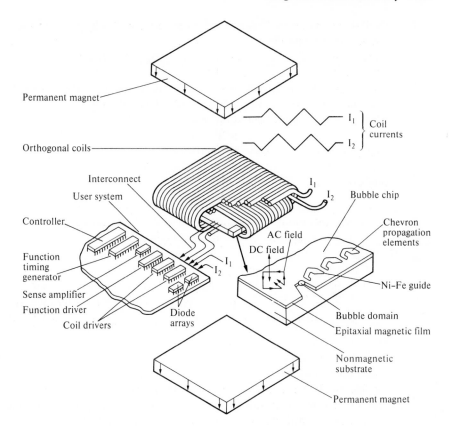

Fig. 6.45 The construction of a magnetic-bubble memory module

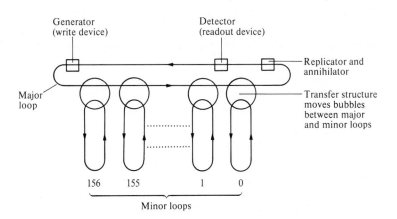

Fig. 6.46 Major–minor loop organization

characters. Calculate the fraction of the tape containing useful data if the records are written as:

(a) Single record blocks   (b) Blocks containing 4 records.

3. A movable-head disk drive has 10 disks and 18 surfaces available for recording. Each surface is composed of 200 concentric tracks and the disks rotate at 2,400 r.p.m. Each track is divided into 8 blocks of 256 32-bit words. There is one read-write head per surface and it is possible to read the 18 tracks of a given cylinder simultaneously. The time to step from track to track is 1 ms (10^{-3} s). Between data transfers the head is parked at the outermost track of the disk. Calculate:

(a) The total capacity in bits of the disk drive
(b) The maximum data transfer rate in bits per second
(c) The average access time in milliseconds
(d) The average transfer rate when reading 256-word blocks located randomly on the disk
(e) If the disk has a 12-inch diameter and the outermost track comes to 1 inch from the edge of the disk calculate the recording density (bits per inch) of the innermost and the outermost tracks. The track density is 200 tracks per inch.

4. As video cassette recorders have dropped in price an engineer proposes to use them to store digital data. What is the storage capacity of a one-hour tape (in bits), and at what rate is data transferred?

A TV picture is transmitted as 625 lines, repeated 25 times per second. The useful portion of each line can be used to store 256 bits.

5. The assumption about head-movement in Question 3 is, in general, incorrect. Assume that a disk-drive has N concentric cylinders numbered from 0 to $N-1$. The innermost cylinder is number 0.

Derive an expression for the average random move from one cylinder to another (in terms of the number of head movements). Assume that when seeking the next cylinder, all cylinders have an equal probability of being selected. Hence, or otherwise, show that the average movement approaches $N/3$ for large values of N.

Hint: Consider the Kth cylinder and calculate the number of steps needed to move to the Jth cylinder, where J varies from 0 to $(N-1)$.

7 ADVANCED COMPUTER ARITHMETIC

Advanced computer arithmetic is concerned with those numerical operations involving multiplication and division. Such operations and their derivatives (reciprocals, square roots, exponentiation, trigonometric functions) are very important in many areas of computation, especially numerical computation. At least one good reason for studying multiplication and division is that there is an infinite number of ways of performing these operations and hence there is an infinite number of Ph.Ds (or expenses-paid visits to conferences in the U.S.A.) to be won from inventing new forms of multiplier.

The newcomer to computing is often surprised to find that most of the popular eight-bit microprocessors cannot perform multiplication directly. Any programmer who wishes to multiply two numbers with (say) the 6502, must resort to an algorithm involving instructions the 6502 has (usually shifting and adding). Equally, the newcomer might think that the omission of multiplication from the CPU's instructions set is a horrendous oversight entirely devaluing the microprocessor. This is not so. It is remarkable how little multiplication or any similar 'higher order' arithmetic operations appear in many programs. For example, the principal operation carried out by editors, assemblers, compilers, or text processors is the searching of data areas for a match with a given string. In fact the most frequent application of multiplication is not in arithmetic, but in calculating the addresses of array elements. For example, the location of the element x_{ij} in the m-row by n-column matrix X, is given by $(A + ni + j)$, where A is the address of the first element.

In this section we consider only multiplication and division. Other mathematical functions are normally derived from multiplication. Indeed, division itself will later be defined as an iterative process involving multiplication.

7.1 Multiplication

Binary multiplication is, in principle, no more complex than decimal multiplication. In many ways it is easier as the whole binary multiplication table can be reduced to:

$$0 \times 0 = 0$$
$$0 \times 1 = 0$$
$$1 \times 0 = 0$$
$$1 \times 1 = 1$$

Note that the multiplication of two bits is identical to their logical AND. When we consider the multiplication of strings of bits, things become more complex and the way in which multiplication is carried out, or mechanized, varies widely from machine to machine. Basically the faster (and more expensive) the computer, the more complex the hardware used to implement multiplication. The simpler machines form the product of two numbers by 'shifting and adding', very much as people do. High-speed computers perform multiplication in a single operation by means of a very large logic array involving hundreds of gates.

7.1.1 Unsigned binary multiplication

The so-called 'pencil and paper' algorithm used by people to calculate the product of two multidigit numbers, involves the multiplication of an n-digit number by a single digit followed by shifting and adding. This approach can be applied to unsigned binary numbers in the following way. The multiplier bits are examined, one at a time, starting with the least significant bit. If the current multiplier bit is one the multiplicand is written down, if it is zero then n zeros are written down instead. Then the next bit of the multiplier is examined, but this time we write the multiplicand (or zero) one place to the left of the last digits we wrote down. Each of these n digits is called a partial product. When all partial products have been formed, they are added up to give the result of the multiplication. Example 7.1 should make this clear.

Example 7.1 10×13

---

10 (multiplicand) = 1010_2
13 (multiplier) = 1101_2

1010	
1101	
1010	Step 1
0000	Step 2
1010	Step 3
1010	Step 4
10000010	Step 5

Step 1 first multiplier bit = 1, write down multiplicand
Step 2 second multiplier bit = 0, write down zeros shifted left
Step 3 third multiplier bit = 1, write down multiplicand shifted left
Step 4 fourth multiplier bit = 1, write down multiplicand shifted left
Step 5 add together four partial products

The result, $10000010_2 = 130$, is eight bits long. It should be appreciated from the above algorithm that the multiplication of two n-bit numbers yields a $2n$-bit product.

Digital computers do not implement the 'pencil-and-paper' algorithm in the above way, as this would require the storing of n partial products, followed by the simultaneous addition of n words. A better technique is to add up the partial products as they are formed. A possible algorithm for the multiplication of the two n-bit unsigned binary numbers is given in Table 7.1(a). Table 7.1(b) shows how this algorithm works with multiplier $= 1101_2$ and multiplicand $= 1010_2$.

Table 7.1(a) An algorithm for unsigned multiplication

(a) Set a counter to n.
(b) Clear the $2n$-bit partial product register.
(c) Examine the rightmost bit of the multiplier (initially the least significant bit). If it is one add the multiplicand to the n most significant bits of the partial product.
(d) Shift the partial product one place to the right.
(e) Shift the multiplier one place to the right (the rightmost bit is, of course, lost).
(f) Decrement the counter. If the result is not zero repeat from step (c). If the result is zero read the product from the partial product register.

Table 7.1(b) $1010_2 \times 1101_2$

Step	Counter	Multiplier	Partial product	Cycle
a and b	4	1101	00000000	
c	4	1101	10100000	1
d and e	4	0110	01010000	1
f	3	0110	01010000	1
c	3	0110	01010000	2
d and e	3	0011	00101000	2
f	2	0011	00101000	2
c	2	0011	11001000	3
d and e	2	0001	01100100	3
f	1	0001	01100100	3
c	1	0001	100000100	4
d and e	1	0000	10000010	4
f	0	0000	10000010	4

Multiplication on an 8-bit microprocessor

The above algorithm can readily be applied to a typical eight-bit microprocessor. As the 6502 does not have a 16-bit data register, it is necessary to store the partial product in memory at two consecutive locations. The memory map below shows the arrangement of multiplier (P), multiplicand (Q), and partial product (RU) and (RL).

0000	P	←	multiplier
0001	Q	←	multiplicand
0002	RU	←	product MS byte
0003	RL	←	product LS byte

The flow chart in Fig. 7.1 illustrates the multiplication algorithm for the 6502. The assembly language program corresponding to Fig. 7.1 is given in

Table 7.1(c). In this program the accumulator itself holds the most significant byte of the partial product. Note that the instructions clearing the partial product during the setting up are, in fact, redundant. This is because any data initially in RU and RL is overwritten by the result.

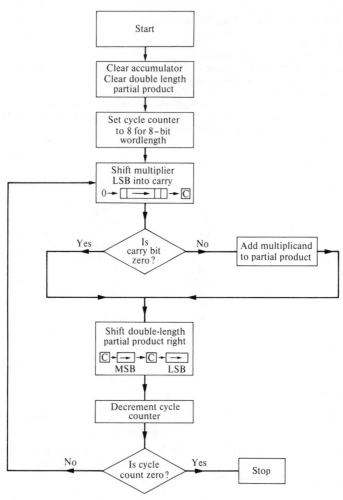

Fig. 7.1 The flow chart for eight-bit multiplication

7.1.2 Signed multiplication

The multiplication algorithm we have just discussed is valid only for unsigned integers or fixed-point numbers. Because many computers represent negative numbers by means of their two's complement it is necessary to find some way of forming the product of two's complement numbers. It is, of

Table 7.1(c) The assembly language program corresponding to Fig. 7.1

P	EQU	0	multiplier location
Q	EQU	1	multiplicand location
RU	EQU	2	destination of result MS byte
RL	EQU	3	destination of result LS byte
	ORG	$0200	origin of program
	LDA	#$00	clear accumulator
	STA	RU	clear partial product MSB
	STA	RL	clear partial product LSB
	LDX	#$08	set counter to 8
LOOP	LSR	P	shift multiplier bit into carry
	BCC	SHIFT	if clear shift partial product right
	CLC		if set add in multiplicand
	ADC	Q	do the addition
SHIFT	ROR	A	rotate partial product MS byte
	ROR	RL	rotate partial product LS byte
	DEX		decrement counter
	BNE	LOOP	loop until all bits done
	STA	RU	store product MS byte

course, possible to convert negative numbers into a modulus-only form, calculate the product and then convert it into a two's complement form if it is negative. This approach wastes time.

Before introducing a suitable algorithm it is worthwhile showing that the two's complement representation of negative numbers cannot be used with 'straight' multiplication. For example, consider the product of X and $-Y$.

Two's complement form of $-Y = 2^n - Y$.

The product $X(-Y) = X(2^n - Y) = 2^n X - XY$.

The expected result, $-XY$, should be represented in two's complement form by $2^{2n} - XY$. Note that the most significant bit is 2^{2n} (not 2^n) because multiplication automatically yields a double length product. In order to get the correct two's complement result it is necessary to add a correction factor of:

$$2^{2n} - 2^n X = 2^n(2^n - X).$$

This is the two's complement of X scaled by 2^n. As an illustration consider the product of $X = 15$ and $Y = -13$ in five bits (Example 7.2) so that

$$X = 15 \rightarrow 01111_2 \text{ and } Y = -13 \rightarrow 10011_2.$$

The final result in ten bits, $1100111101_2 = -195_{10}$ is correct. Similarly, when X is negative and Y positive, a correction factor of $2^n(2^n - Y)$ must be added to the result.

When both multiplier and multiplicand are negative the following situation exists.

$$(2^n - X)(2^n - Y) = 2^{2n} - 2^{nX} - 2^{nY} + XY.$$

In this case correction factors of 2^{nX} and 2^{nY} must be added to the result. The 2^{2n} is a carry-out bit from the MSB position and can be neglected.

Example 7.2 Signed multiplication by adding a correction factor

2^9	2^8	2^7	2^6	2^5	2^4	2^3	2^2	2^1	2^0	
					0	1	1	1	1	(X)
					1	0	0	1	1	(Y)
					0	1	1	1	1	
				0	1	1	1	1		
			0	0	0	0	0			
		0	0	0	0	0				
	0	1	1	1	1					
0	1	0	0	0	1	1	1	0	1	Uncorrected result
1	0	0	0	1						Correction factor
1	1	0	0	1	1	1	1	0	1	Corrected result

Booth's algorithm

The classic approach to the multiplication of signed numbers in two's complement form is provided by Booth's algorithm. This algorithm works for two positive numbers, one negative, or both negative. The algorithm is broadly similar to conventional unsigned multiplication but with the following differences. In Booth's algorithm two bits of the multiplier are examined together, to determine which of three courses of action is to take place next. The algorithm is defined below.

1. If the current multiplier bit is 1 and the next lower order multiplier bit is 0, subtract the multiplicand from the partial product.
2. If the current multiplier bit is 0 and the next lower order multiplier bit is 1, add the multiplicand to the partial product.
3. If the current multiplier bit is the same as the next lower order multiplier bit, do nothing.

Note 1. When adding in the multiplicand to the partial product, discard any carry bit generated by the addition.

Note 2. When the partial product is shifted, an arithmetic shift is used and the sign bit propagated.

Note 3. Initially, when the current bit of the multiplier is its least significant bit, the next lower order bit of the multiplier is assumed to be zero.

The flowchart for Booth's algorithm is given in Fig. 7.2. In order to illustrate the operation of Booth's algorithm, consider the following three products 13×15, -13×15, and $-13 \times (-15)$ (Examples 7.3(a), (b), and (c)).

Example 7.3(a) Multiplicand = 01111 (i.e. + 15), multiplier = 01101 (i.e. + 13)

Step	Multiplier bit	Partial product
		0000000000
Subtract multiplicand	011010	1000010000
Shift partial product right		1100010000
Add multiplicand	01101	10011110000
Shift partial product right		0001111000
Subtract multiplicand	01101	1010011000
Shift partial product right		1101001100
Do nothing	01101	1101001100
Shift partial product right		1110100110
Add multiplicand	01101	10110000110
Shift partial product right		0011000011

The final result is 0011000011_2 which is equal to $+195$. Note that the underlined numbers represent the bits to be examined at each stage.

Example 7.3(b) Multiplicand = 01111_2 (i.e. + 15), multiplier = 10011_2 (i.e. − 13)

Step	Multiplier bit	Partial product
		0000000000
Subtract multiplicand	100110	1000010000
Shift partial product right		1100010000
Do nothing	10011	1100010000
Shift partial product right		1110001000
Add multiplicand	10011	10101101000
Shift partial product right		0010110100
Do nothing	10011	0010110100
Shift partial product right		0001011010
Subtract multiplicand	10011	1001111010
Shift partial product right		1100111101

The result is 1100111101_2 which corresponds to − 195.

Example 7.3(c) Multiplicand = 10001_2 (i.e. − 15), multiplier 10011_2 (i.e. − 13)

Step	Multiplier bit	Partial product
Subtract multiplicand	100110	0111100000
Shift partial product right		0011110000
Do nothing	10011	0011110000
Shift partial product right		0001111000
Add multiplicand	10011	1010011000
Shift partial product right		1101001100
Do nothing	10011	1101001100
Shift partial product right		1110100110
Subtract multiplicand	10011	10110000110
Shift partial product right		0011000011

The result is 0011000011_2 which corresponds to + 195.

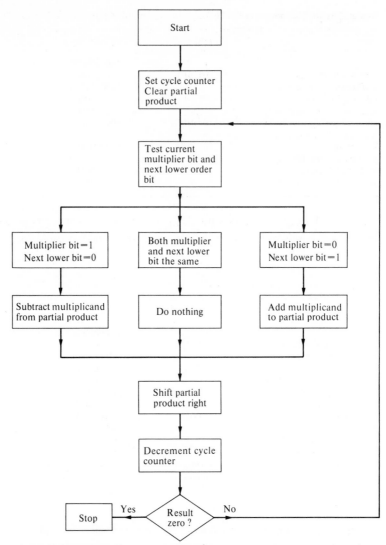

Fig. 7.2 A flowchart for Booth's algorithm

7.1.3 High-speed multiplication

I do not intend to delve deeply into the subject of high-speed multiplication as large portions of advanced textbooks are devoted to this topic alone. Here some ways of forming products alternative to the method of shifting and adding are explained.

We have seen in an earlier example that it is possible to construct a two-bit by two-bit multiplier by means of logic gates. This process can be extended to larger numbers of bits. Currently, 16-bit by 16-bit single-chip multipliers can be bought which will generate the 32-bit product in approximately 50 ns. Figure 7.3 illustrates the type of logic array used to multiply two numbers directly.

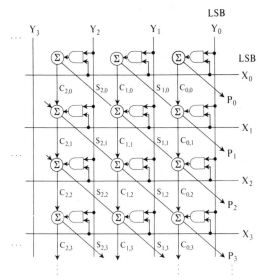

Fig. 7.3 The multiplier array

An alternative approach is to use a look-up table where all the possible results of the product of two numbers are stored in read-only memory. The table below shows how two four-bit numbers may be multiplied by storing all $2^8 = 256$ possible results in a ROM. Table 7.2 is a larger version of the type of table found in Fig. 2.73 in Chapter 2.

The 4-bit multiplier and 4-bit multiplicand together form an eight-bit address which selects one of 256 locations within the ROM. In each of these locations the product of the multiplier (most significant 4 address bits) and the multiplicand (least significant 4 address bits) are stored. For example, the product of 2 and 3 is given by the contents of location 00100011, which is 00000110.

The disadvantage of this technique is the rapid increase in the size of the ROM as the number of bits in the multiplier and multiplicand increases. Table 7.3 illustrates this effect.

The multiplication of two 8-bit numbers requires a memory capacity of 1 048 576 bits. Forming the product of even larger numbers directly by look-up table becomes impracticable. Fortunately, it is possible to calculate the product of two $2n$-bit numbers by using an n-bit multiplier.

Table 7.2 Multiplication by look-up table

Address		Data
multiplier	multiplicand	result
0000	0000	00000000
0000	0001	00000000
.	.	.
.	.	.
.	.	.
0000	1111	00000000
0001	0000	00000000
0001	0001	00000001
.	.	.
.	.	.
.	.	.
0001	1111	00001111
0010	0000	00000000
0010	0001	00000010
0010	0010	00000100
0010	0011	00000110
.	.	.
.	.	.
.	.	.
0010	1111	00011110
.	.	.
.	.	.
.	.	.
.	.	.
.	.	.
1111	1101	11000011
1111	1110	11010010
1111	1111	11100001

Table 7.3 The relationship between word size and table size

Multiplier bits n	Address bits $2n$	Lines in table 2^{2n}	Total of bits in ROM $2n \times 2^{2n}$
2	4	16	64
3	6	64	384
4	8	256	1024
5	10	1024	10240
6	12	4096	49152
7	14	16384	229376
8	16	65536	1048576

Before showing how we proceed with binary numbers, let's take a look at the product of two 2-digit decimal numbers, and then extend the technique to binary arithmetic.

$$34 \times 27 = (3 \times 10 + 4)(2 \times 10 + 7)$$
$$= 3 \times 2 \times 10^2 + 3 \times 7 \times 10 + 4 \times 2 \times 10 + 4 \times 7$$
$$= 6 \times 10^2 + 21 \times 10 + 8 \times 10 + 28$$
$$= 6 \times 10^2 + 29 \times 10 + 28$$
$$= 600 + 290 + 28$$
$$= 918$$

Now consider the generation of the product of two 8-bit numbers by means of 4-bit multipliers. Let the two 8-bit numbers A and B be represented by:

$$A = \boxed{A_u \mid A_l} \quad B = \boxed{B_u \mid B_l}$$

$\leftarrow 4 \rightarrow \quad \leftarrow 4 \rightarrow \qquad \leftarrow 4 \rightarrow \quad \leftarrow 4 \rightarrow$

A_u represents the 4 most significant bits of A, and A_l the 4 least significant bits. We have already encountered the idea of splitting up numbers when we performed 16-bit addition on an 8-bit microprocessor in Section 3.6.

A and B can be represented algebraically as follows.

$A = A_u \times 16 + A_l$ and $B = B_u \times 16 + B_l$

Consequently, $AB = (A_u \times 16 + A_l)(B_u \times 16 + B_l)$

$$= 256A_uB_u + 16A_uB_l + 16A_lB_u + A_lB_l$$

This expression requires the evaluation of four 4-bit products (A_uB_u, A_uB_l, A_lB_l), the shifting of the products by 8 or 4 positions (i.e. multiplication by 256 or 16), and the addition of four partial products. Figure 7.4 shows how this may be achieved.

7.2 Division

Division is the inverse of multiplication and is performed by repeatedly subtracting the divisor from the dividend until the result is either zero or less than the divisor. The number of times the divisor is subtracted is called the quotient, and the number left after the final subtraction is the remainder. That is:

$$\frac{\text{dividend}}{\text{divisor}} = \text{quotient} + \frac{\text{remainder}}{\text{divisor}}$$

Alternatively, we can write:

$$\text{dividend} = \text{quotient} \times \text{divisor} + \text{remainder}$$

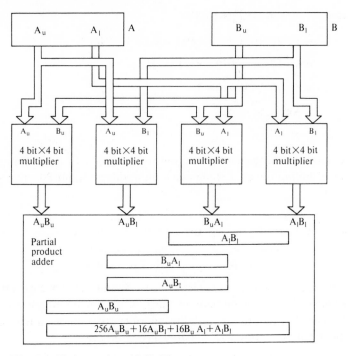

Fig. 7.4 High-speed multiplication

Before we consider binary division let's examine decimal division using the traditional pencil-and-paper technique. The following example illustrates the division of 575 by 25.

$$\text{divisor } \overline{\big|\text{ dividend}}^{\text{quotient}} \qquad 25\;\overline{\big|\,575}$$

The first step is to compare the two digits of the divisor with the most significant two digits of the dividend and ask how many times the divisor goes into these two digits. The answer is 2 (i.e. $2 \times 25 = 50$), and 2×25 is subtracted from 57. The number 2 is entered as the most significant digit of the quotient to produce the situation below.

$$
\begin{array}{r}
2 \\
25\;\overline{\big|\,575} \\
50 \\
\hline
7
\end{array}
$$

The next digit of the dividend is brought down, and the divisor is compared with 75. As 75 is an exact multiple of 25, a three can be entered in the next position of the quotient to give the following result.

```
          23
25 |  575
      50
      75
      75
      00
```

As we have examined the least significant bit of the dividend and the divisor was an exact multiple of 75, the division is complete, the quotient is 23 with a zero remainder.

A difficulty associated with division lies in estimating how many times the divisor goes into the partial dividend (i.e. 57 was divided by 25 to produce 2 remainder 7). While people do this 'mentally', some way has to be found to mechanize it for application to computers. Luckily this process is easier in binary arithmetic. Consider, the above example using unsigned binary arithmetic.

$$25 = 11001_2 \qquad 575 = 1000111111_2$$

```
11001 |  1000111111
         11001
```

The five bits of the divisor do not go into the first five bits of the dividend, so a zero is entered into the quotient and the divisor is compared with the first six bits of the dividend.

```
             01
11001 |  1000111111
         11001
         001010
```

The divisor goes into the first six bits of the dividend once, to leave a partial dividend 001010(1111). The next bit of the dividend is brought down to give:

```
             010
11001 |  1000111111
         11001
         010101
         11001
```

The partial dividend is less than the divisor, and a zero is entered into the next bit of the quotient. The process continues as follows.

```
                010111
11001 | 1000111111
        11001
        00101011
         11001
        000100101
          11001
        000011001
           11001
        0000000000
```

In this case the partial quotient is zero, so that the final result is 10111, remainder 0.

7.2.1 Restoring division

The classic pencil-and-paper algorithm we have just discussed can be implemented in digital form with little modification. The only real change is to the way in which the divisor is compared with the partial dividend. People do the comparison mentally; computers must perform a subtraction and test the sign of the result. If the subtraction yields a positive result, a one is entered into the quotient, but if the result is negative a zero is entered in the quotient and the divisor added back to the partial dividend to restore it to its previous value. A suitable algorithm for restoring division is given in Table 7.4. The flowchart corresponding to this algorithm is given in Fig. 7.5. As an example of this algorithm consider the division of 01100111_2 by 1001_2. This corresponds to 103 divided by 9, and should yield a quotient 11 and a remainder 4. Table 7.5 illustrates the division process, step by step.

Table 7.4 Algorithm for restoring division

1. Align the divisor with the most significant bit of the dividend.
2. Subtract the divisor from the partial dividend.
3. If the resulting partial dividend is negative, place a zero in the quotient, and add back the divisor to restore the partial dividend.
4. If the resulting partial dividend is positive, place a one in the quotient.
5. Perform a test to determine end of division.
   If the divisor is aligned so that its least significant bit corresponds to the least significant bit of the partial dividend, stop. The final partial dividend is the remainder. Otherwise, continue with step 6.
6. Shift the divisor one place right. Repeat from step 2.

7.2.2 Nonrestoring division

It is possible to modify the restoring division algorithm of Fig. 7.5 to achieve a reduction in the time taken to execute the division process. Basically, the nonrestoring division algorithm is almost identical to the restoring algorithm. The only difference is that the so-called restoring operation is eliminated. From the flowchart for restoring division, Fig. 7.5, it can be seen that

Table 7.5 Restoring division: 1001 $\lceil$ 01100111

Step	Description	Partial dividend 01100111	Divisor 00001001	Quotient 00000000
1	Align	01100111	01001000	00000000
2	Subtract divisor from partial dividend	00011111	01001000	00000000
4	Result positive shift in 1 in quotient	00011111	01001000	00000001
5	Test			
6	Shift divisor one place right	00011111	00100100	00000001
2	Subtract divisor from partial dividend	−00000101	00100100	00000001
3	Restore divisor, shift in 0 in quotient	00011111	00100100	00000010
5	Test			
6	Shift divisor one place right	00011111	00010010	00000010
2	Subtract divisor from partial dividend	00001101	00010010	00000010
4	Result positive shift in 1 in quotient	00001101	00010010	00000101
5	Test			
6	Shift divisor one place back	00001101	00001001	00000101
2	Subtract divisor from partial dividend	00000100	00001001	00000101
4	Result positive shift in 1 in quotient	00000100	00001001	00001011
5	Test			

Quotient = 1011_2, remainder = 100_2

after a partial dividend has been restored by adding back the divisor, one half the divisor is subtracted in the next cycle. This is because each cycle includes a shift-divisor-right operation which is equivalent to dividing the divisor by two. Thus, the restore-divisor operation in the current cycle followed by the subtraction of half the divisor in the following cycle is equivalent to a single operation of adding half the divisor to the partial dividend. That is, $D - D/2 = +D/2$ where D is the divisor. Figure 7.6 gives the flowchart for nonrestoring division. After the divisor has been subtracted from the partial dividend, the new partial dividend is tested. If it is negative, zero is shifted into the least significant position of the quotient and half the divisor is added back to the partial dividend. If it is positive, one is shifted into the least significant position of the quotient and half the divisor is subtracted from the partial dividend. Table 7.6 repeats the example of Table 7.5 using nonrestoring division.

7.2.3 Division by multiplication

Because both computers and microprocessors perform division far less frequently than multiplication, there is less special-purpose hardware for division. It is, however, possible to perform division by means of multiplication, addition, and shifting. As high-speed multipliers are readily available, they can be applied to division.

Suppose we wish to divide a dividend N by a divisor D to obtain a quotient Q, so that $Q = N/D$. The first step is to scale D so that it lies in the range:

$$\tfrac{1}{2} \leqslant D < 1$$

The above operation is carried out by shifting D left or right and recording the number of shifts. This is entirely analagous to normalization in floating-point arithmetic. A new number, Z, is defined in terms of D as $Z = 1 - D$. As D lies between $\frac{1}{2}$ and unity, it follows that Z lies between zero and $\frac{1}{2}$.

An elementary rule of arithmetic states that if the top and bottom of a fraction are multiplied by the same number, the value of the fraction remains unaltered.

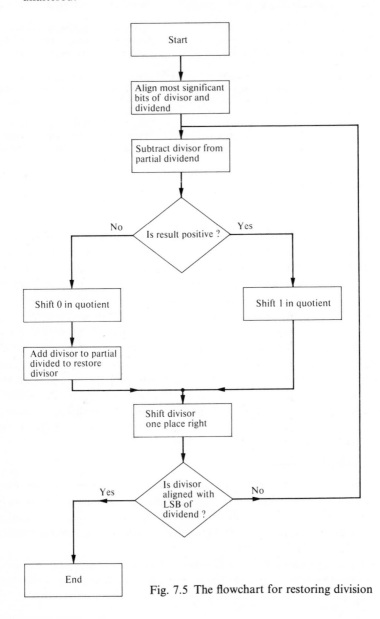

Fig. 7.5 The flowchart for restoring division

Thus, $Q = N/D = KN/KD$.

Suppose $K = 1 + Z$ then:

$$Q = \frac{N}{D} = \frac{N(1+Z)}{D(1+Z)} = \frac{N(1+Z)}{(1-Z)(1+Z)} = \frac{N(1+Z)}{1-Z^2}.$$

If we now repeat the process with $K = 1 + Z^2$, Q becomes:

$$\frac{N(1+Z)}{1-Z^2} \cdot \frac{1+Z^2}{1+Z^2} = \frac{N(1+Z)(1+Z^2)}{1-Z^4}.$$

This process may be repeated n times with the result that:

$$Q = \frac{N}{D} = \frac{N(1+Z)(1+Z^2)(1+Z^4)\cdots(1+Z^{2^{n-1}})}{1-Z^{2^n}}$$

Since Z is less than unity, the value of Z rapidly approaches zero as n is increased. Consequently, the approximate value of Q is given by:

$$Q = N(1+Z)(1+Z^2)(1+Z^4)\ldots(1+Z^{2^{n-1}}).$$

For 8-bit precision n need be only 3, and if $n = 5$ the quotient yields a precision of 32 bits. As the divisor was scaled to lie between one half and unity, the corresponding quotient, Q, calculated from the above formula must be scaled by the same factor to produce the desired result.

Table 7.6 An example of nonrestoring division

Step	Description	Partial dividend	Divisor	Quotient
		01100111	00001001	00000000
1	Align divisor	01100111	01001000	00000000
2	Subtract divisor from partial dividend	00011111	01001000	00000000
3	Shift divisor right	00011111	00100100	00000000
4	Test partial dividend enter 1 in quotient and subtract divisor from partial dividend	−00000101	00100100	00000001
6	Test for end of process	−00000101	00100100	00000001
3	Shift divisor right	−00000101	00010010	00000001
5	Test partial dividend enter 0 in quotient and add divisor to partial dividend	00001101	00010010	00000010
6	Test for end of process	00001101	00010010	00000010
3	Shift divisor right	00001101	00001001	00000010
4	Test partial dividend enter 1 in quotient and subtract divisor from partial dividend	00000100	00001001	00000101
6	Test for end of process	00000100	00001001	00000101
3	Shift divisor right	00000100	0000100.1	00000101
4	Test partial dividend enter 1 in quotient and subtract divisor from partial dividend	−00000000.1	0000100.1	00001011
6	Test for end of process	−00000000.1	0000100.1	00001011
7	Restore last partial dividend	00000100	0000100.1	00001011

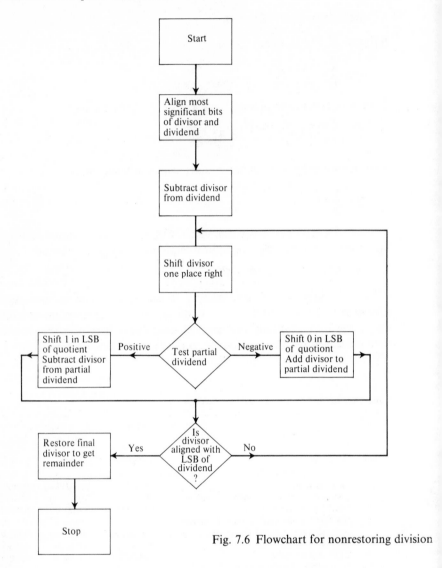

Fig. 7.6 Flowchart for nonrestoring division

8 COMPUTER COMMUNICATIONS

This chapter examines the way in which computers communicate with each other. 'Why should one computer wish to communicate with another?' I hear you ask. Computers communicate with each other for the same reason that people cooperate with each other—efficiency. By sharing skills and resources a group of *n* people can achieve more than *n* times what one person alone can achieve. This is summed up by the phrase 'The whole is greater than the sum of its parts'.

As a simple demonstration of the advantage of linking computers together to form a network, consider the following example. A scientist is using a minicomputer to control an experiment. One day he has to perform a numerical calculation so complex that it will require all the minicomputer's time for several days. During this period the experiment may have to be shut down. If it is necessary to run the experiment continuously, the scientist can buy a new and more powerful computer capable of handling both experiment and calculation. Unfortunately, this approach is terribly wasteful as, once the calculation has been completed, the new computer is underused. A much better solution is to buy time on a large mainframe, and pay only for the work actually done. This can be effected in one of two ways. One is to take the problem physically to the mainframe on magnetic tape or disk. The other is to transmit the problem over some data-carrying network from the minicomputer to the mainframe, and then receive the results from the mainframe.

Because it is very expensive to lay down physical connections between computers, the existing public switched telephone network is often used to link them. This is not an ideal solution as the telephone network was never designed to handle high-speed digital data. Such networks connecting computers together over considerable distances (say more than 1 km) are called wide area networks (WANs).

In the last few years a considerable change in the pattern of computer use has taken place. The flood of low-cost microcomputers and minicomputers has led to a corresponding increase in the number of peripherals capable of being controlled by a computer. It is now common to connect together many different computers and peripherals on a given site—for example a factory. This enables data to be shared, control centralized, and efficiency improved. Such a network is called a local area network (LAN).

A good example of a LAN can be found in the Computer Science Department at Teesside Polytechnic. Figure 8.1 shows how clusters of computers and peripherals are connected to NIUs (network interface units),

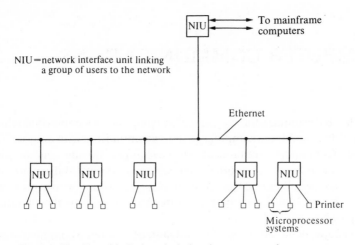

Fig. 8.1 The Teesside Polytechnic local area network

and the NIUs interlinked by an Ethernet, one of the types of LAN available off-the-shelf from several suppliers. The NIUs each have their own microprocessor and serve to link a group of devices with each other and the network. Conceptually, they perform the same function as a telephone exchange. A VDU is located in each lecturer's room, allowing him to communicate with a UNIVAC 1100 or a PRIME 750 mainframe on the adjacent site. This book was itself edited on the PRIME from my own office. Beside the mainframes, a number of mini- and micro-computers are also connected to the network, together with printers and other peripherals.

In the near future it is envisaged that software will be written to provide automated-office facilities. For example, a lecturer will be able to consign a memo to a backing store making it available to those who need it. When a user accesses the memory he will be able to ask for those memos relevant to him. The memo can be displayed on the VDU and a hard copy printed in the unlikely event of it being important.

The first part of this chapter, Section 8.1, deals with the way in which digital data is moved from one point to another, a bit at a time. The techniques by which the data is converted from parallel form to serial form, and by which data is transmitted over telephone channels, are included here.

Simply moving data from one point to another is not the whole story. Section 8.2 provides an introduction to the protocols (rules) enabling computers to exchange data in an orderly fashion. Protocols make sure that the data gets to its correct destination, and deal with the problems of lost or corrupted data.

Section 8.3 is devoted to local area networks, and describes the features of some of the LANs in current use. An important aspect of LANs is the way in which the computers and peripherals are able to share the same network without apparent conflict.

8.1 Serial data transmission

Ideally, information should be moved from one computer to another a word at a time, with all the m bits of a word transmitted simultaneously. Conceptually, this involves linking the data bus of one computer to that of another. While this is feasible for computers separated by up to several metres, it is impracticable for greater distances. An m-bit parallel data highway requires at least m wires to carry the data, and between two and four additional wires to control the flow of information.

Almost all networks transmit data from point to point serially a bit at a time. This arrangement requires only two lines, one to carry the data and one to be the ground return. Note that a voltage has a meaning only when specified with respect to some reference point such as the ground or the earth. If two points are linked by a single path, data can be moved in only one direction at a time. This mode is illustrated in Fig. 8.2 and is called half-duplex transmission. If an extra path is provided for a return channel as in Fig. 8.3, simultaneous two-way transmission becomes possible. This is called full-duplex, and corresponds to a telephone conversation where both parties can talk and listen simultaneously.

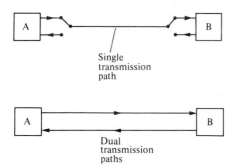

Single transmission path

Fig. 8.2 Half-duplex transmission

Dual transmission paths

Fig. 8.3 Full-duplex transmission

Serial data transmission brings with it two problems. How is the stream of data divided up into individual bits, and how are the bits divided into separate words? How is the data physically transmitted over long distances? The division of the data stream into bits and words is handled in one of two ways: asynchronously and synchronously. These will be treated separately. The transmission of data over long distances involves the concept of modulation and demodulation and is dealt with later in this section.

8.1.1 Asynchronous serial transmission

In an asynchronous serial transmission system the clocks at the transmitter and receiver responsible for dividing the data stream into bits are not synchronized. Figure 8.4 shows the waveform corresponding to a single seven-bit character. The output from the transmitter sits at a logical one state whenever data is not being transmitted and the line is idle. This corresponds

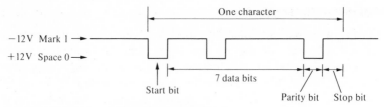

Fig. 8.4 Asynchronous serial transmission

to a 'mark' condition and is represented by a -12 V in many systems operating over short distances.

In what follows, a bit period is the shortest time for which the line may be in a logical one or a logical zero state. When the transmitter wishes to transmit a word, it places the line in a logical zero (space) state for one bit period. A logical zero is represented by $+12$ V. When the receiver sees this logical zero, called a start bit, it knows that a character is about to follow. The incoming data stream can then be divided into seven bit periods and the data sampled at the centre of each bit. The receiver's clock is not synchronized with the transmitter's and the bits are not sampled exactly in the centre. However, if the receiver's clock is within approximately 4 per cent or so of the transmitter's clock, the system works well.

After seven data bits have been sent, a parity bit is transmitted to give a measure of error protection. If the receiver finds that the received parity does not match the calculated parity, an error is flagged, and the current character rejected.

Following the parity bit are one (or optionally two) stop bits at a logical one level. The stop bit carries no information and serves only as a spacer between consecutive characters. After the stop bit has been transmitted, a new character may be sent at any time. Asynchronous serial data links are used largely to transmit data in (ASCII-encoded) character form.

If the duration of a single bit is T seconds, the length of a character is given by

$$\text{start bit} + \text{seven data bits} + \text{parity bit} + \text{stop bit} = 10T.$$

Note that asynchronous transmission is inefficient because it requires ten data bits to transmit seven bits of useful information. There are several formats for asynchronous data transmission in common use. Some transmit seven bits of data per character, others eight. Some have odd parity bits, some even, and some have no parity.

The speed at which a serial data link operates is expressed in bits per second, and is typically in the range 110 to 96 000 bps. For a binary (i.e. two-level) signal, one bit per second is called one Baud, so that a VDU transmitting data at 2400 bps is said to operate at 2400 Baud. The Baud-rate of a transmission system is defined as the number of changes of state of the signal per second, and is also called the signalling speed. If the data were transmitted in the form of an eight-level signal at 2400 Baud, the bit rate would be 7200 bps, as each signal element is equivalent to three bits ($8 = 2^3$) of information.

Once the receiver has assembled all the bits of a character, the character is read by the computer using any of the techniques discussed in Chapter 5. In fact, because the transmission and reception of serial data is performed entirely by special-purpose integrated circuits, the computer itself does not have to worry about the fine details of data transmission.

8.1.2 Synchronous serial transmission

Asynchronous data links are largely used to link peripherals (VDUs, printers, modems, etc.) with computers. Where information has to be passed between the individual computers of a network, synchronous serial transmission is generally employed. In a synchronous serial data transmission system information is transmitted continuously with no gap between adjacent groups of bits. I use the expression 'groups of bits' because synchronous systems often transmit entire blocks of pure binary information at a time, rather than a sequence of ASCII-encoded characters.

There are two problems facing the designer of a synchronous serial system. One is how to divide the incoming data stream into individual bits, and the other is how to divide the data bits into meaningful groups.

Bit synchronization

If a copy of the transmitter's clock were available at the receiver there would be no difficulty in breaking up the data stream into individual bits. Unfortunately, this would require an additional transmission path for the clock, and hence increase the cost of the data link. A better solution is found by encoding the data in such a way that a synchronizing signal is included with the data signal. In Chapter 6 ways of encoding digital data for recording on magnetic media were introduced. Some of these techniques can readily be applied to data transmission. If the data stream is phase encoded, a separate clock can be derived from the received signal and the data extracted. Figure 8.5 shows a phase-encoded signal.

Word synchronization

At first sight it might appear that dividing a continuous stream of bits into meaningful units is a difficult task.

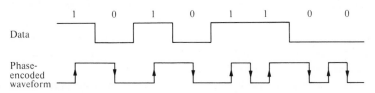

Fig. 8.5 Phase-encoded synchronous serial transmission

Infactitisquiteaneasytasktoformbitsintowords. Here I have removed inter-word spacing in plain text making it harder, but not impossible, to read. This is because the reader surveys the string of letters and looks for recognizable groups corresponding to words. This technique can be applied to binary data streams. Synchronous transmission systems operate in one of two modes: character oriented and block transmission. The former splits the data stream into individual characters, and the latter splits the stream into much longer blocks of pure binary data.

Character-oriented transmission

In character-oriented transmission the data to be transmitted is encoded in the form of (usually) ASCII characters. For example, the string 'Alan' would be sent as the sequence of four seven-bit characters below. The individual letters are coded as: 'A' = $41, 'l' = $6C, 'a' = $61, 'n' = $6E.

    1000001001101110000110111011

This string is read from left to right, with the first bit representing the least significant bit of the 'A'.

What is needed is some method of identifying the beginning of a message. Once this has been done the bits can be divided into groups of seven (or eight if a parity bit is used) for the duration of the message.

The ASCII code has a number of special characters specifically designed to control a data link. The character SYN ($16 or 0010110) is used to denote the beginning of a message. The receiver reads the incoming bits and ignores them until it sees a SYN character. Unfortunately, this simple scheme is flawed; the end of one character together with the beginning of the next may by chance look like a SYN character. To avoid this problem two SYN characters are transmitted sequentially. If the receiver does see a SYN it reads the next character. If this is also a SYN the start of a message is assumed to have been located, otherwise a false synchronization is assumed and the search for a valid SYN character continued. Further details on character oriented transmission systems will be provided when we come to the subject of protocols.

Block-oriented transmission

The ASCII code is excellent for representing text, but is ill-fitted to representing pure binary data. Pure binary data can be anything from a core dump (a block of memory), a program in binary form, to floating point numbers. When data is represented in character form it is easy to choose one particular character (e.g. SYN) as a special marker. When the data is in a pure binary form it is apparently impossible to choose any particular data word as a reserved marker or flag.

However, a remarkably simple but very clever technique can be used to solve this problem. The start of a block of data is denoted by the binary sequence 01111110. Whenever the receiver sees the bit pattern 01111110, it knows that it has found the start of a new block of data. This unique pattern is called a 'flag'. But what happens if the binary sequence 01111110 occurs naturally in the data block to be transmitted? How do we avoid it being regarded as a flag? Whenever the pattern 011111 occurs in the data, the transmitter says, 'If the next two bits are a one followed by a zero a flag pattern will be created'. The transmitter avoids this by deliberately inserting a zero after the fifth logical one in succession. In this way the flag can never appear in the data stream by accident.

This process is called 'bit-stuffing'. At the receiver the data stream is examined for the binary pattern 01111110. When encountered it is deleted and the following data regarded as the message. As the data is read, consecutive ones are counted. When five ones are detected the following bit, which must be zero, is deleted, as it must have been inserted at the transmitter. Figure 8.6 illustrates this process.

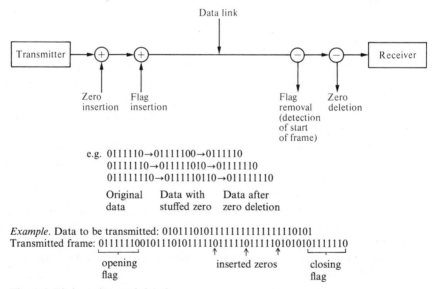

e.g. 0111110→01111100→0111110
     01111110→011111010→01111110
     011111110→0111110110→011111110

Original	Data with	Data after
data	stuffed zero	zero deletion

Example. Data to be transmitted: 01011101011111111111111110101
Transmitted frame: 01111110010111010111101111101111101010101111110
                   └──┬──┘   ↑   ↑   ↑   └──┬──┘
                   opening   inserted zeros   closing
                   flag   flag

Fig. 8.6 Bit insertion and deletion

Modern synchronous serial data transmission systems have largely been standardized and use the HDLC format. HDLC stands for 'high-level data link control'. Data is transmitted in the form of packets of frames, each separated by a flag as above. Bit stuffing is necessary to keep the flag (01111110) unique. The format of a typical HDLC frame is given in Fig. 8.7. Following the opening flag is an address field corresponding to the address of the slave station. HDLC is intended for transmission between a master station and a number of slaves (Fig. 8.8). This allows the master to send a

Fig. 8.7 The HDLC frame format

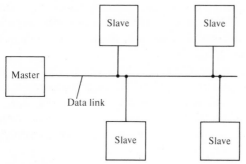

Note. All communication is between a slave and the master. Direct slave-to-slave communication is not allowed.

Fig. 8.8 Master–slave transmission with HDLC

message to one of many slaves without ambiguity. Any slave receiving a frame whose address does not match its own address ignores the message. Unlike humans, computers do not listen to third-party traffic. When a slave sends a message to the master station, the address field identifies the slave sending the message.

Following the address field is an eight-bit control field which controls the operation of the data link ensuring an orderly flow of messages, and deals with the effects of lost messages. This aspect is dealt with in more detail in the section on protocols.

The control field is followed by an optional data field (or information or I-field) containing the actual data to be transmitted. This field is optional because sometimes frames are sent for control purposes only. The length of this field may be any integer number of 5, 6, 7, or eight-bit words. Immediately following the data field is a 16-bit frame check sequence (FCS). This is a powerful method of detecting errors during transmission. It is impossible to go into detail about the FCS here, but the following should convey an idea of its generation and application.

The p bits in the packet between the opening flag and the FCS itself are regarded as forming the coefficients of a polynomial of degree p. This polynomical is divided by a standard polynomial using modulo two arithmetic to generate a quotient and a remainder. The quotient is discarded. The 16-bit remainder is the FCS and is transmitted after the data field. At the receiver the bits from the start of the address field up to the FCS are divided by the same polynomial and the new remainder compared with the received FCS. If they are the same as the received FCS all is well, and if they are not, the entire frame is rejected. By carefully choosing the generator polynomial it is possible to detect the vast majority of transmission errors.

Following the FCS is a closing flag which denotes the end of the frame. Indeed, the receiver determines the end of the data field only by counting back 16 bits from the closing flag.

Modulation and data transmission

The transmission of digital data predates the digital computer by over a century. As early as 1809 King Maximilian asked the Bavarian Academy of Sciences to suggest a scheme for high-speed communication over long distances because he had seen how the French visual semaphore system had helped Napoleon's military campaigns. As a result, Sommering designed a crude telegraph which used 35 conductors (one for each character). When electricity was passed along a conductor it was detected at the receiver by passing the current through water and observing the bubbles formed as the current decomposed the water into hydrogen and oxygen.

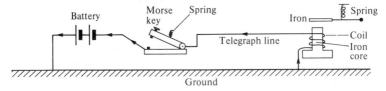

Fig. 8.9 The telegraph

Shortly after the connection between electricity and magnetism had been discovered, the telegraph was invented, and became well-established in the 1830s. Figure 8.9 illustrates the operation of the telegraph. When the key is depressed a current flows in the circuit, energizing the solenoid (i.e. magnetizing the iron core inside the coil). This produces an audible click as a small iron plate is attracted to the iron core. In 1843 Morse sent his assistant A. Vail to the printer's to count the relative frequencies of the letters they were using to set up their press. The resulting code consisted of four symbols: the dot, the dash (= 3 dots), the space between dots and dashes, and the space between words. Frequently occurring letters such as 'E' were given short codes ('E' = '·'), and infrequently occurring letters were given long symbols ('Q' = '— —·—'). It is interesting to note that the Morse code is fairly close to the optimum Huffman code for the English language.

As transmission paths increased in length with the advances in technology during the nineteenth century, it became apparent that signals suffer distortion during transmission. A sharply rising pulse at the transmitter is received as a highly-distorted pulse with long rise and fall times. Figure 8.10 illustrates the effect of this so-called telegraph distortion. The sponsors of the trans-atlantic cable project were worried by the effect of this distortion and the problem was eventually handed to Lord Kelvin. In 1855 Kelvin presented a

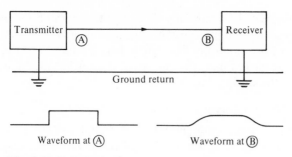

Fig. 8.10 Telegraph distortion

paper to the Royal Society analysing the effect of pulse distortion. This paper is the cornerstone of what is now called transmission line theory.

The cause of the problems investigated by Kelvin lies in the physical properties of electrical conductors. At its simplest, the effect of a transmission line is to reduce the speed at which signals can change state.

From 1880 onwards the telephone dominated information transmission systems. Unfortunately, the telephone transmits analogue signals, and telephone networks are ill-suited to the transmission of digital data. This is because the telephone network is not able to transmit either slowly changing signals or rapidly changing signals. Interestingly this is the same problem from which magnetic recording devices suffer.

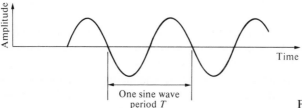

Fig. 8.11 The sine wave

The fundamental waveform of electronics is the sine wave of Fig. 8.11. Any transmission system can be characterized in terms of the attenuation (i.e. reduction in power) experienced by a sine wave transmitted across the network. Figure 8.12 shows the frequency response of a telephone channel, where frequencies in the range 300 Hz to 3000 Hz are transmitted with little attenuation. Frequencies above or below these limits are attenuated. It can be shown that a digital pulse is made up of a series of sine waves with frequencies of f, $2f$, $3f$, . . . , where f is related to the width of the pulse. In theory the sine waves extend up to infinite frequencies.

If a sequence of binary signals were presented to the telephone network, they would be so severely distorted that they would be unusable at the receiving end of the circuit. This is because both the high and low frequency sine waves which make up the pulse are not transmitted by the network.

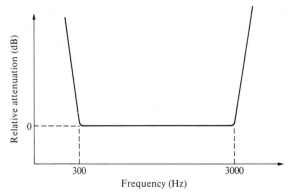

Fig. 8.12 The characteristics of the telephone network

As the telephone network can transmit speech signals, various ways of converting digital information into speech-like signals have been investigated. Figure 8.13 shows how the digital data can be used to change, or modulate, the amplitude of a sine wave. This is known as amplitude modulation or AM. The equipment needed to generate such a signal is called a modulator, and that needed to extract the digital data from the resulting signal is called a demodulator. The interface between a computer and a telephone system is called a modem (modulator–demodulator). Because AM is more sensitive to noise (i.e. interference) than other modulation techniques, it is not widely used in data transmission.

Instead of changing the amplitude of a sine wave it is possible to vary its frequency in sympathy with the digital data. In a binary system one frequently represents one binary value, and a different frequency represents the other. Figure 8.14 shows a frequency modulated (FM) signal. FM is widely used because it has a better tolerance to noise than AM.

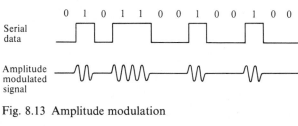

Fig. 8.13 Amplitude modulation

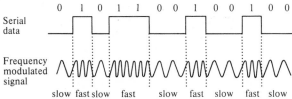

Fig. 8.14 Frequency modulation

Another form of modulation illustrated in Fig. 8.15 is phase modulation (PM). In this case the phase of the sine wave is changed in sympathy with the digital signal. PM is widely used and has fairly similar characteristics to FM.

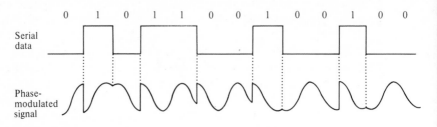

Fig. 8.15 Phase modulation

If the phase change corresponding to a logical one is 180 degrees, and 0 degrees (no change) corresponds to a logical zero, one bit of information can be transmitted at each time slot (Fig. 8.15). If however, the phase is shifted by multiples of 90 degrees, two bits at a time can be transmitted (Fig. 8.16, Table 8.1).

Table 8.1   Phase encoding a multi-level signal

Transmitted bits	Phase change
00	0
01	90
10	180
11	270

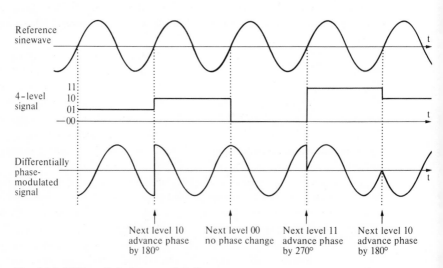

Fig. 8.16 Differential phase modulation

Modems operate over a wide range of bit rates from 300 bps to 9600 bps. In general, low bit rates are associated with the switched telephone network where some lines are very poor and signal impairments reduce the data rate to 2400 bps or below. The higher rates of 4800 bps and 9600 bps are generally found on privately leased lines where the telephone company offers a higher grade of service.

Today it is possible to transmit data at 19 200 bps over ordinary telephone lines by using very sophisticated transmission and reception techniques. By simultaneously changing the amplitude and phase of a signal it is possible to transmit several bits of information at once. This is called quadrature amplitude modulation (QAM). Typically, 16-point QAM uses sixteen different waveforms to transmit four bits at one go. This means that the data rate is four times the signalling rate.

Because the telephone channel severely distorts the transmitted waveforms at high signalling rates, some method of reconstituting the original signal is required. This is called equalization and is found on some high-speed modems. As the characteristics of the telephone channel change from call to call, it is necessary for an equalizer to adapt to the characteristics of the channel currently in use.

8.2 Protocols

In Section 8.1 we dealt with the physical aspects of data transmission. Here we will look at the way in which 'conversations' between two parties are governed. Suppose I have a bank overdraft and I send a cheque to cover it. If after a few days I receive a threatening letter from the manager, what am I to conclude? Was my cheque received after the manager's letter was sent? Has one of my debits reached my account and increased the overdraft? Was my cheque lost in the post?

The above situation demonstrates that the blind transmission of information can lead to confusing situations. It is necessary for both parties to know exactly what messages each has and has not received. The set of rules governing such an exchange between two or more parties is called a protocol. We have already met the basic idea of a protocol for the exchange of data in Chapter 5 when dealing with input/output and handshaking.

There are a number of internationally agreed protocols for the transmission of messages between two points. These fall into two classes: byte control-oriented protocols (BCP) designed for data transmitted in character form, and bit-oriented protocols (BOP) intended for use with streams of pure binary data. Here we shall look at one of each type of protocol. BISYNC is a BCP protocol designed by IBM, and HDLC (high-level data link control) is a widely used BOP. In general, bit-oriented protocols are rapidly becoming a universal standard, and character-oriented protocols like BISYNC can be expected to decline in use.

BISYNC

The BISYNC message is presented in Fig. 8.17. BISYNC uses special characters in the ASCII code to perform certain control functions. Two synchronizing characters, SYN, denote the start of the message. The next field is the header field which begins with the SOH (start of header) character. The header field is really a control field and is used to control the flow of data by means of special ASCII characters. After the header field comes the text

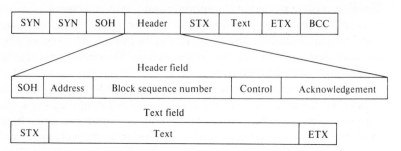

Fig. 8.17 The format of a BISYNC frame

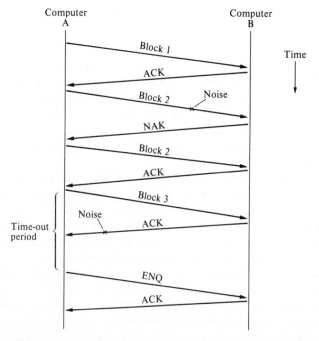

Block 2 from A is corrupted by noise. This is detected by B which then sends a negative acknowledge (NAK) to A, inviting A to retransmit its message. Block 3 is received satisfactorily by B but its acknowledgement is lost on the way to A. After a suitable delay A sends an enquiry request (ENQ), and B repeats its acknowledgement. This arrangement is not reliable and contains an ambiguity (see text).

Fig. 8.18 Two-way communication with BISYNC

field preceded by an STX (start of text) character. Following the text field is an ETX (end of text) character and an error detecting code (BCC).

Figure 8.18 shows how an exchange of messages between two systems, A and B, can be presented graphically. The vertical axis represents increasing time so that the diagram is read from top to bottom. Initially computer A sends a message, Block 1, to computer B. This is acknowledged by B which sends an acknowledge message, ACK.

The second block is corrupted by noise and B sends a negative acknow- ledge message, NAK, inviting A to repeat its transmission. Block 3 is received satisfactorily by B, but B's acknowledgement gets lost. If nothing were done, the system would hang up, with A waiting for a reply forever. To get out of this deadlock, A starts a timer when it sends a message. If a reply is not received within a reasonable interval, a time-out is generated, forcing A to send a reply-request (ENQ) message to B. B will then reply with an ACK or a NAK depending on whether it received the last message.

Unfortunately, the above scheme contains a potential ambiguity. If A sends a message which is entirely lost in transmission, it will receive no ACK or NAK, and after a timeout it will send a reply-request. When B gets the reply-request it sends an acknowledgement to the last message it received. This is not A's most recent message but the one before it. The last message sent by A has been lost and neither A nor B is aware of this. When A receives the ACK from B it sends its next message instead of repeating the last message.

A way round this ambiguity is to resort to numbered acknowledgements. The simplest arrangement employs two acknowledgement codes, ACK-0 and ACK-1. These codes are used alternately. Figure 8.19 shows how the two ACKs resolve this ambiguity.

The above treatment of a character-oriented protocol is intended only to give an idea of how messages are exchanged in an orderly fashion. The setting up of calls and their 'clearing-down' after a transmission are not included here. Readers wishing to pursue this further should consult the bibliography. Housley, in particular, provides a very clear introduction to protocols.

HDLC

The high level data link control scheme for the transmission of pure binary data is now an international standard, and found in many different types of data link. We have already seen that the HDLC frame format is divided into a number of fields. The eight-bit control field is devoted to the sequencing of messages. The format of the control field is determined by bits zero and one as in Fig. 8.20.

Whenever bit zero of a control field is zero, the frame is said to be an information frame because there is an information field in the frame. The control field of an information frame carries two three-bit numbers, N(S),

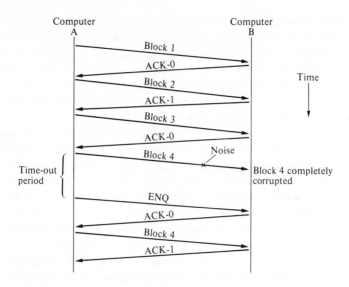

In this case two alternative values for the acknowledgement message are used. These are ACK-0 and ACK-1, and are always sent alternately: ACK-0, ACK-1, ACK-0, ACK-1, ACK-0 . . . . After receiving an ACK-0, A sends Block-4 which is severely corrupted and is not received by B. After a timeout A sends an enquiry request and receives ACK-0 as a response. A knows that ACK-0 is a response to Block-3. If Block-4 had been received, A would have seen an ACK-1.

Fig. 8.19 The use of ACK-0 and ACK-1

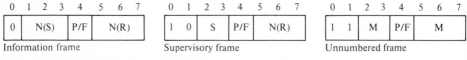

N(S) = Send-sequence count, N(R) = Receive-sequence count, S = Supervisory function bits, M = Modifier function bits, P/F = poll/final bit

Fig. 8.20 Message type

and N(R) whose function is to keep track of the flow of messages between two computers in communication with each other.

The send sequence count, N(S), uniquely identifies the current information frame. For example, if N(S) = 101 this frame is numbered 5. When this frame is received the value of N(S) is examined and compared with the previous value. If the previous value was 4, the message is received in sequence. But if the value was not 4, there is a gnashing of teeth and grieving over a lost message. Note that the sequence count is modulo 8 so that it goes 67012345670 . . . Consequently, if eight messages are lost the next value of N(S) will apparently be correct.

The receive sequence count, N(R), corresponds to the number of the next information frame expected by the receiver. That is, it informs the transmitter that $N(R) - 1$ frames have been correctly received. Suppose A is communicating with B, and is sending to B an information frame with $N(S) = 3$, $N(R) = 6$. This means that A is sending frame number 3, and has safely received frames up to 5 from B. It is saying that it expects to see an information frame from B with its value of $N(S)$ equal to 6.

The P/F bit has a dual meaning. The master station uses it as a poll bit to elicit a response from the slave station with which it is in communication. The master may send (say) five information frames, each with the P bit equal to zero. The next I-frame is sent with $P = 1$, which forces the slave to respond. the master can then determine whether its messages have been received by examining the value of $N(R)$ obtained from the slave. When the slave uses the P/F bit, it is called the final bit and simply tells the master that there are no more I frames to be sent in the current batch.

When bits zero and one of the control field are 1,0, respectively, the frame is said to be a supervisory frame and contains no information field. The supervisory frame (or S-frame) has a three-bit $N(R)$ count, and can therefore be used to acknowledge the receipt of I-frames. Bits two and three of the control field (labelled S) are reserved for four supervisory functions as in Table 8.2.

Table 8.2 Four types of S-frame

S	Mnemonic	Meaning
00	RR	Receiver ready. The station sending this message is in a condition to receive information frames,
01	REJ	Reject. This is a request for the transmission of all messages starting with the frame number $N(R)$.
10	RNR	Receiver not ready. This denotes a busy condition and tells the transmitter not to send any I-frames.
11	SREJ	Selective reject. The REJ message above tells the transmitter to send all messages starting with $N(R)$. The selective reject asks for the retransmission of message $N(R)$.

The third type of control field is called 'unnumbered' because it has no $N(R)$ field. It is used to control the data-link by defining the operating mode, setting up calls, and ending them.

Figure 8.21 shows an exchange of messages between A (the master) and B (the slave) operating in a half-duplex mode. Each frame is denoted by 'type, $N(S)$, $N(R)$, P/F', where type is I (for an information field), RR, REJ, RNR, or SREJ.

Figure 8.22 shows the operation of an HDLC system operating in full-duplex mode, permitting the simultaneous exchange of messages in both directions.

So far we have dealt with two types of protocol. The protocol dealing with the transmission of bits between two points is called the 'physical layer protocol' and is concerned with the electrical characteristics of the trans-

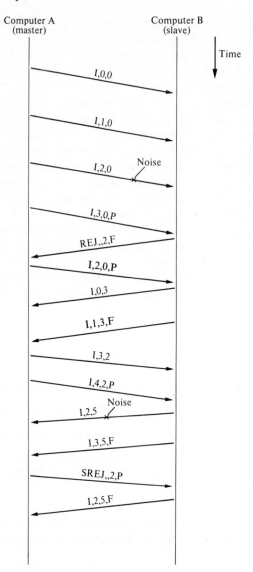

Fig. 8.21 HDLC half-duplex transmission

A message is denoted by: type,N(S),N(R),P/F. For example, I,3,0,P indicates an information frame numbered 3, with an N(R) count of 0, and the poll bit set indicating that a response is required. Note that message 2 from A (i.e. I,2,0) is lost. Therefore, when A sends the message I,3,0,P with the poll bit set, B responds with REJ,,2,F. This indicates that B is rejecting all messages from A numbered 2 and above, and that the F bit is set denoting that B has no more messages to send to A.

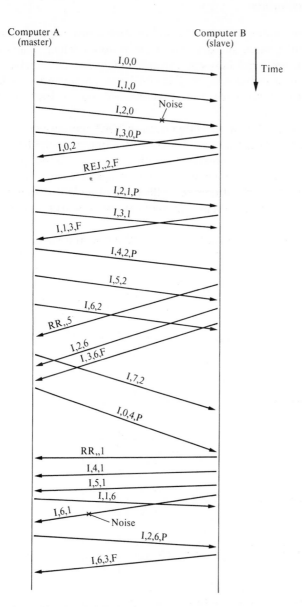

Fig. 8.22 HDLC full-duplex transmission

In this case messages can be transmitted between A and B in both directions simultaneously. Consider the first seven messages. (1) *A sends* a frame 1,0,0 (information frame numbered 0, A is expecting a frame from B numbered 0). (2) *A sends* frame I,1,0 (information frame numbered 1, A is still expecting a frame from B numbered 0). (3) *A sends* frame I,2,0. This frame is corrupted by noise and is not correctly received by B. (4) *B sends* frame I,0,2 (information frame numbered 0, B is expecting a frame from A numbered 2). Note that because A's frame I,2,0 has been lost, B is still expecting to see a frame from B labelled with $N(S) = 2$. (5) *A sends* I,3,0,P (information frame numbered 3, A is expecting a frame numbered 0 from B). A is also polling B for a response. At this point A does not know that its previous message has been lost, and A has not yet received B's last message. (6) *B sends* a reply to A's poll. This is REJ,,2,F indicating that all A's messages numbered 2 and above have been rejected. The final bit, F, is set indicating that B has nothing more to send at the moment. (7) *A now sends* I,2,1 (information frame numbered 2, and A is expecting to see a frame from B numbered 1). This frame is a repeat of A's information frame numbered 2 which was lost earlier.

mission path, the timing of the bits, and the mechanical aspects of the link.

On top of this layer is the data-link layer protocol which deals with the transmission of messages between two adjacent points in a network. The HDLC protocol corresponds to the data-link layer and includes the facilities necessary to provide error-free transmission by asking for lost frames to be repeated.

The International Standards Organization (ISO) has provided a seven-layered reference model for open systems interconnection (OSI). An open system is one that can be connected to other systems. The purpose of this model is to provide a framework for the design and description of all communications networks. Figure 8.23 illustrates ISO OSI reference model. This model is able to deal with all communications networks, no matter how complex.

The network layer is built on the data-link layer and carries packets of

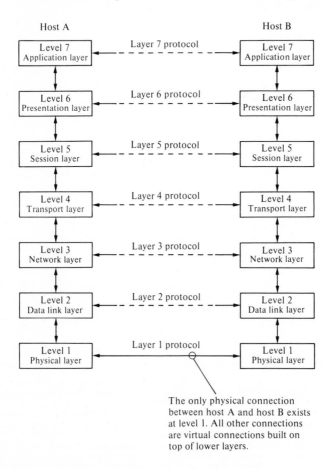

Fig. 8.23 The ISO reference model

information across the network. In a long-haul network several data links may be used in tandem, and the network layer is responsible for routing the packets of information from point to point through the network.

The transport layer provides end-to-end communication using the layers below it. A message handed to the network layer at one point in the network will appear at another point in the network error-free, and in the order in which it was sent. The system uses the network layer to carry the message across the network.

The session layer is responsible for managing the interconnections. It sets up and clears down the call, and is able to convert the session address into the network address. The session address is the address of the distant node from the point of view of the user, while the transport address is the actual address of the node taking part in the information interchange.

The presentation layer performs certain user-specific functions. This may include, for example, the translation of the data format between that used by the application layer, and that transported by layers below the presentation layer.

The application layer is the highest layer of the OSI model. The protocol of this layer directly serves the end user by providing the services appropriate to the application.

8.3 Local area networks

It is not an exaggeration to say that local area networks are changing the face of computing today. The impact of LANs is due to their high performance and low cost, making it feasible for even the smallest organizations to link together all their computers and allied digital equipment.

During the last two decades a whole branch of engineering has been developed to facilitate the transmission of digital information from point to point. This new engineering has been called variously 'computer communications', 'data transmission', or 'teleprocessing', and represents a marriage between traditional electronics, information theory, and computer science. As long as only modest quantities of data were being transmitted over long, often intercontinental, distances, the overall impact of data transmission on computing was essentially minimal. With the advent of low-cost microprocessor and minicomputer systems together with the clustering of a number of such devices in a relatively small area (an office, factory, polytechnic, university, or laboratory), a need for a specialized form of inexpensive communications network was felt. Because of this pressure, a branch of data transmission dealing with the transfer of large quantities of information at high speed between 'geographically distributed computers' arose. This new field is, of course, known as local area networks.

There is no absolute definition of a local area network, and most authors tend to describe them in terms of their primary characteristics. A LAN serves to link together the computer facilities on a given site. This may be a single room, a building, or a group of buildings. The LAN at Teesside Polytechnic links together all the major computing facilities, and terminals. There are plans to implement a number of different LANs and to link them together at points known as 'gateways'. A gateway is an interconnection between two or more separate networks. In everyday terms, the Leicester Square underground station is a gateway because it allows travellers on the Northern line to move on to the Piccadilly line.

Because the LAN covers a single site it is a private system. That is, it does not form part of the public telephone network and is therefore not subject to the mass of constraints normally associated with a public network.

The LAN is inexpensive. It has been devised to connect low-cost systems and therefore the use of expensive technology or transmission media cannot be tolerated. Typical LANs link their nodes by twisted-wire pairs or coaxial cables. They are not only cheap, but require little labour in their installation. In this context, a node is a station which uses the network to send messages to, or receive them from, other nodes linked to the network.

The LAN is a highly reliable means of communication. This is because it links a system over relatively short distances and is not subject to the forms of interference which plague the long-haul transmission paths of the telephone network. Furthermore, the LAN does not employ the fault- and noise-prone mechanical or electronic message switching techniques associated with the telephone system.

Local area networks can offer very high transmission rates. As the transmission path is relatively short and does not involve the type of equipment which limits the bandwidth of the signals it is carrying (like the telephone network) it is possible to transmit data at rates of tens of kilobits/ second with ease. Some networks operate at a data-rate of 10 Mbits/second, which is almost the speed at which data is moved from point to point within a typical microcomputer.

Network topology

The topology of a network describes the way in which the individual users of the network are linked together. There are four basic topologies suitable for use in a LAN. These are: the unconstrained topology, the star network, the bus, and the ring.

The unconstrained network. The most general topology is the unconstrained network of Fig. 8.24(a). The individual nodes are connected together in an arbitrary fashion. Its advantage is that additional links can be provided to reduce bottlenecks where heavy traffic passes between a group of nodes. Further nodes and links can readily be added without disturbing the hardware of the existing system. The road network of most countries is an unconstrained topology, with new roads being added when and where necessary.

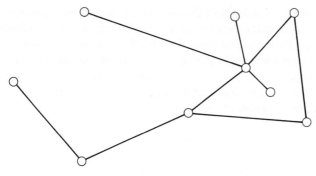

Fig. 8.24(a) The unconstrained topology

The disadvantage of the unconstrained topology is that a decision must be made at each node on the best way to route a message on the way to its destination. In terms of the analogy with the road system, the driver must have a road map to enable him to drive from one place to another. A message cannot just be transmitted from one node to each other node to which it is connected as this would lead to the message being multiplied at each node and propagated round the network forever. Instead, each node must have its own 'road-map' and make a decision on which link the message is to be transmitted on the way to its destination. This process carries with it the computational overhead of working out routing algorithms. Furthermore, whenever a new link or node is added to the network, the routing information must be changed at each node. Figure 8.24(b) shows how a message may be routed through an unconstrained topology.

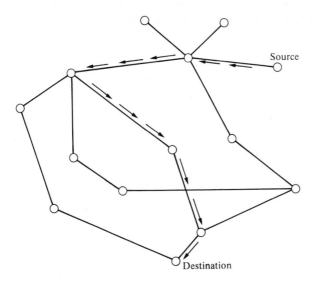

Fig. 8.24(b) Routing a message through an unconstrained topology

The star network. Figure 8.25 shows how the star network eliminates the need for nodes to make routing decisions, by routing all messages from source to destination via one central node. The star has a simple topology and has advantages when the physical topology of the network matches its logical topology. Clearly, there are circumstances where the nodes are distributed in such a way that the links between some of the nodes and the central node are economically unviable.

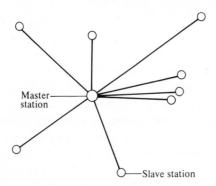

Master station

O—Slave station

Fig. 8.25 The star

The star network has two obvious disadvantages. As all messages pass through the central node, the loss of the central node totally wrecks the network. Other networks may offer a degraded but useful service if part of the network fails. Furthermore, because all traffic passes through the central node, it must be capable of working at a sufficient high speed to handle all nodes to which it is connected.

The bus. The bus topology is illustrated in Fig. 8.26(a), (b). The bus (and also the ring) are attempts to minimize the complexity of a network by both

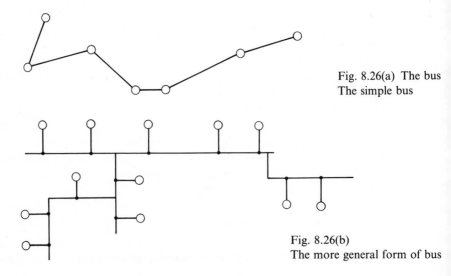

Fig. 8.26(a) The bus
The simple bus

Fig. 8.26(b)
The more general form of bus

removing a special purpose central node and the need for individual nodes to make routing decisions.

In a bus all nodes are connected to a common data highway. This highway may be a single bus linking nodes, or it may be a number of buses with branches linking the individual buses. Such a topology is called an 'unrooted tree'. When a message is put on the bus by a node, it flows outwards in all directions and eventually reaches every point in the network. The bus has one topological and one practical restriction. Only one path may exist between any two points, otherwise there would be nothing to stop a message flowing round a loop forever. The practical limitation is that the bus cannot normally exceed some maximum distance from end to end.

The principal problem faced by the designers of a bus is how to deal with a number of nodes wanting to use the bus at the same time. This is called bus contention and will be dealt with laer.

The ring. Figure 8.27 illustrates the ring topology, where the nodes are

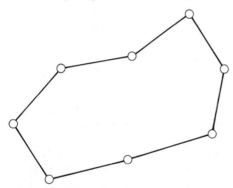

Fig. 8.27 The ring

connected together in the form of a ring. Like the bus this leads to a decentralized structure, as no central node is needed to control the ring. Each node simply receives a message from one neighbour and passes it on to its other neighbour. Messages flow in one direction round the ring.

The only routing requirement placed on each node is that it must be able to recognize a message intended for itself. The ring does not suffer from contention like the bus topology. However, a node on the ring has the problem of how to inject a new message into the existing traffic flow.

In the early days of LANs, the ring was considered prone to failure. A broken link makes it impossible to pass messages all the way round the ring. There are now a number of 'double ring' structures with two links between each of the nodes. If one of the links is broken it is possible for the ring to reconfigure itself and bypass the failure.

Contention control in buses

In a contention net any node wishing to transmit just goes ahead and puts its message on the bus. As there is no control over when a node may transmit, there is nothing to prevent two or more nodes transmitting simultaneously. If this does happen, all messages being transmitted are irretrievably scrambled and lost. The simplest form of contention control would be to let the transmitters retransmit their messages. Unfortunately, such a scheme would not work, as the competing nodes would keep retransmitting the messages which would keep getting scrambled. There are two things to note here. The technical term for two or more messages being lost due to overlapping transmission is a collision. This problem is identical to that of two people approaching the same revolving door together: they cannot both get in, they step back, and advance together causing a collision, so they step back again, advance together, collide, ...

A better strategy on detecting a collision is to 'back-off' or wait a random time before trying to retransmit the frame. Under these circumstances it is less likely that the competing nodes would reschedule the transmissions for the same time. In terms of our revolving door, as soon as the two people collide, they each immediately throw a dice, and then wait the number of seconds the dice shows before trying again. It is unlikely that they would each get the same number, so they can go through the door separately. Networks operating under this form of contention control are well suited to bursty traffic. That is, the arrangement works as long as the average traffic is very low (much less than the maximum capacity of the bus). If the amount of traffic rises, there comes a point where collisions generate repeat messages which generate further collisions and further repeats, and the system eventually collapses.

A better form of contention control is to allow the node to listen to the bus before trying to send its frame. Obviously, if one node is already in the process of sending a message, other nodes are not going to 'butt in'. A collision will now occur only if two nodes attempt to transmit at nearly the same instant. Once a node has started transmitting and its signal has propagated throughout the network, no other node can interrupt. For almost all systems this danger zone, the propagation time of a message from one end of the network to the other, is very small and is only a tiny fraction of the duration of a message.

A further modification of this arrangement is to allow the transmitters to listen to the bus while they are transmitting. Suppose a transmitter, thinking the bus was free, had started transmitting, and at the same time another transmitter had done likewise. After a very short time both transmitters become aware that the bus is in use and abort their messages. In this way the effect of a collision is reduced, because the transmitters stop as soon as they detect the collision. In the absence of a listen-while-transmitting mechanism, a collision is detected indirectly by the absence of any acknowledgement to the message.

One of the earliest LANs is the ALOHA network at the University of Hawaii, designed to allow communication between a number of stations distributed throughout the Hawaiian islands. ALOHA is not a bus network but a star network with a master station at its centre through which all messages between nodes must pass. However, the early work done on ALOHA, and the techniques used to implement contention control led directly to today's bus-oriented LANs. Because of the mountainous nature of the islands, VHF radio was chosen as the communication link. One frequency is dedicated to master–slave communications (no problem of contention here as there is only one transmitter and many receivers). Another frequency is shared by all the slave stations and used for their messages to the master. It is here that contention problems arise, because two or more slaves can start transmitting simultaneously. As the transmission medium is a radio broadcast, a collision will occur.

Pure ALOHA uses packets with a 32-bit header, a 16-bit header parity check, and up to 80 bytes of data followed by a data parity check. Each packet takes about 73 milliseconds to transmit, and has a negligible propagation delay (compared to the packet length of 73 ms). If a station does not receive an acknowledgement from the central node within a fixed time, it assumes its packet has been lost and retransmits a new packet after a random wait. ALOHA does not listen to the channel before transmitting or while transmitting, and therefore represents the crudest possible form of contention control.

Assuming that the probability of a station wanting to transmit a packet has a Poisson distribution, it can be shown that the maximum throughput of this system approaches 18 per cent of the maximum channel capacity. To make this clearer, consider our revolving doors. If people arrive at the doors at random, and the maximum capacity of the doors is 1000 people per hour when all the people follow one after the other (polite behaviour without contention), then with people using a random wait every time they collide, the maximum throughput cannot exceed 180 people per hour.

By dividing the channel time into fixed slots of a duration equal to the maximum packet length (so-called slotted ALOHA), and by permitting the transmission of a packet only at the start of the time slot, the chance of collision is much reduced and the maximum efficiency is increased to 36 per cent. If packets are transmitted at random, the beginning of one packet can collide with the end of another and a period of time equal to two packet lengths is lost. If all packets are transmitted in fixed time slots, a collision cannot affect two adjacent slots, and a time equal to only one packet length is lost. Of course, this arrangement requires that all transmitters have access to an accurate clock in order to schedule their messages to fall within the time slots.

One of the most popular derivatives of ALOHA is Ethernet, which is supported by DEC, Xerox, and Intel. This uses a baseband coaxial cable with phase-encoded data transmitted at 10 Mbits per second. The term baseband means that the digital data is transmitted directly without the need for modems. The contention mechanism adopted by Ethernet is called 'carrier sense multiple access' (CSMA). When an Ethernet station wishes to transmit a packet, it first listens to the state of the bus. If the bus is in use, it waits for the bus to become free. In Ethernet terminology this is called deference. Once a station has started transmitting it acquires the channel, and after a delay equal to the end-to-end round trip propagation time of the network, a successful transmission without collision is guaranteed.

Before the packet has propagated throughout the network, a 'collision window' exists where two stations may begin transmitting unknown to each other. When a station realizes that its packet is being corrupted by another packet, it reinforces the collision by transmitting a 'jam' packet. If it stopped transmitting immediately, the other transmitter might not detect the collision. The collision would be detected indirectly much later by the error-detecting code which forms part of the transmitted frame. This process is inefficient and wastes time. The sending of a short jam packet makes the collision obvious to all listeners. After the jam has been sent, another attempt is made after a random delay. If repeated attempts fail, the random delay is increased as the sender tries to adapt to a busy channel.

The ring

A ring network connects all stations to each other in the form of a continuous loop. Unlike the stations of a bus network, which listen passively to data on the bus unless it is meant for them, the stations of the ring must take an active part in all data transfers. Basically, when receiving incoming data they must test it and decide whether to keep it for themselves or to pass it on to their next neighbour. In general, the mechanisms used to determine which station may gain access to the ring are more varied than those for buses. Three popular control techniques are: token passing, register insertion, and slotted rings. Contention control in the sense of bus networks is not found in rings. I bet somebody will report at least one exception to me!

Token rings

One of the fascinating things about LANs is the way in which many of their seemingly abstract technological aspects can be related to everyday life. A classic railway problem is the control of trains on a single line. Collisions occur if two trains travel in opposite directions from the ends of a single line. These collisions tend to be more harmful than those on data networks. One solution is to provide a metal ring or token for the stretch of line. Only the driver in possession of the token has a right to use the line. If a driver arrives at one end of the line and the token is not there he must wait; if it is there he can pick it up, enter the line, and hang up the token at its other end. While he has the token no one can enter the line behind him or ahead of him. After he has hung up the token, another train can take it and go back down the line.

In a token ring a special bit pattern (the token) is passed round the ring from station to station. The station currently holding the token is the station which can transmit data if it so wishes. If it does not wish to take the opportunity to send data itself, it passes the token round the ring. For example, suppose the token has the special pattern 11111111, with zero stuffing used as in the case of HDLC to keep the pattern unique. A station on the ring wishing to transmit monitors its incoming traffic. When it has detected seven ones it inverts the last bit of the token and passes it on. Thus, a pattern called a 'connector' (11111110) passes on down the ring. The connector is created to avoid sending the eighth '1' and thereby passing on the token. The station may now transmit its data. After it has transmitted its data, it sends a new token down the ring. As there is only one token, contention cannot arise on the ring unless, of course, a station becomes antisocial and sends out a second token. In practice, a real system is rather more complex because arrangements must be included for dealing with lost tokens.

Register insertion rings

The concept of a 'register insertion ring' is illustrated in Fig. 8.28. A message

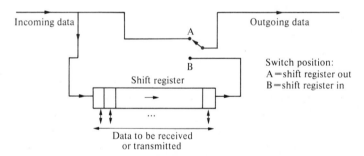

Fig. 8.28 The register insertion ring

to be transmitted is first loaded into a shift register. This shift register is, initially, not part of the ring. When the station notices that the ring is either idle or is at a point between two separate messages, it breaks the loop and inserts the shift register. The message to be transmitted is clocked out of its shift register at the same rate data is moved round the ring. As the message leaves the shift register at one end, any data on the ring is shifted in at the other end. In effect, the register has 'lengthened' the ring. Since the shift register is now part of the ring, it can neither be removed nor used to send other messages.

When the message has moved round the ring it eventually arrives in the originating shift register. At this instant the register can be switched out of the circuit, and the message 'swallowed'. If the message is ever damaged on its journey round the ring, the sender must wait for the ring to become idle before the shift register can be switched out.

Slotted rings

In a slotted ring one or more packet 'carriers' (the slots) are passed round the ring. A carrier is not a physical entity (like a railway carriage). It is just a special type of packet whose bits can be modified by the nodes through which it passes. Up to now we have considered that all packets (i.e. frames) are only generated or received but never modified. Each carrier has a header, a tail, and a full/empty bit. Whenever an empty carrier passes a station wishing to transmit data, the station fills the packet with data and marks the carrier as full by setting the full/empty bit. At its destination the data is 'removed' from the carrier, and the full flag is cleared. The Cambridge ring operates on this principle.

Fig. 8.29 shows the format of the packet used by the Cambridge ring. The

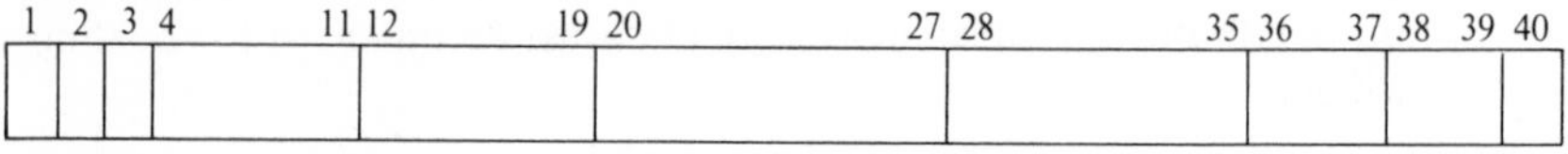

1	2	3	4		11	12		19	20		27	28		35	36		37	38	39	40

1: Leader or slot framing bit (always 1)
2: Full/empty bit (1 = full)
3: Monitor control bit
4–11: Destination address
12–19: Source address
20–27: Data byte 1
28–35: Data byte 2
36: Type bit A
37: Type bit B
38–39

Response bits		
38	39	Response
0	0	BUSY—destination node cannot deal with packet
0	1	ACCEPT—destination node accepts packet
1	0	NOT SELECTED
1	1	IGNORE—no node has read the packet

40: Even parity bit

Fig. 8.29 The format of data on the Cambridge ring

first bit is a synchronization bit and denotes the start of the packet—rather like the start bit of asynchronous systems. The second bit is the full/empty bit. The third bit is used by a master station called the monitor. A ring structure is moderately democratic but it needs a special station, the monitor, to generate empty packets on power-up, and to ambush corrupted packets.

The packet includes an eight-bit destination address, followed by a 16-bit data field. Following the data field are a two-bit control field and a single parity bit. Compared to the HDLC format or the Ethernet format, the packets flowing round the Cambridge ring are relatively crude.

There are many published papers on the relative advantages and disadvantages of the various types of local area network. Some prefer the Ethernet, others the token ring. Some like the bus because it is very easy to extend, others say that they would not use it because it cannot guarantee the receipt of a message within a finite period as it is theoretically possible for a message to suffer an infinite sequence of collisions. Other (wiser) engineers say that the actual form of a LAN is often unimportant as the interface between the user program and the LAN (i.e. the operating system) is normally much slower than the most primitive forms of LAN.

9   OPERATING SYSTEMS

The relationship between an operating system (frequently abbreviated to OS) and a computer is almost identical to the relationship between a conductor and his orchestra. The great conductor is an international celebrity; he gets invited on all the chat shows on television, and is showered with society's highest awards. And yet he does not add a single note to a concert. The importance of a conductor is well known. He coordinates the other players. Moreover, he knows their individual strengths and weaknesses and can therefore apply them in such a way as to optimize their collective performance.

An operating system is frequently the most important piece of software in a computer system, and yet it solves no problems and does no useful calculations. Its role is to coordinate the work of all the functional parts of the computer (including its software), and hence maximize the efficiency of the system. Here efficiency may be taken as the fraction of time for which the CPU is actually executing user programs. It would be more accurate if we were to say that the operating system is designed to remove inefficiency from the system. For example, if a program calls for a listing on a line printer, the CPU is held up while the printer is in operation. The operating system would normally intervene to give the CPU something else to do while it is waiting for the printer to finish. A secondary role of the operating system is to act as the interface between user and computer. By means of a job control language (JCL), the user is able to ask the computer to perform a number of tasks (e.g. to edit a program, load and execute it) without having to know about the detailed operation of the system.

In fact, from the user's point of view, the operating system should behave like the perfect bureaucrat. It should be efficient, helpful, and (like all the best bureaucrats) should remain in the background. For example, a poor operating system, when asked to edit a file, may reply 'ERROR 53'. The programmer now has to find the operating system manual to look up ERROR 53. It's all a waste of time really because the last user ripped out the page with the translation of error messages because he got fed up with having to refer to them.

A really good operating system would have replied 'Hi there, Sunshine. Sorry about this, but my disks are full. Tell you what, I've noticed you've got a lot of back up copies of your program, and if you delete a couple I think we'll be able to find room for your file. Have a nice day.'

It could be argued that a section on operating systems in an introductory hardware course is a little out of place. My reasons for including this topic here are two-fold. The first is that the operating system is intimately connected with the hardware. It controls the operation of the hardware, and also allocates hardware facilities to user programs. Secondly, most students following a course in computer hardware also take a parallel course in high-level languages, data processing, and data structures, removing the need to deal with these topics. However, the formal treatment of operating systems is not normally encountered by students until much later in their course. I have therefore provided this short introduction and overview of operating systems.

Not all computers have an operating system. Where the computer is acting as a controller, or is dedicated to a single task, there is no need for an operating system. The task is simply held in memory (usually ROM) in machine code form. Whenever functions normally performed by an operating system are required, they are incorporated into the task itself. Some personal computers which fall between the dedicated controller and the general purpose computer have a range of operating system facilities built into their high level languages.

General-purpose operating systems were once found only on large computers but are now available on some personal computers. Some computer manufacturers call their operating systems an 'executive', others call it a 'monitor' or a 'supervisor'. Before looking at the details of an operating system it is necessary to present an example of what an operating system actually does.

A student wishes to edit a program and then run it. We will assume that the computer is a mainframe or a mini, although many of the 16-bit microprocessors and a few of the 8-bit machines have sophisticated operating systems. He goes to a terminal and logs on. By logging on he makes his presence known to the computer (a request for service), and at the same time the operating system is able to verify his user identity and (if necessary) password. This prevents unauthorized users from gaining access to the system, and may also perform an accounting function by measuring the total resources consumed.

If we assume that the computer has several terminals, another function of the operating system is to allocate processing time and memory space to each of the users. The operating system must also prevent one user from accidentally (or maliciously) interfering with another user's programs.

The student wishes to edit his program so he loads the editor and his program to be edited, and tells the computer what the new version is to be called. For example, if his program is called EQUATIONS.3, he may enter the command EDIT,EQUATIONS.3,EQUATIONS.4. This is an example of a job-control language and illustrates how little the student need know about the internal operation of the system. The operating system then locates the editor, transfers it from disk to the IAS, loads EQUATIONS.3, and prepares the disk to receive the edited version called EQUATIONS.4. If at any time one of these activities cannot be completed, the operating system reports back to the user.

When the editing is complete, the student submits his job for running. As the program is in source-code form, it must be compiled into object code before it can be executed. Source code refers to a program in a high-level or assembly-level language form as written by a programmer. Object code is the actual binary information which will be executed by the computer. The operating system will perform all these tasks by means of the following command:

PASCAL RUN, EQUATIONS.4

It is then the job of the operating system to locate the PASCAL compiler and the source program EQUATIONS.4, to perform the compilation, load the compiled version of EQUATIONS.4, and execute it. What's more, the operating system must decide where the program is to go in memory and to calculate all addresses of instructions and data accordingly.

At the end of the session the student logs off, freeing his terminal and the resources he has been consuming. The operating system returns all these resources to its pool, and prepares the necessary accounting information and statistics of his job. These statistics include the time for which he has been connected to the terminal, the actual CPU processing time used, the amount of disk space allocated, and the number of lines of output generated.

Types of operating system

Operating systems can be divided into four classes: single-user, batch-mode, demand-mode, and real-time. Any real operating system may have characteristics belonging to two or more classes. The single-user operating system is the most primitive type and is found on many microprocessor systems (e.g. CP/M, Flex). It allows one user to access the system at a time. In general it provides little or no resource management. The oldest forms of operating system work under the batch-mode. The jobs to be executed are fed into the computer, usually in the form of punched cards. Each user's job begins with a number of job-control cards telling the operating system which of its facilities are required. The operating system then schedules the jobs according to the resources they require and their priority, and eventually generates the output—usually on a line printer. Batch-mode is analogous to a dry cleaning service. Clothes are handed in and are picked up at some later date after they have been cleaned. The disadvantage of batch-mode systems is their lengthy turn-round time. It's very frustrating to wait five hours for a print-out only to discover that the job did not run because of a simple mistake in one of the cards.

In the demand mode each user has access to a terminal from which he is able to run his own jobs. This is a great improvement over batch mode because the user can complete each step before going on to the next one. Such an arrangement is also called interactive because the operating system and the user are engaged in a dialogue. Each time the user correctly completes an operation (say editing a file), he is informed of its success and invited to continue by some form of prompt message. If a particular command results in an error, he is informed of this by the operating system and can therefore take the necessary corrective action.

A real-time operating system belongs, largely, to the world of process control in industry. Its primary characteristic is that it must respond to an event within a well-defined time. Consider a computer-controlled petrochemical plant. The computer running it invariably has a real-time operating system. The conditions at many parts of the plant are measured and reported to the computer on a regular basis. It is obvious that control actions must be taken as the conditions in the plant change. A sudden build-up of pressure in a reaction vessel cannot be ignored. The computer must either respond to an interrupt generated by the event, or poll the measuring equipment sufficiently often. Real-time operating systems are found wherever systems are computer-controlled and the response time of the computer must closely match that of the system it is controlling.

Real-time operating systems are so called because the computer is synchronized with what people call 'clock time', in the sense that programs must respond to external events within a meaningful period. 'Meaningful' is a vague term, as the response of a computer to, say, changes in a nuclear reactor may need to be rather faster than to changes in a computer-controlled greenhouse. Non-real-time systems operate in computer time. A job is submitted, and its results delivered after some elapsed time. There is no particular relationship between the elapsed time and the time of day. The actual elapsed time is a function of the loading of the computer and the particular mix of jobs it is running. In a real-time system the response time of the computer to any stimulus is guaranteed.

9.1 The system software

The system software is a collection of programs designed to make the user's life an easier one, if not an actually happy one. Some of the system programs to be described briefly are: the operating system utilities, the editor, the text processor, the assembler, the debugger, and the compilers.

The operating system utilities

The operating system utilities are those functions provided by the operating system which the user is able to access explicitly. These facilities allow the creation of files which may later be manipulated by other system software such as editors, assemblers, and compilers.

Each operating system has its own particular set of utilities. As an example of a typical system, I have chosen the Flex 09 utilities which run on many

6809-based microcomputers. In what follows, 'filename' is the name of a file and consists of up to eight characters. Appended to a filename is a three-character extension which defines the type of the file. For example, the extention TXT indicates that the file is a text file, BIN indicates a binary file, and CMD indicates a command file. The filename is formally defined as:

[⟨drive⟩.]⟨name⟩[.⟨extension⟩]

The '⟨ ⟩' characters enclose a field which is supplied by the user. The '[' and ']' delimiters enclose an optional parameter. If no disk drive is specified, the operating system assumes the default drive (initially drive 0). Typical valid filenames are:

1.Pascal.TXT
RunJob
TEST.CMD

Below are some of the most useful utilities provided by Flex 09.

CAT.　The catalogue function allows the user to list on the terminal all the files currently in the catalogue or directory of a particular disk. The catalogue is really a portion of the disk reserved for a list of the names of the files on it, together with their sizes, and the location of the first sector of each file. It tells the user what files are on the disk.

COPY.　The copy command allows a file to be copied from one disk to another. Its syntax is: COPY,⟨filename1⟩, ⟨filename2⟩. The effect of this command is to copy 'filename1' into a new file called 'filename2'. For example, COPY,0.PROGRAM7.TXT,1.PROG7 has the effect of copying a file called PROGRAM7 on disk 0 to a file which will be named PROG7 on disk 1. The extension of the new file will also be TXT.

DELETE.　This command permits the removal of unwanted files. Entering DELETE,1.PROG7.TXT has the effect of deleting PROG7.TXT from the catalogue on disk 1. Note that it is not necessary to remove the file physically. Simply removing its name from the catalogue causes it to become an un-file.

LIST.　This command has the effect of listing the contents of the named file on the terminal.

PROT.　The protection function has the syntax

[PROT,⟨filename⟩[,option list]]

and provides a measure of protection against accidental damage to the named file. The option list contains one or more of the following parameters: D,W,C,X. A 'D' delete-protects the file and stops it being deleted by any command involving an implicit or explicit delete. A 'W' write-protects the file and has the effect of stopping any further information being written into the file. It also stops the file from being deleted. A 'C' catalogue-protects the file and stops it appearing in the list of contents whenever the catalogue function is used. A catalogue-protected file becomes 'invisible' (i.e. secret) to the user unless he already knows that it is there! An 'X' has the effect of removing any protection afforded to the file by any of the other functions.

SAVE. The general syntax of the SAVE command is

SAVE,⟨filename⟩,⟨begin address⟩,⟨end address⟩[,⟨transfer address⟩].

This command creates a file which is a binary image (copy) of the data in the processor's IAS from 'begin address' to 'end address'. The default extension of the file is BIN. The optional parameter 'transfer address' denotes the entry point at which execution begins when the saved data is later loaded into memory. The command SAVE,Prog6,0100,1F0C,0200 has the effect of storing the data between memory locations $0100 and $1F0C on disk 0 in a file called 'Prog6'. If this file is later loaded in memory, the program counter will be set to the value $0200, at which point execution of the program will commence.

The editor

The editor is a program designed to manipulate text files, and to format the text in the way desired by the operator. Most editors are intended for on-line operation, rather than batch-mode operation. Before VDUs and on-line operation became so popular, information was often submitted to the computer in punched card form. Editing consisted largely of throwing away unwanted cards and replacing them by new cards. Editing punched paper tape involved cutting and splicing the punched tape and did not lead to that goal known as job satisfaction.

Today there are a vast number of editors. They vary from computer to computer, and any given computer often has a number of different editors, varying in sophistication. This is bad news for computer users who have to learn the syntax of each new editor they encounter. The basic functions of most editors are similar, but their commands vary just enough from editor to editor to be a real pain in the bit bucket. Once, when changing from one editor to another, I typed D50 which was meant to delete line number 50. Instead it deleted the next 50 consecutive lines. I should have entered D # 50, the ' # ' sign meaning 'line number'.

Traditionally, most editors regard the text they are editing as a sequence of lines, as if the text were printed on cards. All operations apply to a line of text, although they may be repeated and applied to a number of lines. Such an editor is known as a line editor. Other editors operate on the page of text currently displayed on a VDU. These editors are called screen editors and are rapidly replacing line editors as they can manipulate entire paragraphs or columns of text in one operation.

Although most line editors have a host of sophisticated facilities, only the basic functions are described here. The five most important operations provided by a line editor are:

I Insert, D Delete, R Replace, F Find, C Change.

A line editor regards the text file as a collection of lines numbered from line 1 to line N. At any time a line pointer is positioned at what is called the current line. A command without a parameter acts on the current line. The 'insert' command allows a new file to be entered, or an insertion (i.e. one or more new lines) made to an existing file. The 'delete' command allows the removal of one or more unwanted lines. Typically, D deletes the current line, D3 deletes the next 3 lines and D#3 deletes the line whose number is 3.

The 'replace' command causes one line to be replaced by another. Its use is equivalent to a delete followed by an insertion. The 'find' command enables the operator to search through the text for a given string of characters. A 'string' is the term given to any sequence of consecutive characters. Without this command the programmer would either have to know all the line numbers or have a listing of the program (with line numbers) in front of him. For example, if the operator wishes to locate the line containing 'LDA DATA7' he enters the following command.

F/LDA DATA7/

The slash characters, /, form a delimeter for the string. The editor may reply by displaying the following line:

0023 START   LDA DATA7   get 'DATA'

Now line 23 is the current line and may be edited as required. The 'change' function allows one string to be replaced by another, and avoids the need to replace an entire line. In the above example it may be necessary to replace DATA7 by VAL9, in which case C/DATA7/VAL9/ is entered.

Editors often allow global commands which operate on a number of lines. For example, the change command is used to alter all occurrences of DATA7 within the next 12 lines of the text file in a single operation by means of the command C/DATA7/VAL9/12.

The text processor

The text processor, or word processor, takes over where the editor left off. An editor is employed to create either programs and other structured data forms, or to create pure text. For example, the text for this book has been generated and manipulated by an editor. The function of the text processor is to operate globally on the text file created by the editor to produce a form suitable for printing. The text processor is able to perform left- and right-hand justification, which means that both the left- and right-hand margins of the text are straight. This enables people to produce letters and other text looking like the text of books or newspapers.

Text processors also handle the heading and numbering of pages, and deal with footnotes.

The assembler

An assembler is a program which takes an assembly-language program, consisting of assembly directives and executable instructions, and converts them into machine-code form. The machine code created by the assembler may be saved as a file on disk, or loaded into the computer's memory for immediate execution.

As we have already dealt with assemblers, only a few details will be added here. An assembler frequently generates machine code for the machine on which the code is to be executed. However, it is sometimes more convenient to assemble a program on one machine to generate the code for another. For example, a UNIVAC 1100 can be employed to assemble a program for later running on a 6502-based computer. Such an assembler is called a cross-assembler.

Closely associated with the assembler is the emulator. An emulator is a program which executes (i.e. interprets) machine code in software. For example, a 6502 program may be assembled on a UNIVAC 1100 and the resulting 6502 machine code interpreted, line by line. That is, a program in UNIVAC machine code reads the 6502 op-codes, and then executes them. These operations are performed on 'synthetic' 6502 registers, which are, of course, locations in the UNIVAC's memory. Interpreting machine code in this way is relatively slow and inefficient, but it does provide a way of checking the code for errors before it is actually run on the machine for which it is intended.

The debugger

A debugger is a program designed to monitor the running of another program. Here we shall concern ourselves with the debugger of machine-level programs. Once a program has been assembled, it can be executed. Sometimes the program does not work, or does not achieve the expected results. When this happens a debugger is often needed to help find the problem. Note that the debugger and the program being tested must be in memory at the same time. A debugger is so called because it means 'remove bugs (errors) from'. The basic functions of a debugger are to examine memory locations, to set breakpoints, and to trace the execution of a program.

The 'display memory' function is employed to examine the contents of specified memory locations and to check if the data has changed in the way expected. It can also be used to reset the contents of memory locations prior to the running of a program. This enables a program to be tested with known data.

A breakpoint is a marker inserted in a program which, when encountered during the course of executing the program, causes a predetermined event to take place. The breakpoint takes the form of a machine code instruction. The 6502 calls this 'BRK' (break), and the 6800 calls it 'SWI' (software interrupt). Suppose a program is not behaving as expected. By inserting a breakpoint in the region where the problem is thought to lie, a check on the program's operation may be made. When the program is run, normal operation proceeds until the breakpoint is encountered. Then the execution of the program is halted and the contents of all the CPU's internal registers are printed. This provides the programmer with a 'snapshot' of the state of the computer immediately preceding the breakpoint. After the breakpoint has been encountered it is (sometimes) possible to continue execution.

The 'trace' function of a debugger is rather like an automatic breakpoint which is slowly moved through the program. After each instruction has been executed, the state of all registers is displayed. In this way, it is possible to monitor exactly what is happening while the program is being run.

The compilers

A compiler is a program (often as complex as, or more complex than, the operating system) which takes a source program in a high level language, and compiles it into machine code suitable for execution. The operation of compilers is well beyond the scope of this book.

9.2 Multiprogramming

Multiprogramming is the ability of a computer to handle more than one job at once. Students often ask me in a slightly surprised tone, 'But how can a computer run more than one program at a time? After all, it has only one program counter and one ALU'. The answer I give is that they are, strictly speaking, correct: a computer cannot execute two or more programs simultaneously, but it can give the impression that it is running several programs concurrently. The following example shows how such an illusion is possible.

Consider a game of 'simultaneous chess'. A first class player is pitted against a number of weaker opponents, and moves from board to board making a move at a time. As he is so much better than his opponents, one of his moves takes but a fraction of the time they take. Consequently, each player shares the illusion that he has a single opponent of his own.

The organization of a game of simultaneous chess may readily be applied to the digital computer. All that is needed is a periodic signal to force the CPU to switch from one job to another, and a mechanism to tell the computer where it was up to when it last executed a particular job. The jobs are normally referred to as tasks or processes, and the concept of executing several tasks together is called concurrent programming, or multiprogramming.

Before looking at the implementation of multiprogramming, its advantages should be pointed out. If each task required nothing but CPU time, then multiprogramming would have little advantage over running tasks consecutively. If we re-examine the example of simultaneous chess, we find that its success is based on the great speed of the master player when compared with that of his opponents. While each player is laboriously pondering his next move, the master player is busy making many moves.

A similar situation exists in the case of computers. While one user is busy reading or printing information, or accessing a disk drive, another user can take control of the CPU. A further advantage of multiprogramming is that it enables several users to gain access to a computer at the same time. This is very important today when 40 or more students wish to have access to a mainframe at any given instant.

Figure 9.1 illustrates the advantages of multiprogramming by considering two tasks, A and B. Each of these tasks requires a number of different activities (e.g. VDU input/output, disk access etc.) to be performed during the course of its execution. The sequence of activities carried out by each of these two tasks as they are executed, is given in Fig. 9.1(a).

Fig. 9.1 An example of multiprogramming

| Task A | VDU 1 | CPU | DISK | CPU | VDU 1 | time→ |

| Task B | VDU 2 | CPU | DISK | VDU 2 | CPU |

(a) Two tasks in terms of the sequential activities they require

Resource	Activity				
VDU 1	Task A				Task A	
VDU 2	Task B				Task B	
DISK			Task A	Task B		
CPU		Task A	Task B	Task A		Task B

(b) The scheduling of the two tasks

If task A were allowed to run to completion before task B were started, valuable processing time would be wasted while activities not involving the CPU were carried out. Figure 9.1(b) shows how the tasks may be scheduled to make more efficient use of resources. The boxes indicate the period of time for which a given resource is allocated to a particular task. For example, after task A has just used the CPU, it accesses the disk. While the disk is being accessed by task A, task B is able to gain control of the processor.

The fine details of multiprogramming operating systems are far beyond the scope of an introductory book. However, the following principles are involved:

388   *Operating systems*

1. The operating system has complex algorithms built into it enabling it to schedule a job in the most efficient way, and to make best use of the facilities available. The algorithm may adapt to the type of jobs it is running, or the operators may feed system parameters into the computer to maximize efficiency. Where the parameters are adjusted by human operators, this is called tuning the operating system.

2. Possibly the greatest problem faced by the operating system is that of memory management. If more than one task is to be run, the operating system must allocate memory space to each of them. Moreover, the operating system should locate the tasks in memory in such a way as to make best possible use of the memory. Clearly, large gaps in memory should not be left between tasks.

3. If the CPU is to be available to one task while another is accessing a disk or using a printer, then these devices must be capable of autonomous operation. That is, they must either be able to take part in DMA operations without the active intervention of the CPU, or they must be able to receive a chunk of high-speed data from the CPU and process it at their leisure.

Switching tasks

It has already been pointed out that this book cannot go into the inner workings of an operating system. However, it is possible to outline the way in which task switching takes place. An important reason for including task switching is that it illustrates two hardware mechanisms described earlier— the interrupt and the stack.

Suppose an electronic pulse generator (i.e. a clock) were to be connected to a CPU's $\overline{\text{NMI}}$ line. On each pulse (say every 0.01 seconds) a nonmaskable interrupt is generated. This results in the program counter and PSW being saved on the stack, and a jump made to the interrupt-handling routine. If at the end of the interrupt-handling routine an RTI (return from interrupt) is executed, the program counter and PSW are restored, and execution of the program continues from the point at which it was interrupted.

Suppose now that the interrupt-handling routine does a devilishly cunning thing—it modifies the stack pointer before the RTI is executed. Now, when the RTI is executed, the value of the program counter retrieved from the stack is not that belonging to the program being executed just before the interrupt, but is the value belonging to some other program. It is the act of modifying the stack pointer that effects the task switching.

Figure 9.2 shows how task switching works. Two tasks, A and B, are located in memory. To keep things simple, the regions of memory allocated to the tasks do not change during the course of their execution. Each task has its own stack, and at any instant the system stack pointer may be pointing to either A's stack or B's stack. In Fig. 9.2(a) task A is running. In Fig. 9.2(b) an NMI has occurred and the contents of the program counter and PSW have been pushed on to the stack (i.e. A's stack).

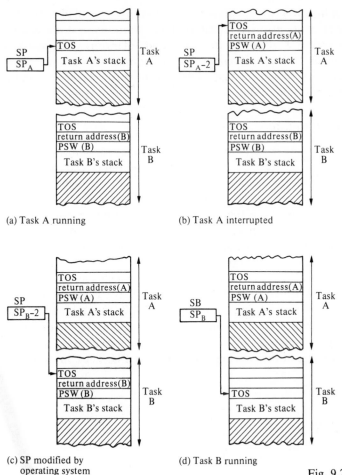

(a) Task A running

(b) Task A interrupted

(c) SP modified by operating system

(d) Task B running

Fig. 9.2 Task switching

In Fig. 9.2(c) the operating system has changed the contents of the system stack pointer so that it is now pointing at task B's stack. Finally, in Fig. 9.2(d) the operating system executes an RTI, and task B's program counter is loaded from the stack, causing task B to be executed.

Thus, at each interrupt, the operating system swaps the stack pointer before the RTI, causing the task to be switched. In a realistic system the operating system maintains a table of tasks to be executed. In addition to the stack pointer, each entry in the table contains further information about the task. Typically, this includes details about the task's priority, its maximum run time, and whether or not it is currently runnable. A task can be in one of the following three states. The task can be running (actually being executed), waiting its turn to be run, or blocked (not runnable as it is waiting for some resource to become available before it can be run). Tasks can be prioritized so that a task with a high priority will always be executed in preference to a task with a lower priority. A task is said to be runnable if it is executed when its turn arrives (subject to the limitations of priority). If the task is not runnable (i.e. blocked), it remains in the computer but is bypassed each time its turn comes. When the task is to be run its run flag is set, and it will be executed next time round.

9.3 Memory management

Up to now we have assumed that the central processing unit of a computer generates the address of an instruction or data, and that this address corresponds to the actual location of the data in memory. Thus, if the computer executes LDA $1234, the operand is found in location number $1234 of the IAS. While this is true of most microprocessor systems, it is not true of many minicomputers and mainframes. The address generated by the CPU does not always correspond to the actual location of the data. Why this is so is the subject of this section.

Memory management is a general term which includes all the various techniques by which an address generated by a CPU is translated into the actual address of the data in memory. Before looking at the reasons for memory management it is necessary to examine some of the concepts underlying the relationship between the location of data within the memory, and the address of the data generated by the CPU. The conventional concept

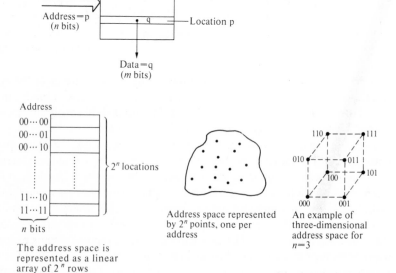

Fig. 9.3 Physical address space

of memory is depicted in Fig. 9.3, where an address, p, is applied to the memory's address input to yield a data word, q, in a read cycle. An n-bit address allows up to 2^n unique locations and can be represented as a linear list from 0 to $2^n - 1$. All these locations can be mapped on to an n-dimensional space called memory space. This memory space is called a physical memory space because each point in the memory space corresponds to a unique location in the actual memory. Figure 9.3 illustrates the concept of physical address space, and provides an example for the case $n = 3$.

Physical address space is a general concept and is not restricted to any particular type of memory. It may even be spread over several devices, from high-speed RAM to low-speed magnetic tape. For our purposes, we will assume that physical memory includes only the IAS, and that backing store is excluded because of its vastly different characteristics. Later we shall see that virtual memory systems allow the backing store to appear as part of the random-access physical memory space.

The programmer is not concerned with physical address space. He is more interested in logical address space, the address space made up of the names of address locations. The following analogy illustrates the difference between logical and physical addresses. A doctor has a filing cabinet in which the records of his patients are stored. These records are stored in logical order by filing them alphabetically. They are never stored in the alphabetic order of the physical addresses of the patients.

As an example of logical address space consider the address space made up of the eight names: ALICE, BRON, CINDY, DAN, EDNA, FRED, GEMMA, and HENRY. Figure 9.4 illustrates this logical address space both as a linear list and a 3-dimensional space. Suppose these names have to be mapped on to a physical address space. One way of doing this is to generate a physical address for each of the names by adding together the ASCII codes for the first three letters of each name. Thus, ALICE is given the physical

Alice
Bron
Cindy
David
Edna
Fred
Gemma
Henry

Logical address space
as a list

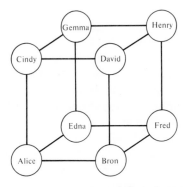

Logical address space in 3 dimensions

Fig. 9.4 Logical address space

hexadecimal address $D6 = 41 + 4C + 49$. From Fig. 9.5 we can see that each of the eight names has a unique location (not guaranteed by this address-generating algorithm), and that the order is not the same as the order of the logical name list. Moreover, the physical addresses of the names are not contiguous.

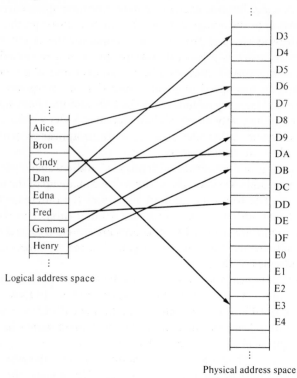

Fig. 9.5 The relationship between physical and logical address space

It's a nice academic exercise to distinguish between logical and physical address space, but how does it actually affect the programmer or the engineer who designs computers? Suppose I bought a cheap microcomputer with 16 K bytes of RAM. I would be able to run programs of up to 16 K bytes, but not larger programs. In other words, although the logical address space of the computer (assuming a 16-bit address bus) allows 64 K locations to be uniquely addressed, the physical address space is limited to only 16 K locations. Similarly, I may be able to afford a block of 256 K bytes of dynamic RAM for a 6502-based computer, but cannot address each physical memory location because the logical address space is limited to 64 K. The address generated by the CPU is a logical address because it represents the name of a location somewhere in physical memory.

In the world of mainframe computers where addresses of 20 bits or more are common, the problem is that the physical address space provided by the high-speed RAM in the IAS is very much less than the logical address space of the CPU, limiting the size of the program that can be executed. The problem which results when the logical address space is far larger than the physical address space is solved by resorting to 'virtual memory' techniques, in which low-speed, high-capacity disk and tape units are made to look like high-speed IAS.

A 68000-based microprocessor system has a 24-bit address bus, corresponding to a logical address space of 16 Mbytes. In a practical system 256 K bytes of IAS may be provided together with 20 Mbytes of hard-disk memory. The problem is how can we run programs greater than 256 K bytes? One possible solution is to 'widen' the immediate-access memory space to include the disk space. That is, an address from the CPU can be used to access either IAS or the contents of the disk, directly. For example, suppose that the instruction LDA DATA1 has the op-code corresponding to LDA located in IAS at address $1234, and the operand DATA1 is located on the disk with the physical address track 7, sector 5, word 9. Figure 9.6 illustrates the memory map corresponding to this situation. The CPU reads the instruction LDA DATA1 from the IAS, and generates the logical address DATA1 which is decoded as track 7, sector 5, word 9. The hardware must now read this location on the disk and transfer its contents to the accumulator. While this read operation is in progress the CPU must be frozen in a wait-state or halted. Although the physical address space is now large enough to deal with the logical address space of the program, the arrangement is unworkable. The average disk access time is of the order of 100 ms which is a hundred thousand times slower than the IAS. A better approach is provided by the use of 'overlays'.

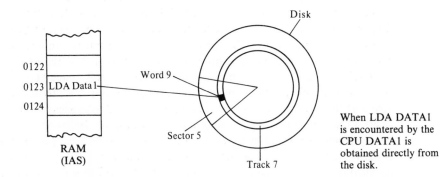

Fig. 9.6 Widening the address space to include disk space

Overlays

The programmer writes his program in the form of a 'main part', and a number of chunks called overlays. These overlays are mutually exclusive in the sense that only one overlay is needed by the main part of the program at any instant. When a program using overlays is to be run, the operating system loads the main part into the IAS, leaving the overlays on disk. The various overlays are written into a region of the IAS reserved by the programmer for overlays, as and when they are required by the main program. Because no two overlays are needed simultaneously, each new overlay is written over the old one. Figure 9.7 shows the relationship between the IAS and disk store when using overlays.

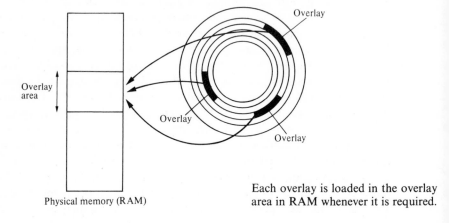

Physical memory (RAM)

Each overlay is loaded in the overlay area in RAM whenever it is required.

Fig. 9.7 Disk overlays

The idea behind overlays is sometimes called the 80/20 rule because of the empirical observation that 80 per cent of the processing is often done by only 20 per cent of a program. Consequently, the active 20 per cent of a program can be loaded in IAS for the whole time the program is running, and the remaining 80 per cent divided into overlays, and loaded as required.

Overlaying solves the problem of the logical address space being greater than the available physical address space by permitting the physical address space of the overlay area to share several logical address spaces. The use of overlays has the advantage of simplicity; no additional hardware is required to implement overlayed memory. Unfortunately, it puts great pressure on the programmer to write programs in a particular way, and, in any case, is applicable only to certain types of program. A good example of this is the operating system where some operations (e.g. DELETE, LIST, RENAME) can be treated as overlays and loaded only when they are actually required. Other parts of the operating system (e.g. the disk file manager) cannot be overlayed as they are constantly in use. A better, and more general, solution to the problem of limited physical address space is provided by 'paging'.

Paging

When dealing with addressing techniques we saw how memory could be divided into a number of units called pages, just as a book is divided into pages. For example, a 16-bit address can be split into an eight-bit page number, and an eight-bit location within a page. This concept can be applied to the problem of limited physical address space by dividing the physical address space of both the IAS and the backing store into pages.

Only the programs actually being executed fill the pages in the IAS, all other programs and data remain on disk. Whenever the CPU requires data which is not currently in a page in the IAS, the page containing this data is moved from disk to the IAS. At first sight this may seem an irrational thing to do. Instead of getting a single word from disk, we now get a whole page of words. Fortunately, most of the information stored in a computer is arranged logically, with the effect that the data stored at address q is highly likely to be related to the data located at addresses close to q. Once a page has been brought from the disk and installed in the IAS, it is very probable that the next few accesses will fall within this page.

A simple example of paging is provided by Fig. 9.8 where a 64 K physical memory space is divided into two pages. The data in page 0, extending from locations 0 to 32 767, is fixed, and does not change during the running of a program. Page 1, extending from locations 32 768 to 65 535, holds the page currently in-use from the disk. A process called address mapping or address translation converts the logical address from the CPU into the physical address of the data in the IAS. The relationship between the logical and physical address can be expressed as follows.

IF   LogicalAddress < 32 768
THEN
       PhysicalAddress : = LogicalAddress
ELSE
       PhysicalAddress : = LogicalAddress mod 32 768 + 32 768

For example, if the CPU refers to a logical address $001234 then it is translated into the physical address $1234. If, however, the CPU refers to address $011234 then $011234 is divided by 32 768 (i.e. $8000) to get the page number (i.e. 2), and the remainder (i.e. $1234) is added to $8000 to get the location of the data (i.e. $9234) in the IAS. Note that we assumed that page 2 is currently in IAS.

At some point in the execution of the program the processor may generate a logical address which falls outside the range of the page currently in IAS. In this case a new page must be brought from disk, and loaded into the physical memory from 32 768 to 65 536. This operation is carried out by the operating system. The address mapping algorithm can now be expanded to include the detection of addresses not currently in IAS.

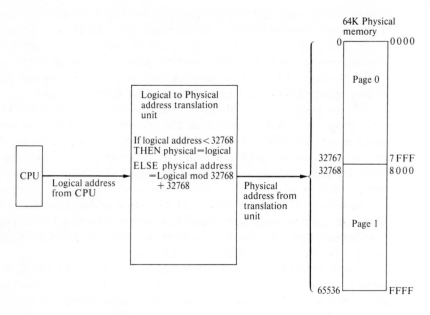

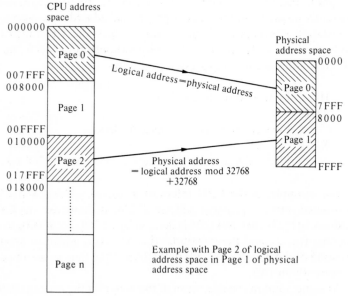

Fig. 9.8 A simple example of paging

```
IF      LogicalAddress < 32 768
THEN
        PhysicalAddress := LogicalAddress
ELSE
        IF      Currentpage = PhysicalAddress div 32 768
        THEN

                PhysicalAddress := LogicalAddress mod 32 768 + 32 768
        ELSE
        BEGIN
                Get Newpage;
                PhysicalAddress: = LogicalAddress mod 32 768
                                                        + 32 768
        END
```

It should now be clear that the page containing the memory location currently being accessed is stored in IAS, and that the logical address generated by the processor is automatically translated into the address of the required data in IAS. This translation is done by high-speed hardware. The process of moving data from disk to IAS is called 'swapping in', and is carried out by the operating system. Whenever a logical address corresponds to a location within a page not currently in IAS, the address translator generates an interrupt, causing the operating system to intervene. Of course, this arrangement is effective only as long as the number of memory references causing a page to be swapped into IAS are few compared to the number of accesses within a page. Clearly, pages should be as large as possible and data well-ordered. Unfortunately, in many real systems the data is not well-ordered and the pages are relatively small—often 2 K or 4 K words. The reader may be tempted to think that paging and overlaying are almost identical. This is not true for two reasons. There is often only one overlay area, while the paging technique is normally extended to a large number of pages. Moreover, when a programmer writes an overlay he chooses the addresses of his program and data to fall within the range provided by the overlay area. But when paging is used, the logical addresses generated by the program and its data are automatically modified to correspond to the physical address of the information in IAS. The above arrangement of paging can be extended to a more general form called 'virtual memory'.

Virtual memory

In a virtual memory system the programmer sees a large array of physical memory (the virtual memory) which appears to be entirely composed of high-speed IAS. In reality, the physical memory is a small high-speed RAM and a much slower sequential access disk store. Virtual memory has two advantages. It allows the execution of programs much larger than the physical memory would normally permit, and frees the programmer from worrying about choosing logical addresses falling within the range of available physical addresses. The programmer is at liberty to choose any logical address he desires for his program and its variables. The actual addresses he selects do not matter; the logical addresses are automatically mapped into the available physical memory space as the operating system sees fit.

Practical virtual memory systems divide the physical random-access memory space into pages of, typically, 512 to 4096 words. This allows several fragments of a virtual program to be in IAS at any instant. Obviously, it is sensible to retain frequently used data in IAS in order to avoid retrieving it from disk everytime it is needed.

Figure 9.9 shows the relationship between virtual memory space and physical memory space. The virtual memory space, corresponding to the logical address space of the processor, spans a total of 256 K words for a CPU with an 18-bit address bus. This virtual address space is divided into 64 pages of 4 K words. The processor's IAS, the physical memory of 64 K words, is divided into 16 pages of 4 K. Each of these 4 K blocks is called a page-frame because it holds one page from the virtual memory. We now have a situation in which the processor can directly address data anywhere in one

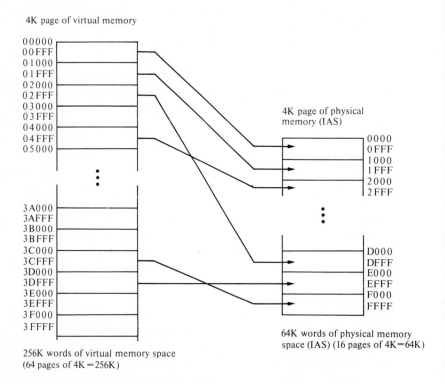

Fig. 9.9 The relationship between virtual and physical address space

of its 64 pages, but only 16 of these pages can be in high-speed IAS at the same time. The rest are stored on disk.

At any given time up to 16 pages of the virtual address space may be in IAS. An example should make Fig. 9.9 more clear. Suppose that the CPU executes LDA DATA1 where DATA1 has the logical address $02AED. The 4 K words corresponding to logical addresses from $02000 to $02FFF are actually stored in physical memory from $D000 to $DFFF. Consequently the logical operand address $02AED must be translated into the physical address $DAED.

The arrangement in Fig. 9.9 raises two questions. Firstly, when the CPU generates a logical address of an operand, how is this address translated into the physical address of the operand in IAS? Secondly, what happens if the logical address has no corresponding physical address because the appropriate page is not in IAS?

The processor maintains a page-table, Fig. 9.10, which maps the pages in IAS on to the processor's own logical address space. The logical address generated by the processor consists of two fields, a 12-bit address which selects a location within a page, and a six-bit page address which selects a particular page. Note that the 12-bit and 6-bit address together span the 18-bit virtual (logical) memory space. From Fig. 9.10 it can be seen that the logical address, 000010 101011101101, causes entry two (i.e. 000010) of the page-table to be interrogated. This yields a page-frame address 13 (i.e. $D), and the data is accessed from location 1101 101011101101 in the IAS.

As only a fraction of a large virtual program can be in IAS at any time, a virtual address will sometimes be generated and the page on which the data lies will not be in IAS. That is, when a page address is applied to the page table, the availability bit corresponding to that page will be zero. The situation is called a page-fault, and the operating system must now intervene. As soon as a page-fault is generated, the operating system fetches the missing page from the backing store, loads it in IAS, and updates the page-table accordingly. A page-fault is rather similar to an interrupt.

This process is called 'demand paging' because a new page is not brought until needed. Once the IAS is full of pages, each new page must overwrite on old one. One possible way of proceeding is to sacrifice the least recently used page every time a new page is brought from disk.

Real virtual memory systems are very complex and require both sophisticated hardware and software. One problem we have not yet considered is the duplication of memory space. Whenever a page is copied from the backing store into the immediate access store it exists in two places. If the CPU never modifies the page in its IAS, there is no problem and the page can be overwritten by a new page at any time. However, if the CPU writes to this page, there is a divergence between the page in IAS and the corresponding page on disk. Under these circumstances the operating system cannot swap-out the page in IAS without writing the updated version on disk. In most

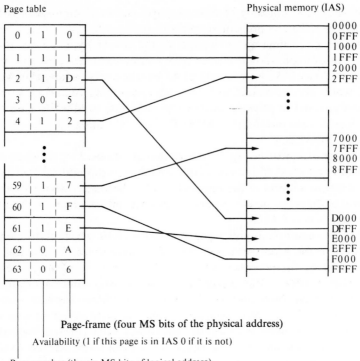

Page table

Physical memory (IAS)

Page-frame (four MS bits of the physical address)

Availability (1 if this page is in IAS 0 if it is not)

Page number (the six MS bits of logical address)

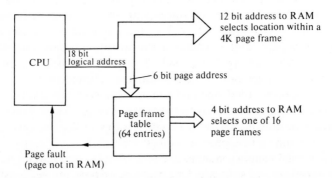

Fig. 9.10 The page-table and address mapping corresponding to Fig. 9.9

systems each page has a 'dirty bit' associated with it. When a word in the page is modified by the processor, the dirty bit is set, reminding the operating system that this page must be re-written to disk when it is swapped-out.

So far we have regarded virtual memory techniques as a solution to the problem of limited IAS. Their ability to translate logical into physical address has two other important implications. The programmer is entirely freed from having to think about where his program and data are going to be in the physical memory. Any logical addresses used by the programmer will automatically be translated into their address in IAS by the page-table. Similarly, in a multiprogramming environment new programs do not have to be located in contiguous blocks of IAS, the page-table address translation permits a program to be located in IAS with its pages scattered at random.

Virtual memories and microprocessors

At first sight it would appear that virtual memory techniques are not applicable to conventional eight-bit microprocessors with 16-bit address buses, because of the microprocessor's limited logical address space of 64 K bytes. However, because the microprocessor's logical address space may be widened by a technique known as 'memory mapping', and because virtual memory techniques are useful in allocating storage to the various tasks in a multiprogramming environment, there is a need to apply virtual memories to microprocessors.

Unfortunately, it is exceedingly difficult to apply virtual address techniques to conventional 8-bit microprocessors. If an access is made to a location currently within the IAS, automatic hardware address translators convert the logical address of the operand to its physical address in a few nanoseconds. This process is entirely transparent to the CPU.

Now suppose the logical address of an operand not currently in IAS is generated. When the address translation hardware sees this address, it signals a 'not in IAS condition' (i.e. a page-fault), and the appropriate page must be brought from disk. Behind this seemingly simple remark lurk two problems. What happens to the current instruction, and how is the new page moved from disk to IAS? Whenever an operand not in RAM is accessed, the current instruction must either be aborted and rerun, or suspended until the operand is in IAS.

If the current operation is suspended, the CPU itself can fetch the page before rerunning the aborted instruction. But if the instruction is suspended by the CPU entering a wait state, another CPU must fetch the page. Figure 9.11 illustrates this sequence of events.

Eight-bit microprocessors do not have facilities for aborting instructions and then re-running them. If virtual memories were to be applied to 8-bit microprocessors it would be necessary to freeze the state of the CPU whenever an operand was not in IAS and to use a second microprocessor to get a new page from disk. Once the page has been installed in IAS, the second processor can 'go back to sleep' and the main processor allowed to complete its frozen instruction now that its operand is in IAS.

Some 16-bit microprocessors are more amenable to virtual memory techniques than their 8-bit counterparts. Both Zilog and Motorola are now producing special versions of their 16-bit machines with an instruction abort

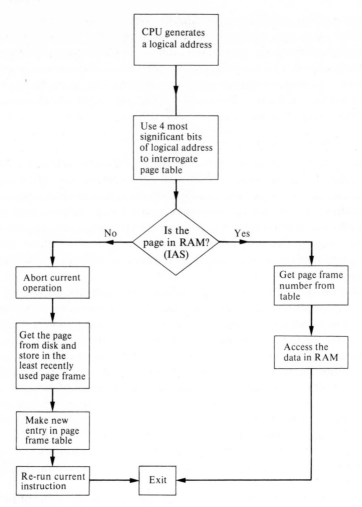

Fig. 9.11 The page-fault

pin, which (when a page-fault is generated) halts the current instruction, saves the machine status, and restores any registers altered by the current instruction to the state they were in before it. This operation is rather like a conventional interrupt, except that it is placed before the interrupted instruction, rather than after it.

Cache memory

The basic concepts involved in virtual memory may be extended to any hierarchical memory structure. In particular, virtual memory techniques are used to speed up the operation of a computer. Suppose that the access time of the processor's IAS is limiting the speed at which the computer can operate.

That is, the processor cycle time is less than the IAS cycle time. By using a relatively small quantity of very high speed IAS, a significant throughput may be achieved by locating part of the contents of the main IAS in the higher speed IAS. Thus, the small high-speed memory has the same relationship to the slower IAS that the RAM has to the backing store. Typically, the high speed IAS may have an access time of 50 ns, while the lower speed IAS has an access time of 400 ns or so.

Cache memory is frequently found in minicomputers where the CPU cycle time is shorter than that of conventional microprocessors. A cache memory maintains a mapping table of the blocks of data currently in it. When a logical address is generated by the processor, the most significant bits interrogate the table and produce a new address giving the location of the data within the cache memory. Of course, as in the case of virtual memory, if the data is not in the cache memory a new page must be transferred from the IAS to the cache memory.

Although the concepts behind cache and virtual memory seem abstract and entirely divorced from everyday life, this is not so. Consider the telephone directory. It contains all the telephone numbers in a given region, and it is time-consuming to locate a particular number because of the size of the directory. What most people do is to record all important, and frequently used, numbers on a blank page at the beginning of the directory. This page may contain no more than 50 numbers out of hundreds of thousands of entries in the directory, and yet 90 per cent of all accesses may be found on this page! You've guessed it—this page is a cache memory.

APPENDIX A1: WORKED EXAMPLES

This appendix contains a number of problems and their solutions. The questions are generally biased towards numerical, algebraic, and calculation-based topics. Questions of a more descriptive nature such as, 'Explain the operation of a ferrite-core memory', have been omitted as they would require a straight repetition of material appearing elsewhere in the text. The problems are generally intended to give additional insight into material covered in preceding chapters, rather than merely repeating earlier work.

A secondary reason for including these problems and solutions is that I find, year after year, some students fail totally to appreciate the purpose of both tutorial work and exam questions. They think that the lecturer is concerned only with the answer to the problem. In fact the answer is unimportant. It is how the student approaches the problem that is the object of the assessment. The final line of the problem counts for very little.

Question 1

A circuit has four inputs, A, B, C, D, representing the sixteen natural binary integers from 0000 (0) to 1111 (15). A is the most significant bit, and D the least significant bit. The output of the circuit, F, is true if the input is divisible by a multiple of 4, 5, 6, or 7, with the exception of 15, in which case the output is false. Zero is 'not divisible' by 4, 5, 6, or 7.

(a) Draw a truth table to represent the circuit.

(b) From the truth table obtain a simplified sum-of-products expression for F by means of Boolean algebraic techniques.

(c) Draw a Karnaugh map and hence obtain a simplified sum-of-products expression for F.

(d) Express F in product-of-sums form.

(e) Design a logic circuit to implement F using NAND gates only.

Solution 1

(a) The truth table for Q1 is given in Table A1.1.

(b) From Table A1.1 a sum of products for F can be obtained by writing down the sum of the minterms.

$$F = \overline{A}\,\overline{B}\,\overline{C}\,\overline{D} + \overline{A}\,B\,\overline{C}\,D + \overline{A}\,B\,C\,\overline{D} + \overline{A}\,B\,C\,D + A\,\overline{B}\,\overline{C}\,\overline{D} + A\,\overline{B}\,C\,\overline{D} + A\,B\,\overline{C}\,\overline{D} + A\,B\,C\,\overline{D}.$$

By means of Boolean algebra the expressions can be simplifed to:

Table A1.1 Solution 1(a)

A	B	C	D	Number value	F	Comment
Inputs						
0	0	0	0	0	0	
0	0	0	1	1	0	
0	0	1	0	2	0	
0	0	1	1	3	0	
0	1	0	0	4	1	divisible by 4
0	1	0	1	5	1	divisible by 5
0	1	1	0	6	1	divisible by 6
0	1	1	1	7	1	divisible by 7
1	0	0	0	8	1	divisible by 4
1	0	0	1	9	0	
1	0	1	0	10	1	divisible by 5
1	0	1	1	11	0	
1	1	0	0	12	1	divisible by 6
1	1	0	1	13	0	
1	1	1	0	14	1	divisible by 7
1	1	1	1	15	0	false by definition

$$F = \overline{A}B\overline{C}(\overline{D} + D) + \overline{A}BC(D + \overline{D}) + A\overline{B}\overline{D}(\overline{C} + C) + AB\overline{D}(\overline{C} + C)$$

$$= \overline{A}B\overline{C} + \overline{A}BC + A\overline{B}\overline{D} + AB\overline{D}$$

$$= \overline{A}B(\overline{C} + C) + A\overline{D}(\overline{B} + B)$$

$$= \overline{A}B + A\overline{D}.$$

(c) The Karnaugh map for F is given in Table A1.2(a). The squares covered by 1's can be formed into two groups of four (Table A1.2(b)). This gives $F = \overline{A}B + A\overline{D}$ which is (reassuringly) the same as the result obtained in part (b) above.

Table A1.2(a)

Table A1.2(b)

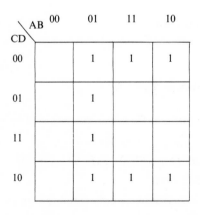

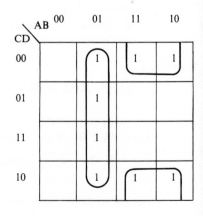

(d) To obtain a product-of-sums expression, it is necessary to generate the complement of F in a sum-of-products form, and then complement it.

$$F = \overline{A}B + A\overline{D}$$

$$\overline{F} = \overline{\overline{A}B + A\overline{D}}$$

$$= (A + \overline{B})(\overline{A} + D) \qquad \text{(complement in product-of-sums form)}$$

$$= A\overline{A} + AD + \overline{A}\,\overline{B} + \overline{B}D$$

$$= AD + \overline{A}\,\overline{B} + \overline{B}D$$

$$= AD + \overline{A}\,\overline{B}$$

$$F = \overline{AD + \overline{A}\,\overline{B}} \qquad \text{(complement in sum-of-products form)}$$

$$= (\overline{A} + \overline{D})(A + B) \qquad \text{(function in required product-of-sums form)}.$$

Note that the complement of F in sum-of-products form could have been obtained directly from the Karnaugh map of F by considering the squares covered by zeros.

(e) To convert the expression $F = \overline{A}B + A\overline{D}$ into NAND logic form, the '+' must be eliminated.

$$F = \overline{\overline{F}} = \overline{\overline{\overline{A}B + A\overline{D}}} = \overline{\overline{\overline{A}B} \cdot \overline{A\overline{D}}}.$$

The inverse functions $\overline{A}$ and $\overline{B}$ can be generated by two-input NAND gates with their inputs connected together. The circuit in Fig. A1.1 implements F in NAND logic only.

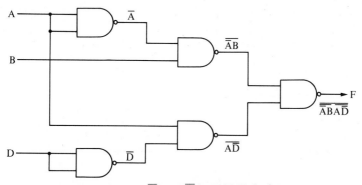

Fig. A1.1 Implementing $F = \overline{A}B + A\overline{D}$ in NAND logic

Question 2

An 8-bit shift register can perform the following operations.

    (i)   Load each stage from an 8-bit data bus (parallel load).
   (ii)   Logical shift left (0 in, MSB lost).
   (ii)   Logical shift right (0 in, LSB lost).

    (iv)   Arithmetic shift left (same as logical shift left).
    (v)   Arithmetic shift right (MSB replicated, LSB lost).
    (vi)   Circular shift left (MSB moves to LSB position).
    (vii)   Circular shift right (LSB moves to MSB position).

The circuit is composed of eight master–slave JK flip-flops and has a clock input which causes operations (i) to (vii) above to be carried out on its falling edge. There are five control inputs, as follows.

S When $S = 1$ perform a shift operation, when $S = 0$ a parallel load.
R When $R = 1$ shift right, when $R = 0$ shift left (if $S = 1$).
L When $L = 1$ perform a logical shift (if $S = 1$).
A When $A = 1$ perform an arithmetic shift (if $S = 1$).
C When $C = 1$ perform a circular shift (if $S = 1$).

Note that illegal combinations of L, A, and C cannot occur, and therefore more than one of L, A, and C, will never be true simultaneously.

For all eight stages of the shift register obtain algebraic expressions for J and K in terms of R, S, L, A, and C, and the outputs of the flip-flops.

Solution 2

Figure A1.2 illustrates five stages of the shift register. These are the end stages Q_7 and Q_0, the most-significant- and least-significant-bit stages, respectively. A non-end stage, Q_i, together with its left-hand neighbour Q_{i+1}, and its right-hand neighbour Q_{i-1} must also be considered.

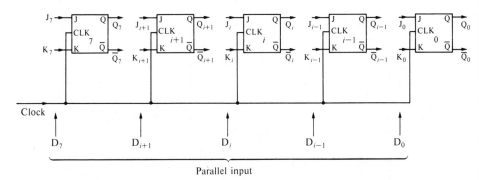

Parallel input

Fig. A1.2 Five stages of the shift register

All stages except 0 and 7 perform the same functions: parallel load, shift right and shift left. As the JK flip-flops always load data from one source or another, only the inputs $J = 1$, $K = 0$, or $J = 0$, $K = 1$ have to be considered. Consequently, $J = \overline{K}$, and we need only derive expressions for J, as the corresponding values for K can be obtained from an inverter.

Stage i:

Parallel load	$J_i = D_i$	$S = 0$
Shift right	$J_i = Q_{i+1}$	$S = 1,\ R = 1$
Shift left	$J_i = Q_{i-1}$	$S = 1,\ R = 0$

Therefore, $J_i = \overline{S}D_i + S(RQ_{i+1} + \overline{R}Q_{i-1})$

Stage 0 (LSB):

Parallel load		$J_0 = D_0$	$S = 0$
Shift right	logical	$J_0 = Q_1$	$S = 1,\ R = 1,\ L = 1$
	arithmetic	$J_0 = Q_1$	$S = 1,\ R = 1,\ A = 1$
	circular	$J_0 = Q_1$	$S = 1,\ R = 1,\ C = 1$
Shift left	logical	$J_0 = 0$	$S = 1,\ R = 0,\ L = 1$
	arithmetic	$J_0 = 0$	$S = 1,\ R = 1,\ A = 1$
	circular	$J_0 = Q_7$	$S = 1,\ R = 1,\ C = 1$

Therefore, $J_0 = \overline{S}D_0 + S(RLQ_1 + RAQ_1 + RCQ_1 + \overline{R}CQ_7)$

$$= \overline{S}D_0 + S(RQ_1 + \overline{R}CQ_7).$$

This expression simplifies because $L + A + C$ must be true as one type of shift, or another, must be taking place if $S = 1$.

Stage 7 (MSB):

Parallel load		$J_7 = D_7$	$S = 0$
Shift right	logical	$J_7 = 0$	$S = 1,\ R = 1,\ L = 1$
	arithmetic	$J_7 = Q_7$	$S = 1,\ R = 1,\ A = 1$
	circular	$J_7 = Q_0$	$S = 1,\ R = 1,\ C = 1$
Shift left	logical	$J_7 = Q_6$	$S = 1,\ R = 0,\ L = 1$
	arithmetic	$J_7 = Q_6$	$S = 1,\ R = 0,\ A = 1$
	circular	$J_7 = Q_6$	$S = 1,\ R = 0,\ C = 1$

Therefore, $J_7 = \overline{S}D_7 + S(RAQ_7 + RCQ_0 + \overline{R}LQ_6 + \overline{R}AQ_6 + \overline{R}CQ_6)$

$$\overline{S}D_7 + S(R(AQ_7 + CQ_0) + \overline{R}Q_6).$$

Question 3

Design a four-bit decade counter to count from 0 to 9 cyclically. Use JK master–slave flip-flops with an unconditional active-low clear input. Provide a timing diagram to illustrate the operation of the circuit.

Solution 3

A decade counter can be derived from a binary counter by resetting it to zero at the appropriate point. A four-stage binary counter counts from 0000 to 1111 (i.e. 0 to 15). To create a decade counter the state ten (1010) must be detected and used to reset the flip-flops.

The binary counter counts normally from 0 to 9. On the tenth count

$Q_d = 1$, and $Q_b = 1$. This is detected by the NAND gate whose output goes low, resetting the flip-flops. The count of ten exists momentarily (see Figs. A1.3(a), (b)).

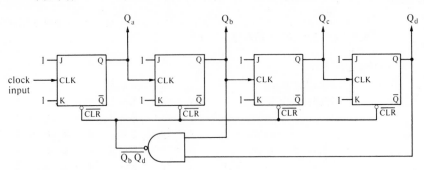

Fig. A1.3(a)

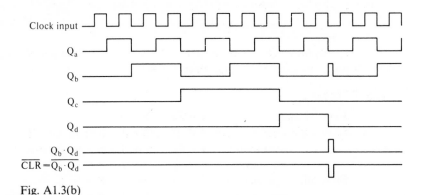

Fig. A1.3(b)

Question 4

When two *n*-bit two's complement integers, A and B, are added together to form a sum S, the possibility of arithmetic overflow exists. The definition of arithmetic overflow is:

$$OV = \overline{s_{n-1}} a_{n-1} b_{n-1} + s_{n-1} \overline{a_{n-1}}\, \overline{b_{n-1}}$$

where s_{n-1}, a_{n-1}, and b_{n-1} are the most significant bits of the sum, A, and B, respectively.

This equation is not generally used in real computers to detect overflow because it requires the storage of a_{n-1} and b_{n-1}, one of which is normally destroyed by the addition.

The actual method of detecting overflow is to compare the carry-in to the most significant stage of the parallel adder with the carry-out from the same stage. If they are different overflow is said to occur. That is:

$$OV = c_n \overline{c_{n-1}} + \overline{c_n} c_{n-1}.$$

Prove that the above method of detecting overflow by examining the carry bits of the parallel adder is valid.

Solution 4

The most-significant stage of a parallel adder can be represented by Fig. A1.4.

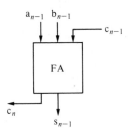

Fig. A1.4

The MSB stage adds together a_{n-1}, b_{n-1}, and c_{n-1} to generate a sum bit, s_{n-1}, and a carry-out, c_n. There are four possible combinations of A and B which can be added together:

$$(+A) + (+B)$$
$$(+A) + (-B)$$
$$(-A) + (+B)$$
$$(-A) + (-B)$$

As adding two numbers of differing sign cannot result in arithmetic overflow, we need consider only the cases where A and B are both positive, or both negative.

Case 1: A and B positive. $a_{n-1} = 0$, $b_{n-1} = 0$.

The final stage adds $a_{n-1} + b_{n-1} + c_{n-1}$ to get c_{n-1}, as a_{n-1} and b_{n-1} are both zero. Therefore, the carry-out, c_n, is zero; and $s_{n-1} = c_{n-1}$. We know overflow occurs if $s_{n-1} = 1$, therefore overflow occurs if the sum is negative and $\overline{c_n}c_{n-1} = 1$.

Case 2: A and B negative. $a_{n-1} = 1$, $b_{n-1} = 1$.

The final stage adds $a_{n-1} + b_{n-1} + c_{n-1} = 1 + 1 + c_{n-1}$, to get a sum, $s_{n-1} = c_{n-1}$, and a carry-out $c_n = 1$. Overflow occurs if the sum is positive and $s_{n-1} = 0$. That is, if $c_n\overline{c_{n-1}} = 1$.

Considering both cases, overflow occurs if $\overline{c_n}c_{n-1} = c_n\overline{c_{n-1}} = 1$.

Question 5

(a) Using AND, OR, and NOT gates only, design circuit diagrams to generate P and Q from inputs X, Y, and Z, where $P = (X + \overline{Y})(Y \oplus Z)$ and $Q = \overline{Y}Z + XY\overline{Z}$. Do not simplify, or otherwise modify, these expressions.

(b) By means of a truth table establish a relationship between P and Q.

(c) Compare the circuit diagrams of P and Q in terms of speed (propagation delay) and cost of implementation.

412   *Appendices*

Solution 5(a)

Figure A1.5(a) gives the circuit diagram for
$$P=(X+\overline{Y})\,(Y\oplus Z)=(X+\overline{Y})\,(Y\overline{Z}+\overline{Y}Z).$$

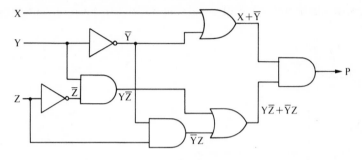

Fig. A1.5(a)

Figure A1.5(b) gives the circuit diagram for $Q=\overline{Y}Z+XY\overline{Z}$.

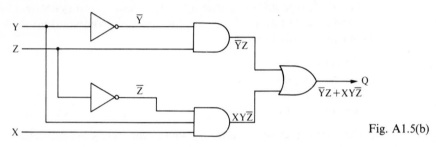

Fig. A1.5(b)

(b) Table A1.3 is the truth table for P and Q. From the truth table it can be seen that $P=Q$.

Table A1.3 Truth table for P and Q

X	Y	Z	$X+\overline{Y}$	$Y\oplus Z$	$P=(X+\overline{Y})(Y\oplus Z)$	$\overline{Y}Z$	$XY\overline{Z}$	$Q=\overline{Y}Z+XY\overline{Z}$
0	0	0	1	0	0	0	0	0
0	0	1	1	1	1	1	0	1
0	1	0	0	1	0	0	0	0
0	1	1	0	0	0	0	0	0
1	0	0	1	0	0	0	0	0
1	0	1	1	1	1	1	0	1
1	1	0	1	1	1	0	1	1
1	1	1	1	0	0	0	0	0

(c) A comparison of the two circuits.

Propagation delay. The maximum delay in the circuit for P is 4 gates in series in the Y path (i.e. NOT gate, AND gate, OR gate, AND gate). Maximum delay in circuit for Q is 3 gates in series in both Y and Z paths (i.e. NOT gate, AND gate, OR gate). Therefore the circuit for Q is 33 per cent

faster than that for P. *Cost.* Total number of gates needed to implement
P = 7. Total number of gates needed to implement Q = 5. Total inputs in the
circuit for P = 12. Total inputs in the circuit for Q = 9.

Clearly, the circuit for Q is better than that for P both in terms of the
number of gates, and the number of inputs to the gates.

Question 6

(a) Show that the EXCLUSIVE OR (EOR) operator is associative, so
that $A \oplus (B \oplus C) = (A \oplus B) \oplus C$.

(b) Show that any logic function can be implemented in terms of EOR and
AND gates only.

Solution 6

(a) $A \oplus (B \oplus C) = A \oplus (B\bar{C} + \bar{B}C)$

$$= A\overline{(B\bar{C} + \bar{B}C)} + \bar{A}(B\bar{C} + \bar{B}C)$$

$$= A(\bar{B} + C)(B + \bar{C}) + \bar{A}B\bar{C} + \bar{A}\,\bar{B}C$$

$$= A(\bar{B}\bar{C} + BC) + \bar{A}B\bar{C} + \bar{A}\,\bar{B}C$$

$$= A\bar{B}\bar{C} + ABC + \bar{A}B\bar{C} + \bar{A}\,\bar{B}C.$$

$(A \oplus B) \oplus C = (A\bar{B} + \bar{A}B) \oplus C$

$$= (A\bar{B} + \bar{A}B)\bar{C} + \overline{(A\bar{B} + \bar{A}B)}C$$

$$= A\bar{B}\bar{C} + \bar{A}B\bar{C} + (\bar{A}\,\bar{B} + AB)C$$

$$= A\bar{B}\bar{C} + \bar{A}B\bar{C} + \bar{A}\,\bar{B}C + ABC.$$

Both these expressions are equal and therefore the operator $\oplus$ is associative.

(b) Consider $F = A \oplus B$.

$F = A\bar{B} + \bar{A}B$.
  If A = 0, F = B.
  If A = 1, F = $\bar{B}$.

In other words, if one input to an EOR gate is connected to a logical one,
the other input appears at the output in a complemented form. Therefore, the
EOR gate can act as an inverter.

If an EOR gate connected as an inverter is applied to the output of an
AND gate, the AND gate is transformed into a NAND gate. As all logic
functions can be generated by NAND gates only, then all logic functions can
be generated by AND gates and EOR gates acting as inverters.

Question 7

Design a BCD-to-7-segment decoder. The decoder has a four-bit natural
binary BCD input represented by DCBA, where A is the least significant bit.

Assume that the BCD input can never be greater than 9. A seven-segment decoder is illustrated in Fig. A1.6, and when one of its seven outputs (a to g) is true, the corresponding segment of the display is illuminated.

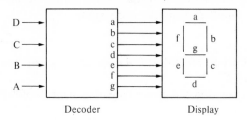

Decoder   Display   Fig. A1.6

Solution 7

The truth table for this problem is given in Table A1.4. We can now solve the equation for segments a to g. By using Karnaugh maps the don't-care conditions can be catered for. The Karnaugh map for segment a is presented in Tables A1.5(a), (b). From this map, $a = CA + BA + D + \overline{C}B$.

Table A1.4

Inputs					Outputs						
D	C	B	A	Character	a	b	c	d	e	f	g
0	0	0	0	*0*	1	1	1	1	1	1	0
0	0	0	1	*1*	0	1	1	0	0	0	0
0	0	1	0	*2*	1	1	0	1	1	0	1
0	0	1	1	*3*	1	1	1	1	0	0	1
0	1	0	0	*4*	0	1	1	0	0	1	1
0	1	0	1	*5*	1	0	1	1	0	1	1
0	1	1	0	*6*	0	0	1	1	1	1	1
0	1	1	1	*6*	1	1	1	0	0	0	0
1	0	0	0	*7*	1	1	1	1	1	1	1
1	0	0	1	*8*	1	1	1	0	0	1	1
1	0	1	0	*9*	X	X	X	X	X	X	X
1	0	1	1		X	X	X	X	X	X	X
1	1	0	0		X	X	X	X	X	X	X
1	1	0	1		X	X	X	X	X	X	X
1	1	1	0		X	X	X	X	X	X	X
1	1	1	1		X	X	X	X	X	X	X

forbidden (bracketing the last six rows)

An alternative approach is to obtain a by considering the zeros on the map shown in Tables A1.5(c), (d). From this map, $\overline{a} = \overline{D}\,\overline{C}\,\overline{B}A + C\overline{A}$. Therefore $a = \overline{\overline{D}\,\overline{C}\,\overline{B}A + C\overline{A}} = (D + C + B + \overline{A})(\overline{C} + A)$

$$= D\overline{C} + DA + C\overline{C} + CA + \overline{C}B + BA + \overline{C}\,\overline{A} + \overline{A}A$$

$$= D\overline{C} + DA + CA + \overline{C}B + BA + \overline{C}\,\overline{A}$$

$$= D\overline{C} + CA + BA + \overline{C}\,\overline{A}.$$

Table A1.5(a)

Table A1.5(b)

DC \ BA	00	01	11	10
00	1		X	1
01		1	X	1
11	1	1	X	X
10	1		X	X

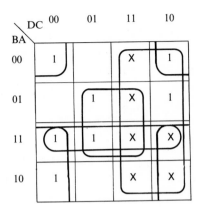

Table A1.5(c)

Table A1.5(d)

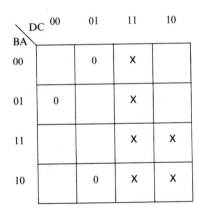

DC \ BA	00	01	11	10
00		0	X	
01	(0)		X	
11			X	X
10		0	X	X

This expression offers no improvement over the first realization of a.

The Karnaugh map for segment b is presented in Tables A1.6(a), (b), giving

$$b = \overline{C} + \overline{B}\,\overline{A} + BA$$

Plotting zeros on the Karnaugh map for b we get (Tables A1.6(c), (d)):

$$\overline{b} = C\overline{B}A + CB\overline{A}.$$

Table A1.6(a)

BA \ DC	00	01	11	10
00	1	1	X	1
01	1		X	1
11	1	1	X	X
10	1		X	X

Table A1.6(b)

BA \ DC	00	01	11	10
00	1	1	X	1
01	1		X	1
11	1	1	X	X
10	1		X	X

Table A1.6(c)

BA \ DC	00	01	11	10
00			X	
01		0	X	
11			X	X
10		0	X	X

Table A1.6(d)

BA \ DC	00	01	11	10
00			X	
01		0	X	
11			X	X
10		0	X	X

Therefore, $b = \overline{\overline{C}\,\overline{B}A + CB\overline{A}} = (\overline{C} + B + \overline{A})(\overline{C} + \overline{B} + A)$

$$= \overline{C} + BA + \overline{B}\,\overline{A}.$$

This expression yields the same result as that obtained directly by considering the ones on the Karnaugh map.

The equations for the remaining five segments can be considered in a similar way.

Question 8

Write a subroutine to input two ASCII-coded hexadecimal characters from a keyboard, and to return with the 8-bit binary representation of these two hexadecimal characters in the accumulator. For example, pressing the keys 'E' and '4' (ASCII codes $45 and $34, respectively) causes a return with $E4 (i.e. 11100100) in the accumulator. If a nonhexadecimal character is entered (i.e. any key not 0 to 9 or A to F), the carry-bit of the PSW is set prior to the return. Assume that the subroutine INALL at $E993 can be used to read a single ASCII character from the keyboard.

Solution 8

This program requires the input of two ASCII-coded characters, their conversion to hexadecimal form, and their packing into a single byte. Figure 3.1 gives the relationship between ASCII characters and their hexadecimal values. The results for 0 to 9, and A to F are repeated below.

ASCII character	0	1 ... 9	A ... F
Hexadecimal value	30	31 ... 39	41 ... 46

From this table it can be seen that numerals from 0 to 9 have ASCII characters equal to their numeric values plus hexadecimal 30, and letters from A to F have ASCII characters equal to their numeric value plus hexadecimal 37. If 'E4' is entered from the keyboard, the following operations must be performed.

Convert the 7-bit ASCII representation of E (i.e. 45_{16}) into a 4-bit binary form (i.e. $14_{10} = 1110_2$). Convert the 7-bit representation of 4 (i.e. 34_{16}) into a 4-bit binary form (i.e. $4_{10} = 0100_2$).

To pack these two 4-bit values into a single eight-bit word, the most significant character is shifted 4 places left to get 11100000, and the least significant character added in to give the final result, 11100100.

The convertion of an ASCII character into hexadecimal form can be expressed as follows:

```
success: = true
char: = char − $30
IF char < 0 THEN success: = false
    ELSE IF char < 10 THEN hexvalue: = char
            ELSE IF (char < 17) OR (char > 22) THEN success: = false
                    ELSE hexvalue: = char − 7
```

The program can be coded into 6502 assembly language as shown overleaf.

```
            JSR   INHEX      get first hex char in LS 4-bits of
                             accumulator
            BCS   END        if carry set then non-hex character
                             and failure
            ASL   A          shift left 4 places to occupy MS 4 bits
            ASL   A
            ASL   A
            ASL   A
            STA   TEMP       save accumulator in TEMP
            JSR   INHEX      get second hex character in LS 4-bits
                             of accumulator
            BCS   END        if carry set then non-hex char and
                             failure
            CLC              clear carry before addition
            ADC   TEMP       add in most significant 4 bits saved in
                             TEMP
END         RTS              return
INHEX       JSR   INALL      get an ASCII character
            SEC              set carry before subtraction
            SBC   #$30       subtract $30
            BMI   FAIL       if negative not valid hex
            CMP   #$0A       check if in range 0 to 9
            BMI   OK         if less than 10 return with success
            CMP   #$11       check if range less than 'A'
            BMI   FAIL       if negative not valid hex
            CMP   #$17       check if range greater than 'F'
            BPL   FAIL       if positive not valid hex
            SEC              set carry before subtraction
            SBC   #$07       subtract 7 to convert to hex form
OK          CLC              clear carry ( = success)
            RTS              return
FAIL        SEC              set carry ( = failure)
            RTS              return
```

Question 9

A palindrome is a word that reads the same forward as backward. For example, HANNAH is a palindrome. A text string is stored in memory started at location $0300 and is terminated by a carriage return, whose ASCII code is $0D. Construct an assembly-language program which will determine whether or not the string is a palindrome. If the string is a palindrome the carry bit of the PSW should be set at the end of the program.

Solution 9

There are two cases to be considered, one in which there are an even number of characters, and one in which there are an odd number of characters.

Even: ABCDDCBA   Odd: ABCDCBA

   ↑   ↑   ↑   ↑

   I   J   I   J

If a pointer is moved in from each end of the string, and the left-hand and right-hand letters being pointed at compared, the string is a palindrome if all pairs match until the middle is reached.

If the left pointer is I, and the right pointer J, the middle is reached when $I = J$ (odd number of letters) or $I + 1 = J$ (even number of letters).

The program may be coded in 6502 assembly language as follows.

```
            NAM  PALINDROME
            ORG  $0000
SAVEY       RMB  1              location of temporary storage for Y
                               register
            ORG  $0080          program origin
            LDX  #00            clear X register (right pointer)
NEXT        LDA  $0300,X        get a character
            INX                 increment pointer
            CMP  #$0D           is it a carriage return?
            BNE  NEXT           if not continue
            DEX                 X now points at righthand char in
            DEX                 string
            LDY  #00            clear Y register (left pointer)
COMP        LDA  $0300,Y        get a lefthand character
            CMP  $0300,X        compare with a righthand character
            BNE  FAIL           if not same then not palindrome
            STY  SAVEY          save Y in memory
            CPX  SAVEY          compare X and Y (odd length)
            BEQ  SUCCESS        if same middle reached
            INC  SAVEY          increment Y in memory
            CPX  SAVEY          compare X and Y (even length)
            BEQ  SUCCESS        if same middle reached
            INY                 move left pointer
            DEX                 move right pointer
            JMP  COMP           repeat
FAIL        CLC                 clear carry
            RTS                 return—not palindrome
SUCCESS     SEC                 set carry
            RTS                 return—it was a palindrome
```

APPENDIX A2: THE 6502 INSTRUCTION SET

There are two reasons for the inclusion of this appendix. It allows the reader to attempt some of the assembly-language problems without referring to additional material. It also illustrates a 'typical' microprocessor instruction set. The instruction sets of eight-bit microprocessors vary from device to device although, in principle, it is possible to tackle any problem with any microprocessor. In practice, some instruction sets are rather unwieldy and lack the elegance making a neat solution possible. Instruction sets are often compared on the basis of 'benchmarks'. A test problem is coded into the assembly language of, say, three different microprocessors and then the programs are executed. By measuring the time taken to execute each program, a figure of merit may be obtained for the microprocessor. Another figure of merit is obtained by examining the size (i.e. number of words) of each program. Ideally, the best microprocessor should execute the program fastest and occupy the least number of bytes.

However, benchmarks are notoriously unreliable. It is difficult to translate a problem into three different machine codes with equal efficiency, so that the programmer's ability to write compact programs often becomes a significant part of the test.

The instruction set of the 6502

Conventionally, the instruction sets of microprocessors are often presented in the alphabetic order of mnemonics. I have decided to group them together logically in terms of the type of operation they perform. The groups chosen are: arithmetic, logical, data movement, branch, and control. The first four groups are self-explanatory while the control group includes all instructions which effect the sequence of operations of the microprocessor (excepting branch instructions). I have also included the miscellaneous instructions in this group. Table A2.1 lists all mnemonics alphabetically in terms of their group.

Table A2.1 The 6502 mnemonics arranged alphabetically

Mnemonic	Name	Group
ADC	Add with carry	A
AND	Logical AND	L
ASL	Arithmetic shift left	A
BCC	Branch on carry clear	B
BCS	Branch on carry set	B
BEQ	Branch on equal to zero	B
BIT	Compare (test) memory bits with accumulator	L

Table A2.1 *contd*

BMI	Branch on minus	B
BNE	Branch on not equal to zero	B
BPL	Branch on plus	B
BRK	Break	C
BVC	Branch on overflow clear	B
BVS	Branch on overflow set	B
CLC	Clear carry flag	A
CLD	Clear decimal flag	A
CLI	Clear interrupt mask	C
CLV	Clear overflow flag	A
CMP	Compare to accumulator	A
CPX	Compare to X register	A
CPY	Compare to Y register	A
DEC	Decrement memory	A
DEX	Decrement X register	A
DEY	Decrement Y register	A
EOR	Exclusive OR	L
INC	Increment memory	A
INX	Increment X register	A
INY	Increment Y register	A
JMP	Jump to address	B
JSR	Jump to subroutine	B
LDA	Load accumulator	T
LDX	Load X register	T
LDY	Load Y register	T
LSR	Logical shift right	L
NOP	No operation	C
ORA	Inclusive OR	L
PHA	Push accumulator on to stack	T
PHP	Push processor status on to stack	T
PLA	Pull accumulator from stack	T
PLP	Pull processor status from stack	T
ROL	Rotate left one bit through carry	L
ROR	Rotate right one bit through carry	L
RTI	Return from interrupt	C
RTS	Return from subroutine	C
SBC	Subtract with carry	A
SEC	Set carry	A
SED	Set decimal mode	A
SEI	Set interrupt mask flag bit of PSW	C
STA	Store accumulator in memory	T
STX	Store X register in memory	T
STY	Store Y register in memory	T
TAX	Transfer accumulator to X register	T
TAY	Transfer accumulator to Y register	T
TSX	Transfer stack pointer to X register	T
TXA	Transfer X register to accumulator	T
TXS	Transfer X register to stack pointer	T
TYA	Transfer Y register to accumulator	T

A = arithmetic
L = logical
T = data movement (transfer)
B = branch
C = control

The operations carried out by the instruction in Table A2.1 are later described in terms of register transfer language, whenever possible. Table A2.2 lists the abbreviations used.

Table A2.2 Abbreviations used in op-code description

Acc	accumulator	PSW bits:	
M	a general memory location	N	negative bit (MSB)
SP	stack pointer	V	overflow bit
X	index register X	B	breakpoint bit
Y	index register Y	D	decimal mode bit
PC	program counter	I	interrupt mask bit
L	a literal value	Z	zero bit
PSW	processor status word	C	carry bit

Addressing modes of the 6502

The 6502 has seven basic addressing modes: implicit, accumulator, immediate (literal), zero page, absolute, indexed, and relative. In the following tables immediate or literal addressing is denoted by L, zero page addressing by Z, absolute addressing by Abs, and indexed addressing by I. The so-called implicit addressing mode is denoted by 'implicit' in the appropriate column, and implies that an explicit memory reference is not required.

Accumulator addressing is denoted by 'Acc' and is a special case of implicit addressing. Accumulator addressing is used to distinguish between an operation on a memory location, and one on the contents of the accumulator. Indexed addressing can be further divided into subgroups. These include absolute indexed using the X or Y register, and are denoted by IX and IY, respectively. In these modes the contents of the X or Y register are added to the 16-bit offset following the operation code to produce a 16-bit effective address. Zero page indexed addressing is denoted by IXZ and is used to access an address on page zero by generating an effective address from the sum of the contents of the X index register and the 8-bit offset following the op-code.

Indexed indirect addressing, denoted by (IX), is also called pre-indexed indirect addressing. The effective address of an operand is given by adding the contents of the index register to the eight-bit value following the op-code. This is then used to interrogate a memory location on page zero containing the true address of the operand. Thus the effective address is defined as $EA = [[X] + OFFSET]]$. The effective address is a 16-bit value spanning the whole 64 K bytes of memory space, and is stored as two consecutive bytes. The value of $[X] + OFFSET$, as calculated above, gives the address of the low byte of the operand, and the memory location $[X] + OFFSET + 1$ gives the address of the high byte of the operand. See Fig. A2.1.

Indirect indexed addressing, denoted by (IY), is also called post-indexed indirect addressing. In this case the effective address of an operand is given by using the offset following an op-code to look up an eight-bit value on page

$EA = [[X] + OFFSET]]$. The effective address is a 16-bit value spanning the

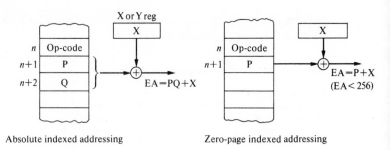

Absolute indexed addressing   Zero-page indexed addressing

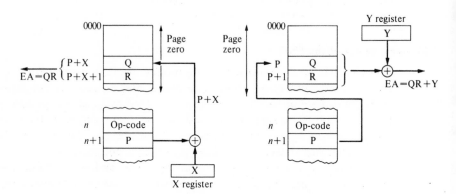

Pre-indexed indirect addressing   Post-indexed indirect addressing

Fig. A2.1 Indexed addressing and the 6502

zero and to add to this the contents of the Y register. Here the effective address is defined as EA = [[OFFSET] + [Y]]. As in the case of indexed indirect addressing, the effective address is a 16-bit value. OFFSET is an eight-bit value pointing at a memory location in page zero. The two consecutive locations pointed at by OFFSET, and OFFSET + 1, are used to form the 16-bit effective address of the operand. See Fig. A2.1. Note that in indexed indirect addressing only the X register may be used, while in indirect indexed addressing only the Y register may be used.

For each of the groups of instructions presented, the following format has been adopted.

Mnemonic Operation in RTL.
Operation in words.
Processor status word flat bits affected by operation.
Addressing modes.

The actual values of the operation codes for a mnemonic (one for each of its addressing modes) are given in Table A2.3 towards the end of this Appendix.

Arithmetic group

ADC $[A] \leftarrow [A] + [M] + [C]$.

Add the contents of memory address M to the contents of the accumulator, together with the carry bit, and deposit the result in the accumulator.

Flags affected: N, V, Z, C.

Addressing modes: L, Z, Abs, IX, IY, IXZ, (IX), (IY).

ASL $\boxed{C} \leftarrow \boxed{7\ 6\ 5\ 4\ 3\ 2\ 1\ 0} \leftarrow 0$.

Shift the contents of the accumulator (or memory location) one place left. The MSB is moved into the carry bit and a zero enters the LSB.

Flags affected: N, Z, C.

Addressing modes: Acc, Z, Abs, IX, IXZ.

CLC $[C] \leftarrow 0$.

Clear the carry flag bit in the PSW.

Flags affected: C.

Addressing modes: implicit.

CLD $[D] \leftarrow 0$.

Clear the decimal mode flag bit of the PSW.

Flags affected: D.

Addressing modes: implicit.

CLV $[V] \leftarrow 0$.

Clear the overflow flag bit of the PSW.

Flags affected: V.

Addressing modes: implicit.

CMP $[A] - [M]$.

Subtract the contents of memory address M from the contents of the accumulator. The result is thrown away, and the contents of the accumulator are unaffected. The purpose of this instruction is to set/clear the appropriate PSW status bit.

Flags affected: N, Z, C.

Addressing modes: L, Z, Abs, IX, IY, IXZ, (IX), (IY).

CPX $[X] - [M]$.

Subtract the contents of memory address M from the contents of the X register. The result is not stored.

Flags affected: N, Z, C.

Addressing modes: L, Z, Abs.

CPY $[Y] - [M]$.

Subtract the contents of memory address M from the contents of the Y register. The result is not stored.

Flags affected: N, Z, C.
Addressing modes: L, Z, Abs.

DEC $[M] \leftarrow [M] - 1$.
Decrement the contents of memory location M.
Flags affected: N, Z.
Addressing modes: Z, Abs, IX, IXZ.

DEX $[X] \leftarrow [X] - 1$.
Decrement the contents of the X register.
Flags affected: N, Z.
Addressing modes: implicit.

DEY $[Y] \leftarrow [Y] - 1$.
Decrement the contents of the Y register.
Flags affected: N, Z.
Addressing modes: implicit.

INC $[M] \leftarrow [M] + 1$.
Increment the contents of memory location M.
Flags affected: N, Z.
Addressing modes: Z, Abs, IX, IXZ.

INX $[X] \leftarrow [X] + 1$.
Increment the contents of the X register.
Flags affected: N, Z.
Addressing modes: implicit.

INY $[Y] \leftarrow [Y] + 1$.
Increment the contents of the Y register.
Flags affected: N, Z.
Addressing modes: implicit.

SBC $[A] \leftarrow [A] - [M] - [\overline{C}]$.
Subtract the contents of memory location M from the contents of
the accumulator. The complement of the carry bit is also
subtracted. The result is left in the accumulator.
Flags affected: N, V, Z, C.
Addressing modes: L, Z, Abs, IX, IY, IXZ, (IX), (IY).

SEC $[C] \leftarrow 1$.
Set the carry flag bit of the PSW.
Flags affected: C. Addressing modes: implicit.

SED $[D] \leftarrow 1$.
Set the decimal mode flag bit of the PSW.
Flags affected: D.
Addressing modes: implicit.

Logical group

AND   [A]←[A].[M].

Carry out the logical AND between the contents of the accumulator and the contents of memory address M. Deposit the
result in the accumulator.

Flags affected: N, Z.

Addressing modes: L, Z, Abs, IX, IY, IXZ, (IX), (IY).

BIT   [A].[M].

Carry out the logical AND between the contents of the accumulator and the contents of memory address M. Discard the
result. This instruction is the logical equivalent of CMP. Note
that the Z bit of the PSW is cleared if [A] and [M] are the same.
Bit 7 of [M] is transferred to the N flag bit of the PSW, and bit
6 of M is transferred to the V flag bit of the PSW.

Flags affected: N, V, Z.

Addressing modes: Z, Abs.

EOR   [A]←[A]⊕[M].

The contents of the accumulator are exclusive ORed with the
contents of the memory address M.

Flags affected: N, Z.

Addressing modes: L, Z, Abs, IX IY, IXZ, (IX), (IY).

LSR   0→ | 7 | 6 | 5 | 4 | 3 | 2 | 1 | 0 | → | C |.

The contents of memory location M, or the accumulator, are
shifted one place right. A zero enters the MSB and the LSB
enters the carry bit.

Flags affected: N, Z, C.

Addressing modes: Acc, Z, Abs, IX, IXZ.

ORA   [A]←[A]+[M].

The contents of the accumulator are ORed with the contents of
memory address M.

Flags affected: N, Z.

Addressing modes: L, Z, Abs, IX, IY, IXZ, (IX), (IY).

ROL | 7 | 6 | 5 | 4 | 3 | 2 | 1 | 0 | ← | C | ↵.

The contents of the accumulator or memory address M are
rotated (shifted) one place left. The carry bit is shifted into the
LSB position, and the MSB is shifted into the carry bit. Note
that this is a nine-bit operation, and no bit is lost.

Flags affected: N, Z, C.

Addressing modes: Acc, Z, Abs, IX, IXZ.

ROR   ↱ | C | → | 7 | 6 | 5 | 4 | 3 | 2 | 1 | 0 | ↰

The contents of the accumulator or memory address M are rotated (shifted) one place right. The carry bit is shifted into the MSB position, and the LSB is shifted into the carry bit. Note that this is a nine bit operation, and no bit is lost.
Flags affected: N, Z, C.
Addressing modes: Acc, Z, Abs, IX, IXZ.

Data movement group (transfer)

LDA $[A] \leftarrow [M]$.
Load the accumulator with the contents of memory address M.
Flags affected: N, Z.
Addressing modes: L, Z, Abs, IX, IY, IXZ, (IX), (IY).

LDX $[X] \leftarrow [M]$.
Load the X register with the contents of memory location M.
Flags affected: N, Z.
Addressing modes: L, Z, Abs, IY, IYZ.

LDY $[Y] \leftarrow [M]$.
Load the Y register with the contents of memory location M.
Flags affected: N, Z.
Addressing modes: L, Z, Abs, IX, IXZ.

PHA $[[SP]] \leftarrow [A], [SP] \leftarrow [SP] - 1$.
Push the contents of the accumulator on to the stack.
Flags affected: none.
Addressing modes: implicit.

PHP $[[SP]] \leftarrow [PSW], [SP] \leftarrow [SP] - 1$.
Push the contents of the processor status word on to the stack.
Flags affected: none.
Addressing modes: implicit.

PLA $[SP] \leftarrow [SP] + 1, [A] \leftarrow [[SP]]$.
Pull the top word from the stack and put it in the accumulator.
Flags affected: none.
Addressing modes: implicit.

PLP $[SP] \leftarrow [SP] + 1, [PSW] \leftarrow [[SP]]$.
Pull the top word from the stack and put it in the processor status word.
Flags affected: none.
Addressing modes: implicit.

STA $[M] \leftarrow [A]$.
The contents of the accumulator are stored at memory address M.
Flags affected: none.
Addressing modes: Z, Abs, IX, IY, IXZ, (IX), (IY).

STX   [M]←[X].
The contents of the X register are stored at memory address M.
Flags affected: none.
Addressing modes: Z, Abs, IYZ.

STY   [M]←[Y].
The contents of the Y register are stored at memory address M.
Flags affected: none.
Addressing modes: Z, Abs, IXZ.

TAX   [X]←[A].
The contents of the accumulator are copied into the X register.
Flags affected: none.
Addressing modes: implicit.

TAY   [Y]←[A].
The contents of the accumulator are copied into the Y register.
Flags affected: none.
Addressing modes: implicit.

TSX   [X]←[SP].
The contents of the stack pointer are copied into the X register.
Flags affected: none.
Addressing modes: implicit.

TXA   [A]←[X].
The contents of the X register are copied into the accumulator.
Flags affected: none.
Addressing modes: implicit.

TXS   [SP]←[X].
The contents of the X register are copied into the stack pointer.
Flags affected: none.
Addressing modes: implicit.

TYA   [A]←[Y].
The contents of the Y register are copied into the accumulator.
Flags affected: none.
Addressing modes: implicit.

Branch group

Note that the value of PC in the conditional branch group is that after the PC
has been incremented in the current fetch cycle.

BCC   IF [C]=0 THEN [PC]←[PC]+OFFSET.
If the carry flag of the PSW is clear, branch to the current address
plus the signed offset following the op-code.
Flags affected: none.
Addressing modes: relative.

BCS   IF [C] = 1 THEN [PC]←[PC] + OFFSET.
       If the carry flag of the PSW is set, branch to the current address
       plus the signed offset.
       Flags affected: none.
       Addressing modes: relative.

BEQ   IF [Z] = 1 THEN [PC]←[PC] + OFFSET.
       If the Z flag bit of the PSW is set, branch to the current address
       plus the signed offset.
       Flags affected: none.
       Addressing modes: relative.

BMI   IF [N] = 1 THEN [PC]←[PC] + OFFSET.
       If the N flag bit of the PSW is set, branch to the current address
       plus the signed offset.
       Flags affected: none.
       Addressing modes: relative.

BNE   IF [Z] = 0 THEN [PC]←[PC] + OFFSET.
       If the Z flag bit of the PSW is clear, branch to the current address
       plus the signed offset.
       Flags affected: none.
       Addressing modes: relative.

BPL   IF [N] = 0 THEN [PC]←[PC] + OFFSET.
       If the N flag bit of the PSW is clear, branch to the current address
       plus the signed offset.
       Flags affected: none.
       Addressing modes: relative.

BVC   IF [V] = 0 THEN [PC]←[PC] + OFFSET.
       If the V flag bit of the PSW is clear, branch to the current address
       plus the signed offset.
       Flags affected: none.
       Addressing modes: relative.

BVS   IF [V] = 1 THEN [PC]←[PC] + OFFSET.
       If the V flag bit of the PSW is set, branch to the current address
       plus the signed offset.
       Flags affected: none.
       Addressing modes: relative.

JMP   [PC]←OFFSET.
       Jump to the 16-bit address given by the absolute offset following
       the op-code.
       Flags affected: none.
       Addressing mode: Abs.

JSR   [[SP]]←[PC]+2, [SP]←[SP]−2, [PC]←OFFSET.
Jump to the subroutine whose address is given by the 16-bit absolute offset following the op-code.
Flags affected: none.
Addressing modes: Abs.

Control and miscellaneous group

BRK   [[SP]]←[PC]+2,   [[SP]−2]←[PSW],   [SP]←[SP]−3, [PC]←[FFFE, FFFF].
The contents of the program counter followed by the contents of the processor status word are pushed on to the stack. The contents of memory locations $FFFE and $FFFF are loaded into the program counter. This instruction is a software interrupt.
Flags affected: B.
Addressing modes: implicit.

CLI   [I]←0.
The interrupt flag bit of the PSW is cleared. This enables interrupt requests.
Flags affected: I.
Addressing modes: implicit.

NOP   No operation.
This op-code has no effect on the execution of the program other than to produce a delay of two clock cycles.
Flags affected: none.
Addressing modes: implicit.

RTI   [SP]←[SP]+1, [PSW]←[[SP]], [SP]←[SP]+2, [PC]←[[SP]].
The PSR and the program counter are pulled off the stack.
Flags affected: all.
Addressing modes: implicit.

RTS   [SP]←[SP]+2, [PC]←[[SP]], [PC]←[PC]+1.
The program counter is pulled from the top of the stack.
Flags affected: none.
Addressing modes: implicit.

SEI   [I]←1.
Set the interrupt mask bit of the PSW. This has the effect of disabling interrupts.
Flags affected: I.
Addressing modes: implicit.

	Instructions	Immediate			Absolute			Zero page			Accum.			Implied		
Mnemonic	Operation	OP	n	#	OP	n	#	OP	n	#	OP	n	#	OP	n	#
A D C	$A+M+C\rightarrow A$ (4) (1)	69	2	2	6D	4	3	65	3	2						
A N D	$A\ M\rightarrow A$ (1)	29	2	2	2D	4	3	25	3	2						
A S L	$\boxed{C\leftarrow 7 \quad 0}\leftarrow 0$				0E	6	3	06	5	2	0A	2	1			
B C C	Branch on C=0 (2)															
B V S	Branch on C=1 (2)															
B E Q	Branch on Z=1 (2)															
B I T	$A\wedge M$				2C	4	3	24	3	2						
B M I	Branch on N=1 (2)															
B N E	Branch on Z=0 (2)															
B P L	Branch on N=0 (2)															
B R K	Break													00	7	1
B V C	Branch on V=0 (2)															
B V S	Branch on V=1 (2)															
C L C	$0\rightarrow C$													18	2	1
C L D	$0\rightarrow D$													D8	2	1
C L I	$0\rightarrow I$													58	2	1
C L V	$0\rightarrow V$													B8	2	1
C M P	$A-M$	C9	2	2	CD	4	3	C5	3	2						
C P X	$X-M$	E0	2	2	EC	4	3	E4	3	2						
C P Y	$Y-M$	C0	2	2	CC	4	3	C4	3	2						
D E C	$M-1\rightarrow M$				CE	6	3	C6	5	2						
D E X	$X-1\rightarrow M$													CA	2	1
D E Y	$Y-1\rightarrow Y$													88	2	1
E O R	$A\forall M\rightarrow A$ (1)	49	2	2	4D	4	3	45	3	2						
I N C	$M+1\rightarrow M$				EE	6	3	E6	5	2						
I N X	$X+1\rightarrow X$													E8	2	1
I N Y	$Y+1\rightarrow Y$													C8	2	1
J M P	Jump to new loc				4C	3	3									
J S R	Jump subroutine				20	6	3									
L D A	$M\rightarrow A$ (1)	A9	2	2	AD	4	3	A5	3	2						
L D X	$M\rightarrow X$ (1)	A2	2	2	AE	4	3	A6	3	2						
L D Y	$M\rightarrow Y$ (1)	A0	2	2	AC	4	3	A4	3	2						
L S R	$0\rightarrow\boxed{7\quad 0}\rightarrow C$				4E	6	3	46	5	2	4A	2	1			
N O P	No operation													EA	2	1
O R A	$A\lor M\rightarrow A$	09	2	2	0D	4	3	05	3	2						
P H A	$A\rightarrow Ms\qquad S-1\rightarrow S$													48	3	1
P H P	$P\rightarrow Ms\qquad S-1\rightarrow S$													08	3	1
P L A	$S+1\rightarrow S\qquad Ms\rightarrow A$													68	4	1
P L P	$S+1\rightarrow S\qquad Ms\rightarrow P$													28	4	1
R O L	$\leftarrow\boxed{7\quad 0}\leftarrow C\leftarrow$				2E	6	3	26	5	2	2A	2	1			
R O R	$\rightarrow C\rightarrow\boxed{7\quad 0}\rightarrow$				6E	6	3	66	5	2	6A	2	1			
R T I	Rtrn interrupt													40	6	1
R T S	Rtrn subroutine													60	6	1
S B C	$A-M-\overline{C}\rightarrow A$ (1)	E9	2	2	ED	4	3	E5	3	2						
S E C	$1\rightarrow C$													38	2	1
S E D	$1\rightarrow D$													F8	2	1
S E I	$1\rightarrow I$													78	2	1
S T A	$A\rightarrow M$				8D	4	3	85	3	2						
S T X	$X\rightarrow M$				8E	4	3	86	3	2						
S T Y	$Y\rightarrow M$				8C	4	3	84	3	2						
T A X	$A\rightarrow X$													AA	2	1
T A Y	$A\rightarrow Y$													A8	2	1
T S X	$S\rightarrow X$													BA	2	1
T X A	$X\rightarrow A$													8A	2	1
T X S	$X\rightarrow S$													9A	2	1
T Y A	$Y\rightarrow A$													98	2	1

(1) Add 1 'N' if page boundary is crossed

(2) Add 1 to 'N' if branch occurs to same page

   Add 2 to 'N' if branch occurs to different page

(3) Carry not = Borrow

(4) If in decimal mode, Z flag is invalid

   Accumulator must be checked for zero result

Z. Page, X			Abs. X			Abs. Y			Relative			Indirect			Z. Page, Y			Processor status Codes								Mnemonic
																		7	6	5	4	3	2	1	0	
OP	n	#	OP	n	#	OP	n	#	OP	n	#	OP	n	#	OP	n	#	N	V	●	B	D	I	Z	C	
75	4	2	7D	4	3	79	4	3										N	V	·	·	·	·	Z	C	A D C
35	4	2	3D	4	3	39	4	3										N	·	·	·	·	·	Z	·	A N D
16	6	2	1E	7	3													N	·	·	·	·	·	Z	C	A S L
									90	2	2							·	·	·	·	·	·	·	·	B C C
									80	2	2							·	·	·	·	·	·	·	·	B V S
									F0	2	2							·	·	·	·	·	·	·	·	B E Q
																		M$_7$	M$_6$	·	·	·	·	Z	·	B I T
									30	2	2							·	·	·	·	·	·	·	·	B MI
									D0	2	2							·	·	·	·	·	·	·	·	B N E
									10	2	2							·	·	·	·	·	·	·	·	B P L
																		·	·	·	1	·	1	·	·	B R K
									50	2	2							·	·	·	·	·	·	·	·	B V K
									70	2	2							·	·	·	·	·	·	·	·	B V S
																		·	·	·	·	·	·	·	0	C L C
																		·	·	·	·	0	·	·	·	C L D
																		·	·	·	·	·	0	·	·	C L I
																		·	0	·	·	·	·	·	·	C L V
D5	4	2	DD	4	3	D9	4	3										N	·	·	·	·	·	Z	C	C MP
																		N	·	·	·	·	·	Z	C	C P X
																		N	·	·	·	·	·	Z	C	C P Y
D6	6	2	DE	7	3													N	·	·	·	·	·	Z	·	D E C
																		N	·	·	·	·	·	Z	·	D E X
																		N	·	·	·	·	·	Z	·	D E Y
55	4	2	5D	4	3	59	4	3										N	·	·	·	·	·	Z	·	E O R
F6	6	2	FE	7	3													N	·	·	·	·	·	Z	·	I N C
																		N	·	·	·	·	·	Z	·	I N X
																		N	·	·	·	·	·	Z	·	I N Y
									6C	5	3							·	·	·	·	·	·	·	·	J MP
																		·	·	·	·	·	·	·	·	J S R
B5	4	2	BD	4	3	B9	4	3										N	·	·	·	·	·	Z	·	L DA
						BE	4	3							B6	4	2	N	·	·	·	·	·	Z	·	L D X
B4	4	2	BC	4	3													N	·	·	·	·	·	Z	·	L D Y
56	6	2	5E	7	3													0	·	·	·	·	·	Z	C	L S R
																		·	·	·	·	·	·	·	·	N O P
15	4	2	1D	4	3	19	4	3										N	·	·	·	·	·	Z	·	O R A
																		·	·	·	·	·	·	·	·	P H A
																		·	·	·	·	·	·	·	·	P H P
																		N	·	·	·	·	·	Z	·	P L A
																		(Restored)								P L P
36	6	2	3E	7	3													N	·	·	·	·	·	Z	C	R O L
76	6	2	7E	7	3													N	·	·	·	·	·	Z	C	R O R
																		(Restored)								R T I
																		·	·	·	·	·	·	·	·	R T S
F5	4	2	FD	4	3	F9	4	3										N	V	·	·	·	·	Z	(3)	S B C
																		·	·	·	·	·	·	·	1	S E C
																		·	·	·	·	1	·	·	·	S E D
																		·	·	·	·	·	1	·	·	S E I
95	4	2	9D	5	3	99	5	3										·	·	·	·	·	·	·	·	S T A
															96	4	2	·	·	·	·	·	·	·	·	S T X
94	4	2																·	·	·	·	·	·	·	·	S T Y
																		N	·	·	·	·	·	Z	·	T A X
																		N	·	·	·	·	·	Z	·	T A Y
																		N	·	·	·	·	·	Z	·	T S X
																		N	·	·	·	·	·	Z	·	T X A
																		·	·	·	·	·	·	·	·	T X S
																		N	·	·	·	·	·	Z	·	T Y A

dex X
dex Y
ccumulator
emory per effective address
emory per stack pointer

+	Add	M$_7$	Memory bit 7
−	Subtract	M$_6$	Memory bit 6
∧	And	n	No. cycles
∨	Or	#	No. bytes
∀	Exclusive or		

BIBLIOGRAPHY

This bibliography has been included to provide the student with a guide to further study.

Lippiatt, A. G. (1979). *The architecture of small computer systems*. Prentice-Hall. This slim volume (173 pages) provides an introduction to the structure of small computers. Here, small means microprocessors and minicomputers. Boolean algebra, assembly-language programming, and peripherals are not included.

Lee, G. (1982). *From hardware to software: an introduction to computers*. Macmillan Press. This large (454 pages) volume covers much of the material in my book. The two major differences are that Lee builds his book around 'A Simple Digital Computer', a hypothetical computer designed for teaching purposes, and also includes considerable detail on software (assembly language, high level language and compiling).

Gibson, J. R. (1979). *Electronic logic circuits*. Edward Arnold. This book is devoted entirely to Boolean algebra and is written at an introductory level. It contains only 114 pages but is very well written and presented.

Cripps, M. (1977). *An introduction to computer hardware*. Edward Arnold. A terse book dealing with a number of hardware topics from the structure of the processor to the design of peripherals. This is a rather short book (130 pages), and should be regarded as a source of additional information rather than a stand-alone text book.

Scanlan, L. J. (1981). *AIM 65 laboratory manual and study guide*. John Wiley. A book intended to be used in conjunction with the AIM 65 microcomputer. It consists of a number of tutorial experiments, each accompanied by the necessary background information. This book is ideal for self-study, and may, with thought, be used by those with other 6502-based microcomputers capable of working in assembly language and having accessible I/O routines.

Ullmann, J. R. (1982). *Micro-computer technology: an introduction*. Pitman Books. Although the title 'Micro-computer Technology' hints at the fabrication of the silicon chips themselves, this book deals almost entirely with Boolean algebra, sequential circuits, microcomputers, and assembly language programming. The Z80 microprocessor is chosen as an example throughout. Many of the examples are presented in terms of Pascal as are the assembly language programs. Professor Ullmann even describes assembly language as 'destructured Pascal'. This is a superb book and is pitched at somewhat higher level than mine. It includes a wealth of worked examples. I would recommend this to anyone wishing to go further into the principles of computer architecture than the majority of introductory texts.

Tanenbaum, A. S. (1981). *Computer networks*. Prentice-Hall. Tanenbaum provides extensive coverage of both wide area and local area networks in this 517-page book. This is an advanced book aimed at third year students and postgraduates. It is well written and is a definitive work on computer communications. The hardware and electronics aspect of data transmission are not included.

Wilkinson, B., and Horrocks, D. (1982). *Computer peripherals.* Hodder and Stoughton. Devoted entirely to input and output devices, backing stores, and (in less detail) computer communications. All these topics are treated fully at an introductory level. This book is strongly recommended to those who wish to learn more about the structure, operation, and characteristics of peripherals.

Housley T. (1981). *Data communications and teleprocessing systems.* Prentice-Hall. This provides a very readable introduction to data communications. It manages to cover a subject, which is often left to post-graduate texts, in a very clear fashion. In particular, Housley provides an excellent introduction to protocols for data transmission systems.

INDEX

@ symbol, assembly language use 198
absolute addressing 197, 208, 209, 423, 424
ABX instruction 227
access times
  definition of 273, 278
  disk drive 297, 308, 314
  ferrite core 291–2
  memory 296, 297
accumulator 135, 165
accumulator addressing 423
accuracy, numbers 141–2
ACK (acknowledgement) codes 105, 361, 362
actuators, magnetic disk 305, 306
ADC instruction 136, 166, 170, 193, 421, 425, 432–3
  RTL description 167, 425
ADCs (analogue-to-digital converters) 268–9
ADD instruction 135, 228
  control signals 177
  sequence of operations 176
adder/subtractor circuit, two's complement numbers 130–1
addition
  binary tables for 120
  Boolean meaning 29
  floating-point arithmetic 148–9
  logical operator 166
  sign-and-magnitude arithmetic 127–8
addition circuits 121–6
address field 190, 191
  data transmission 354
address paths, CPU 163, 164
address-mapping/translation process 395
addressing modes 197–220
  absolute 197, 208, 209, 423, 424
  accumulator addressing 423
  branch relative 222
  direct 197, 222
  extended 222
  immediate 198–201, 221–2
  indexed 201–6, 224–6, 423–4
  indirect 208–9, 226, 423

  inherent 191, 221, 226
  problem questions 231–3
  program-counter relative 223–4
  register 226
  relative 206–8, 222
  RTL definitions 209
  6502-microprocessor 423–4, 432–3
  zero-page 197–8, 221, 423
advanced computer arithmetic 329–46
AIM-65 microputer
  advantages 135
  book on 434
  problem questions 230–1
air gaps, magnetic recording 298, 306
aircraft automatic landing example 7–8
ALOHA network 372–3
alpha particles, semiconductor sensitivity 282
alphabets 14–15
  digital computer 15
ALU (arithmetic and logical unit) 165
AM (amplitude modulation) 357
American Standard Code for Information Interchange (ASCII) 105–6
  control characters 105, 106, 251, 352, 360
  keyboard encoder 251–3
amplitude modulation (AM) 357
analogue input/output devices 267–70
analogue-to-digital converters (ADCs) 268–9
  resolution of 269
  sampling frequency for 269
AND gates 17–19, 22
  in 3-line-to-8-line decoder 183, 184
  logic symbol for 18
  propagation delay effects 90
AND instruction 169, 170, 193, 421, 427, 432–3
AND logical operator 18–19, 29, 30, 166, 330
AND-OR-INVERT gates 53, 55
apostrophe ('), assembly language meaning 216

application layer, data
transmission 336, 367
architecture 3
books on 434
6502 microprocessor 135
arithmetic and logical instructions 193,
227–8, 425–8
arithmetic and logical unit (ALU) 165
arithmetic operators, logical
equivalents 166
arithmetic systems used by computers 3
ASCII (American Standard Code for
Information Interchange) 105–6,
251, 352, 360
ASL instruction 193, 421, 425, 432–3
assembler directives 173
assembler programs 173, 385
assembly language 3, 135, 175
comments in programs 139
label fields in programs 172–3
problem questions 233–4
asterisk (*), as program counter
value 206, 215
asynchronous serial data
transmission 349–51
asychronous systems 70
audio cassette recorders, data storage
using 322
automated-office facilities 348
availability ratio 94–5

B–H curves 287, 289
back-up, system reliability 96
backing stores 4, 297
bandwidth 300
bar, Boolean meaning 29
baseband, definition of 373–4
BASIC interpreters, BCD code
used 113
BASIC programs
branching example 25
loop structure 200
sum-and-multiply 171
batch-mode operating systems 380
Baud, definition of 350
Baud-rates, quoted 350–1, 359
BCC error-detecting code 360
BCC instruction 169, 170, 421, 429,
432–3
BCD (binary coded decimal)
code 112–13
BCPs (byte control-oriented
protocols) 359, 360–1

BCS instruction 137, 169, 170, 421,
430, 432–3
belt printers 264, 265
benchmarks 421
BEQ instruction 169, 170, 197, 421,
430, 432–3
bibliography 434–5
binary alphabet, digital computer 15
binary arithmetic 3, 120–6
division 339–46
multiplication 329–39
problem questions 158–60
binary coded decimal (BCD)
code 112–13
decoder circuit 57–8, 413–14
storage limitations 113
binary counters 78–9
practical packages 83, 85–6
in worked examples 409–10
binary numbers
advantages 107
conversion to/from decimal 108, 109
conversion to/from Gray code 114
conversion to/from hexadecimal/
octal 110
positional notation 106
binary trees, Huffman code 119
bistables 62–74, 272
clocked flip-flops 67, 69–73
D flip-flops 68–9, 74–5, 81–2, 176
definition of 62
JK flip-flops 73–4, 76–9, 183, 184,
408, 410
master–slave flip-flops 72–3
RS flip-flops 63–7, 185–6, 279
T flip-flops 83, 85
BISYNC protocol 359, 369–1
bit (BInary digiT), defined 15, 104
BIT instruction 421, 427, 432–3
bit-organized memory 275
bit-oriented protocols (BOPs) 353–5,
359, 361–6
bit-rates, data transmission 350–1, 359
bit-stuffing 353, 375
bit-synchronized transmission 351
block-oriented transmission 352-5
BMI instruction 169, 422, 430, 432–3
BNE instruction 169, 170, 207, 208,
422, 430, 432–3
Boolean algebra 29–32
basic rules 30
books on 434
example of use 32–9

graphical presentation 39–45
misconceptions 32
problem questions 100–1
theorems 31
Boolean expressions
simplification 32–4
simplification using Karnaugh
maps 42, 44–5
symmetry of 37
Booth's algorithm 334–6
BOPs (bit-oriented protocols) 353–5,
359, 361–6
BOT (beginning of tape) marker 318
BPL instruction 169, 422, 430, 432–3
BRA instructions 135, 206
branch, meaning of term 168
branch instructions, listed 169, 429–31
branch relative addressing 222
breakpoint markers 385–6
BRK instruction 386, 422, 431, 432–3
buffers
I/O device 241
tri-state gate 60–1
burn-in of components 95
bus contention 371
bus networks 370–1
contention control in 371–4
maximum throughput 373
bus topology 370–1
buses 58–9
connection problems 59–60
and three-state circuits 60–1, 278
BVC instruction 169, 422, 430, 432–3
BVS instruction 137, 169, 422, 430,
432–3
byte control-oriented protocols (BCPs)
359, 360–1
byte-organized memory 275
bytes (eight- or six-bit words) 104

cache memory 402–3
Cambridge ring 376
data format for 376
capacitive switched keyboard 250–1
carrier sense multiple access
(CSMA) 374
carry flip-flop 167
carry look-ahead circuits 126
carry-flag bits 122, 167
cartridges, tape transport 322
CAS (column address strobe) 280
cassette recorders 9, 320, 322
cassettes, tape transport 320–2

catalogue function 382
cathode-ray tube (CRT) 253–5
point-plotting display 253
raster-scan mode 255
CCR (condition code register) 136, 168
CCW (channel control word) 249
census-takers, D flip-flops as 68
central processing units (CPUs)
access times 296
address paths 163, 164
connections to RAM 276
control of data flow 175, 176, 246
in data processing 5
execution of programs 12, 162
internal registers 296
programming example 169–72
structure 163–8
channel control word (CCW) 249
channel I/O 248–9
character generator ROM 258
character-oriented transmission 352,
360–1
characters, as words 105–6
check bits 116
chess games, simultaneous playing 386
chevron elements, magnetic-bubble
memory 326
circle, program for area 162
circuit conventions 17
circuit representations, gates 18, 19, 20
CLC instruction 136, 166, 170, 173,
193, 422, 425, 432–3
CLD instruction 422, 425, 432–3
clear, meaning of 65
CLI instruction 422, 431, 432–3
clock generator, VDU display 256
clock pulse intervals 165
clock skew 71–2
clocked flip-flops 69–73
comparison of modes 73
edge-sensitive 71–2, 73, 75
level–sensitive 71, 73
master–slave 72–3, 75
type in shift registers 75
clocked RS flip-flops 67
closed-loop data transfers 238–9
CLR instruction 228
CLV instruction 422, 425, 432–3
CMOS semiconductor memory
chip 274, 275, 285
CMP instruction 193, 196–7, 215, 422,
425, 432–3
code-converter circuits 57–8

coincident-current selection
  technique 291
collisions, bus network 372
column address strobe (CAS), dynamic
  memory 280
COM instruction 170, 228
combinational circuits, definition of 62
comments, assembly language
  program 139
communication systems 4
  book on 435
  reasons for 347
compiled programs 380
compiler program 386
complementary arithmetic 128–34
  one's complement 133–4
  two's complement 129–33
  ten's complement 128–9
complementation
  Boolean meaning 29
  Karnaugh map 46
complementors 20–1
components, microprocessors as 8–9
composite video 256
composite video signal 258
computer, definition of 5
computer scientists, view of
  microprocessors 8
concurrent programming 386
condition code register (CCR) 136, 168
conditional branches 24–5, 168, 169,
  179, 194
contention control, bus networks 371–4
control characters
  ASCII code 105, 251, 360, 361
  data transmission protocol 360, 361
  keyboard-generated 258–9
  VDU usage 258–9
control elements, computers as 7–8
control fields, data transmission
  protocol 354, 360, 361–2
control instructions 386, 431
control keys 251
control store 179
control units (CUs) 165, 174–88
  comparison of 188
  microprogrammed 175–80, 188
  random logic 180–8
conventions, logic element 17
COPY command 382
correspondence-quality printers 262
costs
  cassette recorders 321

disk drives 283, 306
  microcomputers 11
  minicomputers 10
  printers 259, 261
counter circuits 77–9
counters, practical packages 83, 85–6
CPUs: *see* central processing units
CPX instruction 204, 422, 425, 432–3
CPY instruction 204, 422, 425–6, 432–3
crash (system failure) 6; *see also* head-
  crash
cross-assembler program 385
cross-coupled NOR gates 62–3, 65
CRT (cathode-ray tube) 253–5
CRT terminals 236; *see* visual display
  units
CSMA (carrier sense multiple
  access) 374
cursors, VDU display 259
CUs (control units) 165, 174–88
cylinder printers 262

D flip-flops 68–9, 74
  in CPU registers 176
  in octal registers 81–2
  in shift registers 74–5
D register 227
DACs (digital-to-analogue
  converters) 269–70
daisy-wheel printers 263
data encoding techniques 299–305
data movement instructions 192–3, 227,
  428–9
data paths, CPU 175, 176
data processors, computers as 5–6
data transmission 349–59
  book on 435
  open-ended vs. closed-loop 238–9,
  359
data-link layer protocol 366
de Morgan's theorem 31
  applications 34–9
debugger program 385–6
debugging, definition of 135
DEC, network used by 373
DEC instruction 169, 170, 193, 194,
  228, 422, 426, 432–3
decade counters, in worked
  examples 409
decimal numbers
  conversion to BCD code 112
  conversion to/from binary/octal/
  hexadecimal 108, 109

conversion to/from Gray code 114
positional notation 106
decoders
BCD-to-seven-segment 57–8, 413–14
three-line-to-eight-line 183, 184
two-line-to-four-line 57, 82–3
deference, bus contention control 374
delay effects, logic element 69–70,
89–90
delay elements, D flip-flops as 68
delay-line memory 272
delete commands 382, 384
demand paging 399
demand-mode operating systems 380–1
demultiplexers 56
destructive readout (DRO) devices 290,
291
device selector circuits 56–7
DEX instruction 201, 204, 422, 426,
432–3
DEY instruction 204, 422, 426, 432–3
differential phase modulation 358
digit lines, thin-film memory 294
digital input/output devices 266–7
digital nature of computer 14–15
digital-to-analogue converters
(DACs) 269–70
digits, definition 106
DIL (dual-in-line packages) 53, 54,
80–5, 280, 283
direct addressing 197, 222
direct memory access controller
(DMAC) 237, 246–7
direct memory access (DMA) 237,
246–8
cycle-stealing mode 247–8
directives, assembly language 173, 215
dirty bit, virtual memory system 400
disk controller 307
disk drives 237, 305–15
access times for 297, 308, 314
cost of 306
fixed head 308
glossary of terminology 308–9
head settling times for 308
moving-head 308, 309
rotational latency of 308
storage capacity of 297, 306, 308,
311–12, 314
disk files 5
disk formats 307, 312
disks
described 305

hard/soft-sectored 309, 312
see also floppy ... ; Winchester ...
display memory function 385
division 4, 339–46
absence in Boolean algebra 63
multiplication method 343–5
nonrestoring operation 342–3, 345, 346
restoring operation 342, 344
DMA (direct memory access) 237,
246–8
DMAC (direct memory access
controller) 237, 246–7
domains, ferromagnetic material 287–8,
289, 293
don't care conditions 49–52, 65, 174,
225
dot clock, VDU display 256
dot graphics, printing of 261
dot-matrix printers 261–2
print quality of 261–2
double-precision mode 145
DRO (destructive readout) devices 290,
291
drum printers 263–4
dual-in-line (DIL) packages
combinational logic element 53, 54
dynamic RAM 280
ROM 283
sequential logic element 80–5
duplication of memory space 399–400
dynamic memory 274
control circuitry 281–2
dynamic semiconductor
memory 278–83
disadvantages 282

EAROM (electrically alterable read-
only memory) 285
economics, digital design 86–7, 91–3
editor programs 383–4
eight-bit numbers, multiplication using
4-bit multipliers 339, 340
eighty-twenty (80/20) rule 394
elastrometric keyboard 251
electrically alterable read-only memory
(EAROM) 285
electron spin interaction 272, 287
electron weight expression 141
electronic engineers, view of
microprocessors 8
emulation microprograms 179–80
emulator programs 385
ENABLE inputs 60, 81

encoders
  binary/Gray code 113–15
  optical 113–15
  see also decoders
encoding techniques 299–305
end-around carry 134
ENQ (reply-request) message 105, 361
EOR instruction 193, 422, 427, 432–3
EOR operator 19, 166
  in worked example 413
EOT (end of tape) marker 318
EPROM (erasable programmable read-only memory) 284–5
equality tester circuit 27, 28
erasable programmable read-only memory (EPROM) 284–5
  erasure by UV light 285
error detecting codes 115–18, 350
error messages 378
Ethernet 348, 373–4
  contention control used by 374
ETX control character 105, 360
exchange instructions 193, 227
exchangeable disk packs 309
EXCLUSIVE OR gates 19, 22, 26–7
  equality tester application 27, 28
  logic symbol for 26
  two's complement adder/subtractor 130
execution of instructions
  microprogrammable control-unit 176–9
  random-logic control-unit 183–7
execution of programs 12
executive system 379
EXG instruction 193, 227
EXNOR gates 22
exponent, floating-point number 142
extended addressing 222
extensions to filenames 382

failure rate, definition 94
fan-fold paper 259
FCS (frame check sequence) 354–5
FEPs (front-end processors) 248–9
ferrite-core memory 285–92
  advantages 286
  core memory plane 290–2
  hysteresis loop curve 287, 290
  obsolescence 286
  reading effects 290, 291, 292
  reasons for teaching theory 286
  writing 291, 292

ferromagnetism 272, 287–8
fetch cycle 165
fetch/execute cycle 165
  sequence of operations 176
FETCH/EXECUTE flip-flop 186
field-effect transistors 274, 279
figure of merit, microprocessor 421
filename, definition 382
fire detection circuit, Karnaugh map example 47–9
first-in-first-out queue 241
fixed-head disk drives 308
fixed-point arithmetic 140
flags, data transmission 353, 376
Flex operating system 380
  utilities 381–3
flip-flops 3, 62–74, 272
  applications listed 81
  as basis of sequential circuits 62, 79
  as memory cells 272, 274, 275
  see also bistables . . .
floating/indeterminate conditions 60, 65
floating point arithmetic 147–50
  problem questions 160–1
  worked example 150–5
floating point numbers 139–41
  normalization 142–4
  representation 141–2
  storage method 142, 146–7, 150
  typical systems 144–7
floating precision 148
floating-shuttle tape buffers 317
floppy disk, described 309
floppy-disk drives 309-12
  worked example 314–15
flow charts
  Booth's algorithm 336
  eight-bit multiplication 332
  floating-point addition 149
  nonrestoring division 346
  program 171
  restoring division 344
flux reversal 299
flyback, CRT display 255
FM (frequency modulation) 303, 311, 357
font, VDU display 256
formats, disk 307, 312
formatting, soft-sectored disk 309
FORTRAN programs, branching example 25
fractions
  floating-point arithmetic 140

number-base conversion 111
 problem questions 156–7
frame check sequence (FCS) 354–5
FRED (memory location) 135
frequency modulation (FM)
 audio cassette 322
 data transmission 357
 encoding technique 303, 311
friction-feed printer mechanisms 259
front-end processor (FEP) 248–9
full-adders 122–4
 two half-adders in tandem 123–3
full-duplex transmission 349, 363, 365
full-subtractor 126
fully interlocked handshaking 239
fuse-blowing, general-purpose logic
 array 92

gadolinium gallium garnet
 (GGG) 322–3
gates 3, 16–22
 analogue example 16–17
 applications 22–9
 definition of 16
 electrical characteristics 87–91
 propagation delay effects 89–90
 types of 14
 see also AND . . .; EXCLUSIVE OR
 . . .; NAND . . . .; NOR . . .; NOT
 . . .; OR gates
gateways, local-area network 368
GCR (group code representation)
 encoding technique 304–5
GGG (gadolinium gallium
 garnet) 322–3
glitches 90–1
golf-ball printers 262
Gray code 113–5
grid, CRT 253–4
group code representation (GCR)
 encoding technique 304–5

half-adders 121
half-duplex transmission 349, 363, 364
Hall-effect switch 250, 251
Hamming distances, unit distance
 code 113
handshaking 238–40
hang-up of system 240, 361
hard-disk drives: *see* disk drives;
 Winchester . . .
hard-sectored disks 309
hardware, definition of 1

hash sign (#)
 in assembly language
 instructions 196, 198, 199
 as program line number 383
Hawaii University local area
 network 372–3
HDLC (high-level data link
 control) 353–5, 359, 361–6
head crash 6, 307
Hertz (Hz) 300
hexadecimal numbers
 advantages 106–7
 conversion to/from binary 110
 conversion to/from decimal 108, 109
 in worked examples 416–17
high-level data link control
 (HDLC) 353–5, 359, 361–6
 message types 362–3
high-level languages, compiler
 translation 3
high-permeability material 297–8
high-speed multiplication 336–9, 340
Huffman codes 118–20, 355
hysteresis loop curve, ferrite-core
 memory 287, 290
Hz (Hertz) 300

I/O: *see* input/output
IAS (immediate-access store) 4, 5, 8,
 296–7, 398–9
IBM
 data transmission protocol 359,
 360–1
 electric typewriters 262
 floppy-disk drive development 309
 floppy-disk format 311–12
 front-end processors 248
ICL-1900 series computer, word-length
 used 104
IEEE floating-point formats 145–7
IEEE-488 bus 249
IF . . . THEN branches 25
immediate access, definition 273
immediate-access store (IAS) 4, 5
 access times 296–7
 read-only memory 8
 virtual memory mechanism 398–9
immediate addressing 198–9, 209,
 221–2
 examples 199–201
impact printers 260
INALL subroutine 217

INC instruction 169, 170, 193, 194,
    228, 422, 426, 432–3
index hole, floppy disk 310
index registers 162–3, 200–1
    problem questions 234–5
    various microprocessors
        compared 204, 224
    see also X . . .; Y registers
indexed addressing 201–4, 224–6, 423–4
    examples 205–6
indirect addressing 208–9, 209, 226,
    423, 424
infant mortality, component
    reliability 95
information frames, HDLC
    protocol 361–3
inherent addressing 191, 221, 226
ink-jet printers 265–6
input/output (I/O)
    areas of interest 236
    channel 248–9
    interrupt-driven 242–6
    memory-mapped 240–1
    programmed 240–2
    stategies 238
input/output (I/O) devices 3, 249–70
    book on 435
    keyboard 250–3
    printers 259–66
    VDU screens 253–9
Institution of Electronic and Electrical
    Engineers (IEEE)
    bus 249
    floating-point formats 145–7
instruction counters 79, 164
instruction decoder, random-logic
    control-unit 183, 184
instruction register (IR) 164
instructions
    applications 194-7
    arithmetic operations 425–6
    branching 169, 429–31
    control 431
    data movement 192–3, 227, 428–9
    effects on data 194–5
    index register 204
    listed for 6502-microprocessor 169,
        170, 192–7, 421–33
    listed for 6809-microprocessor 226–8
    logical operation 193, 227–8, 427–8
    transfer 192–3, 227, 428–9
    as words 104–5
intelligent peripherals 249

interactive operating systems 380–1
interfaces
    data transfer 236
    user-oriented 266–70
interlacing, VDU 225
International Standards Organization
    (ISO), protocol reference
    model 366–7
interpretation, machine-code
    instructions 175, 187
interrupt acknowledge mechanism 244
interrupt mechanism 219
interrupt request inputs 242
interrupt-driven I/O 242–6
interrupts, disadvantages of 246
inverters 14, 20–1
    propogation delay effects 89–90
INX instruction 201, 204, 422, 426,
    432–3
INY instruction 204, 422, 426, 432–3
IR (instruction register) 164
ISO (International Standards
    Organization), protocol reference
    model 366–7
iterative calculations 6–7

jam packets, bus contention
    control 374
JCL (job control language) 378, 379
JK flip-flops 73–4
    binary counter 78–9
    pulse effect 77–8
    shift register 76–7
    state diagram 77
    three-line-to-eight-line decoder 183,
        184
    worked examples 408, 410
JMP instruction 170, 194, 197, 422,
    430, 432–3
job control language (JCL) 378, 379
JSR instruction 214–15, 216, 422, 431,
    432–3
jump, meaning of term 168
jump instructions 170, 194, 197,
    214–15, 216, 430–1

K, memory capacity expressed in terms
    of 274
Karnaugh maps (K maps) 14, 39–44
    applications 45–7
    Boolean expressions simplified
        using 42, 44–5

don't care conditions 49–52
  examples 44–5
  four variables 40, 42–5
  one variable 40
  plotting of 40–4
  practical example 47–9
  shape of 44
  three variable 40–2
  two variable 40
  worked examples 406, 415, 416
keyboard encoder 251–3
keyboards 250–3
  software to operate 253, 254
keystroke encoding 251
keystroke detection 250

label fields, assembly language
  program 172–3
landing area, Winchester disk drive 313
LANs (local area networks) 347–8,
  367–77, 434–5
large numbers, 8-bit word
  representation 137–8
large scale integration (LSI) circuits 52
LDA instruction 136, 166, 170, 192,
  422, 428, 432–3
LDX instruction 192, 204, 422, 428,
  432–3
LDY instruction 204, 422, 428, 432–3
LEA instruction 227
LEDs (light-emitting diodes) 57–8
left-shift registers 77, 83
life curves, reliability 95
LIFO (last-in-first-out), stack
  queueing 210
light-emitting diodes (LEDs), decoder
  circuit 57–8
limit switch 266
limitations, hardware 2
line editors 383–4
line printers 263–4
line sync, VDU display 256
LIST command 382
listen-before-transmitting strategy, data
  transmission 372
listen-while-transmitting strategy, data
  transmission 372
local area networks (LANs) 347–8,
  367–77, 434–5
  advantages/disadvantages 368, 376–7
  book on 434–5
  topology 368–71
logic circuit design, factors

  affecting 28–9, 86–93
logic elements 3
  binary states of 15
  combinational 14; *see also* gates
  current maximum 88–9
  electrical characteristics 15–16, 87–91
  guaranteed noise immunity 16
  input vs. output ranges 15–16
  inputs 18
  noise margin 88
  performance data 87
  problem questions 98–100
  sequential 14; *see also* flip-flops
  special-purpose 52–8
  temperature effects 87–8
  timing characteristics 89–90
  voltage characteristics 15–16, 88
logic values, defined 16
logic variables
  active-high/active-low 16
  names 16
logical address space 391
  relationship to physical address
  space 392
logical instructions 193, 227–8, 427–8
logical operators 29–30
  arithmetic equivalent 166
look-up tables, multiplication 91–2,
  337, 338
loop structures 199–210
LSI (large-scale integration) circuits 52
LSR instruction 193, 194, 422, 427,
  432–3

machine-code instructions 3, 175
  interpretation 187
macroinstructions 175
magnetic anisotropy 293, 322–3
magnetic disks
  compared with audio records 305–6
  memory characteristics 297
  tracks/sectors 305, 307
  see also disk . . .
magnetic recording, theory 297–305
magnetic tape
  memory characteristics 297
  see also tape . . .
magnetic-bubble memory 272, 322–6,
  327
  detection mechanism for 326
  major–minor loop organization 326,
  327
  module for 327

. . .—*continued*
    as shift register 325, 326
    two-state logic of 323
main store (MS) 164
mainframe computers, described 9–10
majority-logic circuit 8, 22–3
Manchester encoding technique 301–2
mantissa, floating-point number 142, 146
MAR (memory address register) 164
mark condition, asynchronous serial transmission 350
master/slave data transmission system 353–4, 363
master/slave flip-flops 72–3
MBR (memory buffer register) 164
mean time between failure (MTBF) 94
mean time to repair (MTTR) 94
medium scale integration (MSI) circuits 52, 55
memory
    binary storage form 271
    data and program coexistence 13, 136
    definition of 271
    location addresses 13, 136, 173–4
    reasons for 271
memory address register (MAR) 164
memory buffer register (MBR) 164
memory cell, definition 272–3
memory characteristics, ideal memory 296
memory hierarchy 296–322
memory management 4, 388, 390–403
memory map 173–4
    bit-organized 274
    byte-organized 275
    nybble-organized 275
    word-organized 293–4
memory refreshing 274, 279, 281
memory size 274
memory storage devices 4, 272
    electrical with feedback 272
    electrical with stored charge 272
    magnetic 272
    spatial 272
    structural 272
    see also ferrite-core . . .; magnetic-bubble . . . .; plated-wire . . .; semiconductor . . .; thin-film memory
memory technology 272–3, 296–326
    problem questions 326, 328

memory-mapped I/O 240–1
memory-mapping technique 401
MFM (modified fequency modulation) encoding technique 303–4, 311
microcomputers, *see also* microprocessors
microinstructions 167, 174, 175
microprocessors
    data transmission requirements 367
    operating systems used 380
    6502 188–97
        adressing modes 197–220, 423–4
        branch instructions 169, 194, 207, 429–31
        data movement instructions 192–3, 428–9
        data words used 135
        index register 204
        indirect addressing 209, 423
        instruction set 170, 192–7, 421–33
        applications 194–7
        internal structure 189
        interrupt-handling logic 242–4
        multiplication algorithm 331–2, 333
        op-codes listed 432–3
        registers 191–2
        relative addressing mode 206
        stack 211–13
        zero-page addressing 197–8, 423
    6800 223
        addressing modes 197–8, 206, 221
        branch instructions 207
        index register 204
        relative addressing mode 206
        subtraction instructions 129
        zero-page addressing 197–8, 221
    6809 169, 220–30
        addressing modes 198, 221–6
        index register 204
        internal registers 221
        zero-page addressing 198, 220–1
    word-length used 104
    Z80 188, 192, 205, 223
microprogrammed control
    units 175–80, 188
    compared with random logic control units 188
    structure of 178
microprogramming 167, 175–80
minicomputers
    cache memory used 403

data transmission requirements 367
described 10
mini-floppy disks 311
mini-Winchester disk drive 314
minterms 24
Karnaugh map plotting 42, 44
mnemonics, assembly language 135,
    421–3
    see also instructions
modelling calculations 6–7
modems 357, 359
modified frequency modulation (MFM)
    encoding techniques 303–4, 311
modulation systems 335–9
modulo-eight counting 362
modulo-two arithmetic 120
monitor system 379
Morse code 14–15, 118, 355
most-significant bit (MSB)
    parity bit as 116
    as sign bit 127, 131
Motorola microprocessors
    6800 223
    6809 169, 188, 220–30
    virtual memory techniques
        used 401–2
moving-head disk drives 308, 309
MPLX (multiplexer) circuits 23
MS (main store) 164
MS (master/slave) flip-flops 72–3
MSB (most-significant bit) 116, 127,
    131
MSI (medium-scale integration)
    circuits 52, 55
MTBF (mean time between failure) 94
MTTR (mean time to repair) 95
multidisk drive 306
multiplexers
    application 25–6
    Boolean expressions for 32–3
    DIL packages 55–6
    two-input 23–4, 76
multiplication 4, 329–39, 340
    absence in microprocessors 205, 329
    algorithm for 6502-
        microprocessor 331–2, 333
    binary tables for 120, 329
    Boolean meaning 29
    decimal 171–2
    division by 343–5
    high-speed 336–9, 340
    logical operator 29, 166, 330
multipliers

design using logic gates 35–6, 38–9,
    336–7
    ROM look-up table 91–2, 337, 338
multiprogramming 4, 386–90
    advantages 387

NAK message 105, 361
NAM directive 173
NAND gates 21–2
    cheapness/speed of 34, 38
    logic circuits designed with 47–8
    logic functions implemented
        using 38–9
    logic symbol for 21
    speed/cheapness of 34, 38
    types of 38
NAND operator 166
NDRO (nondestructive readout)
    mode 295
NEG instruction 228
negation
    Boolean meaning 29
    logical operator 29, 166
negative numbers 126–34
    multiplication 332–3
    sign/magnitude representation 127–8
negative-flag bit 167
nested subroutines 215
network interface units (NIUs) 347–8
network layer, data transmission 366–7
networks 4, 347–8, 367–77
    book on 434–5
NIUs (network interface units) 347–8
NMI (nonmaskable interrupt) 244–5,
    388
nodes, local-area network 368
noise
    definition of 88
    electronic 115
noise immunity, data codes 300
nondestructive readout (NDRO) mode,
    thin-film memory 295
nonmaskable interrupt (NMI) 244–5,
    288
nonrestoring division 342–3, 345, 346
nonreturn-to-zero, modified, (NRZ1)
    encoding technique 301, 302
NOP instruction 422, 431, 432–3
NDR gates 21–2
    cross-coupled 62–3, 65
    logic functions implemented using 39
    logic symbol for 21
    truth tables for 62, 64

NOR operator 22, 166
NOS (next-on-stack) position 210
NOT gates 20-1, 22
    logic symbol for 20
    propagation delay effects 89-90
NOT operator 21, 29, 166
NRZ1 (modified nonreturn-to-zero)
    encoding technique 301, 302
number bases 106-7
    conversion 107-20
        problem questions 156
    listed 106
number crunchers, computers as 6-7
numbering system, computer
    memory 13
numbers
    formats 105
    range/precision/accuracy 141-2
    as words 105
nybble-organized memory 275

object code 380
octal numbers
    advantages 106-7
    conversion to/from binary 110
    conversion to/from decimal 108, 109
octal registers 81-2
    in register arrays 82-3
offsets
    indexed addressing 203, 224, 424
    relative addressing 206
on/off switches 266-7
one's complement arithmetic 133-4
op-codes 164-5
    microprogrammable control-unit 182
    6502-microprocessor 432-3
open systems interconnection (OSI)
    reference model 366-7
open-ended data transmission 238, 359
operating system (OSs) 4, 378-90
    batch-mode 380
    compared with orchestral
        conductor 378
    demand-mode 380-1
    example of use 379-80
    functions 378
    interactive 380-1
    real-time 381
    single-user 380
    types 380-1
operating system utilities 381-3
optical encoders 113-15

OR gates 19-20, 22
    logic symbol for 19
OR operator 19, 20, 29, 30, 166
ORA instruction 170, 193, 422, 427,
    432-3
ORG directive 173
OSs (operating systems) 4, 378-90
OSI (open systems interconnection)
    reference model 366-7
OUT instruction 169, 170
overflow
    definition of 410
    two's complement arithmetic 132
overflow-flag bit 167
overlays 393-4
    contrasted with paging 397

P/F bits, HDLC protocol 363, 364, 365
page-fault 399, 401, 402
page-tables 399, 400
paging 190, 395-7
    contrasted with overlaying 397
    example 396
paper tape 15, 272, 383
parallel adders 125-6
    in worked examples 410-11
parallel circuits, definition 126
parallel-load capability, shift
    register 76, 83
parallel-to-serial converters, shift
    registers as 75
parameter passing 217-20
parity bits/codes 116-17, 350
    even/odd 116
    horizontal/longitudinal 117
partial dividends 341
partial products 330
partial quotients 342
PC (program counter) 25, 79, 164
PE (phase encoding) techniques 301-2,
    318, 321, 351
per cent symbol (%) 196, 199
peripheral processing unit (PPU) 248
peripherals 3, 236, 249-70
    book on 435
    mainframe/minicomputer 10
    microprocessors in 249
    see also input/output devices
Permalloy, in magnetic-bubble
    memory 324
PHA instruction 192, 193, 212, 422,
    428, 432-3

phase encoding (PE) technique 301–2, 318, 321, 351
phase modulation (PM) 358
PHP instruction 422, 428, 432–3
physical address space 390, 391
  relationship to logical address space 392
  relationship to virtual memory space 398–9
physical layer protocol 363, 366
PLA instruction 192, 193, 212, 422, 428, 432–3
plated-wire memory 292, 295–6
PLP instruction 422, 428, 432–3
PM (phase modulation) 358
point-plotting CRT display 253
poll/finish (P/F) bits, HDLC protocol 363, 364, 365
polled interrupts 245–6
polling loop 241–2
polling mechanism 245
ports
  data transfer 236
  input/output (I/O) 236, 240
  keyboard 252
position-independent code 206
positional notation 106
postbyte, 6809-addressing 223–4, 225
power supply interruption, system shut-down 245
PPU (peripheral processing unit) 248
precision, floating-point number 141, 145
presentation layer, data transmission 366, 367
preset, flip-flop 80–1
pressure-sensitive switch 266–7
print heads
  cylinder 262
  golf-ball 262
  movement mechanism 260–1
printers 259–66
  belt 264, 265
  daisy-wheel 263
  dot-matrix 261–2
  drum 263–4
  functions listed 259
  impact 260
  ink-jet 265–6
  line 263–4
  paper-feed machanism 259
  speed of cheap 242
  thermal 260

prioritized interrupts 245, 389–90
problem questions
  addressing modes 231–3
  AIM-65 microcomputer 230–1
  assembly language 233–4
  binary arithmetic 158–60
  Boolean algebra 100–1
  floating-point arithmetic 160–1
  fractions, number-base conversion 156–7
  index registers 234–5
  logic elements 98–100
  memory technology 326, 328
  number-base conversion 156
  sequential circuits 101–3
procedures, programming 213
processor status register (PSR) 25–6, 136–7, 167
processor status word (PSW)
  bits listed 136–7, 167, 423
  interrupt flag bit 242
processors: *see* microprocessors
product-of-sums form, conversion from sum-of-products form 45–7
program counter (PC) 25, 79, 164
program-counter relative addressing 223–4
program examples
  branching 25
  CPU demonstration 169–72
  hexadecimal characters 418
  keyboard operation 254
  keyboard/printing 215, 216
  loop construct 200, 201
  6809-microprocessor 228–9
  sum-and-multiply 171
  text/string-matching 228–9
programmable logic arrays 92
programmable read-only memory (PROM) 285
programmed I/O 240–2
programmers, hardware knowledge needed by 1, 2
programming, orderly approach 170
programs, comparison with cookery recipes 12
PROM (programmable read-only memory) 285
propagation delays
  full adder 123, 124
  logic element 69–70, 89–90
  random logic control unit 182
  in worked examples 412–13

protection function 382–3
protocol layers 363, 366–7
protocols 238–40, 359–67
  bit-oriented 353–5, 359, 361–6
  book on 435
  byte control-oriented 359, 360–1
pseudo-ROM 285
PSH instruction 227
PSR (process status register) 25–6,
    136–7, 167
PSW (processor status word), 136–7,
    167, 242, 423
PUL instruction 227
pulse effects
  JK flip-flop 77–8
  RS flip-flop 66
  telegraph distortion 355–6
pulse generators 256, 388
pulse intervals, clock 165
punched cards
  editing of 383
  as strucural memory 272
punched paper tape
  data on 15
  editing of 383
  as structural memory 272

QAM (quadrature amplitude
    modulation) 359
quantization 268
quotient, definition of 339
QWERTY keyboard 251

RAM (random-access memory) 273
random-access, definition 273
random-access devices, disk drives
    as 307
random-access memory (RAM) 273
  read/write cycle timing diagrams 277,
    279, 281
  size 274–5
  video display 258
random logic control units 180–8
  compared with microprogrammable
    control units 188
random-rescheduling strategy, data
    transmission 372
range, floating-point number 141, 145
RAS (row address strobe) 280
raster-scan 255
RB (return-to-bias) data-encoding
  technique 300–1

read-only memory (ROM) 8, 274
  character generator 258
  dedicated controller 283
  logic elements replaced by 91–2
  mask-programmed 283
  multiplication look-up table 337–8
  semiconductor technology 283–5
read/write heads 298, 306, 310
  cassette recorder 321
  tape transport 317
real-time operating systems 381
real-time systems, interrupt-
    handling 245
redundancy, system reliability 96
redundant bits 116
reed relay switches 250, 267
refreshing, dynamic memory 274, 279,
    281
register addressing,
    6809-microprocessor 226
register insertion rings 375
register-transfer language (RTL) 163,
    165, 167, 176, 183, 209, 226,
    424–31
relative addressing 206–8, 222
relays, as I/O devices 250, 267
reliability
  definition 93
  misconceptions about 93
reliability factors 93–8
reply-request (ENG) message 105, 361
reset, meaning of 65
restoring division 342, 344
return-to-bias (RB) data-encoding
  technique 300–1
return-to-zero (RZ) data-encoding
  technique 300
right-shift registers 74–7, 83
ring networks 371, 374
  control techniques for 374–7
  double-ring structure 371
ripple-through carry 126
RMB directive 173
ROL instruction 170, 173, 422, 427,
    432–3
ROM: *see* read-only memory
ROR instruction 170, 422, 427–8,
    432–3
rounding technique, floating-point
    arithmetic 150
row address strobe (RAS) 280
RS flip-flops 63–7
  applications 66–7

as FETCH/EXECUTE flip-flops 185–6
pulse effects 66
static RAM 279
RTI instruction 243, 388, 389, 422, 431, 432–3
RTL (register-transfer language) 163, 165, 167, 176, 183, 209, 226, 424–31
RTS instruction 214, 216, 422, 431, 432–3
RZ (return-to-zero) data-encoding technique 300

SAVE command 383
SBC instruction 139, 193, 422, 426, 432–3
scientific notation, floating number 141
screen editors 383
SEC instruction 170, 193, 422, 426, 432–3
sectors, magnetic disk 307
SED instruction 422, 426, 432–3
SEI instruction 422, 431, 432–3
self-clocking codes 300, 302, 303, 304
self-modifying programs 202
    arguments against 202–3
    memory map of 203
semiconductor memory 274–85
    dynamic RAM 278–83
        disadvantages 282
    ROM 283–5
    static 274–8
    static RAM 274–8
sense wires, ferrite-core memory 289, 290
sequential circuits 74–9
    definition of 62
    problem questions 101–3
    special purpose packages 79–86
sequential logic elements, DIL packages 79–86
serial-access, definition 273
serial-access devices 297, 299
serial adders 124–5
serial data transmission 349–59
    asynchronous 349–51
    full-duplex mode 349, 363, 365
    half-duplex mode 349, 363, 364
    synchronous 351–9
serial-to-parallel converters, shift registers as 75–6

session layer, data transmission 366, 367
set, meaning of 65
SET instruction 169, 170
SEX instruction 228
sharp sign (#) 196, 198, 199, 383
shift key 251
SHIFT operator 166
shift registers 74–7
    D flip-flop composition 74–5
    JK flip-flop composition 76–7
    magnetic-bubble memories as 325, 326
    with parallel load capacity 76
    as parallel-to-serial convertors 75
    practical packages 83, 84
    as-serial-to-parallel converters 75–6
    in worked examples 407–8
shifting-and-adding, multiplication method 330
shifts, types of 77
sign-and-magnitude notation
    floating-point number mantissa 146
    negative numbers 127–8, 134
signed binary multiplication 332–6
simultaneous chess, multiprogramming compared with 386, 387
single-user operating systems 380
sixteen-bit microprocessors
    virtual memory techniques used 401–2
sixteen-bit words, 8-bit word representation 138
slash characters (/) 384
slipper, disk drive 307
slotted ALOHA 373
slotted rings 376
small scale integration (SSI) circuits 52, 53
snap-disk switches, in keyboards 250
soft-sectored disks 309, 312
software, definition 1
software interrupt instruction 386, 431
SOH control character 105, 360
solenoid switches
    in cassette recorders 9
    NOT gate function 20
Sommering telegraph 355
source code 380
SP (stack pointer) 211, 212
special-purpose logic elements
    combinational circuits 52–8
    sequential circuits 79–86

sprocket-feed printer mechanisms 259
square brackets [ ], meaning of 13, 163
SSI (small-scale integration) circuits 52,
    53
STA instruction 136, 166, 170, 192,
    422, 428, 432–3
stack 193, 210–13
    6502-microprocessor 211–13
    subroutines use 213–16
stack clearing process 220
stack pointer (SP) 211, 212
star networks 370
    ALOHA example 373
    disadvantage 370
state diagrams 77–8
static memory, definition 274
static semiconductor memory 274–8
staticizers, D flip-flops as 68
stepping motor 310, 311
STOP instruction 170
storage capacities, disk drive 297, 306,
    308, 311–12, 314
storage devices, types 272
stored-program computer 271
    comparison with brain 11–12
streaming tape drives 319–20
STX control character 105, 360
STX instruction 192, 204, 422, 429,
    432–3
STY instruction 204, 422, 429, 432–3
SUB instruction 135, 170
subroutines 213–16
    data input/output 216–19
    return mechanism 213–14
subtraction
    absence in Boolean algebra 63
    assembly language instruction 139
    binary tables for 120
    logical operator 166
    sign-and-magnitude arithmetic 128
subtraction circuits 126
sum-of-products form, conversion to
    product-of-sums form 45–7
sun, weight expression 140–1
supercomputers 7
supervisor system 379
supervisory frames, HDLC
    protocol 362, 363
SWI instruction 386
switching, gate application 23
SYN control character 105, 352, 360
synchronous (clocked) systems 70
synchronous serial data

transmission 351–9
    bit-synchronized 351
    character-oriented 352, 360–1
    word-synchronized 351–5
system reliability
    parallel circuit 96–8
    series circuit 95–6
system software 381–6

T (toggle) flip-flops 83, 85
tape: *see also* magnetic . . .; paper . . .
tape buffer systems
    floating shuttle 317
    tension-arm 316–17
    vacuum column 316
tape cartridges 322
tape cassettes 320
tape dump 6
tape streamers 319–20
tape transport 315–22
task-switching 388–90
TAX instruction 192, 193, 204, 422,
    429, 432–3
TAY instruction 204, 422, 429, 432–3
TEAC MT-2 tape cassette 321
Teesside Polytechnic local area
    network 347–8, 368
telegraph distortion effect 355–6
telegraph systems 355
telephone directory, cache memory
    for 403
telephone networks
    characteristics 356, 357
    data transmission via 356–7
temperature effects, logic element 87–8
ten's complement arithmetic 128–9
tension-arm tape buffer 316–17
text filenames 382
text processors 384–5
TFR instruction 227
thermal printers 260
thin-film memory 292–6
    easy/hard axes 293, 294
    read/write processes 294–5
timing diagrams, memory 277, 279, 281
timing pulse generators
    random-logic control-unit 184
    outputs 185
token passing 374–5
token rings 374–5
topology, local-area network 368–71
TOS (top-of-stack) position 210
trace function, debugger program 386

tracks, magnetic disk 305, 307
tractor-feed printer mechanisms 259
trade-off, money vs. speed 1
transfer instructions 192–3, 227, 428–9
transport layer, data transmission 366, 367
trellis diagram 119
tri-state gates 60
  bus application 60–1
tri-state logic 58–62
truncation technique, floating-point arithmetic 149, 150
truth tables
  air conditioning example 51
  BCD-to-7-segment 414
  Boolean operators 30
  D flip-flop 68
  demultiplexer 56
  flip-flops 65, 68, 74
  full-adder 122, 123
  gates 18, 19, 20, 21, 22, 23, 62
  half-adder 121
  inverter with tri-state output 60
  NOR gate 62
  ROM as multiplier 91
  RS flip-flop 64, 65
  two-bit multiplier 36
  X symbol, meaning in 51, 60, 65
TSX instruction 204, 422, 429, 432–3
TTL logic element, manufacturer's data 87
two's complement arithmetic 129–33
  multiplication 332–3
two's complement numbers 129–30, 134
  adder/subtractor circuit 130–1
  alternative view 132–3
  properties 131–2
TXA instruction 192, 204, 422, 429, 432–3
TXS instruction 204, 422, 429, 432–3
TYA instruction 204, 422, 429, 432–3

ULAs (uncommitted logic arrays) 93
unconstrained-topology networks 368–9
  disadvantage 369
unit distance codes 113–15
Univac computers, number range/precision 145
UNIVAC tape transport 318
UNIVAC-1100 computers
  network using 348
6502 program assembled on 385
  word-length used 104
unnumbered frames, HDLC protocol 362, 363
unpacking, floating-point number 146–7, 150
unsigned binary arithmetic
  division 341–2
  multiplication 330–2, 333
user-oriented interfaces 266–70
utilities
  operating system 381–3
  as overlays 394

vacuum-column tape buffers 316
VCR (video cassette recorder), as tape streamer 320
VDUs: *see* visual display units
vectored interrupts 246
vectors, inner-product evaluation 205
very large scale integration (VLSI) circuits 52–3
video cassette recorder (VCR), as tape streamer 320
video RAM 258
virtual memory space, relationship to physical address space 398–9
virtual memory systems 297, 391, 393, 397–401
  example 399
  in microprocessors 401–2
visual display units (VDUs) 249–59
  data direct input/interrogation 6
  data transfer to/from 236–7
  display format 255–6
  keyboard as input 250–3
  screen as output 253–9
VLSI (very-large-scale integration) circuits 52–3
voice coil 313–14
volatile memory, definition 274
von Neumann computer 271

WANs (wide-area networks) 347, 434–5
weather model example 6–7
Whirlwind computer 286
wide-area networks (WANs) 347, 434–5
Winchester disk drives 312–14
  back-up storage for 319
word lines, thin-film memory 294
word processors 384–5

word-lengths 10, 104
word-organized memory 293–4
word-sychronized transmission 351–5
words
    addition 124–6
    representation 104–6
worked examples 150–5, 314–14, 405–9

X registers 192–3, 210, 224
Xerox, network used by 373
XOR functions/gates 19; *see also*
    EXCLUSIVE OR ...

Y registers 192, 224

zero
    complementary arithmetic 131, 134
    floating-point value 143–4
    sign-and-magnitude arithmetic 127
zero-flag bit 167, 169, 183
zero-page addressing 197–8, 221
zero-stuffing 375
Zilog microprocessors
    virtual memory techniques
        used 401–2
Z80 microprocessor 188, 223
    book with examples using 434